THE SINGING COWBOYS

Also by David Rothel:
Who Was That Masked Man?: The Story of the Lone Ranger

THE SINGING COWBOYS

David Rothel

San Diego • New York
A. S. Barnes & Company, Inc.
In London:
The Tantivy Press

Second Printing
Manufactured in the United States of America

For information write to:
A. S. Barnes & Company, Inc.
P.O. Box 3051
La Jolla, California 92038

The Tantivy Press
Magdalen House
136-148 Tooley Street
London, SE1 2TT, England

Library of Congress Cataloging in Publication Data

Rothel, David, 1936-
    The singing cowboys.

    Bibliography: p.
    Includes filmographies and index.
    1.   Western films—History and criticism.
2.   Cowboys—Songs and music.   3.   Moving-picture
actors and actresses—United States—Biography.
4.   Country musicians—United States—Biography.
I.   Title.
PN1995.9.W4R67   791.43′0909′32   77-89646
Isbn No.: 0-498-02523-3

1 2 3 4 5 6 7 8 9   84 83 82 81 80

To

Mom and Dad

who, in addition to everything else, always provided the thirty-five cents for the ticket, the popcorn, and the soft drink

Contents

Preface

Things are looking grim for our fringe-shirted, spur-jingling, six-gun-toting cowboy hero and his lady fair. To their backs is the canyon wall with its jagged and unscalable rocks. On their left lies the forbidding rattlesnake-infested desert, stretching mile upon parched mile into the mirage-filled haze. Off to the right the outlaw boss and his gang of cutthroats are safely entrenched behind granite boulders, their rifle barrels catching the rays of the blistering sun. As their squinting eyes take careful aim at our hero, lust-filled thoughts of the fair maiden fill their minds' eyes.

The only possible route to safety lies straight ahead toward Deadwood. As the hawklike eyes of our cowboy hero scan this yawning expanse, they suddenly become aware of tiny moving specks on the faraway horizon. Is it the cavalry come to the rescue? Is it the Deadwood sheriff, the maiden's father, with a posse of outraged townspeople to save them and rout the villain and his outlaw pack? No, God help them, it's the renegade redskins come to rape, torture, and scalp.

"What are we going to do?" screams the terrified, tearful damsel to our Stetson-topped, neckerchiefed, cowboy crusader.

"I'm not sure, Ma'am, but first I'm gonna' sing ya' a little song."

And thus the singing cowboy musical Western was born.

Acknowledgments

I would like to express my sincere thanks and appreciation to the singing cowboys—Rex Allen, Gene Autry, Eddie Dean, Monte Hale, Roy Rogers, and Jimmy Wakely—who graciously took time to share with me their recollections of the years they spent as the stars of the musical Westerns and to bring me up to date on their lives. No book on the singing cowboys and their films could hope to be complete without this input from the men who said the lines and sang the songs in front of the cameras.

I extensively used the research facilities of the University of South Florida library, both the Tampa and Sarasota New College branches, in the preparation of this book. My thanks to the librarians and assistants who made my work easier, especially Pat Bryant of the Sarasota New College branch who was so helpful.

Thanks are in order to Frank McDonald for his reminiscences and rare photographs that add so much to the Gene Autry and Roy Rogers chapters. I offer a deep bow and thank you to Ted Rogers for his remembrances of the "Melody Ranch" radio days and other times he spent with Gene Autry.

Appreciation is extended for the many courtesies of Pat Pounds, Gene Autry's secretary, and Marie Duffey of radio station WHLO in Akron, Ohio.

Credit and thanks for much of the Jimmy Wakely filmography goes to Don Martin, who also provided many Jimmy Wakely photographs.

All photographs used in the book are from my personal collection except where credited elsewhere.

Most especially, thanks are due to my wife, Nancy, whose assistance and support in the preparation of this book went far beyond the call of love and marriage.

THE SINGING COWBOYS

1 A Few Words Before Saddling Up. . .

This book, as the title indicates, is about the singing cowboys of the Western films. Much of it is in the words of the performers, directors, and others I interviewed as I did my research for the book. In order to corral my subject area somewhat, I found it necessary to limit my view to just the singing cowboy *stars* of feature films. As a result, such stellar sidekick singing cowboys as Smiley Burnette, Bob Nolan, Foy Willing, Ray Whitley, and others are dealt with only as they relate to a singing cowboy star of features. In addition to shedding some new light and, perhaps, insight on the singing cowboy stars and their musical Westerns, I have tried to spin a lasso around some of the mood, tempo, atmosphere, and aura of what it was like to toil as a singing cowboy in the stables of such B Western factories as Republic Pictures, Monogram, and Producers Releasing Corporation.

The two major chapters in this book examine the undisputed leaders in the field of musical Westerns—Gene Autry and Roy Rogers. I suspect that I may rankle some readers when I pass so lightly on the career of Tex Ritter, a movie singing cowboy who never seemed to find his proper niche on the screen, but was, without a doubt, a country music legend by the time of his death in 1974. Despite some of the nasty things said and written about the Monte Hale and Eddie Dean films of the mid to late forties, I generally found them enjoyable, adequately produced (many in color), and musically very appealing. The early Monte Hale pictures had the added musical treat of featuring Bob Nolan and The Sons of the Pioneers and then Foy Willing and The Riders of the Purple Sage for many episodes. Eddie Dean, though often maligned by critics for his acting, was a personal favorite of mine because he had such a terrific

singing voice. Jimmy Wakely, although he starred in some twenty-eight features for Monogram, never seemed comfortable as a movie singing cowboy and action star. His greatest fame, of course, came later as a recording and radio star.

I believe Rex Allen, the last of the movie singing cowboys, should be slotted right behind Gene Autry and Roy Rogers in any ranking of film singing cowboys. If fate had placed Rex on the Republic Pictures' lot ten years earlier, he very likely would have given the other cowpoke crooners a ride for the singing cowboy crown. For the record, a few pages are devoted to the also-rans in the field—Dick Foran, Jack Randall, Fred Scott, Bob Baker, et al.

I have tried to make the filmographies as complete as possible given the problems I encountered while doing the research. For example, some of the films (particularly those of the lesser-known singing cowboys) were never reviewed even in the trade papers. I also discovered that credit listings were not always kept as completely and/or as accurately as one would wish. Therefore, I ask your understanding when bits of information are occasionally missing from a particular filmography. I would hope that film buffs who possess some of the missing information might share it with me for future editions.

I have annotated the Gene Autry and Roy Rogers filmographies with critical comments, plot summaries, occasional titles of songs featured in the scores, tidbits on performers in the pictures, and other such memorabilia that I thought would be of interest to the Western film fan. I have provided such information only on the Autry and Rogers films because their pictures were the most popular of this genre; they were the most prolific of the singing cowboys (starring in close to two hundred features between them); their films covered almost the entire span of years (1935-53) that musical Westerns were produced; their films were discussed and reviewed more comprehensively in trade journals, fan magazines, and film books than the films of the other singing cowboys; and, finally, because Gene and Roy were my personal favorites.

Although they are no longer playing at the local Bijou, the films of the singing cowboys are still available for viewing. Film rental companies such as Ivy Film (165 West 46th Street, New York, 10036) and NTA (711 5th Avenue, New York, 10022) rent many of the films of Roy Rogers, Tex Ritter, Monte Hale, and Eddie Dean. Also, there are private dealers who sell and buy for home viewing the films of all the singing cowboys included in this book. Many dealers advertise their films in such tabloids as *The Big Reel* (Empire Publications, Drawer B, Summerfield, North Carolina, 27358).

Another good opportunity to see the musical Westerns that are discussed in this book is at Western film festivals, which in recent years have been popping up in hotel convention facilities all over the country—Nashville, Houston, Orlando, and Los Angeles, to name only a few of the bigger ones. These three- or four-day festivals usually have four or five viewing rooms going continuously from morning until late at night. Late each afternoon of the festivals a panel of guest stars usually meets in a large room to answer questions from the fans.

There is always a dealer's room at the festivals where films, movie posters, lobby cards, stills, comics, books—you name it!—are bought and sold. If it pertains to the cowboy films, you can generally find it in a festival dealer's room. Quite often the festivals conclude with an evening banquet at which the Western stars perform. The Western film festivals are fascinating affairs and are heartily recommended as a brief sojourn into the past.

The discography for each of the singing cowboys includes only the recordings that are currently available in record stores or through mail-order dealers. It should be noted that many of the records listed are re-releases, collector's editions, or hard-to-find "specials" of discontinued stocks. For the reader who wishes to locate out-of-date recordings by these performers, I suggest that you canvas the discount bins of record shops. Occasionally an old album no longer listed will turn up in the $1.98 bin and prove to be a rare singing cowboy treasure.

Also, I would recommend keeping a watchful eye on the classified ad pages of the newspaper. Through just such an advertisement I recently acquired eight, ancient Gene Autry 78 rpm recordings on the Okeh label that date back to the late thirties. The price was seventy-five cents each, which was quite a bargain.

*   *   *

For the uninitiated of today who never experienced the singing cowboys in their proper time and milieu, their never-never Western-screen-land of twenty-five to forty years ago may be a strange incarnation of the old (and not so old) West compared with recent movie and television treatments. The singing cowboy musical Westerns at their best were able to blend the musical and action aspects without detriment to either. They were neither boring nor graphically violent. Unlike the plodding, actionless, palavering television "adult Westerns" of a few years ago (and mostly reruns today), the Gene Autry et al. musical Westerns had the good sense to break into song whenever the script temporarily tied up to a hitching post between shoot-outs. Conversely, even a director with a proclivity for action and violence, such as William Witney (who directed all of Roy Rogers's later, more violent, musical Westerns), was required to show restraint with the screen mayhem. No Sam "Wild Bunch" Peckinpah blood-and-guts abandonment was to be tolerated in the musical Westerns. The singing cowboy musical Westerns certainly didn't present the West as it actually was—just as it should have been, and that is much of their charm.

Except for some of the Gene Autry and Roy Rogers films, the scripts for the musical Westerns were mostly gussied-up rewrites of the same B saddle sagas that had entertained us mightily minus the singing and strumming.. Usually the main differences between the B Westerns and the B musical Westerns were that the cowboy star could sing and wore a much fancier shirt than the nonsinging cowboy. In the cases of Gene and Roy, however, the musical aspects were heightened considerably during their peak years (for Gene this would be during the late thirties until 1942, when he entered the service; Roy reached his zenith between 1943 and 1947). During those years their films often became musicals with a Western motif rather than Westerns with some music. "Production" numbers (staged in nightclubs, theaters, on radio, or at fiestas) heavily punctuated their films, occasionally leaving the traditional Western aspects of horses, cattle, rustlers, hold-up men, ranches, fist fights, and shoot-outs somewhat in disarray. For the rest of the singing troubadours there were no production numbers and the songs were just worked in in-between the action sequences.

Gene Fowler once wrote,

> Memory . . . is a Coney Island mirror. Its distortions reflect a mistake in a thinner form than that in which it originally appeared, and a good deed in a wider aspect than it deserves.

For those who remember the singing cowboy musical Westerns of the thirties, forties, and early fifties with unbridled and uncritical enthusiasm, let me caution you that they may not be as good, over all, as you remember them. But, to mount the horse from the other side, for those Western film critics and buffs who show distain whenever a singing cowboy film is broached in a conversation, let me voice the opinion that they weren't that bad either.

We should not attempt to make the singing cowboy films any more than they were—prairie fantasies for kids of all ages who plunked down the admission price and stepped into a magical world for an hour or so of escapism with a favorite cowboy hero. Perhaps that's why thousands of now grown-up fans of these films remember them so fondly. The films were what they were: rootin'-tootin' action, sidekick laughs, Western music, and escapism—pure, empty-headed escapism with the only message in the script provided by the Pony Express or the new-fangled telegraph.

But in another sense there *was* something for us to take with us as we reluctantly trod up the dimly lighted aisle, past the "Cooled by Refrigeration" valanced marquee, out into the blazing heat of a July afternoon. And it wasn't something *just* from the singing cowboys; it was available from all the B Western movie cowboys. I'm referring to the heroic demeanor of the cowboy stars on the screen—the "Code of the West," if you will, that we cowboy buckaroos were often inclined, both consciously and unconsciously, to model after we left the darkened room with the silver screen. Gene Autry is credited with writing the set of "Cowboy Commandments" that Arthur F. McClure and Ken D. Jones quote in their fine book, *Heroes, Heavies and Sagebrush:*

1. He must not take unfair advantage of an enemy.
2. He must never go back on his word.
3. He must always tell the truth.
4. He must be gentle with children, elderly people and animals.
5. He must not possess racially or religiously intolerant ideas.
6. He must help people in distress.
7. He must be a good worker.
8. He must respect women, parents and his nation's laws.
9. He must neither drink nor smoke.
10. He must be a patriot.

Times and styles have changed just as we have changed from Saturday matinee cowboy buckaroos to businessmen, teachers, plumbers, whatever. To properly explore that world again you must seek the child within you that in times long past thrilled to the screen adventures of these crooning cowpokes—Gene Autry, Roy Rogers, and the rest. To assist you in finding that child, I offer the chapters of this book. May these pages help you to take an armchair horseback ride to some of the adventures of your youth.

2   Gene Autry

He is a combination of Sherlock Holmes in a ten-gallon hat, Don Quixote with common sense, and Bing Crosby on horseback.

—Alva Johnson (1939)

As a youngster in the wilds of rural Ohio in the early forties—just beginning to discover a little of the world around me—I had two heroes: my oldest brother, Bob (who was a budding baseball player and would later play for the Cleveland Indians), and Gene Autry. Gene Autry usually ranked first in my ratings (for a brother to even qualify was quite an accomplishment) and I didn't mind having to share my cowboy hero with thousands of other mostly rural kids around the country who also idolized "America's Favorite Cowboy."

We didn't realize it then, but it *was* a mostly rural audience that the movie cowboys—singing or otherwise—were playing to at that time. A story from the late thirties recounts how a national sweat shirt manufacturer by the name of J. T. Flagg from Florence, Alabama, was looking for a new public hero whose image he could emblazon on the front of sweat shirts—Mr. Flagg being a precursor for the T-shirt entrepreneurs of today. Babe Ruth had provided him with bases-loaded, grand-slam-homerun sweat-shirt sales for some years, but now the time was ripe for a new hero and Mr. Flagg was at a loss for a suitable replacement.

As fate would have it, a Mr. Gene Autry, singing movie cowboy, came riding into Florence one day on a personal appearance tour and captured and enraptured the citizenry—young and old. Mr. Flagg, always a cautious man, checked to see that this musical mesquite mesmeriser was not a one-town wonder. He found that city after town had

reacted similarly; that at least one preteenager had walked some fourteen miles to Birmingham just to see the singing cowboy and his horse, Champion; and that it was not uncommon for the cowboy's studio in Hollywood to receive some twelve thousand fan letters a week addressed to Gene Autry, Hollywood, California.

Convinced that he had found his new national sweat-shirt hero, J. T. Flagg finally caught up with

Gene Autry.

Autry in Nashville and proposed a deal, to which Autry replied, "I'm afraid you're too late. I think they sold my sweat-shirt rights to a chap in New York."

Not giving up easily (and not wanting to be outclassed by some New York hotshot), Flagg asked Autry to check on the rights. A series of phone calls revealed that the deal had not been quite consummated. Flagg instantly outbid the "chap in New York" and got the Gene Autry sweat-shirt rights.

Now all of this sounds like the typical success story of an enterprising businessman who would not give up easily. Unfortunately the tag line on the story reveals that Flagg had in reality outbid himself—the "chap in New York" being J. T. Flagg's business representative who had not been overly disturbed at losing the Gene Autry deal because (as he told J. T. Flagg), "Most people *here* never heard of Gene Autry."

This story points up a fact that we country kids who idolized the singing cowboys of the thirties and early forties did not realize. We may not have had paved roads and indoor plumbing throughout the countryside the way most big-city kids did, but we did have Gene Autry, Roy Rogers, and Tex Ritter on our movie screens, which the big-city kids generally did not have. It was not until quite a few years into the phenomenon of the singing cowboys that their films started playing the big-city theaters.

Anyway, Gene Autry was an authentic hero to this generation of youngsters who were by-products of the great depression and/or children of the war years—the children who would come of age with the Korean War of the early fifties and who would wonder what went wrong with The American Dream; the children who had been raised on the principles of right and wrong, victory or defeat, and who now had to learn to cope with the dissolutionment of a "cold war" where there apparently would be few of the clean-cut options or tidy resolutions that could be found on the movie screens each week.

But it was still early then, and heroes still wore white hats and rode charging, magnificent steeds to right wrongs. And for many of us, nobody did it better than Gene, up there on the silver screen. *That* was still what every kid wanted to grow up to do.

Orvon "Gene" Autry was born in the tiny community of Tioga, Texas, to struggling horse trader and cattle dealer Delbert Autry and his wife, Nora. The date was September 29, 1907. He was to be one of four children that would be born to the Autry family. When Gene was still a youngster, the family moved to Oklahoma, where he grew up working on his father's cattle ranch. His grandfather (who was a Baptist minister) was the first to notice Gene's singing talent and trained the youth to sing in the church choir.

By the time Gene was in his late teens, he was singing in local nightspots for pocket money. During his choir singing days a plate had been passed for church contributions; now in the nightspots it was a hat and Gene got to keep what the audience put into it. In a recent interview Autry commented on those early singing engagements, "I don't think I ever made more than fifty cents a night."

It was about this same time that he briefly joined a traveling medicine show as a Western singer (following what was to be a portion of the plot in his first starring film feature, *Tumbling Tumbleweeds* (1935), in which he joined a medicine show led by the redoubtable Dr. Parker, played by Gabby Hayes).

Despite the temptations engendered from his beginning success as a singer, Autry gave little thought at this time to devoting his life to entertaining. Instead, driving cattle from his father's ranch near Achille, Oklahoma, to the railhead, young Autry became fascinated with railroads and the telegraph. Soon he learned the Morse code and found himself working the graveyard shift as telegrapher for the Frisco Line in Chelsea, Oklahoma.

Often, to while away the long, lonely early morning hours, Gene would sing the Western songs he had grown to love, accompanying himself on his guitar. In the darkness of one early morning a stranger shuffled into the telegraph office while Gene was "a hummin' and a strummin' " his guitar. While the stranger was preparing his message, he asked the tuneful telegrapher to sing a song. Finally, his message taken care of, the stranger commented to young Autry about his singing: "I think you have something. Work hard at it and you may get somewhere." It was only after the stranger left that Gene saw the name on the wire—Will Rogers.

It was not to be the last time that the famous Will Rogers (who used to visit the old Rogers homestead and a sister who lived nearby) was to stop at the telegraph office to send his newspaper column to his syndicate and to swap a few words with the young troubadour. He gave Autry encouragement by saying, "You know young fella', you ought to get yerself a job on the radio." In a recent interview Autry commented, "I didn't pay too much attention to him. I thought he was just trying to make me feel good. But later on, when things got pretty rough on the railroad, I said well, if Will Rogers thought I was good enough to be on the radio, maybe I should take a shot at it." Gene packed his things and left for the big city, New York, using a free railway pass. The year was 1928.

Deciding to try his luck first in the recording field, Gene started knocking on the doors of record companies in an attempt to get an audition. Encountering the usual rejections that accompany most ill-conceived audaciousness of this sort, a dejected Gene Autry finally ended up in the reception room at Victor records, unable to get beyond the anteroom door for an audition. Finally, in utter frustration, Gene took his guitar from its case and sang an audition for the office secretary. Typical of the good fortune that was to shine on Gene throughout his future career, a Victor executive by the name of Nat Shilkret happened to walk through the office while the impromptu audition was under way. Shilkret, a big-time bandleader, was intrigued with the young Texan's ability and invited him into his office for further consideration. After more songs and a heart-to-heart talk, Shilkret advised Autry, "You've got a voice, but you haven't had enough experience with the microphone. Go back and get on the radio." He gave Gene a letter of introduction for use when seeking a radio job.

Gene journeyed back to Oklahoma, where his letter got him a singing job on radio station KVOO in Tulsa. The financial remuneration being what it was—nothing—Gene found it necessary to take a part-time job again with the railroad. But as the months passed, recognition came his way as his radio singing became popular throughout the territory and he became known as "Oklahoma's Singing Cowboy" or "Oklahoma's Yodeling Cowboy," depending on whom you talked with.

It was inevitable that, as his radio popularity spread, a recording company would eventually discover him. Finally, Gene was asked to journey back to New York to make a recording for Victor. As he explained to me, "I cut a recording for Victor; I've forgotten what it was. Johnny Marvin, a friend of mine from Oklahoma who was a top Victor recording artist at the time, and his brother, Frankie, played with me for the recording session. [Frankie later became one of Gene's best friends and worked with him in many films.] I had a date after that to talk to Loren Watson. He was the A & R director for Victor. In the meantime, though, Arthur Satherley, who had just gone to work for American Record Corporation, got a hold of me. I

told him that I had a date to see Mr. Watson and he said, 'Well, if I were you, I'd talk to him, but before you sign, I'd like to talk to you, too. I'm just starting out here with American Record and if you'll sign with me, I'll do everything in the world I can to promote you. You'd be my first artist. Victor is a big company and they have several big artists that they have to concentrate on. I don't think you'll get the promotion from Victor that I can give you.' I thought it over and I decided that perhaps he was right. So I went back to Satherley and told him I'd decided to go with him."

The American Record Corporation produced records under private labels for many chain stores at that time. Gene was soon to be featured on the Okeh label and became a popular recording artist, with the major outlet being the Sears-Roebuck catalogue and stores.

Lady Luck's smile broadened again and Gene was "blessed" with a hit song from his first recording session, "That Silver-Haired Daddy of Mine," a song he had written back in the Oklahoma telegraph office with a pal by the name of Jimmy Long. An unbelievable thirty thousand copies of the record were sold in the first month of its release (remember, this was 1930); three-hundred-thousand were sold during the initial popularity; and several million copies were eventually sold over the years. (Gene's friend Jimmy Long not only collaborated with him on the writing of his first hit recording, but he also introduced Gene to his future wife. When Gene went to Springfield to visit Jimmy and his wife, he met Ina Mae Spivey, Jimmy's niece. A few weeks later the Longs and Ina Mae traveled to St. Louis where Gene had a theater date. They spent the weekend there. During this brief interlude love blossomed and the usually very unimpetuous Autry shyly proposed, "Ina Mae, let's get married." And they did—on April Fools' Day. She was only eighteen, he was twenty-two.)

Sears-Roebuck, needless to say, was ecstatic over this young cowboy who could sell record platters faster than a chuck-wagon cook could flip flapjacks. The feeling around Sears was that the young cowboy singer's recording and radio popularity could probably be utilized to sell washing machines and work clothes on their Chicago radio station, WLS (the call letters stood for the store's slogan, "World's Largest Store"). For the next four years Sears presented "The Gene Autry Program" on WLS, starting the cowboy star at the bargain basement salary of thirty five dollars per week.

While Gene may not have been getting rich singing for Sears, he was gaining valuable experience and exposure. In addition to his own show, he eventually appeared on the "National Barn Dance" radio program, "the first country and Western radio program in the country that I know of," Gene told me. "The fellow that produced the 'National Barn Dance,' George Hay was his name, was the first emcee on the program. Maybe five years later he left the 'National Barn Dance' and went to Nashville and started the 'Grand Ole Opry.'"

At various times Gene went on tour with the "National Barn Dance" performers. On one such tour the troupe made a stop in Danville, Illinois, at the Tivoli Theater, which was to receive a most unusual autograph from the future cowboy star. Either in jest or utter frustration (no one seems to know for sure) Autry scribbled the terse message in large letters on his dressing room door: "Gene Autry, America's Biggest Flop." When later he became famous throughout the country, the theater management took the door from its hinges, framed it behind glass, and displayed it in the theater lobby with the following message:

> This is a door taken from a dressing room backstage of the Tivoli Theater, upon which Gene Autry painted the above inscription when he appeared with Jimmy Long in person on the Tivoli Theater stage, March 19-20, 1932.

One day in 1934 the wheel of fortune took another whirl for Gene Autry and came up with his number again—Hollywood beckoned. The participants in the events surrounding Autry's entry into films were Nat Levine, producer and head of Mascot Pictures at the time; Herbert J. Yates of American Record Corporation, Consolidated Film Laboratories, and later head of Republic Pictures (which in 1935 came into being as a combine encompassing Monogram, Mascot, Liberty, and Republic Pictures); Moe Siegel, then president of American Record Corporation; and Gene Autry, radio and recording singing cowboy.

In an early recounting of the Gene Autry "Hollywood beckons" story (as reported by Alva Johnston in the *Saturday Evening Post* of September 2, 1939) Nat Levine, fearing that the Legion of Decency was about to clamp down on the "flaming-youth pictures" of the early thirties era, speculated in his infinite film wisdom that a genre likely to survive the scythe of censorship was the American heritage film, the Western. The only problem was that the venerable genre was at the time riding low in the saddle from overexposure. Noting, however, that the occasional tunes in his

The singing cowboy is pictured here near the beginning of his movie career.

Ken Maynard pictures had been getting a good response, Levine decided to go all-out to develop a singing cowboy movie star.

After considerable scouting around, Levine finally narrowed the singing cowboy candidates to three: a Broadway performer who couldn't ride, but could sing and act; a film actor who couldn't sing, but could ride and act; and Gene Autry, who couldn't act, but could sing and ride. While the first two candidates could overcome their deficiencies (through riding lessons, use of doubles, and lip-synching the vocals), Levine decided to go with Autry. Gene Autry was an authentic cowboy already popular as a Western singer on radio and records. As writer Johnston reported Levine's thinking, "The fact that he couldn't act was at first considered a negligible flaw, and later an asset. Like Gary Cooper and Jimmy Stewart, Autry has the kind of awkwardness and embarrassment that audiences like."

Recently Gene Autry added his own recollections of these events when I visited him at his Hollywood office.

GENE AUTRY: Nat Levine was an independent producer that owned Mascot Pictures. He was famous for his serials; he had made several of them. He was in New York talking about financing with Herbert Yates, who owned Consolidated Film Laboratories, which developed, I would say, seventy-five to ninety percent of the movies that were made here in Hollywood. Yates also financed them.

Levine was talking about making a feature with Ken Maynard and also a serial. Moe Siegel, who at that time was president of American Record Corporation, was sitting in with Levine and Yates when Nat was talking about financing this Western. Siegel said to Levine, "Instead of doing a regular formula Western, why don't you try a musical-type Western? Everybody is making movies of regular program Westerns—Hoot Gibson, Buck Jones, Ken Maynard. Why don't you try something musical? We have a young man out in Chicago on WLS that's selling a hell of a lot of records and is very popular on the radio. Why, I think you ought to talk to him." So Nat said he would.

I got a call from Moe Siegel and Art Satherley, who told me that Nat Levine would be in Chicago on a certain day, I forget when it was, and that he wanted to talk to me. So I met with Levine; I had a talk with him. He said, "I'm thinking about making a Western feature with some music in it and you were recommended to me. Siegel and Yates told me how big your records are going and of your popularity on the 'National Barn Dance.' I want to give it a lot of consideration. I'll be in touch with you." I said, "Fine."

So time rocked along and I got another offer—from Monogram Pictures. I wrote Levine a letter and told him [about the Monogram offer] and asked him if he'd given up on his idea. Because if he had, I was going to talk to these other people. He wrote me back and said, "We are making a picture with Ken Maynard called *In Old Santa Fe* and I will give you a part in the picture and a chance to do some songs. It can be a screen test." So I took it; I came out in June.

In Autry's first screen appearance in the Ken Maynard starrer *In Old Santa Fe* (1934), he sang a couple of Western ballads and self-consciously delivered the few lines that were assigned to him. Supposedly, upon viewing himself on the screen for the first time at a preview, Gene grabbed his wife, Ina, and rushed from the theater. Outside, the ashen-faced cowboy exclaimed, "Let's go back to Chicago fast and get my job back before they release that thing." "You'll do no such thing," Mrs. Autry countered. "You're not as bad as you think you are."

And he wasn't—at least many fans wrote to the studio praising the singing of Autry and complaining that he had too little to do in the picture. In my conversation with Gene he commented, "I thought I was probably the world's worst actor, but I've never found a star yet that likes himself on the screen. It's the greatest second-guessing game that you can ever get into. You see yourself and you often think, 'I could have done that so much differently and better.' A lot of actors won't even look at their pictures. Very seldom are you happy with the scenes when you look at the rushes. You want to do them over, so it's better that you stay out and let just the producer or director see them. Years later I saw very few rushes."

Before the public reaction to Gene Autry could be determined, he was cast in his second film, a Ken Maynard serial entitled *Mystery Mountain* (1934) in which his part was even smaller, and he, inexplicably, did not have a single opportunity to sing. But Dame Fortune was again about to blow on Gene Autry's dice. As Gene told me, "After *In Old Santa Fe* came out on the screen and I got a good reaction [from the fans], well, that's when they called me in and said, 'Look, we've decided we'd like to make a serial with you called *Phantom Empire.*' The idea for the serial came up when a writer named Wally MacDonald went to have some teeth pulled. They put him under the gas and somehow or another during the time he was under he dreamed up this idea of the *Phantom Empire.*" The *Phantom Empire* (1934) was a vanguard production in that it was the bizarre mating of science fiction with the Western genre.

Gene's neophyte status as an actor was very apparent in the twelve chapters of *Phantom Empire* even though he was essentially playing himself—a radio singing cowboy by the name of Gene Autry. (This was the first time that a performer played a fictional version of himself on the screen and it was a habit that would soon be acquired by other movie cowboys.) It has been wryly commented by some reviewers that the basic plot for each chapter of *Phantom Empire* called for Gene to get out of the clutches of the steel-helmeted inhabitants of the underground world of Murania and back to Radio Ranch in time to sing "That Silver-Haired Daddy of Mine" on his next broadcast.

The critics also tweaked Gene for his acting ability at this time (actually this was common practice for some critics throughout his career). Some *Phantom Empire* reviewers commented that Gene sounded as if he had just come from elocution class; he spoke his words with extreme

Director Frank McDonald, Gene, and Smiley Burnette.
Photo courtesy of Frank McDonald.

clarity and precision, but with little emphasis or meaning. Not unexpectedly, his most "natural" moments in the serial took place when he was back at Radio Ranch singing about his "Silver-Haired Daddy."

In a recent conversation with director Frank McDonald (an Autry favorite) I asked him about Gene's acting ability:

DAVID ROTHEL: Was he basically playing himself on the screen?

FRANK MCDONALD: Yes, yes. Moe Siegel [producer Sol's brother] asked me when he engaged me—he was the head of Republic in those days before Yates came out to California—Moe asked me, "Have you ever seen any Autry pictures?" This was 1939. I said, "No, Sir, I haven't." It was a Sunday afternoon at his house. He said, "Well, I want you to look at a couple of them tomorrow, Monday. I'll set them up for you. Now don't expect to see a great actor. Gene is what he is, and whatever he's doing, that's what they're buying. It's what they like, so don't change a thing

and don't try to direct him. Direct everybody else; have everybody else do what you want them to do, but Gene does what he does and that's all he can do, and that's what they [the fans] like."

DAVID ROTHEL: Some critics have said that he isn't a very good actor.

FRANK MCDONALD: Gene said that himself. He told me one day while we were having lunch, "I know I'm no great actor, and I'm not a great rider, and I'm not a great singer; but whatever it is I'm doing, they like it. So I'm going to keep doing it as long as I can."

When I later met with Autry, he jokingly repeated Frank McDonald's comment with the slight variation, "I'm not a great actor; I'm not a great rider; I'm not a great singer; but what the hell is my opinion when fifty million people think I do pretty good." He then continued in a more serious vein, "Naturally, I had never had any experience in front of a camera when I came out here. Nowadays most beginning movie actors have worked on TV and know at least a little bit about working in front of a camera. Back in those days, though, you didn't. But I was fortunate to work with some very fine actors like Noah Beery in *Mexicali Rose,* Jack Holt, and Monte Blue. I was fortunate enough in those pictures that I worked with an awful lot of good people around me that helped me a lot."

Although the budget for *Phantom Empire* was a meager seventy-thousand dollars, the production values suggested a more tidy sum. Gene, under contract to Mascot at the time, was a hundred-and-fifty-dollar-a-week employee. But it turned out to be a good deal for producer Nat Levine and Autry. The fans flocked to the serial each week; Levine made a pile of money on the serial and was thus encouraged to go ahead with plans for a series of Gene Autry singing cowboy features, the first to be *Tumbling Tumbleweeds.*

Not everyone at the studio was as confident of Autry's ability or of the future of singing cowboy Westerns as Nat Levine. Armand "Mandy" Schaefer, an associate of Levine's, for one, thought the idea was ridiculous. After being told of the plans by Levine, Schaefer went home and announced to his wife, "I'm going to quit." Not only did he see little future for serenade-sodden Western films, but he felt that Autry was the antithesis of the Western hero—too complacent-appearing, soft-voiced, and lacking the "rootin'-tootin' " cowboy toughness that film fans expected.

"Mandy had made those shoot-'em-up Western pictures with Hoot Gibson and people like that," Gene told me. "He just didn't think a singing cowboy could ever click. Finally he went with me up north when I appeared in a rodeo. When I rode out in the arena and did a couple of songs, he saw the reaction of the crowd and later said that that was the one thing that did more to change him than anything else. He said, 'By God, there *might* be room for somebody like that.' " Armand Schaefer later, of course, went on to spend most of his career as a producer for and business associate of Gene Autry.

And so with the production of *Tumbling Tumbleweeds* the basic format for the next fifty Gene Autry features (carrying him through 1942 and his entrance into the service) was established: there was always the singing cowboy (Gene) with his "World's Wonder Horse" (Champion) and comic sidekick (Smiley "Frog" Burnette) involved in a situation with some ne'er-do-well businessman who attempted to bilk the local cattlemen/ranchers/citizens out of their cattle/land/oil rights. The beautiful leading lady was often unwittingly involved with the baddies or at the very least convinced that Gene was "just a dumb cowboy." Generally there was an encounter early on between Gene and his leading lady so that their relationship got off on the wrong foot. This gave Gene the rest of the picture to prove himself to the girl and to platonically woo her with cowboy ballads. Quite often the leading lady was only secondarily involved with the main plot. Although a few episodes took place in the old West of the late 1880s, the traditional Autry opus was set in the "modern" West, where cars, radios, machine guns, and airplanes were a part of everyday life for almost everyone. Autry and his pals, however, usually leaned to simple ranch life and had little use for these modern devices unless they needed them to capture the outlaws. The bad guys were usually the ones who utilized the devices to accomplish their evil deeds. Gene Autry and his good guys would generally overcome the outlaws and the new-fangled gadgets and vehicles with only their fists, six-guns, and horses.

Somewhere between five and eight times per film Gene would find cause to break into song. If possible, the plot would provide him a logical reason and setting for such excursions into melody (such as a hoedown or a radio broadcast), but other times Gene would break into song with full accompaniment regardless of the illogic of the setting and situation. The classic example of this can be found in *Mexicali Rose* (1939) when, captured and tied-up by a gang of Mexican bandits, Gene learns that the leader's greatest joy is listening to Autry records on the little wind-up phonograph that the bandits carry from camp to camp. When the bandido's favorite record is inadvertently broken, the trussed-up Autry—under a prairie campfire moon—sings the title song with full orchestral accompaniment.

While there were usually a couple of songs in each film that bore faint connection with the plot situations, it was more typical to find that the songs had some fairly logical reason for being in the story and, in addition, in many, many cases they were integrated into the plot in a way to push the story line along. For example, in *Tumbling Tumbleweeds* a song was used to lure and trap the outlaws. The story situation puts the outlaws in a position where they must kill a witness before he testifies against them. At night they approach the cabin in which the witness and Autry are staying. They see through the window what appears to be Gene sitting in a rocking chair, playing a guitar and singing while the other man is asleep on the bed. Listening to Autry sing the Western ballad, they become overconfident at the apparent ease of their evil mission. They check no closer, slip around to the door, and (as the song ends, of course) they start shooting at the figure in the rocking chair and the other on the bed. The outlaws' chagrin is considerable when they realize that the bed contains only pillows and a blanket, and that the rocking chair houses only a stuffed dummy with a guitar. Autry, hiding in the corner, had manipulated the rocking chair with a heavy string tied to his boot while he played and sang.

Utilizing this basic format for story and music, the Autry films were tremendously popular during the second half of the thirties and the early forties. From 1937 through 1942 Gene Autry placed first in the Motion Picture Herald Poll of Top Money-Making Western Stars as indicated by motion picture exhibitors. From 1947 (when he returned to film theaters after the war) through 1954, Gene placed second on the poll, following Roy Rogers, who moved to first place after Autry went into the service.

One should not forget the popularity of Gene's horse, Champion, commonly billed in films and personal appearances over the years as the "World's Wonder Horse." Although Champion did not get the publicity and "humanizing" that Roy Rogers's Trigger did, he nonetheless was a mighty popular critter to Western fans of all ages.

GENE AUTRY: The horse came from Oklahoma. It was different, a dark sorrel, and I liked a blaze-faced horse.

DAVID ROTHEL: I heard that you got the horse from Tom Mix.

GENE AUTRY: No. That's not actually true. When Tom Mix quit making films, he went on tour with the circus. A fellow named Johnny Agee, who had been the top horse trainer for Ringling Brothers-Barnum and Bailey Circus for many, many years, had this horse that he had trained—what we called "high schooled"—to do tricks. He called the horse Lindy because he was born on the day Lindbergh flew the Atlantic. He looked exactly like Mix's original Tony. When Tom Mix went on tour with the circus, he made a deal with Johnny. He hired him and leased the horse [Lindy] to ride in the circus. They called the horse Tony, Jr. After Mix retired, Agee came over to me—that was about '36 or '37—and had a talk. He said he'd like to go to work for me taking care of

Gene Autry and Champion (circa 1940).

26

Gene Autry and the original Champion are pictured here in
an often-seen photo from the early forties.

my horses and he'd like for me to use his horse Lindy when I did any stage appearances because the horse was trained for the stage and for rodeos.

So I made a deal and Johnny went to work for me taking care of all my horses. He worked the original Champion, too, as to certain tricks he had to do in pictures. When I went on rodeos I used Lindy because he looked like Champion, too. He had four stockings and a bald face.

DAVID ROTHEL: Then you used this horse Lindy when you made personal appearances, but it was another horse that was the original Champion in the films. There were two entirely different horses.

GENE AUTRY: Yes, that's right.

The original Champion was Autry's movie mount throughout the years prior to the war. The "Lindy" Champion was the first horse to be flown coast to coast for an appearance with Autry at the Madison Square Garden Rodeo. All in all the horses probably would have settled for a big bag of oats and peaceful anonymity. But then, they weren't just any bangtails; they were Champion, "World's Wonder Horse."

While Gene was in the service overseas during World War II, the original Champion died. When Gene returned to films in late 1946, he introduced a similar-appearing horse called Champion, Jr., who would carry him in future films. Eventually the "Jr." was eliminated. Gene commented that Champion, Jr. was still alive on the ranch at the time of our conversation in early 1977.

Gene Autry was to learn early in his career the value of good business acumen. He quickly comprehended that an inequity was being perpetrated on him. He had made eight features in 1936 and another eight in 1937, with each one costing between fifty and seventy-five thousand dollars to produce. Each film proceeded to gross at least three times that figure at the box office. Gene, however, was still working for around one hundred and fifty dollars a week on contract.

Finally Gene demanded a more equitable arrangement. Herbert J. Yates, head of Republic Pictures, tried to negotiate with Gene but found him intractable. Autry seemed unfazed when informed that if he took a walk Republic had a young singing cowboy named Roy Rogers ready to take his place. When at last Gene determined that Yates would only understand overt action on his part, he called his director Joseph Kane and told him, "Don't break your neck getting ready for the next picture, because I won't be there."

Kane (talking with Charles Flynn and Todd McCarthy for *Kings of the Bs*) said of the walkout, "They chased him all over the South [where he was making personal appearances] —he was very big in the South. Process servers trying to catch him. He was so popular in these small towns, the people would just surround those process servers and gently walk them out of town. They never did catch him! . . . They didn't know it, but Autry had a nice nest egg. They thought he was broke . . . But he was far from broke. Autry was never broke . . . They finally had to settle with Autry because he wouldn't come back, except on his terms. They paid him what he wanted because they wanted him back."

Autry commented to me, "They [Republic] wanted to settle it because they not only were making money on me, but they were selling their whole product on me. In other words they'd go to an exhibitor and say, 'Look, we've got eight Autrys but in order to get the eight you're going to have to buy so many of these others.'" When the haggling was over, Autry went back to work with a contract calling for $12,500 for each film with six to eight films to be made each year.

This photograph of Gene with Champion, Jr. was taken during the late forties. The horse is over thirty years old and still alive at this writing. *Photo courtesy of Gene Autry.*

28

Along with this very healthy increase in film salary, it was reported that Autry was receiving approximately twenty-five-thousand dollars each year from the sale of Gene Autry licensed products including holsters, cap pistols, sweatshirts, games, comic books, hair oils, spurs, chaps, wristwatches, and the Autry Stampede Suit, which was promoted as "Western Made for Western Man."

In January of 1940 Gene was signed by Wrigley's Doublemint Gum for a weekly Sunday evening thirty-minute radio program called "Melody Ranch." Each program consisted of a passel of Western tunes and about ten minutes given over to Gene galloping "through a foam-flecked drama of the range calculated to make Autry votaries champ their Doublemint in double-quick time." (That's the way *Time* described it.) For his efforts on radio's "Melody Ranch" Gene collected fifteen-hundred dollars each week from Doublemint. Eventually his salary was to rise to five-thousand dollars for his weekly "Melody Ranch" get-togethers.

For Gene's guest starring role in the 1940 Twentieth Century-Fox film *Shootin' High* he received twenty-five-thousand dollars. The sale of his phonograph records around this time was paying him royalties of ten to twelve thousand dollars for such hit recordings as "Mexicali Rose," "The Yellow Rose of Texas," "South of the Border," "Deep In the Heart of Texas," "Maria Elena," "El Rancho Grande," "My Old Pal of Yesterday," "Back in the Saddle Again," and "You Are My Sunshine."

In the fall of 1939 his fan mail was peaking at a reported fifty-thousand letters per month (which was a thousand over the Clara Bow record number of some years past). In 1940 he appeared for the fourth straight year at the head of the *Motion Picture Herald's* poll of movie exhibitors' top money-making Western stars. Even more impressive, he ranked fourth among *all* Hollywood money-making stars at the box office. Only Mickey Rooney, Spencer Tracy, and Clark Gable ranked higher. In 1941 Gene placed sixth and in 1942, seventh, on this prestigious list. (The only other B Western cowboy star to ever get on this classy list was Roy Rogers in 1945 and 1946, but he only *just* made it in tenth place.) Another thing that made Gene's appearance on this list so impressive was the fact that his pictures rarely played the first-run theaters in the major cities throughout the country. As Gene commented at the time, "Some of 'em play in towns so small even Mrs. Roosevelt hasn't been there."

In 1939 Gene toured the British Isles and was

This Gene Autry watch from the late forties is now valued at $125 by nostalgia buffs.

mobbed by cheering crowds. He even broke attendance records set by Britain's inimitable Gracie Fields. Half a million fans came out to see his parade in Dublin. The adoring fans that attended his show in Dublin's Theater Royal jammed the alley behind the theater after each show chanting, "We want Gene." He would go out on the fire escape and sing them songs and talk with them. The last night he was there they packed the alley and, as Gene fondly remembers, "I never heard anything like it. They sang 'Come Back to Erin,' and weaved back and forth, and it was a very heart-touching scene."

Two years later back in the little Oklahoma community of Berwyn—227 inhabitants strong—the town's folk voted unanimously to change their community's name from Berwyn to Gene Autry, Oklahoma. *Life* quoted Gene as saying of Gene Autry, Oklahoma, "You could spend weeks and never find such a natural location for a movie." Ah yes, those were palmy days for Mr. Autry.

Gene Autry served in the military service during most of World War II.

But the storm clouds of war loomed on the horizon, and the Nazi storm troopers had already invaded Poland. Presently the United States was drawn into the war. In July of 1942, despite the cries of anguish from Republic Pictures, Gene volunteered for the service. At first he was put to use recruiting, entertaining the troops, and selling war bonds. But this was not what he had in mind when he enlisted; he wanted a more direct role in the war effort. Earning his pilot's wings on his own time, Gene was finally placed in the Air Ferry Command co-piloting huge cargo planes of men and materials to such far outposts as North Africa, India, China, and Burma.

In 1946 Gene returned to Republic Pictures to continue his film career. But he wasn't the same Autry that had gone off to war; he was older now and beginning to think about his future and the fact that his performing years were numbered. No longer did he wish to work under the tight-fisted Herbert J. Yates unless there was a drastic change in the working relationship.

Gene wanted a piece of the picture action; he wanted to establish his own Gene Autry Productions to produce his features so that he could have a greater say in production matters, but mostly so that he could have a split of the proceeds. Yates would have none of it, so Autry started negotiations with Columbia Pictures and in mid-1947 signed a very lucrative contract that gave him everything that Yates had refused.

Between mid-1946 and the time in 1947 when he signed with Columbia, Gene made five Republic features—all pleasant, but mostly lackluster. They were top heavy with music (usually six songs with many reprises in the approximately seventy minutes of running time), with action sequences woefully lacking. To the dismay of action fans, Gene seldom had his six-guns strapped on in these final features for Republic. There had been slow moments in the prewar features, but nothing to compare with most of these final ho-hum features at Republic. It is easy to speculate that Autry, unhappy with his Republic pact, was riding out his contract.

Variety's critics had these comments on the postwar Republic features: *Sioux City Sue*—"Except for a few shots of Autry jockeying his horse Champion in a hard gallop across the plains, most of the celluloid is taken up with his crooning"; *Trail to San Antone*—"standard fare" . . . "made from the pat formula of Gene Autry vehicles"; *Twilight On the Rio Grande*—"filler product"; *Saddle Pals*—"a bit below entertainment level usually achieved by Gene Autry"; *Robin Hood of Texas* (Gene's last Republic feature and, ironically, the best of the last batch)—"goes along in the slickest Autry tradition" . . . "This is right in the groove for Autry fans" . . . "He's the Autry of old, singing better than ever."

Perhaps it took five films for Autry to get back into the picture-making groove, or perhaps he just wanted to leave Republic with a winner to show Yates that he still had the old magic. Regardless, it was all over at Republic; the Columbia "Proud Lady" was carrying the torch for Gene Autry and he would eventually, between 1947 and 1953, produce thirty-two pictures under her imprimatur.

* * *

It was during the war years that Gene Autry acquired his first deep appreciation for the business term "diversification." The year before he went into the service he had grossed half a million dollars in show business. Suddenly he found himself working for Uncle Sam for a paltry $150.00 per month. The adjustment in income was a difficult one for Autry. Years later he commented to AP writer John Barbour about his wartime financial plight: "If it had not been for royalties I collected for the Gene Autry pistols and the Gene Autry sweatshirts and the Gene Autry hats and all that kind of stuff—and my records—why I could have been in a tough situation. So I said to myself, by God as long as you work and perform you better keep on because the time will come when you can't perform any more. You better have a business to bring you in an income." And a businessman he did become.

During 1947 and 1948 the national magazines were beginning to take note of Autry's big business ways in feature stories with such titles as "Gene Autry, Inc." *(Life)* and "Cowboy in Clover" *(Time).* His very diversified holdings and/or sources of income were reported to include his own movie company (Gene Autry Productions, Inc.); radio stations (KOOL, Phoenix; KOWL, Santa Monica; KOPO, Tucson); Gene Autry Radio Productions, Inc. (which produced his radio programs and booked his guest appearances); oil wells in Texas and New Mexico; cattle ranches in Texas, Arizona, and Nevada; two Phoenix newspapers; a two-million-dollar traveling rodeo; major stock in the publishing company that produced the comic books bearing his name; five movie theaters in Dallas; music publishing companies; record royalties; a California flying school and charter plane service; the licensing of the many products that bore his name (these products alone were bringing in royalties of a hundred thousand dollars a year by this time); and (of all things) a grocery store in Oklahoma City. Gene's net income in 1948 was estimated at six-hundred-thousand dollars—that was *net* income, not gross.

Director Frank McDonald recently commented to me that one day while he was making a movie with Gene at Columbia Pictures, "Gene said, 'Excuse me, I've got to sell a radio station.' He got on the phone and sold his radio station in Arizona, hung up and made nothing of it as though it were done every day. He was shrewd. He wasn't any John D. Rockefeller, but he certainly made good deals. Of course, some of them went sour like with anybody who gambles that kind of money. He was bound to make a mistake now and then, but by and large Gene did all right."

The Columbia-released Gene Autry features of 1947 through 1953 represent some of the finest B Western films ever made. Though the films were popular at the time, they were often overshadowed by the Roy Rogers films, which were flashier—Trucolor specials with elaborate musical produc-

tion numbers, flowery, flamboyant costuming, and large casts. Then, too, there was perhaps the feeling among many critics and fans that Autry was a "comfortable old shoe" that had been around for a long time and was thus allowed to be taken for granted. Whatever the reason, the Columbia films were not fully appreciated until years later when in retrospect and in comparison with others of the same type their worth shone through.

During these years Autry was initiating subtle changes in his films that were not immediately

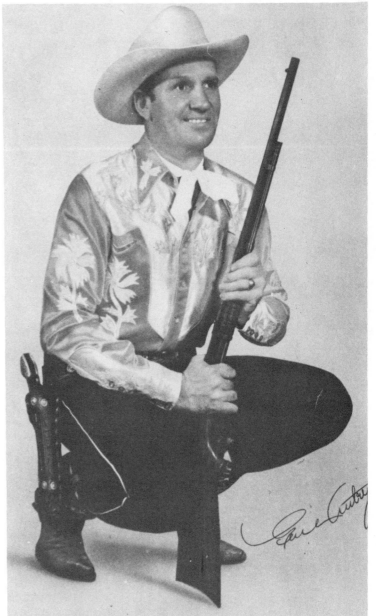

This flamboyant Western costuming was generally forsaken in Gene's Columbia films of the late 1940s and early 1950s. However, it was still stock costuming for rodeo and other personal appearances.

While most of Gene's Columbia Pictures' attire was not this conservative, the contrast with his Republic films was rather sharp.

songs generally functioning logically in the proceedings.

Pat Buttram, another of the popular alumni from Chicago's "National Barn Dance," eventually became Gene's new comic sidekick for the Columbia series. (Smiley Burnette, Gene's prewar sidekick, was under contract at Columbia for the Charles Starrett series and, thus, unavailable.) Pat had made many personal appearances with Gene over the years and had become a regular on the "Melody Ranch" radio program after the war. In 1950 he became Gene's comic cohort on television, too, as the Gene Autry half-hour television series commenced.

Action, which had so often in years past taken a seat at the back of the buggy, was now in the driver's seat. Eighteen of the films between 1947 and 1951 were directed by Republic's old action ace, John English, who kept the Autry Columbia films at full gallop in such episodes as *The Last Roundup* (1947), *The Cowboy and the Indians* (1949), *Mule Train* (1950), and *Gene Autry and the Mounties* (1951), which featured a couple of bully brawls between the heavies and Autry, and closed with a blistering town-burning.

Frank McDonald, who had directed a number of Autry films prior to the war and who would later direct many of his television films, only helmed two of the Columbia features, one of which was *The Big Sombrero* (1949), a singular return to the lavish Autry musical Westerns (nine tunes no less) of earlier years, this time in the rainbow hues of Cinecolor. McDonald commented to me that *The Big Sombrero* was his favorite of the Gene Autry films he directed. *Texan's Never Cry* (1951) was the other McDonald postwar feature, standard Autry fare, but pleasing nonetheless.

I asked Frank about the budgets for the Columbia features in comparison with the Republic budgets.

FRANK MCDONALD: They were higher but nobody knows how much because Mandy [Armand Schaefer, Gene's producer] never told anybody what they were. Very seldom could you get a budget from the director unless he was personally involved in the business. The studios would rather a director didn't know the budget because then he would know how much he could spend and would be tempted to go overboard. So they would keep that a dark secret. Mandy Schaefer was a darned good producer. He could get more out of a dollar than most producers could get out of a hundred dollars. He was quite deaf, you know, but he could hear anything you didn't want him to hear—like most deaf people.

obvious to the casual viewer. The fancy, flowery cowboy outfits of the thirties and early forties were gradually toned down or in some cases eliminated altogether in favor of more subdued Western shirts, and occasionally even the traditional Levi-type pants found their way into his film wardrobe. Generally the fancy duds appeared only if there was a logical reason for them, such as a social event or special occasion. Soon, also, the song content of the films was reduced to around two or three per feature with far fewer reprises than had previously been the case and with the

DAVID ROTHEL: Do you know what the average gross was on an Autry film?

FRANK McDONALD: No, nobody knew that. That they *didn't* want you to know because then you might ask for a raise. (laugh)

The final twelve entries in the series (1952-53) were directed by veteran George Archainbaud, who was capable but lacked the flair for action sequences that John English had. If it can be said that the English features generally galloped at breakneck speed, the Archainbaud films moved at a leisurely trot.

For the six 1953 features Gene was reteamed after many years with sidekick Smiley Burnette, who was available now that the Charles "Durango Kid" Starrett series had concluded at Columbia. Pat Buttram, Gene's regular comic partner, was unable to appear in the last six because of an accident that had occured during the shooting of the Gene Autry television series. Director Frank McDonald recounted the incident for me.

FRANK McDONALD: We were making a television show in the Gene Autry series called "The Rainmaker." Gene and Pat were in it, of course. It was about six o'clock at night—we would work until 7:30 or 8:00 P.M. because it didn't get dark until then; we always worked until the sun went down. We were shooting up on a mountain and doing a scene involving a little cannon the property man had picked up in an antique shop. It was about three feet long, made out of brass, and had little wooden wheels. We didn't have a powder man on the set, so the property man fixed it up to fire when Pat pulled the string attached to it.

We started to shoot the scene with Pat saying, "Now, you see, Gene, you put the powder in here and shoot the cannon off by pulling the string, and then you'll have rain—it'll bring rain." As he pulled the string, you never heard such a noise in your life. It sounded like a bomb; it *was* a bomb. The powder exploded inside the cannon and threw shrapnel all over the place.

Well, all hell broke loose. Pat was nearly killed; his whole chest was cut open and his foot was cut badly, too. Gene's horse, Champion, had a badly cut nose, the sound man got a piece of shrapnel in his knee, and several others were hurt and bleeding. Now, remember, we were on the top of a mountain in the desert. We had to get four miles down to the gas station to call an ambulance, and one ambulance wouldn't take care of all the people that were hurt. I said, "Call up Yucca; I know there's an ambulance there because I helped dedicate it last year." Finally, two ambulances arrived. They put

Pat and another man in the one and put the other wounded in the second ambulance. They rushed to Twentynine Palms, California, to a Dr. Ince, who was a brother of the Ince that was the famous motion picture director of years ago, Thomas Ince. He said, "My God, I've seen bad cases during the war, but this is one of the worst I ever saw." Pat was still conscious, which was terrible.

Finally, they sent a plane to Hollywood for blood and a Dr. Imerman who was going to assist Dr. Ince. [Gene subsequently told me that the plane was his own—a seven-passenger, twin-engine Beechcraft—flown by his personal pilot, Herb Green.] When the plane arrived in Twentynine Palms, there wasn't enough light for it to land so the citizens of Twentynine Palms got out their cars, formed a line, and turned their headlights on so that the plane could see to land. It was a very dramatic thing. Pat was in the hospital for a long time but, of course, eventually recovered.

DAVID ROTHEL: Gene Autry wasn't hurt in the explosion?

FRANK McDONALD: He wasn't touched. I was standing right by Gene, and about a foot away from me was the windshield that had been completely torn out of a jeep. It missed us by inches. It was a terrible, terrible thing.

With the final series feature, *The Last of the Pony Riders* (1953), it was all over; Gene Autry brought his Western motion picture series to a close. He was indeed the last of the "veteran," singing pony riders, closing out his feature movie career almost simultaneously with the last "new" singing cowboy, Rex Allen, over at Republic. The trail dust had settled more than two years before on the Roy Rogers oatuners and even earlier for all the other singing cowboys. Except for the break during the war years, Gene Autry had been a star of Western films from 1935 until the end of 1953, and he had made more singing cowboy movies— ninety-one—than any other performer in his genre. His own personal favorite from the long list was *The Last Roundup* (1947), his first picture for Columbia under his own banner, Gene Autry Productions, Inc.

During the last half of the forties through the early 1950s, Gene was a best-selling recording artist on the Columbia label. His hits included "Buttons and Bows," "Mule Train," "Ghost Riders in the Sky," and the seasonal favorites, "Frosty the Snow Man," "Here Comes Peter Cottontail," "Here Comes Santa Claus," and "Rudolph the Red Nosed Reindeer," his biggest seller. Of the forty million or so records he sold during his career, "Rudolph" accounted for ten million. Gene has said that his

This portrait of Gene was taken in the late 1940s.

personal favorites are "That Silver-Haired Daddy of Mine," "South of the Border," and his "Back in the Saddle Again" theme song.

With his return from the service, Gene had also re-commenced broadcasting his very popular weekly "Melody Ranch" radio program on CBS, sponsored by Wrigley's Doublemint Gum. At first the program was on at 7:00 P.M. on Sundays; later it moved to Saturdays at 8:00 P.M.; finally, it moved back to Sundays at 6:00 P.M. for the last three years. The final broadcast was on May 13, 1956. Gene explained to me the time changes for the program over the years.

GENE AUTRY: Jack Benny had been on NBC for many years when CBS made a deal with him to come over to their network. Jack Benny's new CBS contract was to the effect that he was to have the same time on NBC. Well, when they [CBS] looked that over, they found out that Gene Autry owned the time. I had the packaged show for Wrigley. I had bought the time and produced the show. When CBS came to me and wanted me to switch over to Saturday, I said, "Well, I'll do that, I'll switch to Saturday, but in return I would like the CBS outlet for the two radio stations I have in Tucson and

Phoenix. I'll trade with you. If you'll give me the affiliate stations in Phoenix and Tucson, I'll go over to Saturday night." So they agreed. Frank Stanton said, "You got a deal!" Finally, though, six o'clock came open on Sunday night and they moved me back over there. They thought it was better for me on Sunday than it was on Saturday.

I asked Gene's friend Ted Rogers, at present a successful radio station owner and operator in Florida, about the production of the "Melody Ranch" programs after the war.

TED ROGERS: I was assigned by CBS to be the CBS Network representative and director on the program. That meant that I was responsible for its production quality in terms of censorship and acceptability; I was in charge of the length of the script to make sure that the program got on and off on time; and I saw that the commercials adhered to company policies. To perform these responsibilities I sat in the control room right next to the program director (the man who was actually throwing the cues), in this case Autry's man, Bill Burch. Because I was involved with "Melody Ranch" for almost three years, I got to know Gene and most of the performers: Pat Buttram, Carl Cotner, Johnny Bond, the Cass County Boys, and all the other guys whose names escape me right now.

DAVID ROTHEL: Were the Autry shows live or on tape?

TED ROGERS: They were done live in the largest studio that CBS owned, Studio A, in the CBS Radio headquarters at Sunset and Gower in Hollywood. That was sort of the broadcasting capital of the world. CBS was at Sunset and Gower. (It was called Gower Gulch because you'd see all these out-of-work Western extras in their cowboy boots and spurs standing on the corner looking for a job at Columbia Pictures, which was around the corner.) Right up the street was the Hollywood Paladium; up the street from that was NBC Radio, at the corner of Sunset and Vine.

DAVID ROTHEL: What was Gene like on the job?

TED ROGERS: Gene was very, very serious during his rehearsal periods. He was businesslike; he didn't bridge any horsing around, "futsing" around by the stage hands or by the band; that was out. It was very quiet, very serious. Let's face it, Gene would be the first guy to tell you that he's not the world's greatest dramatic actor. Okay, each one of those "Melody Ranch" programs had a little dramatic piece in it, a little slice of the West, you know. There wasn't that much time to rehearse because there wasn't that big a budget on the show. So when Gene came in, most of the time he had only seen the script the night before and he had maybe "woodshedded" it a little bit at home. But there was an eight- or ten-minute little dramatic piece that he had to perform. It was live, it had music in it, it had lots of sound effects in it, lots of dissolves and scene changes in it. So it was quite a challenge in a restricted, minimum amount of time to get that dramatic piece rehearsed, get it set and done for the dress rehearsal along with the songs and other dialogue, and then, of course, get it on the air.

DAVID ROTHEL: How long did they rehearse the program?

TED ROGERS: Not very long. Whatever the minimum was; I would say three hours.

DAVID ROTHEL: Did you perceive any differences between the public and the private man?

TED ROGERS: No, no. He was exactly the same. I never saw him lose his temper; I never saw him get really irritated; I never saw him blow his stack at anybody in well over three years. I never saw him not have enough time for someone. Let's face it, he was buffeted and shielded from the public by studio guards and the rehearsals were always closed and that sort of thing, but after the show and before the show if any fans somehow got through the stagedoor, somehow got to the lip of the stage when the program was over, Gene'd stoop over and sign autographs and talk with them for ten or fifteen minutes. I never heard him make any derogatory comments about the public; I never heard him make one derogatory comment about the sponsor, the Wrigley people.

You know, there are a lot of cynical stars who take the money and run. I've worked with one hell of a lot of them. The minute the sponsor left the client's booth they'd say, "Well, I hope that's his last trip for thirteen weeks!" I never heard Gene say a derogative word. He was very grateful to CBS and to Wrigley.

DAVID ROTHEL: Jon Tuska in his book *The Filming of the West* tends to present Autry with a rather harsh appraisal as a performer and intimates a certain aloofness [my word] at times. Tuska suggests this when he says, " . . . he did come to have his own network radio show. His performances were quite the same here as in his films, with all the stooges and heavies clustered around the microphone, Autry at the opposite end of the stage, alone before his silver microphone, gaudily dressed, singing his non-Western ditties."

TED ROGERS: I can tell you why he was on that microphone. By having Gene by himself at the microphone closest to the control room, we didn't have any problem with music isolation or sound balance. We had the Cass County Boys, Carl Cotner and his big band, and sound effects—they all needed isolation flats and isolated microphone pickups. We would feed them [the microphones] onto pots so that we could fade them up and down—fade the horse sound effects in and out, fade the background music, fade the "ooh-waas" of the Cass County Boys. Gene required total isolation for sound like any star. If you went to a Bing Crosby broadcast, you'd see John Scott Trotter and the singers, Ken Carpenter, and everybody else way, way down at one end of the studio and Crosby way up at the other end. He's the star and he's the guy you've got to pick up [with the microphones].

In addition, for the dramatic scene, by placing his mike close to the control room—separated only by glass—Bill Burch could damned near walk him through or, to be more precise, he could gesture him through. Bill stood during almost the whole show. He'd say to the technical director, "down" and "up" and "bring him in"; and he gave Gene a lot of hand signals. Gene was very good on hand signals. You could do almost anything with Gene by giving him hand signals.

By the early 1950s Autry had diversified even more and was heavily into television programming with his newly established company, Flying A Productions, producing not only his own "Gene Autry Show" (eighty-five half-hour films produced between 1950 and 1954) with Champion and sidekick Pat Buttram, but also "The Range Rider" (seventy-six half-hour films beginning in 1951) with Jock Mahoney and Dick Jones. Next came the production of the first thirty-nine episodes of "Death Valley Days" (1952) with Stanley Andrews as the Old Ranger. That program was followed by "Annie Oakley" (eighty half-hour films produced beginning in 1953) starring Gail Davis with supporting players Brad Johnson as Deputy Sheriff Lofty Craig and Jimmy Hawkins as Tagg. In 1955 Flying A launched its last two television series: "Buffalo Bill, Jr." (forty half-hour films produced; the first twenty-six on a budget of $850,000) starring Dick Jones (late of "The Range Rider") with Nancy Gilbert and Harry Cheshire; and "Champion" (yes, the horse had his own series of twenty-six half-hour films!) which was promoted as the "story of a wild stallion, a twelve-year-old boy and his dog, with Barry Curtis, Jim Bannon, and Rebel the dog and Champion the horse—leader

Gene is seen here planning the first six "Gene Autry Show" television films with director Frank McDonald (hatless) and producer Louis Gray. *Photo courtesy of Frank McDonald.*

Jimmy Hawkins (Tagg), Gail Davis (Annie), and director Frank McDonald on location for the "Annie Oakley" television series. *Photo courtesy of Frank McDonald.*

Gene Autry (here with Champion, Jr.) was the first movie cowboy star to make films especially for television. *Photo courtesy of Gene Autry.*

of a herd of wild horses in America's Southwest in the 1880s."

I asked Gene about his temerity in entering television series production before other movie stars.

GENE AUTRY: I made the first series of half-hour films for television. I was the first movie star to make pictures for television. Well, I caught all kinds of hell from theater owners, exhibitors, and even from Columbia Pictures [Autry's movie releasing company]—they were all over me for making this first series, which was released over the CBS network. Mr. Wrigley bought them.

About that time there was a Theatre Owners of America convention held in Chicago, I think it was. I made a speech before them and said, "Look, you fellows are hollering about progress. Whether you like it or not, television is coming in and you might as well get ready to face the fact. I remember when radio first came in you said that it was going to ruin the theaters. Instead of that it developed a lot of stars for you fellows in the theaters. Look at Bing Crosby; he's a radio artist. Also, look at Bob Hope; he was first in radio and then came into

pictures. Radio has developed some very fine talent for you. I think television is going to do the same thing and the time will come when all of you producers in Hollywood are going to be making television pictures. And you'll probably wind up selling your old product to television." And it all came true.

Gene's television series went into reruns after 1954. In the spring of 1956 when his "Melody Ranch" radio program went off the air, he pretty much completed the long under way transition from cowboy performer-tycoon to just plain cowboy tycoon.

In the early 1960s *Newsweek* reported that Gene had purchased his fifth hotel and was awaiting FCC approval to "run KTLA-TV, a Los Angeles station that one of his several holding companies recently purchased for twelve million dollars." Gene commented that he was involved in these business dealings "to own and build a secure future."

Along with such wealthy partners as Robert Lehman of Wall Street's Lehman Brothers and Leonard Firestone, Gene owned over fifty percent of the stock in the following holdings:

● Golden West Broadcasting, radio stations in Los Angeles, San Francisco, Seattle, and Portland—estimated worth seventeen million dollars.
● Golden West Baseball Company, the Los Angeles Angels—estimated worth eight million dollars.
● The Gene Autry Hotel Company, five hotels—estimated worth eighteen million dollars.

All by himself Gene owned the before-mentioned ranches, television production company, a rodeo, two music publishing companies, radio and television stations in Phoenix and Tucson, and was a minority stock holder in the Los Angeles Rams professional football team.

Over the years Gene has always been uneasy when questioned about his business acumen and his wealth. Especially during his performing years he felt that his simple, home-spun cowboy image might be tarnished by his growing reputation as a wealthy business tycoon. In interviews he would always play down his wealth. He would generally say something to the effect that, "People don't realize that I have an awful lot of expenses, too. You've got to figure all that overhead; this isn't all just profits. After all, I'm in business."

Gene Autry—cowboy business tycoon. *Photo courtesy of Gene Autry.*

In a recent conversation I asked Ted Rogers about Gene Autry, the businessman.

TED ROGERS: Gene was a slow study [in business matters], but he was a very thorough study. Gene wasn't a meteor or a comet, but when he put his mind to something, researched something, whether it was an idea for a new series or a new venture or selling the paper or buying the television station or disposing of a radio property, there wasn't anything about that property he didn't know before he made his decision. He had all the facts at hand, and it would be totally improper to say that anybody made a decision other than Autry. I've seen him do it time and time again—even when he got involved with the Continental Hotel on the strip, which was one of his latter things, and that hotel in Chicago which was such a disaster. He called the shots, no matter how trivial. (Author's note: When Autry opened the Sahara Inn in Chicago he was informed that it would be necessary to rent the linen from one particular company in the city. When he refused to pay the exorbitant costs they demanded, a portion of the hotel was blown up. Gene rebuilt it and was again threatened unless he acquiesced. Again refus-

ing to cooperate with the extortionists, he sold out.)

TED ROGERS: Oh, God, the Midway Mafia! The Midway Airport Mafia watching him come and go, counting the Cadillacs to see how many . . . I think they used to keep score to see how many they could blow up on a Saturday night. Gene was not quite so successful with things he didn't have so much knowledge of, like the hotels. But when it was something he knew about and when he was dealing in areas of business where he had experience, he was in it with two feet and a cane, all the way: radio, television, broadcasting, programming, packaging productions, movies, and newspapers.

Also on the Autry hotel business, in 1973 George Goodale, a long-time business associate of Gene Autry, commented, "He's only got the Gene Autry Hotel in Palm Springs now and it's doing very well for him. The only thing he said when he sold off the Continental Hotel over on Sunset to the Hyatt chain was how he'd miss having his breakfast in the coffee shop."

In 1974 Gene told AP writer John Barbour about the selling of the Continental Hotel, "It would have made a lot of money, but it had a bad environment, all the hippies, all that class of people. I just didn't want to get involved, with my

Gene Autry still oversees his many business enterprises. *Photo courtesy of Gene Autry.*

name on the hotel. It doesn't matter if it's just a brand name up there. But when it's the Gene Autry Continental, that's different. I just didn't want to be in that environment. That's why I got rid of it."

With the passage of time a sort of mystique has developed around Gene Autry because of what appears to be a strange dichotomy in the man. On the one hand he seems to be the simple, uncomplicated, singing cowpuncher from Texas who, through his friendly, "aw-shucks" behavior, won a place in the hearts of his public as he outfought the baddies and saved the trembling heroine from a fate worse than you know what. (Once, after an attempt to tally his screen fights, Gene commented, "I fought more rounds than Dempsey!") On the other hand another Autry gradually has become known to the public. This Autry is a shrewd, calculating, hard-bargaining millionaire-tycoon who has been heading-up business enterprises in a multiplicity of commercial arenas. Pat Buttram once joked, "Gene can't sing. He can't play the guitar. He can't act. But he sure as hell can count!"

As spectators and chroniclers of the passing scene tried to place Gene in a neat, descriptive box, they were frustrated. It just seemed incomprehensible that this shy fellow smiling, singing, strumming, and "aw-shucks-ing" on the silver screen and radio could also be a lion in the world of business.

In separate, informal conversations with two people who knew him professionally and personally, a behind-the-scenes picture of the man gradually began to appear—not crystal clear, of course, but like an SX 70 picture only half-developed.

DAVID ROTHEL: Was he ever temperamental to work with?

FRANK McDONALD: Never! I never saw Gene temperamental in my life.

DAVID ROTHEL: I take it then that his cast and crew liked him as a person.

FRANK McDONALD: They loved him, loved him. Gene is very congenial, a very fine fellow. He is very quiet and unassuming, and there's no stardust in his hair. He never was one to complain. If he had anything to say, he'd tell me quietly. He'd make a suggestion or a production decision, but never mention anything about an actor. He'd say, "That's your department." You know, he was a quick study on a script. He would sit in the car, learn his lines for the next scene and then take a little nap (which I wish to God I could do). He had trained himself to do this apparently. He could go to sleep for ten minutes, wake up, and go on and do the scene fresh as a daisy. It's a great trick; I never knew anyone else who could do that.

He is a very fine person with a great, quiet sense of humor.

TED ROGERS: Did you see the stuffed Indian he has in his office?

DAVID ROTHEL: Yes, I did.

TED ROGERS: Now that's the kind of sense of humor he has and there's no way to explain it—a complete, life-sized, fully-stuffed Indian. For all I know it is real skin. I've always been afraid to ask him. (laugh) I've always had a wild feeling it's a *real* stuffed Indian. There it is, a life-sized, six-foot Indian sitting in a rocking chair with full war dress on. It was a real start when you went in there the first time.

DAVID ROTHEL: When I saw the Indian, he was wearing a California Angels baseball cap on his head.

TED ROGERS: Gene also had the largest pair of Texas longhorns I've ever seen in my life on the wall of his office. God knows he has had thousands of them [on the hoof]; he probably just keeps telling his foreman, "When you get a bigger one, send it to me." Incidently, Gene is always immaculate. I never saw him in disarray in public. I never saw him without a five-hundred-dollar pair of boots on and I never saw him without a thousand-dollar cowboy suit on or without a hundred-dollar shirt on in my life, in my whole life. I'm not kidding. Down in the dirt and mud practicing some stunt we were going to do, it was Gene Autry with the white hat—The Best in the West. "Where the pavement ends and the West begins"—that's the way Lou Crosby brought on "Melody Ranch," you know.

DAVID ROTHEL: I haven't heard that in years.

TED ROGERS: Yeah, that's it. And then he would say, "The Best in the West, folks, Gene Autry." And Gene would come out. He was always concerned about his personal appearance, about his tendency to put on weight. I used to have breakfast with him at the Continental, his hotel on Sunset Boulevard. Even at breakfast at eight o'clock in the morning he was dressed absolutely like he was ready to go on the set. He surveyed the coffee shop of the Continental like the tycoon he'd grown to be.

Gene is one of the most socially shy guys I've ever met that made it big as a public figure. He is just terribly shy. So you can imagine how uncomfortable he is around, say, Eastern establishment people or advertising network, pseudosophisticated, wheeling-dealing kinds of people—lawyers and accountants.

Gene Autry is seen here receiving the American Patriots Medal from Bob Miller, president of the Freedoms Foundation. The award was presented in early 1977.

A happy Gene Autry was caught by the camera in this recent picture as he watched his California Angels practice at Angel's Stadium in Palm Springs.

There was a tight coterie of people that he was comfortable around, that he believed in and trusted. He gravitated to a certain sort of person and, if you weren't that sort of person, it wasn't all that easy to get along with Autry.

DAVID ROTHEL: Can you describe that sort of person?

TED ROGERS: Yes, a little bit I can. I mean I can give you a few clues: nondevious, straightforward, no fast talk or phony con talk. Gene was very straight, the most unphony guy I ever met—not a fake bone in his body.

DAVID ROTHEL: Nobody ever said "Gene, baby" to him, I'll bet.

TED ROGERS: That's right. Gene was a simplistic person. He was a very basic guy comfortable around basic people. He loved his Scotch and soda; he loved jokes with guys. He was very comfortable in that kind of easy, informal masculine idiom. He was one of the kindest, nicest gentlemen I've ever met. He was a gentleman.

DAVID ROTHEL: You know Gene's wife, Ina, too, don't you?

TED ROGERS: I've met her several times. She's the perfect wife for Gene. Gene has always been very, very proud of her, devoted to her. There were always personal expressions of his feelings about Ina in their Christmas cards and things like that.

FRANK MCDONALD: They used to give two Christmas parties at the wonderful house that burned down in Studio City. They'd give one for half the company and crew one night and another the next night for the rest of them because the house was not big enough—they had about 150 people.

TED ROGERS: Ina totally shunned the spotlight. She hardly ever left the ranch. I saw her a few times when Gene was on location and she brought him things in the car. We just sat and rapped for a while.

DAVID ROTHEL: How long has it been since you last saw Gene?

TED ROGERS: I'd say about three or four years. He was still wearing a Western suit with the Western tie and the boots. I never saw him dressed any other way.

*   *   *

It's fascinating, of course, trying to peal away the outer makeup in an attempt to understand the inner workings of the man. But, ultimately, our curiosity remains as we discover yet another layer of makeup. But that's what makes human beings fascinating and in show business what separates mere stars from super-stars.

The Gene Autry we remember is the star of motion pictures, radio, and personal appearances. He's the one who made us stop in mid chomp on that mouthful of popcorn while he rescued June Storey from a runaway buckboard.

And we remember listening to him on "Melody Ranch" singing "Tweedle-O-Twill" and "Be Honest With Me, Dear" and suffering the good-natured humor of sidekick Pat Buttram and his "Mr. Artery" bantering.

And we remember seeing him in one of his personal appearances. I guess the greatest thrill of my young life was going to the Cleveland Arena for a Gene Autry rodeo and personal appearance. After an interminable time of watching bulldoggers and calf ropers, the arena went dark for Gene's appearance. A voice out of the blackness proclaimed, "And now ladies, gentlemen and children, America's favorite cowboy—Gene Autry."

And suddenly there he was on Champion, riding at full gallop around and around the arena, waving and smiling to the packed house as the orchestra blared "Back in the Saddle Again" and one long, shrill scream echoed back and forth, back and forth across the arena from all but one of his young fans. My breath caught in my throat; tears

The situation looks grim for Gene in this scene from *Phantom Empire.*

filled my ten-year-old eyes. There was a silent click as my mental camera still-framed the image in my mind. It remains there to this day.

*   *   *

GENE AUTRY
ANNOTATED FILMOGRAPHY

The filmography only includes information on the films in which Gene Autry starred. The films in which he appeared in secondary roles or as a guest star are simply listed for the record.

*   *   *

In Old Santa Fe (Mascot, 1934)

Mystery Mountain (Mascot, 1934)

*   *   *

Phantom Empire (Mascot, 1935) Serial

Producer, Nat Levine; directors, Otto Brower and B. Reeves Eason; screenplay, John Rathmell and Armand Schaefer; story, Wallace McDonald, Gerald Geraghty, and Hy Freedman.

CAST: Gene Autry, Smiley Burnette, Frankie Darro, Betsy King Ross, Dorothy Christy, Wheeler Oakman, Charles K. French, Warner Richmond, Frank Glendon, Bill Moore, Wally Wales, Edward Piel, Stanley Blystone, Champion.

Gene Autry makes his first starring appearance in this science fiction/Western serial. In the highly fanciful story Gene, a Western radio singer, gets involved with people from an underground city called Murania. As on the earth's surface, there are good guys and bad guys in the scientifically advanced civilization of Murania. Gene, between broadcasts from his Radio Ranch, continually gets involved with the subterranean people and their inner-world conflicts in one cliff-hanging chapter after another.

Gene and his sidekick, Smiley Burnette, get plenty of opportunities over the many weeks of the serial's run to sing some Western ditties—most of which were written by the two of them. Included are "I'm Getting a Moon's Eye View of the World," "My Cross-Eyed Gal," "Just Come On Back," "I'm Oscar—I'm Pete," "Uncle Noah's Ark," and "That Silver-Haired Daddy of Mine."

*   *   *

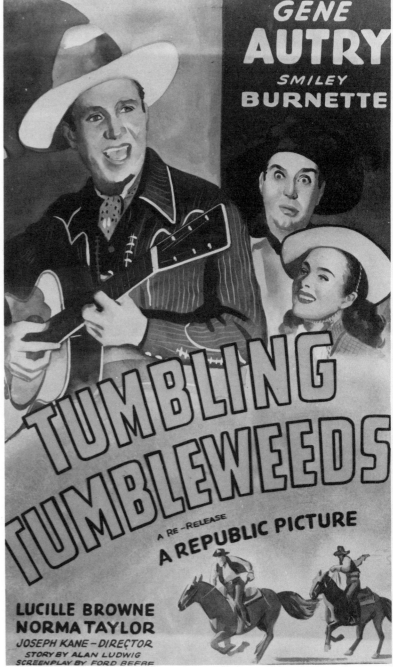

Tumbling Tumbleweeds (Republic, 1935) 57 M.

Producer, Nat Levine; director, Joseph Kane; screenplay, Ford Beebe; story, Alan Ludwig; camera, Ernest Miller.

CAST: Gene Autry, Smiley Burnette, Lucile Browne, Norma Taylor, George Hayes, Edward Hearn, Jack Rockwell, Frankie Marvin, George Chesebro, Eugene Jackson, Charles King, Charles Whitaker, George Burton, Tom London, Cornelius Keefe, Cliff Lyons, Tracy Layne, Champion.

For his first feature Republic gun-galloper the youthful Gene Autry was not immediately recognized as an innovator of Western films by his critics. The film was generally dismissed as "supporting program material."

In the story Gene, returning from a five-year exile from his estranged father, discovers that the prosperous cattleman has been murdered and his (Gene's) childhood companion is accused of the crime. With the assistance of his medicine show companions Smiley Burnette and George (later to be "Gabby") Hayes, Gene actionfully rounds up the real villains in time to sing six or ten more Western tunes. Among them are the title song, "That Silver-Haired Daddy of Mine," and "Ridin' Down the Canyon."

Seeing this first film effort again after viewing many of Gene's later films, it is surprising how inexperienced he appears in all departments— acting, singing, and riding. During these first few films Gene was also plagued with a pudginess that he would lose in a year or so.

*   *   *

Melody Trail (Republic, 1935) 57 M.

Director, Joseph Kane.

CAST: Gene Autry, Smiley Burnette, Ann Rutherford, Wade Boteler, Alan Bridge, Willy Castello, Marie Quillan, Fern Emmett, Gertrude Messinger, Tracy Layne, Jane Barnes, Iona Reed.

Gene teams up for the first time with attractive leading lady Ann Rutherford in this average Autry romp. Outstanding among the songs is "Hold On, Little Doggie, Hold On," written by Gene.

*   *   *

Sagebrush Troubadour (Republic, 1935) 57 M.

Director, Joseph Kane; screenplay, Oliver Drake; camera, Ernest Miller.

CAST: Gene Autry, Smiley Burnette, Barbara Pepper, Frank Glendon, Denny Meadows, Hooper Atchley, Fred Kelsey, Julian Rivero, Champion.

Gene is still learning his trade on-the-job in this

average entry from his first year's supply of features. Murder, mystery, and music (not necessarily in that order of importance) are the plot ingredients that go into this sagebrush stew.

This score-heavy opus seems to have as many songs by Gene and Smiley Burnette as a cactus has prickers. Among them are "On the Prairie," "Lookin' for the Lost Chord," "The Hurdy Gurdy Man," "My Prayer for Tonight," "End of the Trail," and "I'd Love a Home in the Mountains."

*　　*　　*

Singing Vagabond (Republic, 1935) 55 M.

Director, Carl Pierson; screenplay, Oliver Drake, Betty Burbridge; production supervisor, Armand Schaefer.

CAST: Gene Autry, Smiley Burnette, Ann Rutherford, Barbara Pepper, Warner Richmond, Frank LaRue, Grace Goodall, Niles Welch, Tom Brower, Robinson Neeman, Ray Benard, Henry Roquemore, Allan Sears, Chief Big Tree, Champion.

A better-than-average entry in the series, *Singing Vagabond* has the proper blend of music, mayhem, and mesquite to satisfy Western fans. Gene's "shy hero" role is becoming stet at this point as is Smiley Burnette's tenor-bass vocal calisthenics. Songs include "Friends of the Prairie, Farewell" by Smiley Burnette and "Wagon Train" by Autry and Burnette.

*　　*　　*

Red River Valley (Republic, 1936) 60 M.

Producer and director, B. Reeves Eason; screenplay, Stuart McGowan, Dorrell McGowan; camera,

Charles King and George Chesebro are giving Gene a rough time in this scene from *Red River Valley*.

William Nobles; editor, Carl Pierson; sound, Terry Kellum; songs, Sam Stept, Gene Autry, Smiley Burnette; musical director, Harry Grey; production supervisor, Armand Schaefer.

CAST: Gene Autry, Smiley Burnette, Frances Grant, Boothe Howard, Jack Kennedy, Sam Flint, George Chesebro, Charles King, Eugene Jackson, Edward Hearn, Frank LaRue, Ken Cooper, Frank Marvin, Champion.

Again the film title is taken from a popular Western ballad that is reprised frequently within the one-hour ride. The plot concerns the efforts of unknown evildoers to foil the efforts to complete an irrigation project that will bring water to the drought-parched valley. (The song entitled "Where a Water Wheel Keeps Turnin' On" is, as you can imagine, fittingly worked into the score.) Gene and Smiley, working underground, finally thwart and reveal the baddies.

*　　*　　*

Comin' Round the Mountain (Republic, 1936) 60 M.

Producer, Nat Levine; director, Mack Wright; screenplay, Oliver Drake, Dorrell and Stuart McGowan; camera, William Nobles.

CAST: Gene Autry, Smiley Burnette, Ann Rutherford, Roy Mason, Raymond Brown, Ken Cooper, Tracy Lane, Robert McKenzie, John Ince, Frank Lackteen, Champion.

Gene and Smiley are joined by their frequent leading lady Ann Rutherford for more fun and music in this actionful entry in the series. Though the implausible script is best forgotten, there are plenty of laughs and songs ("Don Juan of Sevillio," "When the Campfire Is Low on the Prairie," and "Chiquita") prior to the rip-roaring cross-country horse race that wraps up this zinger.

Champion is very much involved in the goings-on and, according to one trade critic, deserves "top honors" for his performance.

*　　*　　*

The Singing Cowboy (Republic, 1936) 60 M.

Producer, Nat Levine; director, Mack Wright; screenplay, Dorrell and Stuart McGowan; camera, William Nobles and Edgar Lyons; editor, Lester Orlebeck; sound, Terry Kellum; musical director, Harry Grey; songs, Smiley Burnette and Oliver Drake; production supervisor, Armand Schaefer.

CAST: Gene Autry, Smiley Burnette, Lois Wilde,

Lon Chaney, Jr., Ann Gillis, Earl Hodgins, Harvey Clark, John Van Pelt, Earl Eby, Ken Cooper, Harrison Green, Wes Warner, Jack Rockwell, Tracy Layne, Oscar Gahan, Frankie Marvin, Jack Kirk, Audrey Davis, George Pearce, Charles McAvoy, Alfred P. James, Snowflake, Pat Caron, Champion.

The year is 1936, but (would you believe) the plot deals with television on the prairie. It seems that unless Gene and his pals can raise some money for an operation, a little girl will be a cripple for life. Gene goes off to the city and rounds up a sponsor for a radio series. As a stunt to attract a big audience, the prairie broadcasts are televised. (Don't ask who watches!) Sure enough, they get the money for the operation. Among the songs are "Rainbow Trail" and "My Old Saddle Pal."

* * *

Guns and Guitars (Republic, 1936) 55 M.

Producer, Nat Levine; director, Joseph Kane; screenplay, Dorrell and Stuart McGowan; camera, Ernest Miller.

CAST: Gene Autry, Smiley Burnette, Dorothy Dix, Tom London, Charles King, J. P. McGowan, Earl Hodgins, Frankie Marvin, Eugene Jackson, Jack Rockwell, Ken Cooper, Tracy Lane, Wes Warner, Jim Corey, Frank Stravenger, Harrison Greene, Pascale Perry, Bob Burns, Champion.

While slow to get moving, once the action begins about midway, there is nonstop mayhem for the last thirty minutes. The plot has Autry accused of the local sheriff's murder, but through the many plot twists Gene gets himself elected new sheriff and catches the real murderer.

Gene somehow finds time to sing several Western ballads between shootouts. Among them are "Ridin' All Day" and the title tune.

* * *

Oh, Susanna (Republic, 1936) 60 M.

Director, Joseph Kane; screenplay, Oliver Drake; camera, William Nobles; musical director, Harry Grey; songs, Sam H. Stept, Oliver Drake, Gene Autry, Smiley Burnette.

CAST: Gene Autry, Smiley Burnette, Francis Grant, Earl Hodgins, Donald Kirke, Boothe Howard, Clara Kimball Young, Carl Stockdale, Frankie Marvin, Ed Piel, Sr., Light Crust Doughboys Band, Champion.

On his way to Mineral Springs by train, Gene

gets mugged, robbed of his clothes and belongings, and tossed from the moving train like a sack of potatoes. He is befriended by two wandering minstrels (Burnette and Hodgins), who patch him up and accompany him to Mineral Springs. After the usual fisticuffs, bang-bangs, and musical meanderings, Gene finds the one who "done him wrong" and gets his clothes, guns, and honor back. One unhappy critic commented, "Autry is as unemotional as a log."

Songs include the title song and "I'll Go Ridin' Down That Old Texas Trail," written by Autry and Burnette.

Once the proceedings get under way there is almost constant fighting (verbal and physical) among Texas Rangers, the Army, and Comanche Indians.

Autry is a Texas Ranger working undercover as a scout for the Army. He's trying to stop the Comanches from looting a wagon train loaded down with ammunition. When Gene passes word to the Army about a raid, they refuse to believe him. In the end, though, they learn to listen to the singing cowboy in the fancy duds.

*　　*　　*

The Big Show (Republic, 1936) 70 M.

Producer, Nat Levine; director, Mark V. Wright; screenplay, Dorrell and Stuart McGowan; camera, William Nobles and Edgar Lyons; editor, Robert Jahns; songs, Sam H. Stept, Ned Washington and Ted Koehler.

CAST: Gene Autry, Smiley Burnette, Kay Hughes, Sally Payne, William Newell, Max Terhune, Charles Judels, Rex King, Harry Worth, Mary Russell, Christine Maple, The Sons of the Pioneers, The Light Crust Doughboys Band, The Jones Boys, The Beverly Hills Billies, Champion.

This Autry opus lives up to its title. It's really a first-class production. Again the writers are on the mark for Gene in this tailor-made feature.

The story has Gene playing a dual role—a temperamental Western film star and his double. When the star skips out on a personal appearance at the Texas Centennial in Dallas (the scenic background for the story) Gene, the double, is persuaded to take over. The resulting comedy (mistaken identity engagements to two girls) and action (a fracas with Texas gangsters) plus guest appearances by a number of hillbilly music groups (see credits above) make this film the high-point of Gene's film career to this time. (Among those Sons of the Pioneers is a young fellow who will later strike out on his own—Roy Rogers.)

*　　*　　*

The Old Corral (Republic, 1936) 52 M.

Producer, Armand Schaefer; director, Joseph Kane; screenplay, Joseph Poland, Sherman Lowe from original story by Bernard McConville; camera, Edgar Lyons; songs, Sons of the Pioneers, Fleming Allen, Oliver Drake.

CAST: Gene Autry, Smiley Burnette, Hope Manning, Sons of the Pioneers, Cornelius Keefe, Lon Chaney, Jr., John Bradford, Milburn Morante,

*　　*　　*

Ride, Ranger, Ride (Republic, 1936) 63 M.

Producer, Nat Levine; director, Joseph Kane; screenplay, Dorrell and Stuart McGowan from original story by Bernard McConville and Karen DeWolf; camera, William Nobles.

CAST: Gene Autry, Smiley Burnette, Kay Hughes, Monte Blue, George Lewis, Max Terhune, Robert E. Homans, Lloyd Whitlock, Chief Thundercloud, Tennessee Ramblers, Champion.

This one is a real winner, with an ideal combination of music, comedy, and action—action aplenty.

Abe Lefton, Merrill McCormick, Charles Sullivan, Buddy Roosevelt, Lynton Brent, Frankie Marvin, Oscar and Elmer, Champion.

This is not one of the better Autry sagebrushers. The plot brings in everything but Gabby Hayes peddling an elixir on a medicine show wagon. As it is we have Autry portraying himself as a sheriff and local singing cowboy star, a group of singing bandits (The Sons of the Pioneers) who are not taken very seriously by Sheriff Autry, Chicago gangsters loaded down with Tommy guns, and a singing heroine on the lam after witnessing a murder back in gangster-infested Chicago.

The film is distinguished by two occurrences: Gene Autry and Roy Rogers (called Dick Weston here) get into a brawl and have at each other; and Gene kisses the girl on the fade-out. It's worth seeing if only for those two events.

Songs include "So Long Old Paint." and "In the Heart of the West." Autry, who appears pudgy and still uncomfortable in front of the camera, is also not in very good voice this time around.

*　　*　　*

Roundup Time in Texas (Republic, 1937) 63 M.

Producer, Nat Levine; director, Joseph Kane; screenplay, Oliver Drake; camera, William Nobles; editor, Lester Orlebeck.

CAST: Gene Autry, Smiley Burnette, Maxine Davis, Cabin Kids, LeRoy Mason, Earle Hodgins, Dick Wessel, Buddy Williams, Elmer Fain, Cornie Anderson, Frankie Marvin, Ken Cooper, Champion.

The title this time is a real misnomer, since most of the film takes place in the jungles of Africa. It seems that Gene's brother, a diamond prospector in South Africa, has hit a strike and needs some horses to work the mine. He contacts Gene in Texas. Gene hops the next ship to Africa with Smiley and a herd of horses. Villains led by LeRoy Mason have their eyes on the diamonds, too, and cause Gene, his brother, and Frog to get involved with voodoo drums, sneaky native guides, and ferocious wild animals out of the Tarzan stock footage vault before the outlaw roundup time in South Africa. The surprising thing is that it all works out pretty well.

*　　*　　*

Git Along, Little Dogies (Republic, 1937) 60 M.

Director, Joseph Kane; screenplay, Dorrell and Stuart McGowan; camera, Gus Peterson; editor, Tony Martinelli; songs, Sam H. Stept, Sidney Mitchell, Fleming Allen, Smiley Burnette, and the McGowans.

CAST: Gene Autry, Smiley Burnette, Maple City Four, Judith Allen; Weldon Heyburn, William Farnum, Willie Fung, Carleton Young, Will and Gladys Ahearn, The Cabin Kids, Champion.

One of the poorer Gene Autry vehicles, *Dogies* is almost devoid of any action throughout its long hour of running time. The plot concerns the conflict between cattle ranchers and an oil drilling operation. Later, the old chestnut about "the railroad comin' to town" is dusted off and tagged on to confuse matters.

When the story runs out before the expected feature length, there is a theater audience sing-along to the words flashed on the screen. Yes, there is even a bouncing ball. Along with the title number and other familiar folk songs, there is one called "If You Want To Be a Cowboy."

*　　*　　*

Rootin' Tootin' Rhythm (Republic, 1937) 60 M.

Director, Mark V. Wright; screenplay, Jack Natteford; camera, William Nobles; editor, Tony Martinelli.

CAST: Gene Autry, Smiley Burnette, Armida, Monte Blue, Al Clauser and The Outlaws, Hal Taliaferro, Ann Pendleton, Max Hoffman, Jr., Charles King, Frankie Marvin, Nina Campana, Champion.

This better-than-average musical Western finds Gene and Smiley in good form. The plot has the two of them trying to round up some cattle rustlers and in the process being suspected themselves of the cattlenapping. The finale finds them taking a few moments away from the guitars and fiddles to hogtie the outlaws.

*　　*　　*

Yodelin' Kid From Pine Ridge (Republic, 1937) 62 M.

Producer, Armand Schaefer; director, Joseph Kane; screenplay, Jack Natteford, Dorrell and Stuart McGowan; camera, William Nobles; songs, Autry, Burnette, Frank Harford, Jack Stanley, William Lava.

CAST: Gene Autry, Smiley Burnette, Betty Bronson, LeRoy Mason, Charles Middleton, Russell Simpson, Tennessee Ramblers, Jack Dougherty, Guy Wilkerson, Frankie Marvin, Henry Hall, Snowflake, Champion.

This below-par episode could more correctly be called a "Southern" since the story takes place in the Carolinas and Georgia. But it makes no difference since Gene and Smiley are up to their usual righting of wrongs and singing of songs—two of the songs being "Sing Me a Song of the Saddle" and "The Millhouse Wild West Show."

* * *

Public Cowboy No. 1 (Republic, 1937) 60 M.

Director, Joseph Kane; screenplay, Oliver Drake; camera, Jack Marta; editors, Lester Orlebeck, George Reid.

CAST: Gene Autry, Smiley Burnette, Ann Rutherford, William Farnum, James C. Morton, Frank LaRue, Marston Williams, Arthur Loft, Frankie Marvin, House Peters, Jr., Milburn Morante, King Mojave, Hal Price, Jack Ingram, Champion.

The title conveys the type of promotion Republic was using for their singing cowboy star in 1937. Fortunately, this entry in the series helps Gene to live up to that billing.

The plot is the archetype of the Autry films at their best with a featured song telling it all: "The West Ain't What It Used To Be." The story takes place in the West of "today" with cattle rustlers using refrigerated trucks, planes, and two-way radios to purloin the cattle, slaughter them, and send them off to market—all in one quick operation. On the other hand, there are enough touches of the old West (cowboys on horseback, six-guns blazing, and scenic mountains) to make it the best of both times—then and now.

Even the many songs in the story ("I Picked Up the Trail When I Found You," "Heebie, Jeebie Blues," "Defective Detective from Brooklyn," and others) do not get in the way of the whirlwind chases and action.

* * *

Boots and Saddles (Republic, 1937) 60 M.

Producer, Sol C. Siegel; director, Joseph Kane; screenplay, Jack Natteford and Oliver Drake; camera, William Nobles.

CAST: Gene Autry, Smiley Burnette, Judith Allen, Ra Hould, Guy Usher, Gordon Elliott, John Ward,

Frankie Marvin, Chris Marvin, Stanley Blystone, Bud Osborne, Champion.

This first-class production features such songs as "You're the Only Rose That's Left in My Heart" and the title song.

* * *

Manhattan Merry-Go-Round (Republic, 1937)

Gene, along with many other popular recording artists, makes a guest star appearance in this Phil Reagan feature.

* * *

Springtime in the Rockies (Republic, 1937) 60 M.

Director, Joseph Kane; screenplay, Gilbert Wright and Betty Burbridge; camera, Ernest Miller; editor, Lester Orlebeck.

CAST: Gene Autry, Smiley Burnette, Polly Rowles, Ula Love, Ruth Bacon, Jane Hunt, George Chesebro, Alan Bridge, Tom London, Edward Hearn, Frankie Marvin, William Hole, Edmund Cobb, Fred Burns, Jimmy's Saddle Pals, Champion.

It's the old cattlemen-sheepmen fight this time around, but Autry and Republic give it a good going over.

Gene is the foreman of a cattle ranch owned by the absent Polly Rowles. A student of animal husbandry back East, she suddenly arrives on the ranch with a flock of sheep. All of Autry's tact is taxed as he tries to keep peace at home and with the other ranchers in the territory.

* * *

The Old Barn Dance (Republic, 1938) 60 M.

Producer, Sol C. Siegel; director, Joseph Kane; screenplay, Bernard McConville and Charles Francis Royal; camera, Ernest Miller; editor, Lester Orlebeck; musical director, Alberto Columbo; songs, Jack Lawrence, Peter Tinturin, Smiley Burnette, Frankie Marvin, Colorado Hillbillies.

CAST: Gene Autry, Smiley Burnette, Helen Valkis, Sammy McKim, Walter Shrum and His Colorado Hillbillies, Stafford Sisters, Dick Weston (Roy Rogers), Maple City Four, Ivan Miller, Earl Dwire, Hooper Atchley, Raphael Bennett, Carleton Young, Frankie Marvin, Earle Hodgins, Gloria Rich, Champion.

The singing cowboy has another good opus here. This time Gene and his pals earn their living by selling work horses to ranchers at local fairs around the territory. A tractor firm comes along and kills the horse-selling business. While sustaining themselves as singing cowboys on the radio (their sponsor is the tractor outfit), they discover that the ranchers are having a lot of trouble with the malfunctioning horse substitutes. Gene doesn't need a Better Business Bureau to see that his sponsoring company is composed of nothing but a pack of crooks. With a little help from the ranchers, Gene saves the day.

*   *   *

Gold Mine in the Sky (Republic, 1938) 60 M.

Director, Joseph Kane, screenplay, Jack Natteford and Betty Burbridge; camera, William Nobles; editor, Lester Orlebeck; musical director, Alberto Colombo; songs, Charles and Nick Kenny, Gene Autry, Johnny Marvin, Fred Rose.

CAST: Gene Autry, Smiley Burnette, Carol Hughes, Craig Reynolds, Cupid Ainsworth, LeRoy Mason, Frankie Marvin, Robert Homans, Eddie Cherkose, Ben Corbett, Milburn Morante, Jim Corey, George Guhi, Stafford Sisters, J. L. Frank's "Golden West Cowboys," Champion.

This is a standard Autry feature with a very popular title song, good action highlights, and some typical Smiley Burnette slapstick comedy.

The plot is again "simple cowboy in conflict with haughty, pseudosophisticated city girl who thinks he's just a dumb cowpoke." After the usual verbal and physical skirmishes with him, she grows to respect and even—heaven forfend—love him. He is patient with her as he teaches her the "ways of the West," mostly by crooning prairie hymns in the moonlight. It's all been done before and will be done many times again by Autry et al. And usually, as in this instance, it is very enjoyable entertainment.

Songs include the title song, "Dude Ranch Cowboys," "As Long As I Have My Horse," "That's How Donkeys Were Born," and "I'm a Tumbleweed Tenor."

*   *   *

Man from Music Mountain (Republic, 1938) 58 M.

Producer, Charles E. Ford; director, Joseph Kane; screenplay, Betty Burbridge and Luci Ward; original story, Bernard McConville; camera, Jack Marta; editor, Lester Orlebeck; songs, Peter Tinturin, Jack Lawrence, Eddie Cherkose, Smiley Burnette, Gene Autry, Johnny Marvin, Fred Rose.

CAST: Gene Autry, Smiley Burnette, Carol Hughes, Sally Payne, Ivan Miller, Edward Cassidy, Lew Kelly, Howard Chase, Albert Terry, Frankie Marvin, Earl Dwire, Lloyd Ingraham, Lillian Drew, Al Taylor, Joe Yrigoyen, Polly Jenkins and Her Plowboys.

This Republic effort was rated the best of the Autry features to this time by trade critics who felt that it was strong enough to ride single on theater marquees. By this time, too, Gene had acquired some polish as a performer in the acting and action scenes.

While the plot to this episode is no more original than previous scripts—unscrupulous land developers and all that—Autry and company make it seem fresh and fun through their pleasant performances.

A musical menage entitled, classily enough, "Polly Jenkins and Her Plowboys" adds musical merriment to the feature. Autry has fun with "Love, Burning Love" during a lyrical interlude.

*   *   *

Prairie Moon (Republic, 1938) 58 M.

Producer, Harry Grey; director, Ralph Staub; screenplay, Betty Burbridge and Stanley Roberts; camera, William Nobles; editor, Lester Orlebeck.

CAST: Gene Autry, Smiley Burnette, Shirley Deane, Tommy Ryan, Walter Tetley, David Gorcey, Stanley Andrews, William Pawley, Warner Richmond, Raphael Bennett, Tom London, Bud Osborne, Jack Rockwell, Peter Potter, Champion.

An increased budget is apparent in this effort as in other Gene Autry films of 1938. This feature is another winner in the Autry string of hits.

It seems three tough city kids (Chicago, as usual) are left a ranch when their father dies. Autry is the foreman of the ranch and assumes custody of the budding junior hoodlums. The plot utilizes a background of cattle rustling for Autry to teach the neophyte toughs the difference between right and wrong. The windup supports the adage that "there is no such thing as a bad boy."

*   *   *

Rhythm of the Saddle (Republic, 1938) 58 M.

Producer, Harry Grey; director, George Sherman; screenplay, Paul Franklin; camera, Jack Marta; editor, Lester Orlebeck.

CAST: Gene Autry, Smiley Burnette, Pert Kelton, Peggy Moran, LeRoy Mason, Arthur Loft, Ethan Laidlaw, Walter de Palma, Archie Hall, Eddie Hart, Eddie Acuff, Champion.

A little lacking in the action department, this Autry meller is otherwise true to his well-established form. The story concerns a young female ranch owner/Frontier Week Rodeo manager (Peggy Moran) who is in danger of losing the rodeo contract unless this year's show is the best ever and attracts large crowds. Her foreman, Gene Autry, helps her overcome the obstacles of chief heavy, LeRoy Mason, that include a bum murder rap, burning barns, fixed rodeo events, and a to-the-death stagecoach race for the finale.

The film title has no meaning whatsoever.

* * *

Western Jamboree (Republic, 1938) 57 M.

Producer, Harry Grey; director, Ralph Staub; screenplay, Gerald Geraghty from original story by Pat Harper; camera, William Nobles; editor, Lester Orlebeck.

CAST: Gene Autry, Smiley Burnette, Jean Rouverol, Ester Muir, Joe Frisco, Frank Darien, Margaret Armstrong, Harry Holman, Edward Raquelio, Bentley Hewlett, Kermit Maynard, George Walcott, Ray Teal, Eddie Dean, Champion.

Helium gas bandits are the novel owlhoots this time and, as is so often the case in these Autry flickers, plot credulity is stretched to absurdity and back.

When the thieves can't lay claim to the helium well any other way, they secretly lay a pipeline to tap the well. Incredulity creeps in when we are asked to believe that a pipeline—with men, trucks, pipes, and digging equipment—could be laid across the ranch land without anyone noticing. Gene takes time between the three songs he trills ("November Moon" is the most noteworthy) to figure out what's up and to get the sheriff and his posse to help him capture the crooks.

At the bottom of the cast list is Eddie Dean, who would in later years become a singing cowboy star of Western films.

* * *

Home on the Prairie (Republic, 1939) 58 M.

Producer, Harry Grey; director, Jack Townley; screenplay, Charles Arthur Powell and Paul Franklin; camera, Reggie Lanning; editor, Lester Orlebeck.

50

CAST: Gene Autry, Smiley Burnette, June Storey, George Cleveland, Jack Mulhall, Walter Miller, Gordon Hart, Hal Price, Earl Hodgins, Ethan Laidlaw, John Beach, Jack Ingram, Bob Woodward and The Rodeoliers, Sherven Brothers, Champion.

June Storey, nicely playing the young owner of a cattle ranch, makes her first of many appearances in this average Autry actioner—and this time there *is* more action than song.

Gene's a border inspector whose job is to see to it that no germ-carrying materials or animals cross into the territory. With that plot set-up, as you might expect, there is an outbreak of hoof-and-mouth disease that forces Gene to quarantine the area. Some unscrupulous cattlemen attempt to ship their diseased cattle to market anyway causing Gene one heck of a lot of trouble.

One of Johnny Weissmuller's Tarzan elephants must have wandered over to Republic from Metro since much of the film's comedy is supplied by a pachyderm that takes a liking to Frog. The writers conveniently explain that the elephant was once part of a traveling medicine show that ran afoul of the law.

*   *   *

Mexicali Rose (Republic, 1939) 58 M.

Producer, Harry Grey; director, George Sherman; screenplay, Gerald Geraghty from an original story by Luci Ward and Connie Lee; camera, William Nobles; editor, Tony Martinelli.

CAST: Gene Autry, Smiley Burnette, Noah Beery, Luana Walters, William Farnum, William Royle, LeRoy Mason, Wally Albright, Kathryn Frye, Roy Barcroft, Dick Botiller, Vic Demourelle, John Beach, Henry Otho, Champion.

With the help of such film vehicles as *Mexicali Rose,* Autry was rapidly reaching the peak of his form at Republic Pictures. This feature is one of four or five Autry films that possess the quintessence of the Autry film style. All the ingredients are here: a popular title song and other Western ballads sung by Gene; Smiley Burnette's slapstick comedy and novelty songs; some ne'er-do-wells to keep the thrill quota sufficient for action buffs; a charming leading lady; and lots of kids involved in the sentimental story about a mission padre trying to help poor Mexican children while having to protect the mission land from oil land swindlers. At one point the mission provides the setting for a musical fiesta with the whole cast breaking into warmhearted song. Granted, these are pretty stock

ingredients, but when they are blended as they are in this film, the result is Autry at his best and most distinctive. As a bonus, Noah Beery plays a comic Mexican bandito for a delightful fare-thee-well.

"You're the Only Star in My Blue Heaven" is one of the original songs in the score that became popular with Autry fans.

*   *   *

Blue Montana Skies (Republic, 1939) 56 M.

Producer, Harry Grey; director, B. Reeves Eason;

the Blue Montana Sky," "I Just Want You," and "Rockin' in the Saddle All Day."

* * *

Mountain Rhythm (Republic, 1939) 57 M.

Director, B. Reeves Eason; screenplay, Gerald Geraghty from a story by Connie Lee; camera, Ernest Miller; editor, Lester Orlebeck.

CAST: Gene Autry, Smiley Burnette, June Storey, Maude Eburne, Ferris Taylor, Walter Fenner, Jack Pennick, Hooper Atchley, Bernard Suss, Ed Cassidy, Jack Ingram, Tom London, Frankie Marvin, Champion.

Not one of Gene's better efforts, *Mountain Rhythm* concerns shifty deals by land speculators that require the heroe's fists and guns before justice and fair play can once more reign. Autry supplies the heroics while Smiley provides the guffaws, and June Storey the heartthrob. Gene sings (among others) "It Makes No Difference Now."

* * *

Colorado Sunset (Republic, 1939) 58 M.

Producer, William Berke; director, George Sherman; screenplay, Betty Burbridge and Stanley Roberts from an original story by Luci Ward and Jack Natteford; camera, William Nobles; musical director, Raoul Kranshaar.

CAST: Gene Autry, Smiley Burnette, June Storey, Barbara Pepper, Larry "Buster" Crabbe, Robert Barrat, Patsy Montana, The CBS-KMBC Texas Rangers, Purnell Pratt, William Farnum, Kermit Maynard, Jack Ingram, Elmo Lincoln, Frankie Marvin, Champion.

A milk war provides the impetus for this average Autry oatuner. It seems milk ranchers are being coerced into joining a "protective" association, otherwise their milk runs the risk of never making it to market—wrecked milk trains and all that sort of thing. Gene and his singing pals unwittingly get involved when they commission Frog to buy a ranch for them, which they discover when they take possession is a milk cow ranch. The finale has Gene and the other ranchers breaking up the protective association in a thrilling chase involving horses, men, and overturning milk wagons. Yes, the villains do a lot of crying over spilt milk!

* * *

In Old Monterey (Republic, 1939) 74 M.

screenplay, Gerald Geraghty from an original story by Norman S. Hall and Paul Franklin; camera, Jack Marta; editor, Lester Orlebeck.

CAST: Gene Autry, Smiley Burnette, June Storey, Harry Woods, Tully Marshall, Al Bridge, Glenn Strange, Dorothy Granger, Edmund Cobb, Robert Winkler, Jack Ingram, Augie Gomez, John Beach, Walt Shrum and The Colorado Hillbillies, Champion.

Fur smuggling is the plot ploy in this fast-moving Autry adventure. Songs include " 'Neath

Producer, Armand Schaefer; director, Joseph Kane; screenplay, Gerald Geraghty, Dorrell McGowan and Stuart McGowan; camera, Ernest Miller; editor, Edward Mann; songs, Gene Autry, Frank Marvin, Billy Rose, Mabel Wayne, Gus Kahn, Walter Donaldson, Bob Nolan, Fred Rose.

CAST: Gene Autry, Smiley Burnette, June Storey, George Hayes, Hoosier Hot Shots, Sarie and Sallie, The Rand Boys, Stuart Hamblen, Billy Lee, Jonathan Hale, Robert Warwick, William Hall, Eddie Conrad, Champion.

Only an average six-gun serenader, *In Old Monterey* gets by mainly because of the appealing regular cast members and some strong supporting performers (George "Gabby" Hayes, Stuart Hamblen, and guest radio stars).

Like many Autry features, the story is topical—this time dealing with 1939 army preparedness for the war abroad. Gene's an army attache assigned to acquire out-of-the-way land for use in bombing practice exercises. Naturally, there are some unscrupulous un-Americans who try to make an illegal profit from the trying times until Autry straightens things out.

* * *

Rovin' Tumbleweeds (Republic, 1939) 62 M.

Director, George Sherman; screenplay, Betty Burbridge, Dorrell and Stuart McGowan; camera, William Nobles; editor, Tony Martinelli; musical director, Raoul Kraushaar.

CAST: Gene Autry, Smiley Burnette, Mary Carlisle, Douglas Dumbrille, William Farnum, Lee "Lasses" White, Ralph Peters, Gordon Hart, Vic Potel, Jack Ingram, Sammy McKim, Reginald Bartow, Eddie Kane, Gay Usher, Pals of the Golden West, Champion.

"One of his worst duds on record" is the way one critic referred to this tumbleweed saga. The working, prerelease title on the film was *Washington Cowboy,* a moniker more suited to what actually occurs in the story.

A crooked Washington politician is stalling a flood control bill long enough to set himself up for a huge land sale profit when the bill goes through. The poor, common people who are affected by the scheme finally rise up and elect radio singer Gene Autry to Congress. So Mr. Autry goes to Washington, and if you saw that other similarly titled film from 1939 about Mr. Smith, you have some idea what happens.

* * *

South of the Border (Republic, 1939) 71 M.

Producer, William Berke; director, George Sherman; screenplay, Betty Burbridge and Gerald Geraghty from an original story by Dorrell and Stuart McGowan; camera, William Nobles; editor, Lester Orlebeck; songs, Art Wenzel, Michael Carr, Jimmy Kennedy, Johnny Marvin, Gene Autry, Fred Rose, E. G. Nelson.

CAST: Gene Autry, Smiley Burnette, June Storey, Lupita Tovar, Mary Lee, Duncan Renaldo, Frank Reicher, Alan Edwards, Claire DuBrey, Dick Botiller, William Farnum, Selmer Jackson, Sheila Darcy, Rex Lease, The Checkerboard Band, Champion.

This Autry feature has only one thing going for it—a title song that became a standard on two continents. As a matter of fact, the song was written by two Englishmen who had never crossed the Atlantic prior to penning the song.

The stylistic presentation of the title song is a bit forced in the film. It is first heard as part of the prediction of a fortune teller. The camera zooms into her crystal ball and dissolves into Gene voice-overing the song as he is seen as a participant in the song's story. In the main plot line Gene and Smiley are U. S. agents sent to quell a potential Mexican revolution.

* * *

Rancho Grande (Republic, 1940) 68 M.

Producer, William Berke; director, Frank McDonald; screenplay, Bradford Ropes, Betty Burbridge, Peter Milne from an original story by Peter Milne and Connie Lee; camera, William Nobles; editor, Tony Martinelli.

CAST: Gene Autry, Smiley Burnette, June Storey, Mary Lee, Dick Hogan, Ellen E. Lowe, Ferris Taylor, Joseph De Stefani, Roscoe Ates, Rex Lease, Ann Baldwin, Roy Barcroft, Edna Lawrence, Pals of the Golden West, Boys' Choir of St. Joseph's School, Brewer Kids, Champion.

Frank McDonald's first directing effort for Gene Autry finds him suffering with an overworked plot. June Storey is a "madcap Eastern heiress" who takes over Rancho Grande, which was willed to her by her grandfather. She and foreman Gene don't always agree on how the ranch should be run. When some baddies try to upset the new irrigation system, which the financially troubled ranch must have if it's to continue operation, Gene goes into action. Eventually the villains are routed and Miss Storey's heart is won by the singing cowboy.

* * *

Shooting High (Twentieth Century-Fox, 1940) 65 M.

Producer, John Stone; director, Alfred E. Green; screenplay, Low Breslow and Owen Francis; camera, Ernest Palmer; editor, Nick DeMaggio.

CAST: Gene Autry, Jane Withers, Marjorie Weaver, Robert Lowery, Katherine Aldridge, Hobart Cavanaugh, Frank M. Thomas, Jack Carson, Hamilton MacFadden, Charles Middleton, Ed Brady, Tom London, Eddie Acuff, Pat O'Malley, George Chandler, Champion.

This is Gene's first film away from Republic and the first starring feature in which he does not play himself. Unfortunately the results are not very good.

It seems there is a movie company coming to Gene's Western town to film the life of his grandfather, who was quite a hero in his time. Gene, though reluctant at first, is finally induced to play the role. When some gangsters pull a bank robbery while the film is rolling, Gene, himself, becomes a hero by capturing the bandits in an over-hill-and-dale chase finale.

New York Times critic Bosley Crowther commented in his review of the film that "Mr. Autry has a unique way of projecting moods. He does not change expression; he just changes cowboy suits."

* * *

Gaucho Serenade (Republic, 1940) 66 M.

Producer, William Berke; director, Frank McDonald; screenplay, Betty Burbridge and Bradford Ropes; camera, Reggie Lanning; editor, Tony Martinelli; songs, Connie Lee, Gene Autry, John Marvin, John Redmond, James Cavanaugh, Nat Simon, Mack Davis, Dick Sanford, Sammy Mysels, Smiley Burnette.

CAST: Gene Autry, Smiley Burnette, June Storey, Duncan Renaldo, Mary Lee, Clifford Severn, Jr., Lester Matthews, Smith Ballew, Joseph Crehan, William Ruhl, Wade Boteler, Ted Adams, Wendell Niles, The Velascos, Jose Eslava's Orchestra, Champion.

Variety's critic sounded a warning to potential aisle-sitters of 1940 that this film was saddled with a moseying, yawn-producing script:

First horse is not mounted until forty-four minutes have passed; first fist is not flung until fifty minutes have passed; first gun is not fired until fifty-six minutes have passed. What manner of Western is this?

Songs are very good, though, and include "The Singing Hills," "Give Out with a Song," "Wooing of Kitty MacFuty," "A Song at Sunset," and the popular title song.

* * *

Carolina Moon (Republic, 1940) 65 M.
Producer, William Berke; director, Frank McDonald; screenplay, Winston Miller from an original story by Connie Lee; camera, William Nobles;

Director Frank McDonald (center) is seen here on location with popular young star Mary Lee. The camera operator is John MacBurnie.

Photo courtesy of Frank McDonald.

editor, Tony Martinelli; musical director, Raoul Kraushaar.

CAST: Gene Autry, Smiley Burnette, June Storey, Mary Lee, Eddy Waller, Hardie Albright, Frank Dae, Terry Nibert, Robert Fiske, Etta McDaniel, Paul White, Fred Ritter, Ralph Sanford, Jimmie Lewis and His Texas Cowboys, Champion.

This time Gene finds himself in the South trying to save some old plantations from a local land wheeler-dealer. The cast includes teenager Mary Lee, who comes close to stealing the picture away from the cowboy star even though her role is relatively brief.

Songs include "Say Si Si," "Carolina Moon," and some Negro spirituals.

*　　*　　*

Ride, Tenderfoot, Ride (Republic, 1940) 66 M.

Producer, William Berke; director, Frank McDonald; screenplay, Winston Miller from an original story by Betty Burbridge; camera, Jack Marta; editor, Lester Orlebeck; musical director, Raoul Kraushaar; songs, Johnny Mercer, Richard Whiting, E. Di Lazzaro, Harold Adamson, Nick Kenny, Charles Kenny, Johnny Marvin, Gene Autry, Smiley Burnette, Arthur Fields, Fred Hall.

CAST: Gene Autry, Smiley Burnette, June Storey, Warren Hull, Forbes Murray, Joe McGuinn, Joe Frisco, Isobel Randolph, Herbert Clifford, Mildred Shay, Cindy Walker, The Pacemakers, Champion.

Ride, Tenderfoot, Ride is another Autry film that deserves careful study by those who wish to better understand the fantastic success of the Autry pictures with audiences of the late thirties and early forties. All of the Autry gimmicks are packed beautifully into the sixty-six minutes of playing time.

Unassuming, shy cowboy Gene becomes heir to a meatpacking company. Snooty June Storey owns the rival company, whose underhanded executives are trying to run Autry out of business. At first Miss Storey (who early-on has a comic run-in with Gene and is made to look foolish) unwittingly assists her officers in getting control of the Autry company. Mary Lee, playing Miss Storey's younger, precocious sister, again nearly steals the film as she exclaims her undying school-girl love for the singing cowboy.

Gene successfully fends off the amorous advances of the youthful Mary Lee, dodges the verbal darts from snippy June Storey long enough to gain her eventual love, exposes the dirty dealers, and still finds time to sing a slew of appealing tunes. Among them is the hit of the time, "The Woodpecker Song."

* * *

Melody Ranch (Republic, 1940) 80 M.

Producer, Sol C. Siegel; director, Joseph Santley;

screenplay, Jack Moffitt, F. Hugh Herbert; camera, Joseph August; editor, Lester Orlebeck; musical director, Raoul Kraushaar; songs, Jule Styne, Eddie Cherkose.

CAST: Gene Autry, Jimmy Durante, Ann Miller, Barton MacLane, Barbara Jo Allen (Vera Vague), George "Gabby" Hayes, Jerome Cowan, Mary Lee, Joseph Sawyer, Horace MacMahon, Clarence Wilson, William Benedict, Champion.

This Autry special is named after his popular radio series and features some relatively big show-business names of the era. Jimmy Durante is

Members of the cast and crew are seen here on location for *Ride, Tenderfoot, Ride.* Director Frank McDonald is center. The cameraman is Jack Marta. *Photo courtesy of Frank McDonald.*

On the set for *Ride, Tenderfoot, Ride.* Left to right: Gene Autry, unidentified man, director Frank McDonald, and cameraman Jack Marta. *Photo courtesy of Frank McDonald.*

Director Frank McDonald and Mary Lee on location for *Ride, Tenderfoot, Ride. Photo courtesy of Frank McDonald.*

particularly effective playing the radio announcer for the singing cowboy. As one critic commented, "The Schnoz has never been funnier on the screen." Ann Miller, just starting her Hollywood career, hoofs up a storm in the film and displays the moxie that would make her popular with future film audiences.

Radio singing star Gene Autry is invited to return home to Torpedo, Arizona, to be honorary sheriff for the Frontier Days Celebration. Some town hoods rough up acting Sheriff Autry and try to send him packing back to the big city. His dander now up, Gene stays on to clean up the town just as it's done in Western movies.

Songs include "We Never Dream the Same Dream Twice," "Vote for Autry" (song by Durante), "Call of the Canyon," and "Melody Ranch."

This is another Autry flicker for Western buffs to examine to discern the magic of the Autry style.

* * *

Ridin' on a Rainbow (Republic, 1941) 79 M.

Director, Lew Landers; screenplay, Bradford Ropes, Doris Malloy from a story by Ropes; camera, William Nobles; editor, Tony Martinelli; musical director, Raoul Kraushaar; special music and lyrics, Jule Styne and Sol Meyer.

CAST: Gene Autry, Smiley Burnette, Mary Lee, Carol Adams, Ferris Taylor, Georgia Caine, Byron Foulger, Ralf Harolde, Jimmy Conlin, Guy Usher, Anthony Warde, Forrest Taylor, Burr Caruth, Champion.

Only an average Autry thriller, this feature is, for the most part, set on an entertainment showboat.

The investigation of a local bank robbery leads Gene and Smiley to a showboat where teenaged Mary Lee and her father are the entertainers. It soon becomes apparent that Mary Lee's father, worried about how to provide for her future, has cooperated with the robbers. After the regulation fisticuffs and crooning Gene gets the whole matter resolved to everybody's satisfaction.

As has happened in so many other Autry films of this era, the talented Miss Lee holds the spotlight during much of the unreeling time. She sings, dances, makes with the funnies, and tugs at your emotions during the serious moments.

Songs include "What's Your Favorite Holiday," sung by Mary Lee, and "Ridin' on a Rainbow," Autry's biggest musical moment of the film.

Gene and Ann Miller are seen on location for *Melody Ranch.*

Acting Sheriff Autry has lost round one, but the fight is not yet over. Left to right: Ann Miller, Gabby Hayes, Gene, Jimmy Durante.

*   *   *

Back in the Saddle (Republic, 1941) 73 M.

Producer, Harry Grey; director, Lew Landers; screenplay, Richard Murphy and Jesse Lasky, Jr.; camera, Ernest Miller; editor, Tony Martinelli; musical director, Raoul Kraushaar.

CAST: Gene Autry, Smiley Burnette, Mary Lee, Edward Norris, Jacqueline Wells, Addison Richards, Arthur Loft, Edmund Elton, Joe McGuinn, Edmund Cobb, Robert Barron, Champion.

Taking its title from the singing cowboy's theme song, this feature provides a return to the six-shooter mayhem that is in short supply in many other Autrys from this vintage.

*   *   *

The Singing Hills (Republic, 1941) 65 M.

Producer, Harry Grey; director, Lew Landers; camera, Reggie Lanning; editor, Tony Martinelli.

CAST: Gene Autry, Smiley Burnette, Virginia Dale, Mary Lee, Spencer Charters, Gerald Oliver Smith, George Meeker, Wade Boteler, Harry Stubbs, Cactus Mack Peters, Jack Kirk, Champion.

*   *   *

Sunset in Wyoming (Republic, 1941) 65 M.

Director, William Morgan; screenplay, Ivan Goff and Ann Morrison Chapin; camera, Reggie Lanning; editor; Tony Martinelli; musical director, Raoul Kraushaar.

CAST: Gene Autry, Smiley Burnette, George Cleveland, Maris Wrixon, Robert Kent, Sarah Edwards, Monte Blue, Dick Elliott, John Dilson, Stanley Blystone, Champion.

This is another one of Gene's lesser efforts. Critics of the time complained that Gene seemed to be getting farther away from the Western genre that had made him a star.

In this episode he is attempting to teach a logging company a few things about land conservation. His efforts take him to a swanky country club, fancy swimming pools, and even a ball where everyone shows up in formal gowns or tails, including Frog. Gene, unfortunately, spends more time in a convertible than on Champion this time around and the results are disappointing.

* * *

Under Fiesta Stars (Republic, 1941) 68 M.

Producer, Harry Grey; director, Frank McDonald; screenplay, Karl Brown and Eliot Gibbons; camera, Jack Marta; editor, Tony Martinelli.

CAST: Gene Autry, Smiley Burnette, Carol Hughes, Frank Darien, Joseph Strauch, Jr., Pauline Drake, Ivan Miller, Sam Flint, John Merton, Jack Kirk, Elias Gamboa, Inez Palange, Champion.

* * *

Down Mexico Way (Republic, 1941) 77 M.

Producer, Harry Grey; director, Joseph Santley; screenplay, Olive Cooper and Albert Duffy based on a story by Dorrell and Stuart McGowan; camera, Jack Marta; editor, Howard O'Neill; production manager, Al Wilson.

CAST: Gene Autry, Smiley Burnette, Fay McKenzie, Harold Huber, Sidney Blackmer, Joe Sawyer, Andrew Tombes, Murray Alper, Arthur Loft, Duncan Renaldo, Paul Fix, Julian Rivero, Ruth Robinson, Thornton Edwards, The Herrara Sisters, Champion.

This is another "special" in the Autry series, meaning that the budget has been tilted upward to allow for a stronger cast and more impressive production values. It all works dandily resulting in a picture that Autry and company can be proud ot.

The plot takes Gene and Frog south of the border in pursuit of a gaggle of con men who have fleeced the citizens of Sage City out of their hard-earned savings. The concluding roundup is a wild and woolly chase across the badlands featuring horses, cars, and motorcycles.

* * *

Sierra Sue (Republic, 1941) 64 M.

Producer, Harry Grey; director, William Morgan; screenplay, Earl Felton and Julian Zimet; camera, Jack Marta; editor, Lester Orlebeck; songs, J. B. Carey, Gene Autry, Fred Rose, Fleming Allan, Nelson Shawn.

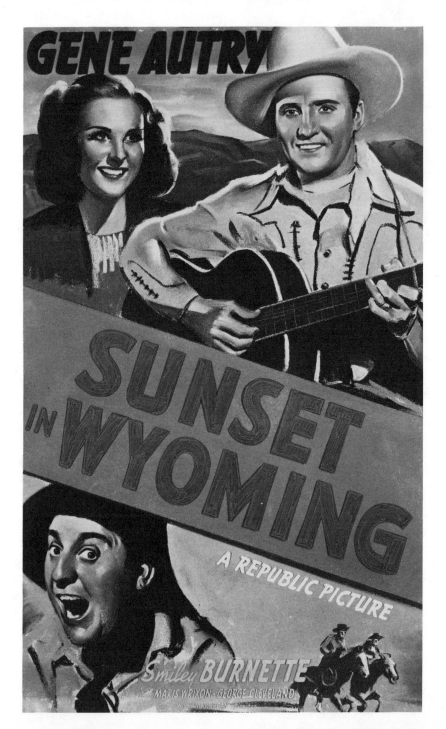

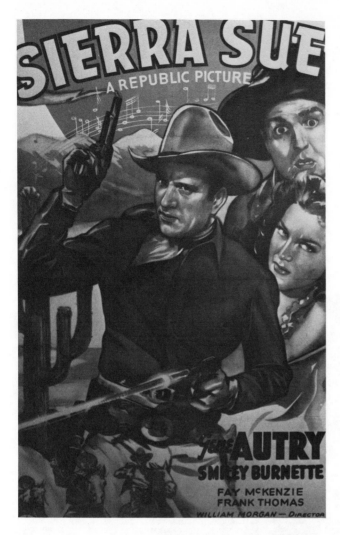

CAST: Gene Autry, Smiley Burnette, Fay McKenzie, Frank Thomas, Robert Homans, Earle Hodgins, Dorothy Christy, Kermit Maynard, Jack Kirk, Eddie Dean, Budd Buster, Rex Lease, Champion.

The plot of this one lazes along for fifty-some minutes until the wrap-up, which features a plane crash and cattle stampede.

It seems that there is a weed growing on the grazing land that has been poisoning the cattle. Government inspector Autry calls for chemical spraying of the area by airplanes, but the troublesome head of the cattleman's association wants to burn the infected area. He finally relents, but during the air spraying, a hired gun who has not gotten the word shoots the plane out of the sky. The resulting explosion causes the cattle stampede. Some days nothing goes right!

Way down in the cast listing is future singing cowboy star Eddie Dean.

* * *

Cowboy Serenade (Republic, 1942) 66 M.

Producer, Harry Grey; director, William Morgan; screenplay, Olive Cooper; camera, Jack Marta; editor, Lester Orlebeck; musical director, Raoul Kraushaar.

CAST: Gene Autry, Smiley Burnette, Fay McKenzie, Cecil Cunningham, Addison Richards, Rand Brooks, Tristram Coffin, Lloyd "Slim" Andrews, Melinda Leighton, Johnnie Berkes, Champion.

This is a good addition to the Autry series. Gene's frequent leading lady, Fay McKenzie, is again on hand for singing and acting duties. While she does not have the looks of a typical Western heroine, her vivaciousness and thesping ability carry her through nicely.

Gene is attempting to break up a gambling ring and finds matters complicated when the leader turns out to be the father of his girl, Miss McKenzie. She refuses to believe her father's guilt and starts her own investigation. The climax brings the death of the old man, who is, of course, guilty as sin. After all, Gene can't be wrong about these things!

* * *

Heart of the Rio Grande (Republic, 1942) 68 M.

Producer, Harry Grey; director, William Morgan; screenplay, Lillie Hayward and Winston Miller from a story by Newlin B. Wildes; camera, Harry Newmann; editor, Lester Orlebeck; musical director, Raoul Kraushaar.

CAST: Gene Autry, Smiley Burnette, Fay McKenzie, Edith Fellows, Pierre Watkin, Joe Strauch, Jr., William Haade, Sarah Padden, Jean Porter, The Jimmy Wakely Trio, Champion.

In this not very successful entry we have the stock situation of the wealthy and spoiled big-city girl taken to a dude ranch out West where the great outdoors and a singing cowboy save her soul. As *Variety's* critic commented, "The script is palpably artificial, situations are hackneyed, characters are almost satirically broad, and the whole picture has an air of ludicrous sanctimoniousness."

Another future singing cowboy star is featured here with his trio—Jimmy Wakely.

* * *

Home in Wyomin' (Republic, 1942) 67 M.

Producer, Harry Grey; director, William Morgan; screenplay, Robert Tasker and M. Coates Webster; camera, Ernest Miller; musical director, Raoul Kraushaar.

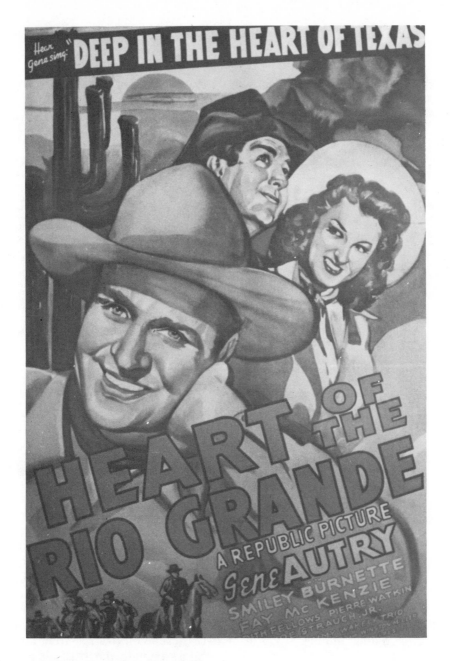

CAST: Gene Autry, Smiley Burnette, Fay McKenzie, Olin Howlin, Chick Chandler, Joseph Strauch, Jr., Forrest Taylor, James Seay, George Douglas, Charles Lane, Hal Price, Champion.

Autry's mind seems to be on other things in this listless Republic episode. Gene plays a singing radio performer who goes home to Wyoming (resulting in a closer link to the title than many of these films have) to help out a friend who's having financial problems with a rodeo he owns.

Joe Strauch, Jr., a moppet look-alike for Smiley "Frog" Burnette, is again on hand to assist with the comedics. The youngster goes by the name of Tadpole in these adventures. Frog—Tadpole, you get it?

* * *

Stardust on the Trail (Republic, 1942) 65 M.

Producer, Harry Grey; director, William Morgan; screenplay, Betty Burbridge from a story by Dorrell and Stuart McGowan; camera, Bud Thackery; editor, Edward Mann.

CAST: Gene Autry, Smiley Burnette, Bill Henry, Edith Fellows, Louise Currie, Emmett Vogan, George Ernest, Vince Barnett, Betty Farrington, Roy Barcroft, Tom London, Champion.

This is another song-laden release in the series. "I'll Never Let You Go," "Goodnight, Sweetheart," "When Roses Bloom Again," "Wouldn't

Gene, Frog (Smiley Burnette), and Tadpole (Joe Strauch, Jr.) on location for *Home in Wyomin'*.

You Like To Know," "Home on the Range," "Deep in the Heart of Texas," "Roll on Little Doggies," and "You Are My Sunshine" are featured in the film's score. The left over few minutes are consigned to the story and action, which have something to do with selling mining stock to cattlemen.

*   *   *

Call of the Canyon (Republic, 1942) 71 M.

Producer, Harry Grey; director, Joseph Santley; screenplay, Olive Cooper from an original story by Maurice Rapf and Olive Cooper; camera, Reggie Lanning; editor, Edward Mann.

CAST: Gene Autry, Smiley Burnette, Sons of the Pioneers, Ruth Terry, Thurston Hall, Joe Strauch, Jr., Cliff Nazarro, Dorothea Kent, Edmund MacDonald, Marc Lawrence, John Harmon, John Holland, Champion.

This is a top-flight addition to the series with its comfortable blend of music, thrills, comedy, and a fairly logical and entertaining story line. It all has to do with cattlemen, a crooked purchasing agent for the packing company, and the head of the packing company (the irrepressible Thurston Hall, who chews up the outdoor scenery in a delightful performance). Gene, the cattlemen's representative, is called on to straighten out the trouble.

Songs include the title song, "Montana Skies," "Boots and Saddle," "When It's Chilly Down in Chile" (song by Miss Terry), and "Somebody Else Is Taking My Place." The Sons of the Pioneers show up here to help out Gene and the others on several songs.

*   *   *

Bells of Capistrano (Republic, 1942) 73 M.

Producer, Harry Grey; director, William Morgan; screenplay, Lawrence Kimple; camera, Reggie Lanning; editor, Edward Mann; musical director, Morton Scott; songs, Jimmy Morgan, Thomas Holer, Milton Ager, Jack Yellen, Fred Stryker, Jerry Charleston, Sol Meyer, Walter Donaldson.

CAST: Gene Autry, Smiley Burnette, Virginia Grey, Lucien Littlefield, Morgan Conway, Claire DuBrey, Charles Cane, Joe Strauch, Jr., Maria Shelton, Tristram Coffin, Champion.

Two traveling rodeos are in competition with each other in this one. Gene goes to help out Virginia Grey, the owner of one of the shows. Prospects start to brighten for Miss Grey until her competitor (who, of course, is unscrupulous and will stoop to anything) introduces a little sabotage into the story. This riles Gene a little, so he proceeds to beat the heck out of anyone who even resembles a bad guy.

This was Gene's last feature before entering the service during World War II.

*   *   *

Sioux City Sue (Republic, 1946) 69 M.

Producer, Armand Schaefer; director, Frank McDonald; screenplay, Olive Cooper; camera, Reggie Lanning; editor, Fred Allen; songs, Jimmy

Gene has just settled a disagreement with Ralph Sanford in this scene from *Sioux City Sue.*

Hodges, Dick Thomas, Gonzale Roig, Jack Sherr, A. Rodriguez, John Rex, Sosnik Adams.

CAST: Gene Autry, Lynne Roberts, Sterling Holloway, Richard Lane, Ralph Sanford, Ken Lundy, Helen Wallace, Pierre Watkin, Kenne Duncan, Cass County Boys, Champion.

This first postwar Autry Western musical is short on Western action and heavy on music.

It seems that a film company is looking for a good Western singing voice for a cartoon donkey series. Lynne Roberts (my favorite Western leading lady) is a film scout who discovers cattleman Gene and lures him to Hollywood with the promise of a starring film career when in reality he turns out to be the tonsils for the animated donkey. Somehow it all ends up back at Autry's ranch where his cattle are stampeded when owlhoots blow up a nearby dam. Don't ask how the dambusters got involved with the donkey plot!

Songs are plentiful and include the popular "Sioux City Sue," "Ridin' Double," "Someday You'll Want Me To Want You," "Chisholm Trail," "Yours," and "You Stole My Heart."

*   *   *

Trail to San Antone (Republic, 1947) 67 M.

Producer, Armand Schaefer; director, John English; screenplay, Jack Natteford, Luci Ford; camera, William Bradford; editor, Charles Craft; songs, Deuce Spriggens, Sid Robin, Joe Burke, Marty Symes, Spade Cooley, Cindy Walker, Gene Autry.

CAST: Gene Autry, Peggy Stewart, Sterling Holloway, William Henry, John Duncan, Tristram

Coffin, Dorothy Vaughan, Edward Keane, Ralph Peters, Cass County Boys, Champion.

The title makes it sound like an old Western thriller, but the film is a horse-racing, human-interest story with Autry trying to help in the rehabilitation of a crippled jockey before the big race of the picture.

The villain of this piece is a wild stallion who breaks into the stable and horsenaps the mare that Autry and the jockey had expected to enter in the race. Autry goes horse hunting via airplane and—hold on to your hats—lassoes the mare from the airplane; yes, that's right! Anyway, the mare wins the big race, the jockey is rehabilitated, and Gene sings another song.

*   *   *

Twilight on the Rio Grande (Republic, 1947) 71 M.

Producer, Armand Schaefer; director, Frank McDonald; screenplay, Dorrell and Stuart McGowan; camera, William Bradford; editor, Harry Keller; songs, Charles Tobias and Nat Simon, Smiley Burnette, Larry Marks and Dick Charles, Jack Elliott.

CAST: Gene Autry, Sterling Holloway, Adele Mara, Bob Steele, Charles Evans, Martin Garralaga, Howard J. Negley, George J. Lewis, Nacho Galindo, Tex Terry, Cass County Boys, Champion.

An undistinguished entry in the series, the plot is mostly a south-of-the-border affair as Gene attempts to locate the killer of his ranch partner. The songs are fine, though, with a hit song of 1947, "The Old Lamplighter," a highlight. Others include "I Tipped My Hat and Slowly Rode Away," and "Pretty Knife Grinder" (how's that for a romantic title?) performed by Adele Mara.

*   *   *

Saddle Pals (Republic, 1947) 73 M.

Producer, Sidney Picker; director, Lesley Selander; screenplay, Bob Williams and Jerry Sackheim from an original story by Dorrell and Stuart McGowan; camera, Bud Thackery; editor, Harry Keller; songs, Harry Sosnik and Stanley Adams, Ray Allen and Perry Botkin, Britt Wood and Hy Heath, Gene Autry.

CAST: Gene Autry, Lynne Roberts, Sterling Holloway, Irving Bacon, Damian O'Flynn, Charles Arnt, Jean Van, Tom London, Charles Williams,

Francis McDonald, George Chandler, Edward Gargan, Cass County Boys, Champion.

A weak film in the action department, *Saddle Pals* gains its only plusses from an appealing cast and a pleasant musical score. Autry sings "I Wish I Had Never Met Sunshine," "Amapola," and "You Stole My Heart." The Cass County Boys warble "Which Way Did They Go?" and "The Covered Wagon Rolled Right Along."

The talky plot about villains attempting to bankrupt a rich land owner so that they can buy him out for a fraction of the true land value does not provide much in the way of thrills.

* * *

Robin Hood of Texas (Republic, 1947) 71 M.

Producer, Sidney Picker; director, Lesley Selander; screenplay, John K. Butler and Earle Snell; camera, William Bradford; editor, Harry Keller; songs, Gene Autry, Carson J. Robinson, Sergio De Karlo, Kay Charles.

CAST: Gene Autry, Lynne Roberts, Sterling Holloway, Adele Mara, James Cardwell, John Kellogg, Ray Walker, Michael Branden, Paul Bryar, James Flavin, Dorothy Vaughan, Stanley Andrews, Alan Bridge, Cass County Boys, Champion.

Autry's last Republic feature is right on the mark. The plot has to do with a bank stick-up and the resulting search for the missing loot. The windup has Autry giving chase to the robbers, who try escaping via buckboard. Gene finally intercepts them by jumping from that familiar rock (all of you remember) into the buckboard and subduing them as the wagon careens along the trail. It's all pretty exciting!

Songs include "Goin' Back to Texas," "You're the Moment of a Lifetime," and "Merry-Go-Round-Up," all performed by Gene. The Cass County Boys provide the musical and vocal back-up for Autry.

* * *

The Last Round-Up (Columbia, 1947) 76 M.

Producer, Armand Schaefer; director, John English; screenplay, Jack Townley and Earl Snell; camera, William Bradford; editor, Aaron Stell; musical director, Paul Mertz.

CAST: Gene Autry, Jean Heather, Ralph Morgan, Carol Thurston, Mark Daniels, Bobby Blake, Russ Vincent, George "Shug" Fisher, Trevor Bardette, Lee Bennett, John Holloran, Sandy Sanders, Roy

Gene is rounding up some strays in this scene from *The Last Roundup*.

Gordon, Silverheels Smith (Jay Silverheels), Frances Rey, Bob Cason, Champion.

This is Gene's first Columbia release and first feature produced under his Gene Autry Productions banner. The film is one of the best features of his career and is his particular favorite. It's filled with fast-tempoed action, scenic backgrounds, a pleasing cast, and good songs. Autry and company can be proud of their work.

The story, placed in the modern West, deals with Autry's attempts to relocate a tribe of Indians onto new lands so that an aqueduct can be built on their barren, former homeland. Some of the Indians don't look too kindly on the projected move; also, some palefaces aren't too happy about it either. Autry has his work cut out for him as he tries to avoid uprisings from both sides.

When Gene's not busy with negotiations, fisticuffs, and chases, he takes time to warble some Western melodies. Among them are "160 Acres in the Valley," "You Can't See the Sun When You're Crying," "An Apple for the Teacher," "Comin' Round the Mountain," and the title song.

* * *

The Strawberry Roan (Columbia, 1948) 76 M. Cinecolor

Producer, Armand Schaefer; director, John English; screenplay, Dwight Cummins and Dorothy Yost from a story by Julian Zimet; camera, Fred H. Jackman; editor, Henry Batista; musical director, Paul Mertz.

CAST: Gene Autry, Gloria Henry, Jack Holt, Dick Jones, Pat Buttram, Rufe Davis, John McGuire,

Gene and Dick Jones are seen here in a tense scene from *The Strawberry Roan.*

Eddy Waller, Redd Harper, Jack Ingram, Eddie Parker, Ted Mapes, Sam Flint, Champion.

This is Gene's first color picture and first outing with Pat Buttram in the cast, albeit in a minor role. But the real star of the film is Gene's horse, Champion, whose strawberry roan beauty and training are nicely highlighted by the Cinecolor camera and the story.

One is hard-pressed to ignore the story similarities between this film and the Roy Rogers 1946 entry, *My Pal Trigger.* Both feature acting veteran Jack Holt as the villain and revolve around a beautiful horse that causes the hero to become a fugitive until a happy ending can be found. Both films are excellent and feature fine casts and production values, but this one has the added plus of beautiful color lensing.

*　　*

Left to right: Cass County Boys, Gene, Leon Weaver (black suit), Barbara Britton dancing with Robert Shayne.

Gene and Russell Arms (Remember him from "Your Hit Parade" on television?) have their hands full trying to control Barbara Britton in this scene from *Loaded Pistols*.

Gene's about to warble a tune for the pawnbroker in this scene from *The Big Sombrero*.

Villains Douglas Dumbrille and Clayton Moore have the drop on Gene and the officer in this scene from *Riders of the Whistling Pines*.

Loaded Pistols (Columbia, 1949) 77 M.

Producer, Armand Schaefer; director, John English; screenplay, Dwight Cummins and Dorothy Yost; camera, William Bradford; editor, Aaron Stell.

CAST: Gene Autry, Barbara Britton, Chill Wills, Jack Holt, Russell Arms, Robert Shayne, Vince Barnett, Leon Weaver, Fred Kohler, Clem Bevans, Sandy Sanders, Cass County Boys, Champion.

An extremely fine cast was rounded up for this excellent Autry action-tuner. These first few Columbia releases had a running time that exceeded the usual B Western allotment, but in most cases the action, fun, and music made the time speed by.

The plot has Autry hiding out a young fellow accused of murder while he investigates the case and finally uncovers the identity of the real murderer.

When he's not on the killer's trail, Gene takes time to sing a few songs. There are five songs in the exceptionally well-constructed plot, but they never seem to intrude. They are "Loaded Pistols," "When the Bloom Is on the Sage," "A Boy from Texas and a Girl from Tennessee," "Pretty Mary," and the standard, "Blue Tail Fly."

*   *   *

The Big Sombrero (Columbia, 1949) 77 M. Cinecolor

Producer, Armand Schaefer; director, Frank McDonald; screenplay, Olive Cooper; camera, William Bradford; editor, Henry Batista.

CAST: Gene Autry, Elena Verdugo, Stephen Dunne, George J. Lewis, Vera Marshe, William Edmunds, Martin Garralaga, Gene Stutenroth, Neyle Morrow, Bob Cason, Pierce Lyden, Rian Valente, Antonio Filauri, Champion.

Another excellent entry in the Autry Columbia series, this feature is Gene's only other color film. Production values are top quality and a Mexican fiesta sequence provides additional local color, music, and some fancy dancing. The plot, though thin, provides the impetus for the usual action sequences required for this type of film.

The featured numbers include "No Word Did I Hear," "Thankful for Small Favors," and the hit, "In My Adobe Hacienda."

*   *   *

Riders of the Whistling Pines (Columbia, 1949) 72 M.

Producer, Armand Schaefer; director, John English; screenplay, Jack Townley; camera, William Bradford; editor, Aaron Stell.

CAST: Gene Autry, Patricia White, Jimmy Lloyd, Douglas Dumbrille, Damian O'Flynn, Clayton Moore, Harry Cheshire, Leon Weaver, Loie Bridge, Cass County Boys (Jerry Scoggins, Fred S. Martin, Bert Dodson), Jason Robards, Britt Wood, Len Torrey, Roy Gordon, The Pinafores, Champion.

This opus is not up to the usual Autry standards. The action is skimpy, the plot slow as Autry gets mixed up with some outlaws in timberland that is under the watchful eye of the Forestry Department. After being framed for a killing and for poisoning cattle, Autry finally captures the real villains, proves his innocence, and saves the woodland from potential destruction at the hands of the baddies.

*   *   *

Rim of the Canyon (Columbia, 1949) 70 M.

Producer, Armand Schaefer; director, John English; screenplay, John K. Butler from a story by Joseph Chadwick; camera, William Bradford; editor, Aaron Stell; musical director, Mischa Bakaleinikoff; songs, Hy Heath, Johnny Lange, Gene Autry.

CAST: Gene Autry, Nan Leslie, Thurston Hall, Clem Bevans, Walter Sande, Jock O'Mahoney, Francis McDonald, Alan Hale, Jr., Amelita Ward, John R. McKee, Champion.

Rim of the Canyon is a fairly good entry in the Autry series. The story begins with a twenty-year flashback where we see Gene's father (played by Gene with a mustache) capturing three thieves who robbed a mine owner of thirty thousand dollars. The money was never found. Now, twenty years later, Autry, Jr. is on the trail of the bandits, who have escaped from prison and are on their way to the hidden loot. A lot of the action takes place in an atmospheric ghost town that adds to the fun and excitement.

*   *   *

The Cowboy and the Indians (Columbia, 1949) 68 M.

Producer, Armand Schaefer; director, John English; screenplay, Dwight Cummins and Dorothy Yost; camera, William Bradford; editor, Henry Batista.

CAST: Gene Autry, Sheila Ryan, Frank Richards, Hank Patterson, Jay Silverheels, Claudia Drake, George Nokes, Charles Stevens, Alex Fraser, Clayton Moore, Frank Lackteen, Chief Yowlachie, Lee Roberts, Nolan Leary, Maudie Prickett, Harry Mackin, Charles Quigley, Champion.

A good episode, this feature deals with the plight of reservation Indians when a crooked Indian agent takes advantage of their vulnerability to bilk them out of their cattle, and then exacts exorbitant costs from them for food and other supplies. Autry and female doctor Sheila Ryan help the starving Indians, and then Gene brings the evil Indian agent to his just reward.

*   *   *

Riders in the Sky (Columbia, 1949) 69 M.

Producer, Armand Schaefer; director, John English; screenplay, Gerald Geraghty from a story by Herbert A. Woodbury; camera, William Bradford; editor, Henry Batista; musical director, Mischa Bakaleinikoff; songs, Stan Jones, Jimmie Davis.

CAST: Gene Autry, Gloria Henry, Pat Buttram, Mary Beth Hughes, Robert Livingston, Steve Darrell, Alan Hale, Jr., Tom London, Hank Patterson, Ben Welden, Dennis Moore, Joe Forte, Kenne Duncan, Frank Jaquet, Roy Gordon, Loie Bridge, Champion.

Titled after the hit song, this feature lives up to the usual expectations of action fans. The plot is the old one about the town that is run by the evil, slick, oily gambler. Gene arrives to help his rancher friend, who has been thrown in the clink on a murder charge. After the regulation number of fights, chases, and tunes, Autry gets the goods on the gambler and wraps it all up. Robert Livingston, who only a few short years before was a cowboy star in his own right, is the villain of the piece.

*   *   *

Sons of New Mexico (Columbia, 1950) 70 M.

Producer, Armand Schaefer; director, John English; screenplay, Paul Gangelin; camera, William Bradford; editor, Henry Batista; musical director, Mischa Bakaleinikoff.

CAST: Gene Autry, Gail Davis, Robert Armstrong, Dick Jones, Frankie Darro, Irving Bacon, Russell Arms, Marie Blake, Clayton Moore, Sandy Sanders, Roy Gordon, Frank Marvin, Paul Raymond, Pierce Lydon, Kenne Duncan, Champion.

This is an average Autry feature about the

singing cowboy's efforts to save potential juvenile delinquent Dick Jones from the evil enticements of gambler Robert Armstrong. Gene is so busy looking after the boy that he only has time to sing a couple of songs in the entire film. (The two-song policy would generally prevail for the duration of his Columbia series.)

Gail Davis (who would be Gene's leading lady in many of the Columbia features and would eventually star for him on television as "Annie Oakley") makes her first appearance here in an Autry Film.

*   *   *

Mule Train (Columbia, 1950) 69 M.

Producer, Armand Schaefer; director, John English; screenplay, Gerald Geraghty from a story by Alan James; camera, William Bradford; editor, Richard Fanti; songs, Johnny Lange, Hy Heath, Fred Glickman.

CAST: Gene Autry, Pat Buttram, Sheila Ryan, Robert Livingston, Frank Jaquet, Vince Barnett, Syd Saylor, Sandy Sanders, Gregg Barton, Kenne Duncan, Roy Gordon, Stanley Andrews, Robert Hilton, Bob Wilke, John Miljan, Robert Carson, Pat O'Malley, Champion.

Gene is back on the beam with this actionful and entertaining feature that takes its title from the popular song hit.

Adventure abounds as U. S. Marshal Autry comes to the aid of an old friend who is about to have his natural cement claim jumped by villainous contractor and freight shipper, Robert Livingston. Livingston wants control of the claim so that he can supply the cement for a dam that is to be constructed in the area. Gene, of course, is victorious in his efforts to save the claim for his old friend.

*   *   *

Cow Town (Columbia, 1950) 70 M.

Producer, Armand Schaefer; director, John English; screenplay, Gerald Geraghty; camera, William Bradford; editor, Henry Batista; musical director, Mischa Bakaleinikoff.

CAST: Gene Autry, Gail Davis, Harry Shannon, Jock O'Mahoney, Clark "Buddy" Burroughs, Harry Harvey, Steve Darrell, Sandy Sanders, Ralph Sanford, Bud Osborne, Robert Hilton, Ted Mapes, Charles Robertson, House Peters, Jr., Champion.

Cow Town raises the question of whether cattle ranches should be fenced in with barbed wire or

Gene and Jock O'Mahoney (later the Range Rider and Yancy Derringer on television) mix it up in this scene from *Cow Town.*

whether range land should remain open. Despite opposition from some ranch hands and rustlers, Gene strings the wire around his ranch. Before it's all over and Autry's will prevails, there is a regular war brewing around the cow town.

*   *   *

Beyond the Purple Hills (Columbia, 1950) 69 M.

Producer, Armand Schaefer; director, John English; screenplay, Norman S. Hall; camera, William Bradford; editor, Richard Fanti; song, Charles and Nick Kenny.

CAST: Gene Autry, Pat Buttram, Jo Dennison, Don Beddoe, James Millican, Don Reynolds, Hugh O'Brian, Roy Gordon, Harry Harvey, Gregg Barton, Bob Wilke, Ralph Peters, Frank Ellis, John Cliff, Sandy Sanders, Champion.

This is another winner in the Autry series. Along with the usual ingredients that make up these features, there is the additional treat of Champion and newcomer Little Champ showing off their bag of tricks for the particular delight of youngsters.

After a wealthy citizen is murdered and his son is held on suspicion of committing the killing, Sheriff Autry conducts an investigation that eventually leads to the town banker. It seems the banker had been fleecing the dead man's estate, was discovered, and had to commit murder in an attempt to cover his tracks. (The unjustly jailed son is played by Hugh O'Brian, later televisions Wyatt Earp.)

Gene finds time to sing two songs in the film—"Dear Hearts and Gentle People" and the title tune.

COLUMBIA PICTURES presents
GENE **AUTRY**
and CHAMPION
INDIAN TERRITORY
A GENE AUTRY PRODUCTION

* * *

Indian Territory (Columbia, 1950) 70 M.

Producer, Armand Schaefer; director, John English; screenplay, Norman S. Hall; camera, William Bradford; editor, James Sweeney.

CAST: Gene Autry, Pat Buttram, Gail Davis, Kirby Grant, James Griffith, Philip Van Zandt, Pat Collins, Roy Gordon, Charles Stevens, Robert Carson, Champion.

As with many of the Autry Columbia features, this one takes place in the old West just after the Civil War. Autry, an Indian agent working undercover in the Union Army, is assigned the task of getting to the bottom of some Indian uprisings that have been taking place in the territory. The action is plentiful, the story taut, and the musical interludes held to two—the popular "Chattanooga Shoe Shine Boy" being the big number.

Kirby Grant (television's Sky King) is featured in the film.

* * *

The Blazing Sun (Columbia, 1950) 69 M.

Producer, Armand Schaefer; director, John English; screenplay, Jack Townley; camera, William Bradford; editor, James Sweeney.

CAST: Gene Autry, Pat Buttram, Lynne Roberts, Anne Gwynne, Edward Norris, Kenne Duncan, Alan Hale, Jr., Gregg Barton, Steve Darrell, Tom London, Sandy Sanders, Frankie Marvin, Champion.

Continuing his string of action-packed features, Gene is in the modern West this time on the trail of a couple of bank robbers who lead him a merry chase across the countryside and use all sorts of modern devices—short-wave radios, cars, and trains—in their attempts to outwit him. The thrilling finale has Gene making his capture on a runaway train.

Two popular songs, "Brush Those Tears from Your Eyes" and "Along the Navajo Trail," are spotted in the proceedings so that they add to the enjoyment of the picture without interrupting the action.

* * *

Gene Autry and the Mounties (Columbia, 1951) 70 M.

Producer, Armand Schaefer; director, John English; screenplay, Norman S. Hall; camera, William Bradford; editor, James Sweeney; songs, Doris Anderson and Gene Andrea.

CAST: Gene Autry, Pat Buttram, Elena Verdugo, Carlton Young, Richard Emory, Herbert Rawlinson, Trevor Bardette, Francis McDonald, Jim Frasher, Gregg Barton, House Peters, Jr., Jody Gilbert, Nolan Leary, Champion.

This is a good feature in the Autry series. Gene and Pat are U. S. Marshals operating near the Montana-Canada border in pursuit of a bank robber and his gang. When the outlaws cross over into Canada, Gene enlists the help of the Mounties in his quest for justice. A subplot concerns Gene's efforts to straighten out a potential juvenile delinquent who idolizes the French Canadian outlaw and his cohorts. The ending finds the outlaw leader dying in the flames of a fire that just about destroys the whole town. The sequence is well filmed and very realistic for the limited budget.

Gene sings "Blue Canadian Rockies" and "Anteora," while heroine Elena Verdugo sings "Love's Ritornella."

*   *   *

Texans Never Cry (Columbia, 1951) 66 M.

Producer, Armand Schaefer; director, Frank McDonald; screenplay, Norman S. Hall; camera, William Bradford; editor, James Sweeney; musical director, Mischa Bakaleinikoff.

CAST: Gene Autry, Pat Buttram, Mary Castle, Russ Hayden, Gail Davis, Richard Powers, Don Harvey, Roy Gordon, Michael Reagan, Frank Fenton, Sandy Sanders, John R. McKee, Harry Mackin, Harry Tyler, Minerva Urecal, Richard Flato, I. Stanford Jolley, Duke York, Roy Butler, Champion.

An average Autry oater, *Texans Never Cry,* as you might expect, has Gene as a Texas Ranger attempting to bring justice to the badlands. A good supporting cast helps to raise the picture to the level it does achieve.

*   *   *

Whirlwind (Columbia, 1951) 70 M.

Producer, Armand Schaefer; director, John English; screenplay, Norman S. Hall; camera, William Bradford; editor, Paul Borefsky; musical director, Mischa Bakaleinikoff.

CAST: Gene Autry, Smiley Burnette, Gail Davis, Thurston Hall, Harry Lauter, Dick Curtis, Harry Harvey, Gregg Barton, Tommy Ivo, Kenne Duncan, Al Wyatt, Gary Goodwin, Champion.

Gene's up to his usual good-guy business in this standard opus in the series. This time he's a postal inspector out to break up a frontier mafia. Smiley Burnette reteams with Gene for this feature while Pat Buttram recovers from an illness.

*   *   *

Silver Canyon (Columbia, 1951) 71 M.

Producer, Armand Schaefer; director, John English; screenplay, Gerald Geraghty based on a story by Alan James; camera, William Bradford; editor, James Sweeney.

CAST: Gene Autry, Pat Buttram, Gail Davis, Jim Davis, Bob Steele, Edgar Dearing, Richard Alexander, Terry Frost, Peter Mamakos, Duke York, Eugene Borden, Champion.

A great supporting cast helps Gene to raise this feature to higher-than-usual quality. There's action aplenty in the story about a Utah guerrilla raider during Civil War days: Gene's a federal scout assigned to handling the problem, and he does it with guns ablaze and fists a-swinging.

*   *   *

Hills of Utah (Columbia, 1951) 70 M.

Producer, Armand Schaefer; director, John English; screenplay, Gerald Geraghty based on a story by Les Savage, Jr.; camera, William Bradford; editor, James Sweeney.

CAST: Gene Autry, Pat Buttram, Elaine Riley, Donna Martell, Onslow Stevens, Denver Pyle, William Fawcett, Harry Lauter, Kenne Duncan, Harry Harvey, Sandy Sanders, Tom London, Champion.

This time Gene is a new doctor setting up practice in a Utah town. Because of the slugfests and shootouts between the local copperminers and ranchers, the doctoring business keeps him pretty busy. Presently Gene's lawman instincts get the best of him. He goes out and conducts an investigation and, finally, captures the outlaws who are egging the two factions on to their mayhem.

Gene sings two songs—"Happy Easter Day" and "Back to Utah."

*   *   *

Valley of Fire (Columbia, 1951) 70 M.

Producer, Armand Schaefer; director, John English; screenplay, Gerald Geraghty from a story by Earle Snell; camera, William Bradford; editor, James Sweeney; musical director, Mischa Bakaleinikoff.

CAST: Gene Autry, Pat Buttram, Gail Davis, Russell Hayden, Christine Larson, Harry Lauter, Terry Frost, Barbara Stanley, Teddy Infuhr, Marjorie Liszt, Riley Hill, Victor Sen Yung, Gregg Barton, Sandy Sanders, Bud Osborne, Fred Sherman, James Magill, Duke York, Champion.

Gene's the mayor of a frontier village very much lacking in female citizens. To assuage the needs of the local males, he arranges for a wagon train of fine ladies to be shipped out to his mesa metropolis. Unfortunately, villains Harry Lauter and Russell Hayden, seeking vengeance on Mayor Autry for past actions against them, plan a hijacking of the wagon train of feminine pulchritude. They and a gang of lonely miners have plans for the femmes. When Gene and the town's males get wind of the scheme, a lot of wild and woolly action transpires. In the end justice prevails and love blossoms in the valley. The fire mentioned in the title, I presume, refers to the fire of passion.

*   *   *

The Old West (Columbia, 1952) 61 M.

Producer, Armand Schaefer; director, George Archainbaud; screenplay, Gerald Geraghty; camera, William Bradford; editor, James Sweeney.

CAST: Gene Autry, Pat Buttram, Gail Davis, Lyle Talbot, Louis Jean Heydt, House Peters, Sr., Dick Jones, Kathy Johnson, Don Harvey, Dee Pollock, Raymond L. Morgan, James Craven, Tom London, Frank Marvin, Champion.

The title could be *Gimme That Old-Time Religion,* since Gene early on in the story is befriended by an old West preacher who hopes to save the town of Saddlerock from sin and degradation—most of which is exemplified by Lyle Talbot and his sleazy henchmen. Gene finds himself in conflict with Talbot, too, because the evildoer is out to get Gene's contract to supply horses for the stage line. The climax is a winner-take-all stagecoach race that Gene wins.

Gene takes time in the film to display the equine talents of Champion and Champ Jr. and to sing "Somebody Bigger Than You and I" and "Music By the Angels."

*   *   *

Night Stage To Galveston (Columbia, 1952) 62 M.

Producer, Armand Schaefer; director, George Archainbaud; screenplay, Norman S. Hall; camera, William Bradford; editor, James Sweeney.

CAST: Gene Autry, Pat Buttram, Virginia Huston, Thurston Hall, Judy Nugent, Robert Livingston, Harry Cording, Robert Bice, Frank Sully, Clayton Moore, Frank Rawls, Steve Clark, Harry Lauter, Robert Peyton, Lois Austin, Champion.

This is a pokey cactus caper that makes up in music what it lacks in action.

We're back in Texas after the days of the Texas Rangers when law is enforced by the state's police—some of whom are corrupt and brutal with the citizens. Gene, a former Texas Ranger, works with some of his old buddies to bring about a return to proper law enforcement.

There are more songs than usual used to fill out the time left by the slim plot. They include "Down in Slumberland," "Eyes of Texas," "Yellow Rose of Texas," and "A Heart as Big as Texas."

*   *   *

Apache Country (Columbia, 1952) 62 M.

Producer, Armand Schaefer; director, George Archainbaud; screenplay, Norman S. Hall; camera, William Bradford; editor, James Sweeney; musical director, Paul Mertz.

CAST: Gene Autry, Pat Buttram, Carolina Cotton, Harry Lauter, Mary Scott, Sydney Mason, Francis X Bushman, Gregg Barton, Tom London, Byron Foulger, Frank Matts, Mickey Simpson, Champion.

Even rampaging Apaches can't bring life to this yawner. The story has bad white guys supplying the Apaches with liquor and guns and then sicking them on settlers while the white outlaws do their own rampaging and robbing in other areas. The Indians serve as a sort of cover for the nefarious activities of the plundering palefaces. Autry, a government man, is sent out to restore the peace—a task he completes in sixty-two minutes with little action, and just a modicum of interest. He doesn't even take much time to sing—"Cold, Cold Heart" being his major crooning effort.

*   *   *

Barbed Wire (Columbia, 1952) 61 M.

Producer, Armand Schaefer; director, George Archainbaud; screenplay, Gerald Geraghty; camera,

William Bradford; editor, James Sweeney; musical director, Mischa Bakaleinikoff.

CAST: Gene Autry, Pat Buttram, Anne James, William Fawcett, Leonard Penn, Michael Vallon, Terry Frost, Clayton Moore, Edwin Parker, Sandy Sanders, Champion.

Barbed Wire is a decided improvement over the first three 1952 entries in the series. In this one Texas cattlemen and farmers are feuding again, causing a delay in the big cattle drive. Autry, a cattle buyer, gets involved to protect his business interests and ultimately brings peace to the range land once more. (Notice that way down in the cast listing is Clayton Moore, who in '49 became television's Lone Ranger, but who at this time was in temporary contractual exile from the television series.)

* * *

Wagon Team (Columbia, 1952) 61 M.

Producer, Armand Schaefer; director, George Archainbaud; screenplay, Gerald Geraghty; camera, William Bradford; editor, James Sweeney.

CAST: Gene Autry, Pat Buttram, Gail Davis, Dick Jones, Gordon Jones, Harry Harvey, Henry Rowland, George J. Lewis, John Cason, Fred S. Martin, Bert Dodson, Jerry Scoggins, Gregg Barton, Pierce Lyden, Carlo Tricoli, Champion.

Wagon Team is, at best, a routine episode in Gene's series—a rambling plot and a paucity of action contribute to the designation.

In this one an army payroll has been stolen from a stagecoach by a gang of outlaws. Gene plays a special investigator for the stage line sent to solve the crime. During his Sherlocking he takes a job as a singer for a medicine show so that he can work undercover on the case. Presently the villains slip up allowing Gene to get the goods and the cuffs on them.

* * *

Blue Canadian Rockies (Columbia, 1952) 62 M.

Producer, Armand Schaefer; director, George Archainbaud; screenplay, Gerald Geraghty; camera, William Bradford; editor, James Sweeney.

CAST: Gene Autry, Pat Buttram, Gail Davis, Carolina Cotton, Ross Ford, Tom London, John Merton, Gene Roth, Don Beddoe, Mauritz Hugo, David Garcia, Cass County Boys, Champion.

1952 was not a very good year for Gene Autry

features. The blame can be shared by most of the hands: Gene at the time was overextended with his weekly radio and television series, his movie series, plus his burgeoning business interests; George Archainbaud, Gene's director, was a competent, but routine film director; and the scripts coming down the chute were nothing to "ya-hoo" about. Perhaps all the participants realized that the long ride of the musical Western was nearing an end and that they would all soon be hanging up their saddles, guns, and guitars for the final time.

* * *

Winning of the West (Columbia, 1953) 57 M.

Producer, Armand Schaefer; director, George Archainbaud; screenplay, Norman S. Hall; camera, William Bradford; editor, James Sweeney.

CAST: Gene Autry, Smiley Burnette, Gail Davis, Richard Crane, Robert Livingston, House Peters, Jr., Gregg Barton, William Forrest, Ewing Mitchell, Rodd Redwing, George Chesebro, Frank Jocquet, Charles Delaney, Champion.

This first episode for 1953 was quite an improvement over Autry's 1952 cinema rides.

The script is a brother-against-brother yarn as Gene discovers his *frère* among a gang of outlaws selling "protection" to townspeople and miners. Eventually family bonds triumph as Gene wins his brother over to the cause of justice and with his help rounds up the no-gooders.

Songs include "Cowboy Blues," "Find Me My Trusty 45," and "Cowpoke Poking Along." Smiley Burnette rejoins Gene for the final year of films.

* * *

On Top of Old Smoky (Columbia, 1953) 59 M.

Producer, Armand Schaefer; director, George Archainbaud; screenplay, Gerald Geraghty; camera, William Bradford; editor, James Sweeney; musical director, Mischa Bakaleinikoff.

CAST: Gene Autry, Smiley Burnette, Gail Davis, Grandon Rhodes, Sheila Ryan, Kenne Duncan, Robert Bice, Zon Murray, Cass County Boys (Fred S. Martin, Jerry Scoggins, Bert Dodson), Champion.

This film had added "want-to-see" appeal because of the title song, which was a revival hit at the time. Gene and the Cass County Boys, traveling troubadours, find themselves impersonating Texas Rangers to help Gail Davis protect her valuable property from mineral poachers. It's all routine film fodder for Western fans.

*   *   *

Goldtown Ghost Riders (Columbia, 1953) 57 M.

Producer, Armand Schaefer; director, George Archainbaud; screenplay, Gerald Geraghty; camera, William Bradford; editor, James Sweeney; musical director, Mischa Bakaleinikoff.

CAST: Gene Autry, Smiley Burnette, Gail Davis, Kirk Riley, Carleton Young, Neyle Morrow, Denver Pyle, Steve Conte, John Doucette, Champion.

This is a typical Autry adventure with perhaps a more involved and intriguing plot than usual. This time Gene is a circuit judge trying a murderer in a mining town out West. The twist is that the murderer claims that he can't be tried for the crime since he already has served his prison sentence for the killing. It seems that years before, the murderer had thought he killed his partner (a fellow swindler in a gold rush fraud), was tried and sent to prison. In reality the victim lived and assumed a new identity. Now, ten years later and released from prison, the convicted man discovers his old victim and this time does him in for good. "If at first you don't succeed" and all that sort of thing.

*   *   *

Pack Train (Columbia, 1953) 56 M.

Producer, Armand Schaefer; director, George Archainbaud; screenplay, Norman S. Hall; camera, William Bradford; editor, James Sweeney; songs, Jimmy Kennedy, Gene Autry, Smiley Burnette.

CAST: Gene Autry, Smiley Burnette, Gail Davis, Kenne Duncan, Sheila Ryan, Tom London, Harry Lauter, Melinda Plowman, B. G. Norman, Champion.

The Cass County Boys watch Gail Davis pin a Ranger's badge on Gene in this scene from *On Top of Old Smoky.*

"Average" is probably the best way to describe this series feature. When he's not engaged in fisticuffs and chases performing his job of getting supplies to boondock settlers, Gene slows down to warble two tunes: "God's Little Candles" and "Wagon Train." His sidekick, Smiley Burnette, gets in some funnies along the way and sings "Hominy Grits."

*   *   *

Saginaw Trail (Columbia, 1953) 56 M.

Producer, Armand Schaefer; director, George Archainbaud; screenplay, Dorothy Yost and Dwight Cummins; camera, William Bradford; editor, James Sweeney.

CAST: Gene Autry, Smiley Burnette, Connie Marshall, Eugene Borden, Ralph Reed, Henry Blair, Myron Healey, Mickey Simpson, John War Eagle, Rodd Redwing, Billy Wilkerson, Gregg Barton, John Parrish, Champion.

We are in northern Michigan in 1827 in this above-average Autry starrer. Gene, a captain in Hamilton's Rangers, is called upon to stop Indian raiding parties that are driving away settlers from the area. The renegades are led by a French fur trapper who fears that the settlers will drive the wild game away.

Gene sings "Beautiful Dreamer," while Smiley gets some laughs with "Learn I Love You."

*   *   *

Last of the Pony Riders (Columbia, 1953) 58 M.

Producer, Armand Schaefer; director, George Archainbaud; screenplay, Ruth Woodman; camera, William Bradford; editor, James Sweeney.

CAST: Gene Autry, Smiley Burnette, Kathleen Case, Dick Jones, John Downey, Howard Wright, Arthur Space, Gregg Barton, Buzz Henry, Harry Mackin, Harry Hines, Champion.

With *Last of the Pony Riders* Gene comes to the end of his long trail of singing cowboy features in satisfactory style. The story concerns the transition period in the old West from Pony Express to stagecoach and telegraph. Gene's setting up a stage line and wants to keep the mail franchise he had with the Pony Express. The bad-guy local banker tries to undermine Gene's success, but as you might expect by now, Gene is well-nigh impossible to defeat in these films.

Gene gets in his usual quota of two songs in this final episode. He solos "Song of the Prairie" and gets a little help from Smiley on "Sugar Babe."

*   *   *

The Silent Treatment (Ralph Andrews Production, 1968)

Gene was a guest star in this film that was never released. Others in the cast included Jerry Lewis, Milton Berle, George Raft, Marty Ingels, and Jackie Coogan.

*   *   *

GENE AUTRY DISCOGRAPHY

Although Gene Autry has not made any new recordings since the early fifties, his old Columbia recordings are still available in reissue. In recent years Gene has made available many musical selections from his "Melody Ranch" radio series on the "Gene Autry's Republic Records" label.

*   *   *

All American Cowboy Republic Records
Selections:

Don't Bite the Hand
There's No Back Door to Heaven

Okeh was an early subsidiary label of Columbia Records, the company for which Gene Autry recorded during most of his career.

You're the Only Good Thing
The West, A Nest, and You
My Old Kentucky Home
Dixie Cannonball
Down in the Valley
Cowboy Blues
Missouri Waltz
Kentucky Babe
When Day Is Done
A Boy from Texas

*   *   *

Back in the Saddle Again Harmony (Columbia)
Records

Selections:

Back in the Saddle Again
You Are My Sunshine
Cowboy Blues
Rolling Along
Blueberry Hill
I Lost My Little Darlin'
Goodnight Irene

Home on the Range
Have I Told You Lately That I Love You?

*   *   *

Christmastime with Gene Autry Mistletoe Records
Selections:

Jingle Bells
Silver Bells
Here Comes Santa Claus
Up on the House Top
Rudolph, the Red-Nosed Reindeer
Santa Claus Is Coming to Town
Sleigh Bells
O Little Town of Bethlehem
Silent Night
Joy to the World

*   *   *

Country Music Hall of Fame Album Columbia
Records
Selections:

Mexicali Rose
(Take Me Back To My) Boots and Saddle
Have I Told You Lately That I Love You
You Are My Sunshine
South of the Border
Sioux City Sue
Mule Train
Someday You'll Want Me To Want You
Goodnight Irene
I Love You Because
That Silver-Haired Daddy of Mine
Red River Valley
Buttons and Bows
Back in the Saddle Again

*   *   *

Cowboy Hall of Fame Republic Records
Selections:

Back in the Saddle Again
Silver Spurs
(Take Me Back to My) Boots and Saddle
Twilight on the Trail
Rainbow on the Rio Colorado
Mule Train
The Last Roundup
Riders in the Sky
Tumbling Tumbleweeds
Red River Valley
Ridin' Down the Canyon
Cowboy's Trademarks
Home on the Range
Let the Rest of the World Go By

*   *   *

Gene Autry Favorites Republic Records
Selections:

You Are My Sunshine
Be Honest with Me
Goodbye Little Darlin'
Hang Your Head in Shame
Trouble in Mind
Tweedle-O-Twill
You're the Only Star
I Hang My Head and Cry
Blues Stay Away from Me
San Antonio Rose
Tears on My Pillow
Lonely River

*   *   *

Live from Madison Square Garden Republic Records
Selections:

Half as Much
Down Yonder
Anytime
It's My Lazy Day
That Silver-Haired Daddy of Mine
The Last Letter
Rounded Up in Glory
Someday You'll Want Me To Want You
Let Me Cry on Your Shoulder
Blue Canadian Rockies
I Was Just Walking Out the Door
There's a Goldmine in the Sky

*   *   *

South of the Border Republic Records
Selections:

Rancho Pillow
Mexicali Rose
Vaya Con Dios
El Rancho Grande
A Gay Ranchero
You Belong to My Heart
In a Little Spanish Town
My Adobe Hacienda
Under Fiesta Stars
Serenade of the Bells
South of the Border
It Happened in Old Monterey

*   *   *

You Are My Sunshine and Other Great Hits Harmony (Columbia) Records
Selections:

When the Swallows Come Back to Capistrano
We Never Dream the Same Dream Twice
Blueberry Hill
When It's Springtime in the Rockies
Tweedle-O-Twill
I Don't Want to Set the World on Fire
Maria Elena
You Are My Sunshine
Twilight on the Trail
Someday You'll Want Me To Want You

*   *   *

The Great American Singing Cowboys Republic Records

Selections:

    Back in the Saddle Again
    The Last Roundup

  and ten additional selections by other singing cowboys

*   *   *

Single recordings available:

    Rudolph, The Red-Nosed Reindeer
      Columbia Records
  Here Comes Santa Claus Columbia Records

3   Tex Ritter

FROM GRAND NATIONAL TO THE "GRAND OLE OPRY"

Within a few months of the release of Gene Autry's first feature, *Tumbling Tumbleweeds,* two more singing cowboys had joined the B musical Western ranks—Dick Foran at Warner Brothers for a short-lived series and Tex Ritter at Grand National. Next to Gene Autry and Roy Rogers, Tex Ritter, between 1936 and 1945, starred in more B musical Westerns than any other singing cowboy—a total of fifty-eight. He appeared seven out of nine years on the Top Money-Making Western Stars poll of exhibitors, although never higher than sixth, and tenth twice.

Despite the fact that Tex made so many musical Westerns and appeared among the top ten Western money-makers, his films were only mildly popular with musical Western fans at the time of their release, and were never any real competition at the box office for Gene Autry or Roy Rogers. It should be noted, however, that the fans who did prefer him over his competitors were a loyal and devoted coterie that remain staunch to this day—years after Tex's death.

The fact that Tex Ritter did not make it to the Gene Autry-Roy Rogers level of popularity was not all his fault. Tex, throughout much of his film career, was plagued with working in third- and fourth-rate studios (Grand National, Monogram, PRC) where his pleasant screen personality, his ability to handle action scenes effectively, and his way with a Western ballad were frequently sand-bagged by inferior production values, anemic scripts, unfunny comic sidekicks, and tired direction. When he did work in the better B studios (Columbia and Universal), he was for the most part playing second fiddle—co-starring with Johnny Mack Brown or Bill Elliott, but always getting the lesser of the two starring roles.

The first studio Tex worked for was Grand National. Grand National was formed in early 1936 by Edward R. Alperson, a film exchange manager, who got together with Jimmy Cagney (who was on the outs with Warner Brothers at the time) and some money men to establish the company. Cagney's arrangement called for him to receive a large bundle of shares in Grand National for agreeing to make one picture a year for the company. Alperson figured that the Cagney box-office strength would assure the film a good playoff and, in addition, through block booking he would be able to force exhibitors to play the company's lesser product to get the Cagney plums. There is no doubt that the Jimmy Cagney pulling power at theater box offices helped to swing financial credit for the fledgling company.

The advertising head for the newly formed Grand National was an enterprising fellow named Edward Finney who had a strong desire to become a film producer. Noting the quick success of the Gene Autry films over at Republic Pictures, young Finney started scouting around for his own singing cowboy.

All the way across the country in New York City, a young Texan by the name of Woodward Maurice Ritter was building a radio and stage reputation that would soon come to the attention of the budding film producer. Ritter was a native of Panola County in the remote wilds of east Texas ("I guess my little section of east Texas was possibly the last place in the country that had an

Tex Ritter.

automobile.")* and the youngest of six kids in his family. He grew up in what he was later to describe as "a rather Victorian society" where the Baptists and Methodists had banned square dancing, card playing, and other similar, sinful indulgences.

Getting his first singing training and experience from a traveling music teacher with the unlikely name of P. O. Stamps, young Ritter got off to a faulty vocal career. Even his family felt the need to hush him up during early family sing-a-longs. ("I remember once my mother said it would be nice if her [three] boys would sing. So we got up in front of the fireplace and sang about a half a song and the others stopped and said, 'Mama, would you make him sit down?' ")

Eventually, though, the youngster's voice changed for the better and he got interested in

*Ritter quotes are from "An Interview with Tex Ritter, Champion of the West" by Kathy Sawyer, *Country Music*, July 1973.

Western music—the kind the cowboys sang around the campfires. While later studying prelaw at the University of Texas, his interest in cowboy songs was heightened by contact with J. Frank Dobie, an English professor whose passion was Western folklore; Oscar J. Fox, Tex's voice teacher and a composer and arranger of Western songs; and John A. Lomax, a collector of cowboy facts and information.

Law school proved to be less stimulating in fact than in anticipation, so the restless and gregarious young Texan decided to see if there might be a place for him in show business as a purveyor of Western songs. In 1928, radio station KPRC in Houston was the first to take a flyer with Tex, assigning him a thirty-minute program that was broadcast every Saturday. The next thing he knew a touring country-Western band offered him the chance to join up with them for a tour through the Midwest, a tour that concluded in Chicago in late

1930 with Ritter, as usual, short on funds.

Eventually, on the advice of his brother-in-law in Ohio, Tex headed for the big city—New York. ("He had always told me that a year or two in the East would be good for a Texas boy, because it moved a little faster and gave you a different outlook.") New York in the early depression years was not exactly a city of refuge for poor Texas boys, or anyone else for that matter. But Tex turned out to be one of the lucky ones. Within a few months he had landed a job in a Broadway show, singing four Western songs and playing a cowhand in the Theatre Guild's production of *Green Grow the Lilacs*. A little over a decade later the show would be converted into a full-fledged musical and called *Oklahoma.*

Broadway led to radio. ("I got on the radio—WOR, 'The Lone Star Rangers.' . . . then we had a program for children called 'Cowboy Tom's Roundup.' It was an older man, an Indian boy from Oklahoma and me. We did five characters and had a script every day. After the Cowboy Tom thing broke up, I had a thing on WHN called 'Tex Ritter's Campfire.' . . . And then I had another show once a week called 'WHN Barn Dance' in 1934.") It was at this time that Edward Finney of Grand National Pictures out in Hollywood heard about the Broadway-radio cowboy singer named Tex Ritter.

Gene Fernett in *Hollywood's Poverty Row* quotes Finney:

> First, of course, I had to convince other Grand National officials that I'd made the proper choice in this case. To do that, I knew that we must prepare a brief screen test. So I sent for Tex. . . .
> I knew a top flight makeup man at Paramount—a fellow named Eddie Senz. We hastily made up a screen test at the Paramount lot, on a sort of western-style saloon set they had there. Well, Tex sang a song, read some dialog, and generally looked the handsome, virile cowboy I was looking for. The test impressed Alperson and the others at Grand National, and we were on our way.

Being shrewd in the ways of Hollywood and, of course, knowledgeable of the shaky financial foundation upon which Grand National was founded, Edward Finney put Tex under personal contract to him (rather than the studio) so that he could negotiate with the studio as producer-agent on the Tex Ritter musical Westerns. Shortly thereafter a deal was made with Grand National for a series of Westerns, each with a budget of eight to twelve thousand dollars, with Tex receiving twenty-four hundred dollars per picture as star. Finney organized his own production unit, which he called Boots and Saddles, and went about the business of making Tex's musical Westerns on a five-day shooting schedule. Considering the shoe-string budgets and the inexperience of the star and producer, it's a wonder the films were as good as they were. Fortunately, what they may have lacked in finesse and skill, they more than made up for in exuberance.

The first of the Ritter films was *Song of the Gringo* (1936), a routine affair that strove to establish Tex as quick with his fists and trigger finger when danger intruded and quick on the musical downbeat in quieter, less frantic, more romantic moments. Fuzzy Knight provided a few laughs as the comic sidekick, and former bank robber turned thespian, Al Jennings, played a role in the picture. Between set-ups he reportedly taught Tex the finer points of gun-slinging and the quick draw.

The fourth entry in the series, *Trouble in Texas* (1937), featured a young "looker" named Rita Cansino who would later become a star under the name of Hayworth. (In the forties the film would be re-released with Rita Hayworth—then a front-ranked star—receiving top billing.) *Trouble in Texas* marked the first appearance of Horace Murphy as main comic backup for Tex [he had had a previous small role in Ritter's *Arizona Days* (1937)]. One critic commented, "Horace Murphy, besides having trouble spitting his tobacco juice through a phony handlebar mustache, is not very funny." Despite the critical rap (and there would be others) Murphy, along with silent movie comic Snub Pollard, would generally provide what comedy there was in these early Grand National pictures (and for many of the later Monogram pictures).

Hittin' the Trail (1937), Tex's next effort, was the first Ritter feature to be really clobbered by a trade critic. *Variety's* critic blasted it by writing, "Film was too obviously made with one eye on the clock and the other on the purse. . . . Made for the lower floor of two-story shops." (Translation for those who are unfamiliar with *Variety*ese: produced for release as the bottom half of a double-feature presentation at a movie theater.) Other early features like *Tex Rides with the Boy Scouts* (1938), *Frontier Town* (1938), *Utah Trail* (1938), and *Rollin' Plains* (1938) ("Film looks like it was tossed together between takes on some other feature.") failed to make passing grades with critics though they did generally average business at ticket windows where they were released—usually in smaller Southern and Western towns.

Early Ritter films that got high or above-average marks by the critics were *Arizona Days* (1937), *Sing, Cowboy, Sing* (1937), *Riders of the Rockies* (1937) (which one critic didn't particularly like, but said of Tex, "He's a life-saver in this entry."), and probably the best of the Grand National features, *Mystery of the Hooded Horsemen* (1937), which had, as the title indicates, a mystery angle—who the chief villain was, hooded horsemen, and seriallike action. It was a real winner with fans of all ages.

By 1938 the financial situation at Grand National had become very grim. The Jimmy Cagney-Grand National alliance, always shaky at best, crumbled completely after the nine-hundred-thousand dollar *Something To Sing About* Cagney feature provided very little to sing about at the box office. By 1940 Grand National would be in receivership. But in 1938 Edward Finney, seeing Grand National's financial ruin imminent, packed up his Boots and Saddles production unit and moved over to the Monogram Pictures stable. The budgets at Monogram were not much better, hovering between twelve and fifteen thousand dollars per picture with Tex continuing to receive his twenty-four hundred dollars per picture. On the whole there wasn't much difference in the Ritter Monogram pictures. Neither awful nor great, they continued for three years and twenty features.

The best of the Monogram features were probably *Roll, Wagons, Roll* (1939), *Rhythm of the Rio Grand* (1940) ("... trim entertainment, likely to enhance the crooning cowboy's rep as an actor"), and *Rollin' Home to Texas* (1941), which featured future singing cowboy star Eddie Dean as a sheriff. The list, unfortunately, is longer on the negative side of the critical ledger with the following films having the dubious distinction of being standouts: *Sundown on the Prairie* (1938) ("... crudest of the action collection to date ... "), *Down the Wyoming Trail* (1939) ("Made with a paste pot and a promise ... "), *Riders of the Frontier* (1939) ("... inferior acting, direction, and story ... "), and *Cowboy from Sundown* (1940) ("... a cactus opera that's got plenty of thorns. It'll be a pain for exhibs, even in the most remote situations"). And so it went.

Tex, regrettably, was never blessed with really first-rate comic sidekicks in his films for Grand National and Monogram. Horace Murphy and Snub Pollard—Murphy of the whiny voice and Pollard of the hangdog look—handled these chores more often than not until 1940, and never really made a strong impression with most fans. One of their greatest drawbacks was that they did not regularly ride alongside Tex on his adventures, although this changed somewhat in later episodes. During 1940 and early 1941 "Arkansas" Slim Andrews took over the sidekick chores and was either a great comic step forward or backward, depending on your cactus comedy taste. I have to agree with Don Miller's assessment of Slim Andrews in his book *Hollywood Corral:* "... Arkansas Slim Andrews [was] a gangly blowhard familiar to back-country audiences on the bucolic circuit.... There was no in-between with Andrews, one either doted on him or loathed him. If a tally had been made, results would probably have tilted in the latter direction."

When Tex's contract with Edward Finney was up in 1941, he decided that it was a good time to strike out on his own. He figured he had to start planning his future more carefully now that he was going to be a married man. Tex had met and fallen in love with Dorothy Fay Southworth, his leading lady in *Rainbow Over the Range* (1940), and they planned to be married on June 14, 1941. (After their marriage, Dorothy decided to retire from pictures to raise the family of two boys that were eventually born to them.)

Columbia Pictures, totally lacking in singing cowboys (which were so popular at the time), quickly snapped up Tex to co-star in a series with Bill Elliott, who was already doing a series for Columbia. Tex was put under contract by the studio and paid a weekly salary (not paid by the picture, as he had been with Finney), which proved to be far more lucrative. Tex really wanted a series of his own at Columbia, but the shared series with Bill Elliott was the best he could negotiate. Elliott wasn't too happy with the arrangement either, but the two men remained personal friends throughout their run of eight pictures together. They may not have been too happy with the situation, but the truth was that they "played" well together on the screen—Tex, the gregarious, folksy cowpoke who would occasionally fly off the handle; Elliott, the "peaceable man," reserved, calculating, slow-to-anger, but a raging buffalo when the inevitable fracas ensued. Often they were pitted against each other for the first three-fourths of a picture. Then, of course, the storyline would have them join forces for the climax to rout the bad guys.

Tex invariably had the weaker of the two starring roles in the pictures regardless of the attempts by the writers to give their characters equal treatment. *Variety's* critic summed up the problem that was to remain with the actors (if not the fans) throughout the series in his review of Tex and Bill's first picture, *King of Dodge City* (1941):

> Interest suffers from attempt to split hero functions equally between the two westerners, and indications are that studio will have to revise formula for teaming Elliott and Ritter whereby either one or the other will have to take secondary importance.

From a production standpoint—scripts, direction, general production values—the Columbia series was a definite step up for Tex, certainly better than he had ever received at Grand National or Monogram. And Tex's acting took on more dimension and flair during this series. Although most of the entries in the series could hold their own in B Western competition, this reviewer would rank *The Lone Star Vigilantes* (1942) and *Prairie Gunsmoke* (1942) as being particular highpoints, packing fast action, solid story lines, interesting characters, and pleasant, unobtrusive musical interludes into the swift-paced features.

After the eight pictures in the Elliott-Ritter series, Elliott went over the hill to Republic Pictures where he was to star in Westerns for a good many years. Tex, then expecting to ride solo for Columbia, was surprised to have his option dropped. As luck would have it, Universal Pictures was in much the same situation as Columbia had been a couple of years before and had a "Singing Cowboy. Co-Star Wanted" sign posted. After the usual negotiations, Tex saddled up his horse, White Flash, and rode on over to Universal where he was to co-star with Johnny Mack Brown for seven features. Tex and Universal had an "understanding" that if things worked out, Tex would eventually get a solo Western series.

Again, as with the Bill Elliott series, Tex was supposed to get equal treatment in the screenplays, but never really did. As the films went into release one by one, anyone could see that regardless of the billing, Johnny Mack Brown was the real star. One film, *Raiders of the San Joaquin* (1943), was reviewed by *Variety* in its standard format of critical commentary, plot summary, and technical references without once even mentioning Ritter's name. You had to check the cast listing to know he was even appearing in the film—much less co-starring. But again, as with Elliott, the two stars complemented each other's performances throughout the seven episodes in the series. The problem was that neither of them really wanted to co-star in a B Western series with *anyone*.

Inexplicably, Tex's musical contribution in each of the Universal features was less than he had provided in any of his earlier series even though the first four episodes were titled after songs that, to one degree or another, were associated with Tex: *Deep in the Heart of Texas* (1942), *Little Joe, the Wrangler* (1942), *Old Chisholm Trail* (1942), and *Tenting Tonight on the Old Camp Ground* (1943). Adding further to the mystery, despite the low budgets, The Jimmy Wakely Trio was hired to supply the majority of the musical content for the films, leaving Tex generally with only one or two songs to warble.

Of the seven Mack Brown-Ritter features, *Little Joe, the Wrangler, Old Chisholm Trail,* and *Lone Star Trail* (1943) stand out as the best entries, combining as they do all the standard ingredients expected in B musical Westerns.

Periodically over the years of its existence, Universal Pictures has had severe financial turnabouts. In 1943 it was over-the-hill-to-the-poorhouse time again for the company. Cutbacks were demanded. One story goes that since Johnny Mack Brown cost the company more than Tex, he was dropped. Another version is that Mack Brown was offered the chance for a solo series at Monogram and took it. Whatever the behind-the-scenes maneuvering, Tex was again (briefly) riding the silver screen alone.

Tex solo starred in only three pictures for Universal before their financial woes worsened and the series was dropped in late 1943. Those three pictures, though, were quite well done from all standpoints—action, acting, music, and production values—and many of Tex's fans rank them the best that he ever made.

Unfortunately, Tex's best days as a film singing cowboy ended with his last Universal feature, *Oklahoma Raiders* (1943). When the Universal series was dropped in late 1943, Tex was asked by PRC (Producers Releasing Corporation), a fourth-rate, shoestring production company, to take over one of the roles in their Texas Rangers series. James Newill, an opera-trained pseudosinging cowboy, was leaving and Tex looked like a good bet to add box-office muscle to the rather limp series. Tex joined regulars Dave O'Brien, a handsome fellow, indeed, when he wore his toupee, but best known as the bald-headed bumbler in the famous Pete Smith shorts, and Guy Wilkerson, a middle-aged, gangly drink-of-water, who provided what few chuckles could be found in the series. From a production viewpoint, the PRC films were little better than the old Grand National series of years before and did not possess nearly the exuberance.

It was an unfortunate ending to a long B musical Western career. In examining the Tex Ritter film

Tex projects a rather somber attitude in this portrait from
his movie singing cowboy days.

career one is always tempted to consider "what might have been" had Tex been hired early in his career by, say, Herbert Yates at Republic Pictures. With the slick Republic production values, plus better direction, scripting, and promotion—who knows? As it was, Tex had another career well underway when the cameras ran out of film.

During the late thirties and early forties, his early film years, Tex had started recording for Decca Records—cutting many of the songs that were highlighted in his films. When Capitol Records was formed in 1942, Tex was put under contract and remained so actively for the rest of his life. By the time his singing cowboy film career ended in 1945, Tex was one of Capitol's major recording artists with such hits to his credit as "There's a New Moon Over My Shoulder," "Rye Whiskey," "Bol Weevil," "You Two-Timed Me One Time Too Often," and "Deck of Cards"—just to name a few.

In addition to his burgeoning recording career, Tex also had put a touring show together and went on the road for extended periods of personal appearances. White Flash, his film horse, and Arkansas Slim Andrews, his comic sidekick from the later Monogram series, appeared with him in many of the shows.

By the early 1950s Tex's career seemed to be winding down; it appeared that he was over the hill. But then one Sunday afternoon he got a call from a man named Tiomkin who wanted him to sing a song off-camera for a movie sound track. The song and the movie were called *High Noon.*

It seems that Stanley Kramer, the producer of *High Noon,* previewed the picture before a theater audience prior to its planned release date and the audience hated it. Taking the film back to the cutting room, Kramer personally re-edited the picture, adding shots of clocks ticking away the time and numerous close-ups of the troubled, agonized face of star Gary Cooper (who was suffering from a painful ulcer throughout the shooting of the film). Then Kramer called in composer Dimitri Tiomkin and told him to add a Western ballad to his score for the picture, which he did, calling upon his regular lyricist, Ned Washington, to add the words. And Tex was asked to sing it. The rest, as they say, is history. A few months later at Academy Awards time, the song, the score, the editing, and Cooper won Oscars. Tex got a hit recording out of *High Noon* and the kind of exposure he needed to give his career added prestige and a big boost.

After his recognition for "High Noon," Tex became a regular performer on a West Coast television program called "Town Hall Party," a country music show. That was followed by a nationally syndicated country-Western television program called "Tex Ritter's Ranch Party," which was produced during the 1957-58 season and consisted of thirty-nine half-hour programs.

During the 1950s Tex occasionally guested on Western adventure television programs such as "Zane Grey Theatre," "Shotgun Slade," and "The Rebel." None of the roles he assayed was memorable and Tex's extra heft and advancing age, unfortunately, took away somewhat from the remembrance of his movie singing cowboy roles of previous years.

By the early sixties Tex Ritter was becoming something of a country-Western music legend. His recordings and personal appearances continued to receive strong support from the public. To many middle-aged people who had followed his career through radio, pictures, recordings, television, and personal appearances, there had never been a time when Tex Ritter was not a show business personality. Now he was becoming an elder statesman in his chosen field.

In 1964 Tex's admiring co-workers elected him to the highest honor the Country Music Association can bestow on one of its own—The Country Music Hall of Fame. The inscription on his Country Music Hall of Fame plaque read in part:

> One of America's most illustrious and versatile stars of radio, television, records, motion pictures, and Broadway stage. Untiring pioneer and champion of country and Western music industry. His devotion to his God, his family, and his country is a continuing inspiration to his countless friends throughout the world.

In 1965 Tex was asked to join the "Grand Ole Opry" program in Nashville. The contract they offered gave some indication of the faith the "Opry" had in Tex—it was a lifetime contract. For years Nashville had been the hub from which his personal appearances and recordings evolved. In 1965, with the "Opry" contract in hand, Tex uprooted himself and his family from their longtime home in California and settled permanently just outside of Nashville.

In 1970 some of the good ole boys of east Tennessee convinced Tex that he should take his country music, elder-statesman prestige to Washington as a United States Senator. After an exhausting campaign throughout the state, the electorate told him from the voting booth that they wanted him to stay in Nashville at the "Grand

PRC Pictures presents

Tex RITTER
DAVE O'BRIEN *as The Texas Ranger*

THREE in the SADDLE
with **GUY WILKERSON**

Screenplay by ELMER CLIFTON   Produced by ARTHUR ALEXANDER   Directed by HARRY FRASER

Tex, Lorraine Miller, Guy Wilkerson (the tall one), and two unidentified actors are pictured in a scene from one of Tex's final singing cowboy films.

Ole Opry." Tex said of the ordeal, "It was a great experience, and I don't regret it at all."

In the early 1970s Tex started to slow down a little—just a little—and lead a slightly more leisurely life with his family. He was proud of his wife, Dorothy, and their two sons, Tom and John. Tom was attending Vanderbilt Law School in Nashville, well on the way to being the lawyer that Tex had studied to be during his college days. John, two years younger than his brother, was seeking a career as an actor and doing quite well for himself. His first major screen roles were in the Disney features *The Barefoot Executive* and *Scandalous John*. On television he appeared in featured roles in such series as "The Waltons," "Medical Center," "Hawaii Five-O," and is one of the stars in a series called "Three's Company."

Tex's wife, Dorothy, had been his constant companion over the years, always looking after his needs, traveling with him on the many tours, and campaigning for him during his senate run in 1970. During free periods through the years she had devoted time to charitable organizations, raising sums of money for such worthy causes as cerebral palsy research (a disease with which their first son was afflicted at birth).

On January 2, 1974, Tex went to visit a friend who was in the Nashville jail. While there, he suddenly slumped over, struck down with a heart attack. Shocked onlookers rushed to Tex's aid, but it was too late. Within a short time he was dead.

Tex Ritter was a fairly popular movie singing cowboy for a few years, but he was a giant in the country music scene for a lot of years—a legend in his own time, and for once the appellation fits. Just go ask anybody in Nashville.

TEX RITTER
SELECTED FILMOGRAPHY

The following filmography only includes the Western films in which Tex Ritter starred.

Song of the Gringo (Grand National, 1936) 62 M.

Producer, Edward Finney; director, John P. McCarthy; screenplay, John P. McCarthy and Robert Emmett.

CAST: Tex Ritter, Monte Blue, Fuzzy Knight, Warner Richmond, Joan Woodbury, Al Jennings, William Desmond, Glenn Strange, Jack Kirk.

* * *

Headin' For the Rio Grande (Grand National, 1936) 61 M.

Producer, Edward Finney; director, Robert N. Bradbury; screenplay, Lindsley Parsons; songs, Tex Ritter, Jack Smith.

CAST: Tex Ritter, Eleanor Stewart, Sid Saylor, Warner Richmond, Charles King, Earl Dwire, Forrest Taylor, William Desmond, Charles French, Snub Pollard, Budd Buster, Bud Osborne.

* * *

Arizona Days (Grand National, 1937) 57 M.

Producer, Edward Finney; director, Jack English; screenplay, Sherman Lowe from a story by Lindsley Parsons; songs, Ted Choate, Jack Smith, Tex Ritter.

CAST: Tex Ritter, Eleanor Stewart, Ethelind Terry, Sid Saylor, William Faversham, Forrest Taylor, Snub Pollard, Glenn Strange, Horace Murphy, Earl Dwire, Budd Buster, William Desmond, Edward Cassidy.

* * *

Trouble in Texas (Grand National, 1937) 53 M.

Producer, Edward Finney; director, Robert N. Bradbury.

CAST: Tex Ritter, Rita Cansino, Earl Dwire, Yakima Canutt, Dick Palmer, Hal Price, Fred Parker, Horace Murphy, Charles King, Tom Cooper.

* * *

Hittin' the Trail (Grand National, 1937) 58 M.

Producer, Edward Finney; director, Robert N. Bradbury; screenplay, Robert Emmett.

CAST: Tex Ritter, Jerry Bergh, Tommy Bupp, Earl Dwire, Jack Smith, Snub Pollard, Archie Ricks, Heber Snow, Charles King, Edward Cassidy, Ray Whitley and His Range Ramblers, The Phelps Brothers, Tex Ritter's Tornadoes.

* * *

Sing, Cowboy, Sing (Grand National, 1937) 59 M.

Producer, Edward Finney; director, Robert N. Bradbury; screenplay, Robert Emmett; songs, Tex Ritter, R. N. Bradbury, Ted Choate, Frank Sanucci.

CAST: Tex Ritter, Louise Stanley, Al St. John, Karl Hackett, Charles King, Robert McKenzie, Budd Buster, Heber Snow, Chick Hannon.

* * *

Riders of the Rockies (Grand National, 1937) 56 M.

Producer, Edward Finney; director, Robert N. Bradbury; screenplay, Robert Emmett from a story by Lindsley Parsons; camera, Gus Peterson; songs, Tex Ritter, Frank Sanucci.

CAST: .Tex Ritter, Louise Stanley, Charles King, Yakima Canutt, Earl Dwire, Snub Pollard, Horace Murphy, Martin Garralaga, Jack Rockwell, Paul Lopez, Heber Snow.

* * *

Mystery of the Hooded Horsemen (Grand National, 1937) 60 M.

Producer, Edward Finney; director, Ray Taylor; screenplay, Edmond Kelso; camera, Gus Peterson; songs, Fred Rose, Michael David, Tex Ritter, Frank Sanucci.

CAST: Tex Ritter, Iris Meredith, Horace Murphy, Charles King, Earl Dwire, Forrest Taylor, Joseph Girard, Lafe McKee.

* * *

Tex Rides with the Boy Scouts (Grand National, 1938) 57 M.

Producer, Edward Finney; director, Ray Taylor; screenplay, Edmond Kelso from a story by Kelso and Lindsley Parsons; camera, Gus Peterson; musical director, Frank Sanucci.

CAST: Tex Ritter, Marjorie Reynolds, Horace Murphy, Edward Cassidy, Tim Davis, Snub Pollard,

Tex takes the advice of the film title, *Sing, Cowboy, Sing,*
in this scene with Louise Stanley and Al St. John.

Charles King, Philip Ahn, Tommy Bupp, Lynton Brent.

* * *

Frontier Town (Grand National, 1938) 60 M.

Producer, Edward Finney; director, Ray Taylor, screenplay, Lindsley Parsons.

CAST: Tex Ritter, Ann Evers, Snub Pollard, Charles King, Horace Murphy, Karl Hackett, Lynton Brent, Edward Cassidy, Forrest Taylor, Jack Smith, Don Marion.

* * *

Rollin' Plains (Grand National, 1938) 57 M.

Producer, Edward Finney; director, Al Herman; screenplay, Lindsley Parsons and Edmond Kelso from a story by Jacques and Ciela Jacquard; songs, Walt Samuels, Leonard Whitcup, Teddy Powell, Frank Harford.

CAST: Tex Ritter, Horace Murphy, Snub Pollard, Harriet Bennett, Hobart Bosworth, Edward Cassidy, Karl Hackett, Charles King, Ernest Adams, Lynton Brent, Hank Carpenter, Hank Worden, Augie Gomez, Oscar Gaghan, The Beverly Hills Billies.

* * *

Utah Trail (Grand National, 1938) 56 M.

Producer, Edward Finney; director, Al Herman, screenplay, Edmond Kelso from a story by Kelso and Lindsley Parsons; songs, Bob Palmer, Frank Harford, Rudy Sooter.

Snub Pollard (with mustache) and Horace Murphy provided the comic relief in many of Tex Ritter's early films.

CAST: Tex Ritter, Horace Murphy, Snub Pollard, Adele Pearce, Karl Hackett, Charles King, Edward Cassidy, David O'Brien, Bud Osborne, Lynton Brent, Rudy Sooter.

* * *

Starlight Over Texas (Monogram, 1938) 56 M.

Producer, Edward Finney; director, Al Herman; screenplay, John Rathmell from an original story idea by Harry MacPherson; camera, Francis Corby; editor, Fred Bain.

CAST: Tex Ritter, Salvatore Damino, Carmen LaRoux, Rosa Turick, Horace Murphy, Snub Pollard, Karl Hackett, Charles King, Jr., Martin Garralaga, George Chesebro, Carlos Villarias, Edward Cassidy, The Northwesterners.

* * *

Where the Buffalo Roam (Monogram, 1938) 52 M.

Producer, Edward Finney; director, Al Herman; screenplay, Robert Emmett; camera, Francis Corby; editor, Fred Bain; musical director, Frank Sanucci; songs, Tex Ritter, Frank Sanucci, Frank Harford.

CAST: Tex Ritter, Dorothy Short, Horace Murphy, Snub Pollard, Richard Alexander, Karl Hackett, Dave O'Brien, Ed Cassidy, Charles King, Jr., Louise Massey's Westerners.

* , * *

Song of the Buckaroo (Monogram, 1938) 55 M.

Producer, Edward Finney; director, Al Herman; screenplay, John Rathmell; camera, Francis Corby; editor, Fred Bain.

CAST: Tex Ritter, Jinx Falkenberg, Mary Ruth, Tom London, Frank LaRue, Charles King, Bob Terry, Horace Murphy, Snub Pollard, Dave O'Brien, Dorothy Fay.

* * *

Sundown on the Prairie (Monogram, 1938) 59 M.

Producer, Edward Finney; director, Al Herman; screenplay, William Molte and Edmond Kelso; camera, Bert Longenecker; editor, Fred Bain.

CAST: Tex Ritter, Horace Murphy, Dorothy Fay, Karl Hackett, Charles King, Hank Worden, Frank Ellis, Wally West, Ernie Adams, Frank LaRue, Edward Piel, Sr., Musical Tornadoes featuring Juanita Street.

Charles King (seen here about to clobber Tex) was one of the most popular Western film villains of the thirties and forties.

* * *

Rollin' Westward (Monogram, 1939) 55 M.

Producer, Edward Finney; director, Al Herman; screenplay, Fred Myton; camera, Marcel LePicard; editor, Fred Bain.

CAST: Tex Ritter, Horace Murphy, Dorothy Fay, Slim Whitaker, Herbert Corthell, Harry Harvey, Charles King, Hank Worden, Dave O'Brien, Tom London, Estrelita Novarro.

* * *

Down the Wyoming Trail (Monogram, 1939) 52 M.

Producer, Edward Finney; director, Al Herman; screenplay, Peter Dixon and Roger Merton; camera, Marcel LePicard; editor, Holbrook Todd.

CAST: Tex Ritter, Horace Murphy, Mary Brodel, Bobby Samson, Charles King, Bob Terry, Jack Ingram, Earl Douglas, Frank LaRue, Ernie Adams, Charles Sergeant, Ed Coxen, Jean Southern, The Northwesterners.

* * *

The Man From Texas (Monogram, 1939) 56 M.

Producer, Edward Finney; director, Al Herman; screenplay, Robert Emmett.

CAST: Tex Ritter, Ruth Rodgers, Nelson McDowell, Hal Price, Charles B. Wood, Charles King, Tom London, Kenne Duncan.

* * *

Riders of the Frontier (Monogram, 1939) 58 M.

Producer, Edward Finney; director, Spencer Bennett; screenplay, Jesse Duffy and Joseph Levering; camera, Marcel LePicard; editor, Fred Bain; musical director, Frank Sanucci; songs, Frank Harford.

CAST: Tex Ritter, Jack Rutherford, Hal Taliaferro, Glen Francis, Nolan Willis, Roy Barcroft, Bill McCormick, Mantan Moreland, Edward Cecil, Bruce Mitchell, Jean Joyce, Marion Sais, Maxine Leslie.

* , * *

Roll, Wagons, Roll (Monogram, 1939) 55 M.

Producer, Edward Finney; director, Al Herman; screenplay, Victor Adamson, Edmond Kelso, Roger Merton; camera, Marcel LePicard; editor, Fred Bain; musical director, Frank Sanucci; songs, Dorcas Cochran, Charles Rosoff.

CAST: Tex Ritter, Nelson McDowell, Muriel Evans, Nolan Willis, Steve Clark, Tom London, Reed Howes, Frank Ellis, Kenneth Duncan, Frank LaRue, Chick Hannon.

* * *

Westbound Stage (Monogram, 1939) 56 M.

Producer, Edward Finney; director, Spencer Bennett; screenplay, Robert Emmett from a story by John Foster; camera, Marcel LePicard; editor, Fred Bain; musical director, Frank Sanucci; songs, Johnny Lange, Lew Porter.

CAST: Tex Ritter, Nelson McDowell, Muriel Evans, Nolan Willis, Steve Clark, Tom London, Reed Howes, Frank Ellis, Frank LaRue, Kenne Duncan, Hank Bell, Chester Gan, Phil Dunham, Chick Hannon.

* * *

Rhythm of the Rio Grande (Monogram, 1940) 53 M.

Producer, Edward Finney; director, Al Herman; screenplay, Robert Emmett; camera, Marcel LePicard; songs, Frank Harford, Johnny Lange, Lew Porter.

CAST: Tex Ritter, Suzan Dale, Warner Richmond, Martin Garralaga, Frank Mitchell, Mike J. Rodriquez, Juan Duval, Tristram Coffin, Chick Hannon,

Tex has the drop on Glenn Strange in this lobby card from *Pals of the Silver Sage*.

Earl Douglas, Forrest Taylor, Glenn Strange, James McNally.

* * *

Pals of the Silver Sage (Monogram, 1940) 52 M.

Producer, Edward Finney; director, Al Herman; screenplay, George Martin; camera, Marcel LePicard; editor, Robert Golden; songs, Johnny Lange, Lew Porter.

CAST: Tex Ritter, Sugar Dawn, Slim Andrews, Clarissa Curtis; Glenn Strange, Carleton Young, John McGuinn, Warner Richmond, Betty Miles.

* * *

Cowboy from Sundown (Monogram, 1940) 58 M.

Producer, Edward Finney; director, Spencer Bennett; screenplay, Rolland Lynch and Robert Emmett from an original story by Lynch; camera, Marcel LePicard; musical director, Frank Sanucci; songs, Tex Ritter, Frank Harford, Johnny Lange, Lew Porter.

CAST: Tex Ritter, Pauline Hadden, Roscoe Ates, Carleton Young, George Pembroke, Dave O'Brien, Patsy Moran, James Farrar, Chick Hannon, Slim Andrews, Bud Osborne, Glenn Strange.

* * *

The Golden Trail (Monogram, 1940) 52 M.

Producer, Edward Finney; director, Al Herman; screenplay, Roland Lynch, Robert Emmett, Roger Merton; camera, Marcel LePicard; editor, Robert Golden.

CAST: Tex Ritter, Slim Andrews, Ina Guest, Patsy Moran, Gene Alsace, Stanley Price, Warner Richmond, Eddie Dean (later singing cowboy star), Forrest Taylor.

* * *

Rainbow Over the Range (Monogram, 1940) 58 M.

Producer, Edward Finney; director, Al Herman; screenplay, Robert Emmett; camera, Marcel LePicard; editor, Fred Bain; songs, Fleming Allen, Johnny Lange, Lew Porter, Garland Edmundson.

CAST: Tex Ritter, Slim Andrews, Dorothy Fay, Gene Alsace, Warner Richmond, Jim Pierce, Chuck Morrison, Dennis Moore, Art Wilcox and the Arizona Rangers.

* * *

Arizona Frontier (Monogram, 1940) 55 M.

Arkansas "Slim" Andrews was Tex Ritter's main comic sidekick for the Monogram pictures from 1939 to 1941. He is seen playing the concertina in the above picture.

Producer, Edward Finney; director, Al Herman.

CAST: Tex Ritter, Evelyn Finley, Slim Andrews, Jim Thorpe, Rocky Cameron, Tristram Coffin, Chick Hannon.

*   *   *

Take Me Back to Oklahoma (Monogram, 1940) 54 M.

Producer, Edward Finney; director, Al Herman; screenplay, Robert Emmett.

CAST: Tex Ritter, Ruth Rodgers, Slim Andrews, Carlton Young, Terry Walker, Robert McKenzie, Bob Wills and The Texas Playboys.

*   *   *

Rollin' Home to Texas (Monogram, 1940) 53 M.

Producer, Edward Finney; director, Al Herman; screenplay, Robert Emmett; camera, Marcel LePicard; editor, Fred Bain.

CAST: Tex Ritter, Slim Andrews, Eddie Dean, Virginia Carpenter, I. Stanford Jolley, Harry Harvey, Cal Shrum and His Rhythm Rangers.

*   *   *

Ridin' the Cherokee Trail (Monogram, 1941) 52 M.

Producer, Edward Finney; director, Spencer Bennett; screenplay, Edmond Kelso; camera, Marcel LePicard; editor, Robert Golden; songs, Jack Gillette, Harry Blair.

CAST: Tex Ritter, Slim Andrews, Forrest Taylor, Betty Miles, Jack Roper, Fred Burns, Bruce Nolan, Gene Alsace, Tennessee Ramblers.

*   *   *

The Pioneers (Monogram, 1941) 59 M.

Producer, Edward Finney; director, Al Herman; screenplay, Charles Anderson; camera, Marcel LePicard; editor, Fred Bain.

CAST: Tex Ritter, Slim Andrews, Red Foley, Doye O'Dell, Wanda McKay, George Chesebro, Del Lawrence, Post Park, Karl Hackett, Lynton Brent, Chick Hannon, Gene Alsace, Jack Smith, Chief Many Treaties, Chief Soldani.

* * *

King of Dodge City (Columbia, 1941) 59 M.

Producer, Leon Barsha; director, Lambert Hillyer; screenplay, Gerald Geraghty; camera, Benjamin Kline; editor, Jerome Thoms.

CAST: Bill Elliott, Tex Ritter, Judith Linden, Dub Taylor, Guy Usher, Rick Anderson, Kenneth Harlan, Pierce Lyden, Francis Walker, Harrison Greene, Jack Rockwell.

* * *

Roaring Frontiers (Columbia, 1941) 62 M.

Producer, Leon Barsha; director, Lambert Hillyer; screenplay, Robert Lee Johnson.

CAST: Bill Elliott, Tex Ritter, Ruth Ford, Frank Mitchell, Bradley Page, Tristram Coffin, Hal Taliaferro, Francis Walker, Joe McGuinn, George Chesebro, Charles Stevens, Charles King, Hank Bell.

* * *

Lone Star Vigilantes (Columbia, 1942) 58 M.

Producer, Leon Barsha; director, Wallace W. Fox; screenplay, Luci Ward; camera, Benjamin Kline; editor, Mel Thorsen.

CAST: Bill Elliott, Tex Ritter, Frank Mitchell, Virginia Carpenter, Luana Walters, Budd Buster, Forrest Taylor, Cavin Gordon, Lowell Drew, Edmund Cobb, Ethan Laidlaw, Rick Anderson.

* * *

Bullets for Bandits (Columbia, 1942) 55 M.

Producer, Leon Barsha; director, Wallace W. Fox; screenplay, Robert Lee Johnson.

CAST: Bill Elliott, Tex Ritter, Frank Mitchell, Forrest Taylor, Ralph Theodore, Dorothy Short, John McGuinn, Art Mix.

*   *   *

North of the Rockies (Columbia, 1942) 60 M.

Producer, Leon Barsha; director, Lambert Hillyer; screenplay, Herbert Dalmas.

CAST: Bill Elliott, Tex Ritter, Shirley Patterson, Frank Mitchell, Tristram Coffin, Lloyd Bridges, Larry Parks.

*   *   *

Mountie Bill Elliott pays a visit to Tex, who seems to be in a lot of trouble in this scene from *North of the Rockies*.

96

BILL TEX
ELLIOTT·RITTER
in
VENGEANCE OF
THE WEST
A COLUMBIA PICTURE

"You're under arrest—for murder!"

Tex saves Adele Mara from the evil clutches of Dick Curtis.

Devil's Trail (Columbia, 1942) 61 M.

Producer, Leon Barsha; director, Lambert Hillyer; screenplay, Philip Ketchum.

CAST: Bill Elliott, Tex Ritter, Eileen O'Hearn, Frank Mitchell, Noah Berry, Sr., Ruth Ford, Joel Friedkin, Joe McGuinn, Edmund Cobb, Tristram Coffin, Paul Newlan.

*   *   *

Prairie Gunsmoke (Columbia, 1942) 56 M.

Producer, Leon Barsha; director, Lambert Hillyer; screenplay, Jack Ganzhorn.

CAST: Bill Elliott, Tex Ritter, Virginia Carroll, Frank Mitchell, Tristram Coffin, Ted Mapes, Glenn Strange.

*   *   *

Vengeance of the West (Columbia, 1942) 60 M.

Producer, Leon Barsha; director, Lambert Hillyer; screenplay, Jack Townley.

CAST: Bill Elliott, Tex Ritter, Frank Mitchell, Adele Mara, Dick Curtis, Robert Fiske, Ted Mapes, Eva Puig, Jose Tortosa, Guy Wilkerson.

*   *   *

Deep In the Heart of Texas (Universal, 1942) 62 M.

Producer, Oliver Drake; director, Elmer Clifton; screenplay, Oliver Drake; camera, Harry Newmann; musical director, H. J. Salter; songs, Johnny Bond, Don Swander, June Hershey.

CAST: Johnny Mack Brown, Tex Ritter, Fuzzy Knight, Jennifer Holt, William Farnum, Harry Woods, Kenneth Harlan, Pat O'Malley, Roy Brent, Edmund Cobb, Jimmy Wakely Trio.

*   *   *

Little Joe, The Wrangler (Universal, 1942) 61 M.

Producer, Oliver Drake; director, Lewis D. Collins; screenplay, Sherman Lowe; camera, William Sickner.

CAST: Johnny Mack Brown, Tex Ritter, Fuzzy Knight, Jennifer Holt, Florine McKinney, James Craven, Hal Taliaferro, Glenn Strange, Jimmy Wakely Trio.

*   *   *

The Old Chisholm Trail (Universal, 1942) 59 M.

Producer, Oliver Drake; director, Elmer Clifton; screenplay, Elmer Clifton from a story by Harry Fraser; camera, William Sickner; musical director, H. J. Salter.

CAST: Johnny Mack Brown, Tex Ritter, Fuzzy Knight, Jennifer Holt, Mady Correll, Earl Hodgins, Roy Barcroft, Edmund Cobb, Budd Buster, Michael Vallon, Jimmy Wakely Trio.

*   *   *

Tenting Tonight on the Old Campground (Universal, 1943) 59 M.

Producer, Oliver Drake; director, Lewis D. Collins; screenplay, Elizabeth Beecher from an original story by Harry Fraser; camera, William Sickner; editor, Charles Maynard.

CAST: Johnny Mack Brown, Tex Ritter, Fuzzy Knight, Jennifer Holt, John Elliott, Earle Hodgins, Rex Lease, Lane Chandler, Allen Bridge, Dennis Moore, Tom London, Jimmy Wakely Trio.

*   *   *

Cheyenne Roundup (Universal, 1943) 59 M.

Producer, Oliver Drake; director, Elmer Clifton; screenplay, Elmer Clifton and Bernard McConville; camera, William Sickner; editor, Otto Ludwig.

CAST: Johnny Mack Brown, Tex Ritter, Fuzzy

Johnny Mack Brown and Tex examine a wounded man in this scene from *Tenting Tonight on the Old Campground.*

Johnny Mack Brown and Tex Ritter in a scene from *Cheyenne Roundup.*

Knight, Jennifer Holt, Harry Woods, Roy Barcroft, Robert Barron, Budd Buster, Gil Patric, Jimmy Wakely Trio.

*　　*　　*

Raiders of the San Joaquin (Universal, 1943) 60 M.

Producer, Oliver Drake; director, Lewis D. Collins; screenplay, Patricia Harper; camera, William Sickner; editor, Russel Shoengarth.

CAST: Johnny Mack Brown, Tex Ritter, Fuzzy Knight, Jennifer Holt, Henry Hall, Joseph Bernard, George Eldredge, Henry Roquemore, John Eliott, Michael Vallon, Jack O'Shea, Jack Ingram, Robert Thompson, Carl Sepulveda, Roy Brent, Budd Buster, Jimmy Wakely Trio.

*　　*　　*

The Lone Star Trail (Universal, 1943) 56 M.

Producer, Oliver Drake; director, Ray Taylor; screenplay, Oliver Drake from an original story by Victor Halperin; camera, William Sickner; editor, Ray Snyder.

CAST: Johnny Mack Brown, Tex Ritter, Fuzzy Knight, Jennifer Holt, George Eldredge, Michael Vallon, Harry Strang, Earle Hodgins, Jack Ingram, Jimmy Wakely Trio.

*　　*　　*

Arizona Trail (Universal, 1943) 57 M.

Producer, Oliver Drake; director, Vernon Keays; screenplay, William Lively; camera, William Sickner; editor, Alvin Todd.

CAST: Tex Ritter, Fuzzy Knight, Dennis Moore, Janet Shaw, Jack Ingram, Erville Alderson, Joseph Greene, Glenn Strange, Dan White, Art Fowler, Johnny Bond and His Red River Valley Boys.

*　　*　　*

Marshall of Gunsmoke (Universal, 1943) 58 M.

Producer, Oliver Drake; director, Vernon Keays; screenplay, William Lively.

CAST: Tex Ritter, Russell Hayden, Jennifer Holt, Fuzzy Knight, Herbert Rawlinson, Harry Woods, Slim Whitaker, Johnny Bond and The Red River Valley Boys.

*　　*　　*

Oklahoma Raiders (Universal, 1943) 56 M.

Producer, Oliver Drake; director, Lewis D. Collins; screenplay, Betty Burbridge.

CAST: Tex Ritter, Jennifer Holt, Fuzzy Knight; Dennis Moore, I. Stanford Jolley, Johnny Bond and The Red River Valley Boys.

*　　*　　*

Gangsters of the Frontier (PRC, 1944) 56 M.

Producer, Arthur Alexander; director, Elmer Clifton; screenplay, Elmer Clifton.

CAST: Tex Ritter, Dave O'Brien, Guy Wilkerson, Patti McCarty, Harry Harvey, Betty Miles, I. Stanford Jolley, Marshall Reed, Charles King, Clark Stevens.

*　　*　　*

Dead or Alive (PRC, 1944) 56 M.

Producer, Arthur Alexander; director, Elmer Clifton; screenplay, Harry Fraser.

CAST: Tex Ritter, Dave O'Brien, Guy Wilkerson, Marjory Clements, Rebel Randall, Ray Bennett, Charles King, Henry Hall, Ted Mapes.

* * *

Whispering Skull (PRC, 1944) 56 M.

Producer, Arthur Alexander; director, Elmer Clifton; screenplay, Harry Fraser.

CAST: Tex Ritter, Dave O'Brien, Guy Wilkerson, Denny Burke, I. Stanford Jolley; Henry Hall, George Morrell, Edward Cassidy, Robert Kortman, Wen Wright.

* * *

Marked For Murder (PRC, 1945) 56 M.

Producer, Arthur Alexander; director, Elmer Clifton; screenplay, Elmer Clifton.

CAST: Tex Ritter, Dave O'Brien, Guy Wilkerson, Marilyn McConnell, Ed Cassidy, Henry Hall, Charles King, Jack Ingram, Bob Kortman, Wen Wright, Milo Twins.

* * *

Enemy of the Law (PRC, 1945) 59 M.

Producer, Arthur Alexander; director, Harry Fraser; screenplay, Harry Fraser.

CAST: Tex Ritter, Dave O'Brien, Guy Wilkerson, Kay Hughes, Jack Ingram, Charles King, Frank Ellis, Kermit Maynard, Henry Hall.

* * *

Three in the Saddle (PRC, 1945) 61 M.

Producer, Arthur Alexander; director, Harry Fraser; screenplay, Elmer Clifton.

CAST: Tex Ritter, Dave O'Brien, Guy Wilkerson, Lorraine Miller, Charles King, Edward Howard, Edward Cassidy, Bud Osborne, Frank Ellis.

* * *

Frontier Fugitives (PRC, 1945) 58 M.

Producer, Arthur Alexander; director, Harry Fraser; screenplay, Elmer Clifton.

CAST: Tex Ritter, Dave O'Brien, Guy Wilkerson,

Tex and Dave O'Brien (white hat) take charge in this scene from *Three in the Saddle*.

Lorraine Miller, I. Stanford Jolley, Jack Ingram, Frank Ellis, Jack Henricks, Charles King.

* * *

Flaming Bullets (PRC, 1945) 59 M.

Producer, Arthur Alexander; director, Harry Fraser; screenplay, Harry Fraser.

CAST: Tex Ritter, Dave O'Brien, Guy Wilkerson, Charles King, Patricia Knox, I. Stanford Jolley, Bob Duncan, Bud Osborne, Kermit Maynard.

* * *

TEX RITTER DISCOGRAPHY

In late 1932 or early 1933 Tex Ritter cut his first recordings for Vocalian Records, a subsidiary of Decca. The songs in the first session included "Rye Whiskey," "Nobody's Darling But Mine," and "Makes No Difference Now." When Capitol Records came into existence around 1940, Tex was one of their first recording artists and stayed on the Capitol label throughout the rest of his career. In the following discography the Buckboard Records LP is a re-release of Capitol recordings and the Shasta and Republic Records are taken from radio program tapes.

American Legend Capitol Records (a three-record album)

Selections:

Jingle, Jangle, Jingle

Jealous Heart
I've Done the Best I Could
There's a New Moon Over My Shoulder
I'm Wastin' My Tears on You
High Noon
Deck of Cards
Pledge of Allegiance
Just Beyond the Moon
Green Grow the Lilacs
I Dreamed of a Hillbilly Heaven
I'm Gonna Leave You the Way I Found You
Love Me Now
You Will Have To Pay
You Two-Timed Me One Time Too Often
Big Rock Candy Mountain
Let Me Go, Devil
Teneha, Timpson, Bobo, and Blair
Bats in Your Belfry
I Can't Get My Foot Off the Rail
When You Leave, Don't Slam the Door
Boll Weevil
From Now On
Blood on the Saddle
Froggy Went A-Courtin'
Rounded Up in Glory
Americans

*   *   *

The Best of Tex Ritter Capitol Records
Selections:

High Noon
We Live in Two Different Worlds
Boll Weevil
Rye Whiskey
Jealous Heart
Deck of Cards
I Dreamed of a Hillbilly Heaven
Green Grow the Lilacs
There's a New Moon Over My Shoulder
Bad Brahma Bull

*   *   *

Comin' After Jinny Capitol Records
Selections:

Comin' After Jinny
Lookin' Back
He Who Is Without Sin
    (Let Him Judge Me)
Wandrin' Star
The Girl Who Carries a Torch for Me
One Night for Willie

Sweet Bird of Youth
Growin' Up
Willie, The Wandering Gypsy and Me
My God, Bless America Again

*   *   *

The First Great Hits of Tex Ritter Shasta Records
Selections:

High Noon
Boll Weevil
Ceilito Lindo
I Dreamed of a Hillbilly Heaven
Froggy Went A-Courtin'
The Fool's Paradise
The Gallows Pole
Green Grow the Lilacs
The Keeper of the Keys
Conversation with a Gun
Have I Stayed Away Too Long

*   *   *

Hillbilly Heaven Capitol Records
Selections:

I Dreamed of a Hillbilly Heaven
Green Grow the Lilacs
Love Me Now
High Noon
The Deck of Cards
Jealous Heart
Have I Stayed Away Too Long
Ol' Shorty
We Live in Two Diff'rent Worlds
There's a New Moon Over My Shoulder
Jingle, Jangle, Jingle
The Pledge of Allegiance

*   *   *

Tex Ritter Buckboard Records
Selections:

Bad Brahma Bull
Home on the Range
Boll Weevil
Thank You
The Deck of Cards
The Old Chisholm Trail
Froggy Went A-Courtin'
The Green Grass All Around

*   *   *

All Star Country Christmas Capitol Records
Selections:

Here Was a Man
Ole Tex Kringle

and additional Christmas selections by other Capitol artists.

*   *   *

Country Hits Of The '40s Capitol Records
Selections:

There's a New Moon Over My Shoulder

and additional selections by other Capitol artists.

*   *   *

Country Hits of the '60s Capitol Records
Selections:

I Dreamed of a Hillbilly Heaven

and additional selections by other Capitol artists.

*   *   *

The Great American Singing Cowboys Republic Records
Selections:

High Noon
Conversation with a Gun

and ten additional selections by other singing cowboys.

*   *   *

Single records available:

Blood on the Saddle, Capitol Records
High Noon, Capitol Records

Deck of Cards, Capitol Records
Rye Whiskey, Capitol Records

I Dreamed of a Hillbilly Heaven,
Capitol Records
Just Beyond the Moon, Capitol Records

4. The Unsung Singing Cowboys

This chapter is "for the record" and devoted to the lesser-known singing cowboys who did not "make it" with the moviegoing public for one reason or another or who, as in the case of Dick Foran, left the musical Western field for other show business pastures.

Gene Autry, the first of the singing cowboys, was generally the model that producers eyed when searching for challengers to his leadership in the genre. But for some unfathomable reason an inordinate number of B Western film producers during the late thirties seemed to hold the belief that mellow-voiced opera singers could be recycled into singing cowboys—that the trail from grand opera to horse opera was a short one and a natural show business progression. This thinking produced such opera-trained singing cowpokes as Fred Scott, George Houston, and James Newill. Dick Foran, Jack Randall, and John "Dusty" King, while perhaps not candidates for grand opera, certainly were influenced by the Nelson Eddy style of vocalizing. And perhaps the success of such Eddy features as *Rose Marie* and *Girl of the Golden West* led to the producers' belief that some of Nelson Eddy's then current popularity would rub off onto the aspiring singing cowboys as they toiled in their shoestring productions, and that the popularity of thin-voiced, yodeling cowboys like Gene Autry would not long endure. Such was not to be the case, of course. Whatever the original reasoning, the mistake was soon recognized and the opera fellows were shipped back East on the next available stage—not, however, before close to a hundred not-very-popular musical Westerns of greatly varying quality were produced starring these cactus Carusos.

Warner Brothers led the way with sound pictures in 1927 with *The Jazz Singer* and they came awfully close to being the first out of the gate in the singing cowboy horse-opera race. Gene Autry's *Tumbling Tumbleweeds* was released in September of 1935, only two months before singing cowboy Dick Foran took to the celluloid range for Warners in *Moonlight on the Prairie*. Through the years Warner Brothers produced only this one singing cowboy series and it lasted a relatively brief

Dick Foran.

103

Dick Foran was the only singing cowboy star that Warner Brothers ever had.

time—from late 1935 through 1937—for a total of twelve features.

Foran, who would later go on to greater success in non-Western roles, came across to audiences as a lovable, sentimental lug of a guy, and for a time enjoyed a fair degree of popularity as a singing cowboy—especially among youngsters who perhaps saw him as a likable older brother. Foran handled himself well in the acting and action departments, and possessed a big, pleasant singing voice that audiences found appealing. Unlike some of his opera-trained counterparts, he did not appear uncomfortable warbling Western ditties on horseback or to a pretty rancher's daughter. Eventually, though, some of Foran's screen sentiment turned to sentimentality and occasionally his by-play with screen moppets became cloying. Generally, however the Dick Foran series was well-produced utilizing the excellent facilities of the Brothers Warner and great stock action footage from some of the old Ken Maynard silent Westerns to spruce up the excitement.

The twelve Dick Foran features were the following: *Moonlight on the Prairie* (1935), *Treachery Rides the Range* (1936), *Song of the Saddle* (1936), *Trailin' West* (1936), *California Mail* (1937), *Guns of the Pecos* (1937), *Cherokee Strip*

Fred Scott.

(1937), *Blazing Sixes* (1937), *Land Beyond the Law* (1937), *Empty Holsters* (1937), *Devil's Saddle Legion* (1937), *Prairie Thunder* (1937).

Fred Scott was the first of the opera trained performers to find his way into series Westerns. Coming from a stint in the San Francisco Opera Company's production of *Salome* to a poverty row film production entitled *Romance Rides the Range* (1936), Scott tried hard to make the transition, but even the comic support of Al St. John (who created his "Fuzzy" character during the Scott series) and Stan Laurel (of all people) as producer for some of his films could not conceal the slapped-together production look of the films. By 1940, after close to two dozen pictures, the Western film trail petered out for Fred Scott, and he eventually mosied successfully into California real estate.

The Fred Scott Western series was produced by an independent company called Spectrum Pictures and included such features as *Singing Buckaroo* (1937), *Melody of the Plains* (1937), *Roaming Cowboy* (1937), *Ranger's Roundup* (1938, produced by Stan Laurel), and *Two Gun Troubadour* (1939).

Certainly one of the most obscure singing cowboys is Smith Ballew, who was the only B

In later non-Western films Foran was often referred to as "the good guy who doesn't get the girl."

105

Smith Ballew.

Western star ever for Twentieth Century-Fox Pictures—and then only for five pictures. During the early thirties Ballew was a fairly popular recording artist, orchestra leader, and singer. He bore the questionable honor of being the singing voice for John Wayne in a few better-off-forgotten "Singing Sandy" Wayne Westerns made for Lonestar Productions in the early thirties. After playing a cowboy role in Paramount's *Palm Springs* (1936), Ballew was selected by producer Sol Lesser for a musical Western series about to roll at Twentieth Century-Fox.

Although Ballew possessed Gary Cooper-like good looks and a pleasant singing voice, his initial film productions in the series were lacklustre and did not catch on with the ticket buyers. (One critic commented that, "The musical numbers are dragged in and prolonged beyond reason.") Even though the final three productions did show considerable improvement, the vote was in and Smith Ballew was out as a singing cowboy. Ballew did, however, continue in supporting roles for many years.

Of special note among Ballew's starring vehicles is *Rawhide*, which co-starred baseball great Lou Gehrig, who played himself. Gehrig, acquitting himself surprisingly well, fought baddies in a pool parlor by pitching billiard balls at them and stopped a contract signing by smashing a baseball through a window. There are those who speculated that Gehrig could have had a successful career in films had he not died two years later.

The five starring Smith Ballew musical Westerns were *Western Gold* (1937), *Roll Along, Cowboy* (1938), *Hawaiian Buckaroo* (1938), *Rawhide* (1938), and *Panamint's Bad Man* (1938).

Addison (Jack) Randall also had one of the briefer stints as a B Western singing cowboy—starting in August of 1937 and concluding in April of 1938, after only five musical Westerns. Prior to his nine-month sojourn as a singing troubadour for Monogram Pictures, Randall had performed without the cowboy gear on Broadway in musical and dramatic productions and at RKO in such pictures as *His Family Tree, Love on a Bet,* and *Follow the Fleet* (with Fred Astaire and Ginger Rogers).

Although he was not destined to have the success as a cowboy star that his brother Bob Livingston achieved, Jack Randall did continue as a star of lesser Western efforts (minus the music and singing) for a number of years. As a singing cowboy for Monogram, Randall is perhaps more to be pitied than censured—to coin a phrase. His unfortunate experiences as a singing cowboy can be traced directly to directorial sloppiness and also to the inept production values of Monogram

Jack Randall.

Pictures. Randall was frequently called upon to lip-sync his prerecorded songs in medium close-up while jouncing along on a trotting horse. His prerecorded, pleasant baritone voice conveyed none of the strain of trying to sing while riding a frisky horse, thus revealing singing cowboy Randall as faking to all but the most dense members of the audience. Also, given the circumstances of the moment, the lip-syncing was none too accurate, leading one trade critic to speculate that Randall was mouthing the vocal abilities of some off-screen singing cowboy. Randall happily left his singing cowboy days behind and continued with limited success as a straight B Western action star.

By the early forties, however, he was reduced to supporting roles. While playing a down-in-the-cast villain role in *The Royal Mounted Rides Again* (1945) serial released by Universal, Jack Randall died of a heart attack during the filming of some horseback riding scenes. He was only thirty-nine years old.

The five Monogram musical Westerns that starred Jack Randall were *Riders of the Dawn* (1937), *Danger Valley* (1938), *Stars Over Arizona* (1938), *Where the West Begins* (1938), and *Land of Fighting Men* (1938).

Tex Fletcher, a New York radio singer who played guitar left-handed, made his one and only cactus opus and found his studio, Grand National, folding around him just as the picture was going into release. With pluck and grit Fletcher carried on as best he could under the circumstances. As *Variety* reported in January of 1940 in a column captioned "Self-Booked Cowboy Star":

> Tex Fletcher no doubt holds the distinction of being the only horse opry star who has literally taken the bull by the horns. His one and only film was delivered to Grand National last spring just as the company was running into serious financial shoals and laying off most of its salesmen. As a result, the picture, "Six Gun Rhythm," got few playdates.
>
> Fletcher, for six years WOR's "Lonesome Cowboy," wasn't stopped by that, however.

Tex Fletcher in a scene from his only feature, *Six Gun Rhythm.*

He's not only now personally getting dates for the film in New England, but also booking himself in to do a p.a. with it. He's got almost 25 dates coming up in as many days.

John "Dusty" King, former radio and band singer (Ben Bernie's) became a member of the Range Busters trio Western series with Ray "Crash" Corrigan and Max Terhune in 1940 for Monogram. A bland screen personality and vocal capabilities more suitable for band singing hindered King's development as a film personality, but he managed to last through three years of the Range Busters series. His films included *Trailing Double Trouble* (1940), *Tumbledown Ranch in Arizona* (1941), *Fugitive Valley* (1941), *Saddle Mountain Roundup* (1941), *Underground Rustlers* (1941), *Thunder River Feud* (1942), *Texas Trouble Shooters* (1942), *Arizona Stagecoach* (1942), and *Texas to Bataan* (1942).

George Houston, a former opera singer, somehow found his way into series Westerns in 1941 with PRC. Houston was teamed with Al St. John for eleven Lone Rider films in which he was often allowed to break into song in his rather stiff, operatic manner. Without the popular comic backup of St. John, it's doubtful if the series would have lasted as long as it did. Houston's bemused demeanor on the screen seemed to suggest that he was somewhat dismayed by where fate had led him. When the Lone Rider series bit the dust in 1942, George Houston retired from the screen. Within two years he had died of a heart attack.

Prior to the Lone Rider series, Houston played Wild Bill Hickok in *Frontier Scout* (1938) for Grand National. His Lone Rider films included *The Lone Rider Rides On* (1941), *The Lone Rider Fights Back* (1941), and *Outlaws of Boulder Pass* (1942).

James Newill was another former opera singer who toiled on the musical Western range after a three-year term in the late thirties up in the wild north country as Renfrew of the Royal Mounted for Grand National Pictures and later Monogram. In 1942 Newill became a member of the Texas Rangers trio series (with Dave O'Brien and Guy Wilkerson) for PRC and stayed on for a couple of years (fourteen bottom-of-the-barrel almost budgetless features) until his singing contribution was cut back by the producers. (Tex Ritter had the misfortune of taking over for Newill when he left the series.) Newill's Texas Rangers series included such episodes as *The Rangers Take Over* (1942), *West of Texas* (1943), *Trail of Terror* (1943), *Gunsmoke Mesa* (1944), and *Pinto Bandit* (1944).

John "Dusty" King.

Much like Fred Scott, George Houston, and Dusty King, Newill never seemed comfortable warbling a Western tune. There was a stiffness or stolidness about his and their demeanors that suggested to audiences that these gentlemen were pretenders and did not really belong in those cowboy outfits or on the cow ponies—and within a couple of years they weren't.

Bob Baker, nee Stanley Leland "Tumble" Weed, grew up living the life that every singing cowboy should have had to experience as a prerequisite for musical Western stardom: an Arizona cowboy in his mid teens; later a rodeo wrangler; then on to Chicago and singing appearances on the WLS "National Barn Dance" radio program; and, finally, a successful Hollywood screen test and a contract with Universal for a series of musical Westerns—a storybook example of success in show business.

Everything seemed to click for Bob Baker until he got into his film series. Technically the films were quite good with fine camera work and above-average use of stock action footage when the skimpy budgets forbade new action shots. The problem lay with the implausible scripts and with Baker himself through the handling he received from his directors. Baker, a handsome and pleasant

George Houston.

enough performer, was occasionally allowed to look foolish while delivering lines or while involved in plot situations. Often what his character was required to do was not consistent with what a rational person would do or say in the same situation. For example, in *Phantom Stagecoach* (1939) when camping at night out in the wilderness, Baker and his sidekick suddenly hear a sneeze in the blackness that surrounds them. Instead of grabbing their guns and investigating the possible danger (as fearless film cowboys were supposed to do) they say, "Let's get out of here." Then seemingly without a concern for a possible ambush or danger to their persons, they take time to pack their things and leave without even investigating the nearby sneeze in the prairie night. We, the audience, are left to speculate on the reason for the sneeze—and who sneezed, for that matter!

Baker was able to handle the singing chores

James Newill.

Bob Baker serenades inmate LeRoy Mason in this scene from an early Baker feature.

quite well, but he needed help from a director on his acting. Unfortunately. he didn't get it, or perhaps he did, but it just didn't help. For example, every once in a while in his early films Baker would have reason to react to a comic situation by laughing. Inexplicably, he would often be allowed to become almost hysterical during these occurrences giving forth with a high-pitched, giddy laugh far out of proportion to the situation—a common pitfall for untrained young actors feeling their way along in a new field. With proper handling and careful direction Baker could have been guided through these early films (the way Autry and, later, Roy Rogers were) so that the cowboy hero image he needed would reach the audience.

As it was, Baker did not get the proper singing cowboy grooming and thus did not catch on with the public. In a little over a year he lost his own starring series and was relegated to second lead status in Johnny Mack Brown's series for Universal. Theirs was an uneasy relationship on the screen and within a year and a half Baker had slipped even farther in popularity and soon left films for good.

At the beginning of his career it had appeared that Bob Baker had it all going for him: looks, a cowboy background, a good singing voice, and a natural, pleasing manner. But the breaks did not come his way and he didn't have someone to guide and protect his career development, something he apparently didn't have the experience or ability to do for himself.

The Bob Baker series included such features as *Courage of the West* (1937), *The Last Stand* (1938), *Honor of the West* (1939), *Desperate Trails* (1939, his first with Johnny Mack Brown), and *Bad Man From Red Butte* (1940, Baker's last series leading role).

5 Roy Rogers

"THE KING OF THE COWBOYS"

During those Saturday afternoons of movie watching in the 1940s I would first see the Western that was up for the weekend—let's say a Johnny Mack Brown—then there would be a detective or mystery film such as *Boston Blackie and the Law* with Chester Morris or *Charlie Chan in Black Magic* with Sidney Toler; that would be followed by the serial, my favorite being *The Sea Hound* with Buster Crabbe; and finally, rounding out the bill would be the previews of coming attractions. The previews (we never called them "trailers" as they did in the trade) were designed, of course, to convince me that the films coming next week were going to be even more super-colossal than the ones I had seen that day.

For some reason I particularly remember the previews for the Roy Rogers musical Western films. It wasn't that they varied so much from previews of other musical Westerns. There were excerpts from the shoot-outs and fistfights, and some Roy Rogers-Roy Barcroft (Roy's frequent and "best" villain) dialogue thrown in to let me know if it was to be the cattlemen versus the sheepmen conflict or the rustled-cattle-in-the-cave-under-the-waterfall plot.

Roy, Dale, and The Sons of the Pioneers would provide a few sample bars from the sagebrush songs included in the episode, and Gabby Hayes would have a few seconds to get in a "Yer durned tootin'!" just so I could know that he would be there, too.

All of these musical, comical, and edge-of-the-seat adventurous teasers were the stock stuff of any musical Western, as were the overlay word blurbs that would flash on the screen to punch up the anticipation for the thrills and excitement that were in store for next week:

> The hard-hitting, straight-shooting hero of the West in an all new chilling, thrilling adventure.

or

> Roy fights his most daring battles and sings his most lilting Western ballads while bringing peace to the warring factions of the West.

All of this was stock, but most effective, hype; but what I remember most vividly was the Roy Rogers preview finish. It was generally a shot of Trigger galloping at full clip with Roy astride, gun drawn and firing, looking ahead grim-faced while dodging and weaving to avoid the bullets of the unseen villain up there just out of camera view.

The camera angle for this shot was always down low, slightly in front and to the right of the charging Trigger. With this breath-stopping shot ongoing, the words,

> Don't miss a thrilling moment!

would flash across the screen. About three seconds more of galloping and shooting would ensue on the unworded screen, then,

> With Roy Rogers, the King of the Cowboys, and Trigger, the Smartest Horse in the Movies.

Roy Rogers. *Photo courtesy of Roy Rogers.*

I would usually be there the next Saturday.

* * *

I could never have imagined in those pistol-packing childhood days that some thirty years later I would be venturing from my home in Sarasota, Florida, to the high desert country of Victorville, California, to interview the still very active Roy Rogers. It had taken some doing and over a year to catch Roy between appearances on television (he had just finished a "Wonder Woman" episode when I talked with him), openings for his Roy Rogers Family Restaurants, and the exhausting task of moving the Roy Rogers and Dale Evans Museum from Apple Valley to its brand new home in nearby Victorville—a task that he and Dale had personally supervised to the tiniest detail.

During the months I was waiting for Roy to find some time to see me, I researched and prepared a draft profile of his life and career and sent it to him to look over. Finally my perseverance and patience paid off—he invited me to meet with him at the museum. During my day-and-a-half visit, Roy not only talked to me about the times of his life, he showed them to me in a two-hour personally escorted tour of the museum. After that we looked at the draft profile and, finally, just shot the breeze about anything in his career that hadn't yet come up.

What follows is the completed profile of Roy's life and career with frequent insertions by Roy—thoughts and comments he expressed at one time or another during my visit. Occasionally he would find errors in the draft copy—most coming from ancient Republic publicity, which, according to Roy, sometimes bore little resemblance to events in the real world. When these surrogates of the

An early publicity photo of Roy Rogers, prior to his acquiring the title "King of the Cowboys."

truth were discovered, Roy would set the record straight for me as he remembered it.

*   *   *

I didn't know in 1946, sitting in the Lincoln Theatre in Elyria, Ohio, watching Roy up there on the screen, that twenty-five years earlier he had been a youngster in my very own state of Ohio, and had been a farm boy the same as I. He wasn't known as Roy Rogers then, at age ten in 1921; his name was Leonard Franklin Slye and he was living on his parents' small farm in Duck Run, a little country place in southern Ohio.

While I in the mid-1940s could not build up much interest in my father's forty-eight acres of farmland, ten-year-old Leonard in 1921 was a member of the 4-H Club, and two years later would win a blue ribbon with his pig, Martha Washington, at the Scioto County Fair, and an all-expense-paid week at the state capital of Columbus.

(ROY ROGERS: That was the first time I had ever been ten miles off the farm. I had never even seen an elevator before. I spent the whole first day just riding up and down the elevator in the old Neil House Hotel, which is still there.)

Farm life in southern Ohio during the 1920s generally did not offer much in the way of thrills and excitement, but Leonard did enjoy riding bareback on their old farm horse named Babe and occasionally he would ride the horse to prayer meetings or to square dances, which he dearly

Roy Rogers stalking the villain (circa early 1940s).

loved. Always a shy boy, he gradually discovered that he possessed a knack for square dance calling and soon worked up enough courage to start calling a few of the dances when the regular callers didn't show up.

In a short time the square dancers of Duck Run considered Leonard one of the best callers they had, and, in addition, they were surprised to discover that he also had a good singing voice and could do "right well" with the country ballads they loved to waltz to after an exhausting set of allemande lefts and do-si-dos. He would accompany himself on his mother and dad's guitar.

When Leonard was seventeen the family gave up the farm and he was forced to go to work alongside his father at the U. S. Shoe Company in Cincinnati, the same work his father had performed years before when Leonard was born.

But fortunately events were taking place that would alter the seemingly dismal future for the boy. In the late 1920s Leonard's older sister Mary wed a young man and left with him to live in far-off California. The family missed their newly wed daughter and often wondered aloud about her new life in the West—the land of mountains and oranges that they could hardly imagine. Many times they talked of visiting Mary, but because there was little money for such a lengthy journey, it seemed that it would only amount to that—talk.

One bleak day in the summer of 1930, when neither Leonard nor his father felt he could endure another day in the shoe factory, Leonard told his father that he had squirreled away almost a hundred dollars. "What do you say, Pop?" he asked. "You must have around a hundred, too. What do you say we all jump in the jalopy and go visit Mary in California?" And so they did.

Abundant with the provincialism of many untraveled Americans at that time, the Slye family really had little idea just how far away Lawndale, California (where Mary lived) was. After almost two weeks of maneuvering the flatlands, mountains, and desert, along with suffering the vagaries of a 1923 Dodge that had no desire to traverse the heartland of the nation, a rather rag tag *Grapes of Wrath*-ish appearing Slye family arrived at their destination.

Leonard and his father immediately sought work and were fortunate in finding employment driving dump trucks. The work was terribly exhausting because the sand and gravel they hauled and dumped first had to be shoveled onto the trucks— by them. Despite the hard labor, Leonard loved California—the year-round warm climate, sunny skies, and mountains were terribly enticing when compared with the frigid, slate-skied flatlands of Ohio—and he hated leaving when the family was ready to make the long journey back to Ohio.

A few months later when Mary's father-in-law drove out to California, Leonard was right there to help out with the driving—a small price for the chance to return to the West Coast that he prophetically saw as a land of milk and honey. He never returned to Ohio to live; from that time forward his home would always be in California.

Like most of the United States, California was a little short on milk and honey during those early days of the depression, and Leonard found himself picking peaches with Okies and again truck driving to keep a few coins in his frayed britches.

The only relief from the long days of drudgery was found strumming his twenty-dollar guitar and singing the hillbilly ballads he had grown up with. After much prodding from his sister Mary, one night he finally got up enough nerve to go to the nearby town of Inglewood to perform on a radio amateur show called "Midnight Frolic." Two days after the admittedly unspectacular performance, a group of country musicians called The Rocky Mountaineers phoned and invited Leonard to join them as vocalist on their weekly radio program heard over a Long Beach station. Leonard jumped at the opportunity even though there was no money in the offer. The group's only "pay" was the opportunity to plug their availability for other appearances where, if they were fortunate, they might receive a small stipend.

Shortly thereafter the group added another voice to the group by advertising "Singer Wanted" in the local paper. A young fellow by the name of Bob Nolan responded to the ad and was immediately "hired." Before very long, however, Nolan, a former Santa Monica lifeguard, found that The Rocky Mountaineers couldn't keep him in eating money, so he quit to become a caddy for the Bel-Air Country Club—a position looked upon by the hungry Nolan as "steady work" during the height of the depression.

Another ad, this time in *Variety,* brought a young lad by the name of Tim Spencer into Leonard's life. Spencer, in addition to sporting a fine voice, also turned out to be an accomplished song writer and would through their many years of association write many of Roy Rogers's finest movie songs. But there was little hint at that time of the gold mine that lay just a few years ahead.

Shortly after Tim Spencer joined The Rocky Mountaineers, the group disbanded and Leonard, eager to see that his toe-hold in show business was not lost, convinced Spencer to stay with him and

was able to get some other out-of-work country musicians to join them in a group they rather capriciously called The International Cowboys. It was the same old stand though—gratis performing on radio in hopes of having their personal appearance sought for pay, and occasionally they did get a paying job.

(ROY ROGERS: During June of 1933 we were playing the Warner Brothers Theatre in downtown Los Angeles as The International Cowboys. They introduced us just as the big earthquake hit—the one that hit Los Angeles and shook Long Beach to the ground. You know the old saying, "The show must go on." Well, we went on. We looked out in the audience and there was only one guy sitting in the middle of the theater. The big chandelier, which was probably fifteen or twenty feet across in the big dome of the theater, was swinging back and forth like a bell clapper. We went ahead and sang "See them tumbling down" from "Tumbling Tumbleweeds," which I thought was very apropos at the time. We did our whole act and every few seconds the after-shocks would come. Every time one of those after-shocks would hit, we'd miss a beat or two of the song.)

Much to their surprise an agent contacted them about a barnstorming tour through the Southwest. It all sounded rather glamorous and exciting to the naive International Cowboys, so they agreed. Besides, prospects were not so tremendous where they were, and the "greener pastures" syndrome served as a lure, too. Later Roy was to describe the tour as "destined for the doubtful honor of being the most unsuccessful of its kind in history."

(ROY ROGERS: We wanted to start off with a new name, so we picked a famous old brand, the O-Bar-O, and called ourselves The O-Bar-O Cowboys. Our first booking was Yuma, Arizona. We went from there to Miami, Safford, and Willcox, Arizona. We also played Lubbock, Texas, and Roswell, New Mexico. Miami, Arizona, turned out to be a ghost town at that time because all of the copper mines were shut down, so we never made anything there. We made four dollars apiece in Safford. We had six blow-outs between Willcox, Arizona, and Roswell, New Mexico. When we got to Roswell, we didn't have nickle.

We got on this little radio station in Roswell and started advertising our personal appearance. We didn't have any money for food so we'd kid one another over the air about what we liked to eat. We picked out a variety of food so that maybe we'd get different things from the listeners. I was supposed to like lemon meringue pies, one other said he liked chicken, and another liked biscuits and gravy. We'd already asked the station manager if we could borrow his rifle because we liked to go hunting; that's what we told him, anyway. We'd go out in the evening and shoot a couple of cottontails and fry them in the little motel where we were staying. I think when we left Roswell the population of cottontails was thinned down quite a bit. That's what we lived on until we got the people who were listening on the radio to bring food to us.)

The only event of lasting significance during the Southwest tour occurred in Roswell. Leonard's radio comment about missing the deliciousness of his mother's homemade lemon pie resulted in a phoned promise of just such a pie if he would do "The Swiss Yodel" on the next day's program. Leonard diligently practiced his yodeling and accommodated the request. The following day a Mrs. Wilkins and her lovely daughter, Arlene, delivered two homemade lemon pies to the radio station. As famished as he was, Leonard's attention was drawn to the yodel-loving daughter of Mrs. Wilkins. By the time the O-Bar-O Cowboys left Roswell, Leonard was completely smitten, as was Arlene.

After the tour the O-Bar-O Cowboys broke up. Leonard went back to Los Angeles and joined a radio group called Jack and His Texas Outlaws, who were performing on KFWB. But he felt he could do better with other performers—people who better understood the kind of music he loved.

(ROY ROGERS: So I went out to see Tim Spencer. I said, "Tim, let's see if we can get Bob [Nolan] and get our trio back together again." Bob was caddying at the Bel Air Country Club at the time. We told him what we had in mind and he went for it. So the three of us got a room in a Hollywood boarding house near the studio so we could walk to the station and save money. We holed up there and started learning songs.)

They called themselves The Pioneer Trio. Long days and nights of practicing followed as their harmonizing style slowly took shape and a different Western music sound emerged—a rich, mellow vocal blend that bespoke the lonely life of the cowboy out on the prairie, especially when they harmonized on "The Last Round-up," "Tumbling Tumbleweeds," and other songs of that genre. Singing for nothing on an early morning KFWB program proved to be their making when Los Angeles columnist Bernie Milligan heard them, was impressed, and listed them in his *Los Angeles Herald Examiner* column as the "Best Bets of the Day."

KFWB, figuring it had a good thing going, put them on the staff of the station, and gave them plenty of exposure. Within a few months the trio added Hugh and Carl Farr to its number, had a sponsor, and were doing a morning program as The Gold Star Rangers and a late afternoon program as The Sons of the Pioneers.

(ROY ROGERS: We were making thirty-five dollars a week then and were tickled to death because up to then we hadn't made anything—just enough to eat on. People who never lived in the depression have a hard time believing the things that went on. The poor people were scratching trying to get something to eat and the rich ones were jumping out of ten-story buildings because they were losing all their money. I thought that thirty-five dollars was all the money in the world— and it was as far as I was concerned at that time. That was thirty-five dollars for each of us.)

Success tends to breed success and The Sons of the Pioneers suddenly were "hot" and in great demand. They were being asked to appear on big-time radio programs with the likes of Phil Regan, Larry Gray, Jo Stafford, and others. In 1935 they made their motion picture debut in a Mary Carlisle feature entitled *The Old Homestead* and immediately followed that with a brief appearance in Gene Autry's first starrer, *Tumbling Tumbleweeds,* a two-reeler with Joan Davis entitled *Way Up Thar,* and the Charles Starrett Western, *Gallant Defender.*

In 1936 they were invited to perform for the Texas Centennial in Dallas. Leonard took this opportunity to stop off in Roswell, New Mexico, to marry Arlene Wilkins, the homemade lemon pie girl he had been corresponding with almost daily since the abortive Southwest tour of two years before.

Back in Los Angeles The Sons of the Pioneers joined Peter Potter's KNX "Hollywood Barn Dance" program and signed a recording contract with Decca Records. But motion pictures were the great hope for anyone performing in California. A film contract truly symbolized that you had "arrived." Leonard Slye kept urging his fellow Pioneers that they had to keep pounding on studio gates if they wanted to make it in films.

With their radio and personal appearance reputations fairly well established, the studio gates opened more easily. In 1936 they again appeared with Gene Autry in his features *The Big Show* and *The Old Corral.* Over at Columbia Pictures— "Gower Gulch," as the lot was often referred to at that time—they appeared in another Charles Starrett Western feature *The Mysterious Avenger.* Their only "prestige" film was a bit in Paramount's

The youthful Leonard Slye, wearing probably the world's largest black cowboy hat, Bob Nolan (playing bass), and the other Sons of the Pioneers accompany vocalist Gene Autry. To the left is Smiley Burnette; ventriloquist Max Terhune and "Elmer" are behind the studio window on the right (*The Big Show*, Republic, 1936.)

Bing Crosby starrer *Rhythm on the Range*, which featured Bob "Bazooka" Burns and Martha Raye.

To ten-year-old Leonard Franklin Slye back in Ohio in 1921, the possibility of becoming a member of a successful Western singing group, making personal appearances, and singing in movies would have been almost incomprehensible; but now that the reality was there, a frustration began to set in. No new doors seemed to be opening. Leonard Slye wondered if this was to be as high as he would go as a Western singer.

His answer came one afternoon in the autumn of 1937 when he happened to be in a hat shop out in Glendale dropping off his white Stetson, which needed to be cleaned and reblocked. While he was there, an excited young actor rushed in and bought a new cowboy hat for (he said) auditions Republic was having the next day for singing cowboys.

(About this time Gene Autry was getting difficult again now that contract time was near, and the story was that Republic planned to hedge its bet by signing a possible successor to keep Autry in line, or to replace him if he proved to be too cantankerous with money demands.) The audition information was not lost upon the enterprising, ambitious Leonard Slye, who now intended to find a way into Republic Studios the next day even though he had not been invited.

The next day proved rougher than he expected. The guard at the studio gate was intractable; "No pass, no entering!" It was after lunch before Leonard managed to slip in with some returning employees. No sooner did he get inside Republic's walls than his luck changed. Who should he encounter but Sol Siegel, the producer, who was auditioning the singing cowboy prospects. Siegel remembered Leonard Slye from The Sons of the Pioneers' singing spots in Republic's Gene Autry films, and suggested that he audition for the new singing cowboy job. Siegel indicated that after listening to about seventeen performers that morn-

117

ing, he still did not feel that he had the right singing cowboy for the job.

Siegel told young Slye to get his guitar from the car and to meet him in his office where the audition would be conducted. A few minutes later in Siegel's office the out-of-breath transplanted Ohioan rather nervously made like a real cowpoke and sang for the film producer. When the final chord was strummed, Siegel told Leonard to relax and sing another song.

(ROY ROGERS: In my audition with Sol Siegel I sang and yodeled because very few of the other cowboys had done any yodeling. I sang a song called "Hadie Brown," which has a fast yodel in it. I forget what else I sang, but that was the main one. While we were talking, he asked me if I was tied up at any other studio. I told him we had just signed as a group for Charlie Starrett's pictures at Columbia. Mr. Siegel asked me if I thought I could get loose if things worked out. I told him I didn't know. I was thinking to myself, "If I break loose of the contract and the screen test doesn't pan out, I'm out both ways." So I went to Irving Briskin at Columbia and told him the situation. I asked him if he would release me from the contract if the screen test worked out. He said he would. I got Pat Brady, a friend of mine, to take my place at Columbia if the situation worked out at Republic.

Time passed and I didn't get my screen test. Then one day we were called to Republic to do background music for another Autry picture—our Columbia contract allowed us to do that. I told Joe Kane, who was directing the picture, what had happened. Joe had always liked me even though I only had a little bit to do in the pictures. He said, "Let me see what I can do." The next morning they had me out there for a screen test. They liked the screen test and signed me up.

A lot of people ask, "How did you get into motion pictures?" I always say that I figure God must have wanted me in pictures because I can look back and see so many little things that happened just right for me. For example, being at that hat shop when the man came in. I never had any idea they were looking for another singing cowboy over at Republic. Another example, Sol Siegel later told me I never once entered his mind until I walked through the gate and he saw me. If I'd been ten feet further ahead or behind, I might never have become a singing cowboy of pictures.)

On October 13, 1937, Leonard Slye signed a contract with Republic Pictures. Included in the deal was a new name—Dick Weston—which Leonard and Republic thought was more suitable for a Western star than his real name. Unfortu-nately, fame and success could not be bestowed as easily as a new name, so Dick Weston, potential cowboy star, languished waiting for lightning to strike him famous.

Republic did give him featured billing in two Western films. One was *Wild Horse Rodeo* starring The Three Mesquiteers (Robert Livingston, Ray "Crash" Corrigan, and Max Terhune). *Variety's* film critic commented, "Dick Weston, who is a ringer for Wayne Morris, sings a couple of guitar-accom-panied ditties, but they're only incidental." The other film was Gene Autry's *Old Barn Dance,* where Dick Weston was listed in the credits as simply "Singer."

Finally in early 1938, Gene Autry, as he had threatened to do many times, went on strike at Republic just before the start of filming on his new feature. After a hurry-up conference with other top brass at Republic, Sol Siegel called Dick Weston and told him to get over to the studio because he was about to become the star of the Republic feature, *Under Western Stars.*

As the picture was getting under way, it was determined that yet another change of name for Leonard Slye should take place.

(ROY ROGERS: We were in Mr. Yates's office at the time of my first starring picture. There were several of us—Sol and Moe Siegel, Mr. Yates—all the officials of the studio. We'd kicked around several names until Rogers came up. I said, "Well, that's one I like because I've loved Will Rogers all my life." So we stopped on that. Then they started naming short first names that would go with it. Finally they hit on Roy; they liked the sound of Roy Rogers. When I was little I had known a kid named Leroy that I didn't like, so I didn't know whether I was going to like Roy. But when you say the two together—Roy Rogers—they kind of go together. So we all settled on it and that's the way the name came about.)

The new moniker did cause some consternation at Republic, though. Shortly after the release of *Under Western Stars,* a vaudevillian by the name of Roy Rogers sued Republic and the film cowboy Roy Rogers for one hundred and fifty-thousand dollars over the use of the name. *Variety,* conclud-ing a report on the incident in an article entitled, "Rep Pays Off Rogers, Keeps Tag For Oat Star," stated:

Cash figure is not disclosed, but Republic retains exclusive picture rights to the disputed name for its Western player, while the vaude-villian retains the right to use his name on the stage. Plaintiff had asked an injunction to

Leonard Slye, alias Dick Weston, alias Roy Rogers.

restrain the studio from using the Rogers handle for its player, whose real name is Leonard Slye.

Perhaps because of the lawsuit, or the impermanency of filmmaking, or just because of his Ohio conservativeness—whatever—Leonard Slye did not legally change his name to Roy Rogers until 1942.

*   *   *

Republic very much wanted *Under Western Stars* to be a critical and box-office success. To help ensure those results, extra money was funneled into the budget of the film. And Republic got exactly what it paid for—an excellent box-

office return and, sure to cause concern in the Autry camp, critical hosannas beyond everyone's wildest expectations. *Variety's* critic exclaimed:

. . . In addition to being entertaining it's plausible sage stuff that will hold the adult mind as well as the credulous kiddies. . . . Unlike majority [of musical Westerns], music and comic situations are injected with rhyme and reason, besides being pleasant to the ear.

About Rogers the critic commented:

. . . Add to the foregoing the presence of a new star, Roy Rogers, a cinch b.o.'er . . . . In Roy Rogers producers present a cowboy who looks like a wrangler, is a looker, an actor, and a singer. Pushed into a quick starring spot . . . he lives up to every expectation, and then some. His appeal to femme mob can also be counted upon. [He] Walks away with the film despite presence of Smiley Burnette and Carol Hughes . . . .

Bosley Crowther in the *New York Times* commented that Republic had discovered,

> . . . a new Playboy of the Western World in the sombrero'd person of Roy Rogers, who has a drawl like Gary Cooper, a smile like Shirley Temple, and a voice like Tito Guizar.

With the success of *Under Western Stars,* Republic rushed Rogers into a follow-up series of Westerns that differed from the Autry output in a number of ways: the Rogers features (unlike Autry's "modern" Westerns) were for the most part "historical" Westerns, that is, set in the period from the Civil War until the late 1880s; music, while always utilized (two or three songs per film), never was stressed to the degree of the Autry films (usually five to eight songs in a seventy-minute film); Autry always played a character named Gene Autry, while Roy was quite often cast as a famous person from history (Billy the Kid, Buffalo Bill, Bill Hickok) or given a "character" name. Until 1942 he would only occasionally play "Roy." [After that he became "Roy Rogers, The King of the Cowboys," and his films became more and more like Gene Autry's (modern Westerns, more songs, etc.) until by the middle 1940s he was out Autry-ing Autry with the inclusion of lavish production numbers in his films.]

Alan G. Barbour in his engrossing pictorial history of the B Westerns entitled *The Thrill of It All,* assesses the Rogers films from 1938 to 1942 as ". . . a continuing string of pleasant, but generally uninspired, period films set in the old West."

In a rather informal ranking of the Rogers films (good, fair, not-so-good) based on *Variety* reviews from 1938's *Under Western Stars* through *Ridin' Down the Canyon* in 1942 (the last Rogers film before the big Republic build-up of Rogers and increased budgets), my results indicate that of the thirty-six films produced during this period of time, four films were in the not-so-good category; sixteen were rated fair; and seventeen ranked as good—certainly a pretty good record for such an inexperienced young performer.

Herbert J. Yates, the president of Republic Pictures, was intrigued with film titles. It is reported that he enjoyed creating titles that he thought would "sell" with movie fans, particularly

Roy is in hot pursuit of the villain in this publicity still from around 1940.

kids, since so many of his films were of the Saturday matinee variety. Unfortunately, Yates acquired a liking for a couple of title formats and repeated them as often as he dared.

One format he grew fond of (as did many other movie title concocters) was "The___and the___." Over the years he utilized the format in such film titles as *The Ranger and the Lady* (1940); *The Lady and the Monster* (1944); *The Cowboy and the Senorita* (1944); *The Plainsman and the Lady* (1946); *The Angel and the Badman* (1947); *The Bullfighter and the Lady* (1951).

But the much-used title format that Yates loved the most was "King of the___." Through the decades Republic feature film and serial titles proclaimed a diversity of royal blood that would give anyone cause for pause. They included the following: *King of the Pecos* (1936); *King of the Royal Mounted* (1940); *King of the Texas Rangers* (1941); *King of the Forest Rangers* (1946); *King of the Rocket Men* (1949); and *King of the Carnival* (1955).

All of the "King of the___" titles tended to blur together—all, that is, except the one created in 1943 for the cowboy performer, who, it was deemed, was to be the new star in Republic's crown (now that Gene Autry had defected into the Army Air Corps), and who was about to be the recipient of one of the biggest promotional campaigns ever accorded a Hollywood performer. Leonard Slye, alias Dick Weston, alias Roy Rogers—a singing cowboy who had faithfully toiled on Republic's "oater" range for five years and forty-some films—was proclaimed "King of the Cowboys" by the Republic Pictures publicity department.

To help ensure that the title stuck, a movie feature by that title was quickly ushered into general release throughout the country, and Republic announced that it was upping the budgets on all future Roy Rogers Westerns to three-hundred fifty-thousand dollars or more, with two-hundred-thousand dollars earmarked annually for national advertising. An additional hundred-thousand dollars was being set aside for promotion and newspaper ads in key cities where the Rogers pictures would be shown. (Roy told me he felt the above figures probably had been inflated by the Republic publicity department.)

In June of 1943 Republic announced the launching of a "twenty-four-sheet" campaign to promote its sagebrush star nationally. The term "twenty-four-sheet" referred to the number of paper sheets needed to cover a roadside billboard. It was the first time in Hollywood history that a film company provided this type of promotion for a performer, since billboards were usually reserved to advertise a product such as cigarettes, a loaf of bread, or a movie, rather than a person.

Republic stated that by July 1st it hoped to cover thirty-five percent of the country with 192 billboard displays and planned to link a spot radio and newspaper campaign to coincide with the billboards. Depending upon whom you talked to at Republic, the cost for this concentrated campaign ranged from one-hundred-thousand to five-hundred-thousand dollars.

The three-pronged drive (billboards, radio, and newspapers) was Republic's attempt to sell the public a star of rip-snorting musical Westerns and movie exhibitors on the idea that a strong Western movie starring an attractive, appealing-to-the-whole-family performer like Roy Rogers would do well in the deluxe downtown theaters as well as the "shooting gallery" theaters where B Westerns usually rode the movie screens. *Idaho* (released early in 1943) was the first Rogers starrer to play the Loew circuit in New York, and Republic wanted to see to it that the coming Rogers features (the next two being *King of the Cowboys* and *Song of Texas*) played the Loew chain of first-run theaters.

The Republic publicity staff found itself in the delightful position of launching a promotional campaign for its Western star precisely at a time when cowboy pictures, the old reliable escapists of the film industry, were moving back into first-run theaters after a lapse of years. As *Variety* put it:

> . . . Republic's Roy Rogers saddlers are galloping into high-admission houses that once refused to recognize Gene Autry. The return of the cowpokes is a completion of the cycle which began about twenty years ago when Tom Mix and Bill Hart were welcomed in first-run houses.

Republic Studios attributed the Western film boom to better production, better scripts, and the popularity of stars like Gene Autry and Roy Rogers. *Newsweek* in an article devoted to the subject commented that "more possibly it [the popularity of Western films] owes something to the fact that, although the war worker can—and does—pay better prices for his movies, his tastes remain unchanged." Whatever the reason, more people were going to movies and a sizable number were choosing those which starred a singing cowboy.

Republic was happy with the situation, of

You'd better not mess around with "The King of the Cowboys"!

course, because it had the corner on the musical Western market and a reputation for making a larger profit per invested dollar than any other movie studio. A Roy Rogers film in 1943 could be expected to play in at least seventy-five-hundred theaters—a healthy portion of the country's eighteen-thousand—and show a profit of around three-hundred-thousand dollars.

During the week of July 16, 1943, more than one hundred twenty-six theaters in the windy city of Chicago and its suburbs were playing Roy Rogers Westerns as the star himself galloped into town on Trigger and presented a week of stage shows at the downtown Oriental Theatre. The feature on the screen was *Song of Texas. Variety* reported that the Oriental had one of its best weeks ever with a gross of twenty-nine-thousand dollars. If that gross does not seem especially outstanding, remember the year was 1943 and the ticket price scale ranged from a low of twenty-eight cents for children to a high of sixty-nine cents for adults.

The capper to this phenomenal, king-making effort by the publicity boys at Republic occurred the week before the Chicago engagement, July 12, 1943, when Roy Rogers, astride the rearing Trigger, made the cover of *Life* magazine. *Life* got the noted writer and humorist H. Allen Smith to write the "King of the Cowboys" feature story for the issue. Smith, obviously somewhat nonplussed by the publicity shenanigans, kept his tongue—as if it were a Gabby Hayes chaw of tobacco—firmly ensconced in his cheek throughout the story.

Taking note of the plethora of puffery that had engulfed Rogers in recent months, Smith wryly commented:

The manufacture of personalities through a process known as The Old Build-up has long been one of Hollywood's most noted contributions to world civilization. No better example of the hand-tailored human exists today than Roy Rogers, who has been trumpeted into the splendid title "King of the Cowboys."

Later in the story Smith sardonically attempted to describe the process of evolution that had overtaken the traditional American movie cowboy and replaced him with a mutation called the singing cowboy.

He is the protagonist in the American morality play. He is purity rampant—never drinks, never smokes, never shoots pool, never spits, and the roughest oath at his command is "shucks!" He never needs a shave, and when it comes to fist-fighting, he seldom takes on a single opponent; he beats their brains out in a group. He always wins the girl though he doesn't kiss her. He kisses his horse. His immense public would have him no other way.

Smith's description failed to take note of the "reel" cowboy's attire—certainly as far removed from a real cowboy's duds as a tuxedo would be. The "regalia" became as much a trademark of the singing cowboy as his guitar and more of a trademark than his six-guns since a number of the singing cowboys wore guns only occasionally, much to the chagrin of many young viewers.

The cowboy clothes worn by Roy Rogers were certainly more gaudy than those worn by any other singing cowboys during the 1940s—and they were expensive, too. A white stetson ran about forty dollars; fancy Western shirts were fifty dollars each; coat and pants were about two hundred dollars; the tooled leather belt to hold up the pants could run as high as forty-five dollars; the gun belt, seventy-five dollars; the six-shooters about sixty-five dollars each; the cowboy boots could be purchased for around seventy-five dollars a pair; silver spurs for the boots, eighty-five dollars.

The "clothes" for Trigger were also very expensive, with the saddle alone costing at least fifteen-hundred dollars. When Rogers bought the palomino horse in 1938, he paid twenty-five-hundred dollars for him, a lot of money for Rogers at the time. In later years he commented, ". . . it was the cheapest $2,500 I ever spent."

Rogers, working with trainer Glen Randall, taught Trigger to perform some sixty tricks for films and personal appearances. As a publicity stunt when Roy and Trigger first went to New York for a Madison Square Garden appearance, Trigger was taken right into the hotel lobby where Roy was staying, and was given a pencil to hold in his teeth while he marked an "X" on the register. Trigger could drink milk from a bottle, walk 150 feet on his hind legs, and do simple addition and subtraction as well as count to twenty. All the cues for the tricks were hand motions by Roy. Undoubtedly the greatest "trick" credited to Trigger was his ability to display "self-restraint" while indoors.

Of course, being "The Smartest Horse in the Movies" was not all hay and oats. During personal appearances Trigger was the constant prey of souvenir seekers, the prize being a few hairs from

Trigger displays his talent here as he poses in a most extra-
ordinary rearing position. *Photo courtesy of Roy Rogers.*

Trigger, "The Smartest Horse in the Movies." *Photo courtesy of Roy Rogers.*

his mane or tail. Rogers has claimed that there were times when the pilfering became such a problem that Trigger was forced to wear a "tail toupee" for a while.

DAVID ROTHEL: How did you come to acquire Trigger?

ROY ROGERS: When we got ready to pick a horse for me when I was starting my series at Republic, all the stables that leased horses to the studios were called and told to send out their lead horses. If a stable could get one of their lead horses on a picture, then they could get a studio to take their posse horses, buggy horses, and the street horses for the picture. So they all brought their horses out—I think there were about six lead horses there that day. I got on a couple of them and rode them down the street and back. Then I got on [the horse that was to become] Trigger and rode him down the street and back. I never looked at the

rest of them. I said, "This is it. This is the color I want. He feels like the horse I want, and he's got a good rein on him." So I took Trigger and started my first picture. About the second or third picture I went to Hudkins Stables and bought him from them.

DAVID ROTHEL: How did he happen to get the name Trigger?

ROY ROGERS: The name came up when we were getting ready to do the first picture. Smiley Burnette and I and some others who were there got to kicking it around. I was fooling around with my guns as we talked. I believe it was actually Smiley who said, "As fast and as quick as the horse is, you ought to call him Trigger, You know, quick-on-the-trigger." I said, "That's a good name." And I just named him Trigger.

DAVID ROTHEL: He was certainly a great-looking horse.

ROY ROGERS: Trigger was not only a beautiful horse, but he was a good "using" horse for all those chases and things. You know, Trigger did those chases through the rocks and over the mountains, down steep grades and never had any ankles, hocks, or knees go wrong—nothing. He was just tough as a boot. I could do those running mounts and dismounts and never have any problem with him at all. He could outrun any horse on the set—just flatfooted outrun them. But you had to be "with him" whenever you gave him the cue to go left or right or he'd spin right out from under you.

He was half Thoroughbred. His sire was a race horse at Caliente and his dam was a cold-blooded palomino. He took the color, white mane, and tail from his mother and the stamina, speed, and conformation from the Thoroughbred side. He took the good parts from both of them. His registered name was Golden Cloud as a palomino.

DAVID ROTHEL: Since he was originally owned by Hudkins Stables for leasing purposes, had he ever appeared in any films prior to yours?

ROY ROGERS: I later found out that the first picture he appeared in was *Robin Hood,* which starred Errol Flynn and Olivia De Havilland. She rode him in the Sherwood Forest scene, sidesaddle. That was when Trigger was three years old. He was four when I made my first picture.

DAVID ROTHEL: Did you have any stand-ins for Trigger?

ROY ROGERS: I always owned four or five extra palomino horses in case anything should happen to Trigger. So in any long-distance shots where they weren't identifiable, we would use one of the other horses to give Trigger a break. But if the shots were close-ups, Trigger had to do them. But he was tough; if you gave him a little breather after each one, he could just go all day. And we took care of him. He was checked thoroughly every six months by a vet.

DAVID ROTHEL: I read somewhere that Trigger was under contract and receiving a salary of about seven-hundred-fifty dollars a week during your biggest years at Republic. Is that right?

ROY ROGERS: No. He never even got scale. He just went along with me. Trigger never got anything but some fine treatment by me and my trainer, Glen Randall.

DAVID ROTHEL: I read in the same article that his contract called for three close-ups in each film, equal billing with you, and that the scripts must show him helping to "motivate" the story.

ROY ROGERS: Well, that's nonsense. That's some publicity guy's daydream.

DAVID ROTHEL: Did Trigger perform in the TV series?

Roy, Trigger, and an unidentified canine are seen here on location for a film. *Photo courtesy of Roy Rogers.*

ROY ROGERS: Yes. I'm the only cowboy in the business, I think, that started and made all my pictures with one horse.

DAVID ROTHEL: What about Trigger, Jr.?

ROY ROGERS: Well, we used him for personal appearances. He wasn't worth a nickle as a cowboy horse, but he could do a beautiful dance routine, so we used him for personal appearances. But Trigger—he was something else! I retired him in 1957 after the TV series we made. He was twenty-five then and he lived to be thirty-three years old, dying in 1965. A horse's life is over three to one in comparison to a man's. So that made Trigger over a hundred years old in human terms.

*   *   *

A new leading lady rode into the Roy Rogers Westerns in 1944, and was to remain for the next twenty consecutive films. Her name was Dale Evans, and she was eventually destined to become Roy's leading lady in more ways than one. Their first picture together was *The Cowboy and the Senorita.*

Dale, a successful radio singer and recording artist, had made a few bit picture appearances for Twentieth Century-Fox in 1942, but it could be said that her real picture debut was in *Swing Your Partner* for Republic in 1943. Dale described the

Roy is putting Trigger, Jr. through his paces. Trigger, Jr.'s specialty was performing dance routines during Roy's personal appearance tours. *Photo courtesy of Roy Rogers.*

picture as a "hayseed musical," but at the time she was glad to have the work because it meant money to support her and her teenaged son, Tommy.

Years before when she was only fourteen, Dale had impetuously run off and married her teenaged boyfriend. In less than a year, a son, Tommy, was born, but by that time her young husband had deserted her, and she was left alone at fifteen years of age to care for her baby.

With the vocal talent she possessed and a vast amount of determination, Dale eventually landed a singing job on a radio station in Louisville, Kentucky. It was at the Louisville station that the program director advised that her real name of Frances Smith might not be classy enough for a young singer on the rise, and suggested Dale Evans because it was easy to spell, pronounce, and remember. From then on she used the name.

Dale later returned to her home state of Texas to sing on the "Early Birds" program over Dallas station WFAA. In 1937 she took an offer to sing at the Edgewater Beach Hotel in Chicago with Jay Miller's Orchestra. Later she toured with Anson Weeks and his band for nearly a year. After that she again returned to Chicago for more radio

singing on WBBM and with Caesar Petrillo and his orchestra. When Ray Bolger headlined at Chicago's Chez Paree nightclub in 1940, Dale was also on the bill. A few months later agent Joe Rivkin wired her from Hollywood that Paramount was looking for a "new face" to appear with Bing Crosby and Fred Astaire in a picture to be called *Holiday Inn,* and indicated that she might have a chance to be that new face.

Dale decided to take a leave of absence to see what Hollywood had to offer. Upon completion of the usual film tests, it was decided that she was wrong for the Crosby picture since she had had no dance training at that time. But Twentieth Century-Fox saw hope for her and signed her to a one-year contract, during which time she only received bit roles. While her movie career was going nowhere, she was doing quite well on radio, having been signed for the extremely popular Edgar Bergen-Charlie McCarthy "Chase and Sanborn Program." In addition, some recordings she had made were selling better than anyone had anticipated.

So that's the way it was for Dale Evans in early 1944 when Herbert J. Yates, Republic's president, said to her, "I'm starting a new brand of Western musicals for Roy Rogers. I'd like to see what you can do with them. The first will be titled *The Cowboy and the Senorita.*"

Dale played the Senorita Ysobel Martinez of the title, a rather off-beat role for the blond, blue-eyed Texas gal, but she played the role well, and was popular with Roy and the other cast members. She was brought back for the next Rogers film, *The Yellow Rose of Texas* (1944), where she got more of an opportunity to sing and dance. The film received excellent reviews and did well at the box office. causing the top brass at Republic to want to continue a good thing—which they did for eighteen more films, running through *Bells of San Angelo* in 1947.

In the fall of 1944 a new opportunity opened for Roy Rogers—his own network radio program. "The Roy Rogers Show," sponsored by Goodyear, went on the Mutual network Tuesday evenings at 8:30 P.M. beginning on November 21, 1944. Roy was able to include his film co-stars, Bob Nolan and The Sons of the Pioneers, in the cast along with female vocalist Pat Friday, Perry Botkin and his band, and announcer Vern Smith. *Variety* reviewed the program by commenting that it was "commercially sound, with the usual format of any Western musical radio program, but lacking comedy."

The program was certainly a good buy for Goodyear with the total production tab for each

Dale is seen here in typical Western attire she wore for motion pictures and personal appearances. *Photo courtesy of Roy Rogers.*

Director Frank McDonald, Dale, and Roy are pictured taking a stroll on the Republic lot (circa 1945). *Photo courtesy of Frank McDonald.*

show set at thirty-five-hundred dollars. Other radio programs of that time were far more costly with "The Great Gildersleeve" coming in for sixty-five-hundred dollars per show, and Jack Benny for twenty-two-thousand five-hundred dollars. About the only network radio show that could boast a higher rating and far lower cost was "The Lone Ranger," coming from Detroit at the bargain basement cost of eighteen-hundred dollars per week for *three* thirty-minute programs.

While Roy's radio program did moderately well in the ratings, Goodyear did not pick up the option and the show went off the air in the late spring of 1945 as World War II was winding down.

As a side note—the military status of Roy Rogers during World War II was always a touch-and-go situation for Republic Pictures and Rogers himself. Roy was married, of course, and had a family to support. He had reported for his pre-induction physical and had passed it. But before he could be called-up for service, V-E Day arrived and

the service stopped inducting anyone over thirty.

A year elapsed before Roy's next radio venture, this time with more of his film regulars. In addition to Bob Nolan and The Sons of the Pioneers, Roy's radio cast this time included Gabby Hayes and Dale Evans. Pat Buttram (who would later be Gene Autry's comic sidekick) was also in the supporting cast along with Country Washburn and his orchestra. In reviewing the new Saturday night at nine o'clock series on NBC, sponsored by Miles Laboratories, *Variety* stated:

> Helping to spread word of the benefits of Alka-Seltzer and One-A-Day Vitamins among the yokelry, Roy Rogers and his supporting cast from Republic Pictures' series is taking over for the National Barn Dance. Program is pretty much a repeat of stock filler from the film series in which every story is padded by the comedics of Gabby Hayes and the singing of Rogers and Dale Evans.
>
> Citizens of the hinterlands are notoriously passionate fans of cowboy stars in general and, because of his exploitation, Rogers in particular. . . . The only thing missing is Trigger.

Though it was fairly popular, Miles cancelled the program at the end of the radio season.

It was during the run of the second radio series—at a time when his movie career was at its peak—that tragedy struck the life of Roy Rogers. On October 28, 1946, Roy's wife, Arlene, gave birth to their third child, a boy. Six days later on November 3rd, Arlene was unexpectedly stricken with an embolism. Within hours she was dead.

I remember listening to Roy's radio program the week his wife died. There was an announcement at the beginning of the show that Roy would not be there because of the death of his wife. I was not quite ten years old at the time, but I remember somehow sensing the devastation that Roy must have been feeling by drawing the only comparison I could at the time—the recent death of the little dog that had been with me all the years of my short life.

In the months that followed Arlene's death, Roy Rogers, with three children to raise alone, turned more and more to his film leading lady, Dale Evans, for comfort and companionship. In time their feelings turned to love, and on December 31, 1947 they were married.

* * *

From his first starring feature film, *Under*

Starting in 1944, Dale appeared with Roy in twenty consecutive Republic Pictures' films. *Photo courtesy of Roy
Rogers.*

Western Stars in 1938 until *Pals of the Golden
West* (1951), his last Republic film, Roy Rogers
was directed by only four men in his regular
Republic Western series: Joseph Kane (forty-two
films, 1938-44); Frank McDonald (eleven films,
1939-46); John English (three films, 1944-45); and
William Witney (twenty-seven films, 1946-51).

When William Witney took over the helm of the
Roy Rogers films in 1946, no shift in direction was
apparent for some time, but change was coming to
the Rogers films—as it was to the country with the

war just ended and television antennas beginning to
sprout ever so gradually like corn shoots on a
Kansas farm in the spring.

Witney, unlike Kane, McDonald, and English,
was to place his individual directorial stamp upon
the Roy Rogers series of films. Witney was a
plain-spoken, hard-drinking, man's man who made
his reputation at Republic as a director of twenty-
four rough-and-tumble serials from 1937 until
1946. Because of the fast action and, to quote
some critics, "violence" he incorporated into those

Roy is pictured here "on location" for the filming of a mid-1940s feature.

In his next film, *Springtime in the Sierras* (1947), Rogers is after a hunting ring that deals in fancy game killed out of season. Before the roundup at the finale, Rogers is thrown into the gang's meat locker and almost ends up frozen stiff.

In 1948's *Eyes of Texas* the villainess uses trained wild dogs to slay her victims. She thus appears innocent of any wrongdoing by claiming that wolves must be responsible. *Variety's* critic commented, "There's a hair-raising, running gun fight as a climax that's loads different from the accepted one."

Francis M. Nevins, Jr. states in his article in *Films in Review,* "Ballet of Violence: The films of William Witney":

Witney . . . set out to change the direction of Roy's movies. He wanted to restore a reasonable measure of fast action and stunting in the serial tradition, and experiment with techniques for making hand-to-hand combat more realistic-looking. In the Rogers films of the late '40s, when people get into fistfights they come out bloodied. . . . Though the front office demanded several country-western ditties per picture (at the proper moment a bored Witney would call out "OK, guys, song time!"), action devotees still got their money's worth in such sequences as the chase in *The Far Frontier* ('49) where the fleeing villains roll oil barrels from the back of a truck and Trigger sidesteps every one; and the scene in *Twilight in the Sierras* ('50) where Roy rescues a man and woman bound and gagged inside a burning runaway stage-coach.

DAVID ROTHEL: We kids loved the wild and woolly action scenes in those William Witney-directed pictures. By today's standards, though, the mayhem was pretty tame. What sort of restrictions did you have on screen violence in those days?

ROY ROGERS: We had what was called the Hays Office. [Will H. Hays was president of the Motion Picture Producers and Distributors Association of America from 1922 until 1945 and was the author of its Production Code, which set the standards for the film industry.] Then, the heroes couldn't even hit a guy in the stomach. Now they can hit them anywhere they can hit, kick, or chop. We could have a bruise or a trickle of blood from our nose or the corner of our mouth. That was the limit that the Hays Office would allow. I'm not too sure that they weren't right when I see all the blood and guts they have in pictures today.

serials, he has been called the Sam Peckinpah of the thirties and forties.

Considering his serial background (he had only directed three features in his career prior to the Rogers films, the last one a Don "Red" Barry Western in 1942) and his gruff, earthy, no-nonsense approach to filmmaking, it seems incongruous that he should agree to direct the fantasy-like, musical-comedy Westerns of Roy Rogers. Nevertheless, Witney told writer Francis M. Nevins, Jr. in 1974 that his years with Rogers were the happiest in his career.

During Witney's first four Roy Rogers films (*Roll On Texas Moon* (1946), *Home in Oklahoma* (1946), *Heldorado* (1946), and *Apache Rose* (1947)) it appeared to be business as usual with the typical blend of action, comedy, and songs. But with the next film, *Bells of San Angelo* (1947), Witney's penchant for rawer screen action became apparent. As one critic commented:

Midway through [the film] Roy Rogers takes a monumental shellacking from McGuire, Sharpe, et. al., and with the aid of the picture's Trucolor tinting, the gore literally runs red. The kids will especially like that.

This is one of the quieter moments in an otherwise rough and tumble film. Pictured are Roy, Dale, Foy Willing (with guitar), the Riders of the Purple Sage, and an unbilled canine friend. *Photo courtesy of NTA.*

In the fall of 1948 Roy began yet another radio series, this time for Quaker Oats on the Mutual Broadcasting System, Sundays at 6:00 P.M. The program proved successful and was retained by Quaker Oats for three years, until the summer of 1951. By the 1950-51 radio season, program costs for the Roy Rogers series had risen to seventy-two-hundred dollars per week. This cost was quite low, though, when compared to the fifteen-thousand dollar weekly tab for the very similar Gene Autry "Melody Ranch" program. It was reported that one of the reasons Quaker Oats cancelled was that Roy's picture contract did not permit him to do television.

In the fall of 1951 General Foods picked up the tab on the "Roy Rogers Show" (broadcast on NBC at 8:00 P.M. on Fridays the first year, Thursdays thereafter) and continued it until 1954 when Dodge Motors took over sponsorship for the last year of the radio series.

Following Gene Autry's lead in radio as he had in films, the Roy Rogers radio stanzas over the years consisted of Western ballads sung by Roy and Dale; some hillbilly comedy provided by Gabby Hayes, Pat Buttram, or Pat Brady; a short Western drama (usually about ten minutes in length); with just enough time left for a closing song and theme.

By 1951 *Variety's* reviewer must have felt that he had heard it all before when he wrote:

... Roy Rogers and his Western meller, song jamboree come through very much like countless other thirty-minute soap opera sessions.... Unfortunately one can't see Roy Rogers and his comely wife, Dale Evans, in action. And this is a handicap since this western film star is mainly a sight actor. His trained mount, Trigger, figures importantly in this plot, story having the horse actually rout the badman when Roy Rogers is cornered.

131

In 1949 Roy and Trigger were asked to put their boot and hoof prints in cement in the famous courtyard of Grauman's Chinese Theatre in Hollywood.

Here again, it is just so many sound effects. . . . Musical portion of the show rates 1-A, but it is not effectively tied in with the plot as per their screen vehicles.

By 1951 the bloom was off the musical Western sage. The multiplicity of singing cowboys that had galloped onto movie screens during the 1940s had pretty much sung their last roundup. Only the two leading exponents of the genre—Gene Autry and Roy Rogers—were still active, plus a new fellow, Rex Allen, who was brought in by Republic Pictures in 1950, a few months after Roy recommended him to Herbert Yates, Republic's president.

On May 27, 1951, Roy Rogers's contract with Republic was up for renewal. Only a few months before, it was assumed that he would re-sign with his long-time boss, but a couple of things happened to change all that: Roy's insistence that the new contract include television rights and Republic's sudden announcement that it intended to release Roy's pictures to television.

(ROY ROGERS: When my second seven-year contract came up in 1951, television had really gotten to rolling. Mr. Yates wanted me to sign another seven-year contract, but I wouldn't sign it unless I got television rights. Well, at that time all of the studios were fighting television teeth and toenails. When he wouldn't give me any TV rights, I wouldn't sign the contract. A few days later he came out with a big publicity announcement that my pictures had been cut and were ready for release to television.)

Rogers, through his lawyer, informed Republic that they had no right to release the films to television and that he would, if necessary, take legal action to stop them. Rogers's claim was that the films were made by Republic for entertainment purposes only and that any attempt to televise them in conjunction with video advertising would be an infringement of his contract, since he retained the one hundred percent rights to his name, voice, and likeness in all commercial tie-ups. This was interpreted to include television sponsorship. In addition, Rogers, like Gene Autry the year before, wished to get into television with a Western series of his own. He rightly saw that a television contract might be hard to come by if his full-length, big-budget Republic features were to be made available to television stations in competition

Perhaps the slightly quizzical expression on Roy's face reflects his concern that the times were changing for the movie industry during the late forties and early fifties.

with a (necessarily) low-budget television series.

As late as May 15, 1951, it was announced that a new contract with Republic giving Rogers video rights would be signed upon the return of Republic president Herbert Yates, who was out of town. In addition, it was announced that Art Rush, Roy's manager, was negotiating with potential sponsors for a series of half-hour "videoaters" (with contracts expected to be signed by the next week) as well as a new radio series contract.

As the Republic contract date approached, Yates became more and more adamant that he was not going to include the right to do television in Rogers's contract. Without the clause Rogers wouldn't sign. May 27th came and passed with no signatures on the contract. In early June Republic went through with its plan to offer the Rogers films to advertising agencies and television stations for immediate telecasting. Rogers's attorney immediately sought and was granted a temporary restraining order forbidding the use of Rogers' name, voice, or likeness for commercial purposes.

While the litigation was under way, Art Rush negotiated a radio-television contract with Post Cereals of General Foods. The Roy Rogers past record was so impressive that General Foods signed without even seeing a television pilot film. The only catch—a cause for cliff-hanging concern—was an escape clause in the contract in case Rogers should lose his legal fight with Republic over the television release of his feature films.

On September 13, 1951, the hearing began on the lawsuit filed by Rogers against Republic Pictures. The case, of course, was closely watched by all of show business because the outcome would very likely have bearing on the future sale of old motion pictures to television. After four and a half grueling weeks of evidence, the hearing ground to an end. The court's ruling was a victory for the Rogers forces. The judge found that Rogers had the right to control the association of his name with commercial advertising and granted a permanent injunction restraining the studio from selling the films for television purposes or even allowing them to be used as a sustaining (noncommercial) program because this in effect would advertise the station that televised the film.

Republic Pictures announced immediately that it would appeal the court's decision. In June of 1954, after almost three more years of litigation, a United States Court of Appeals reversed a portion of the original verdict stating in effect that a motion picture actor could not forevermore claim that the original producer's use of the films was unfair competition to the performer. In addition, the Appeals Court held that Rogers's contract with Republic gave the studio the right to reproduce "any and all acts, poses, plays, and appearances" of the actor. Wall Street sources estimated at the time that Republic would realize some twenty million dollars from the television release of the Roy Rogers and Gene Autry features (which were also involved in similar litigation).

(ROY ROGERS: Many people think that we've made a fortune out of [the televising of] those pictures, but we've never gotten a cent. They've made millions off them.)

But back in October of 1951 it didn't matter what the courts would eventually decide on the case; the way was clear for General Foods's sponsorship of the Roy Rogers television and radio series on NBC.

The premiere of "The Roy Rogers Show" on television (December 30, 1951) was a gala affair featuring a live first half-hour sendoff from the El Capitan Theatre in Hollywood with regulars Roy, Dale Evans, and Pat Brady, and with special guest star Bob Hope. The second half of the program consisted of the initial episode in the regular thirty-minute Western adventure series that would appear on NBC each Sunday at 6:30 P.M., sponsored by Post cereals.

During the live half of the program, Bob Hope, sporting a black ten-gallon Stetson, made with the OK corral comedy at the expense of straight man Roy Rogers. In addition to working in a plug for their just-completed Paramount feature, *Son of Paleface,* the duo socked over their own special rendition of "Tears in My Ears," with Rogers

yodeling a final chorus. Dale Evans and the Whippoorwills (a Western singing group) vocalized a couple of country songs, while Pat Brady got some comedy mileage out of a hillbilly novelty tune. The big finish featured Rogers, Hope, and Trigger in a hilarious poker game that climaxed with "The Smartest Horse in the Movies" shrewdly overturning the table and pushing Hope off the stage.

The second-half adventure was a standard Rogers-Evans contemporary Western, attractively packaged by executive producer-star Roy Rogers and producer Jack Lacey to appeal to a new generation of fans—this time viewing on the tiny living room screen.

In the television series Rogers played the owner of the rambling Double R Bar Ranch located somewhere out West in a place called Paradise Valley. Not far from the ranch was a sleepy little town called Mineral City where Dale operated the Eureka Cafe, a respectable establishment serving nothing stronger to the citizenry than Dale's coffee—no Miss Kitty, she. The time frame for the episodes—as with most of their film features—was the movie make-believe modern West where just about everyone wore a six-shooter and rode a horse, but where modern automobiles, airplanes, and conveniences could be hustled into the story line with hardly a hint of anachronism. Location filming was shot at Iverson's ranch, a site used at one time or another by just about all the Western series. Mineral City was the revamped Western street on the Sam Goldwyn backlot; interiors were also shot at the Goldwyn studio.

Stet cast members for the television series included Roy, Dale, Trigger, Buttermilk (Dale's new horse replacing her movie mount, Pal, who looked too much like Trigger on the small screen), and Bullet, Roy's German Shepherd dog. No Western series was considered complete in those days without a comedy sidekick for the hero. Pat Brady was selected for this chore and given a mount unlike that of any other practitioner of Western comedy relief—a jeep by the name of Nellybelle that seemed to possess a life (and will) of its very own.

With the mixture of these mostly stock ingredients and an appealing cast, a tasty weekly Western adventure stew was cooked up for hungry viewers. Critics had kind words for the winning personalities and the "wholesomeness" of the cowboy star and his co-star wife, Dale Evans, and speculated rightly that these qualities would serve them well in television homes across the country as they had in movie theaters for so many years.

"The King of the Cowboys," "The Queen of the West," and "The Smartest Horse in the Movies."

Roy with Bullet, "The Wonder Dog" of all the television episodes. *Photo courtesy of Roy Rogers.*

Roy, Trigger, and Bullet are hot on the trail to adventure in this scene from the television series. *Photo courtesy of Roy Rogers.*

The series continued on the NBC television network through the 1956-57 season with a total of one hundred black and white episodes produced. In the early 1960s the popular series appeared on the CBS television network in reruns.

During the 1950s a new personal side of the Roy Rogers-Dale Evans team gradually emerged to the public—their deep religious convictions. Through the years they many times stated that only their faith helped them stand the test of personal tragedy when three of their children died as a result of sickness or accidents.

In their many personal appearances at rodeos and circuses throughout the country, the Rogerses added an inspirational segment to their regular routines. Standing in a shaft of tinted light in an otherwise darkened arena, the cowboy hero to millions of youngsters would advise his cowboy buckaroos that it was not sissy to go to Sunday School or to say their prayers at bedtime. And then with Trigger kneeling in imitation of humans in prayer, Roy would sing "Peace in the Valley."

As the late fifties approached, Roy began to slow down his show business career. His film career had, of course, ended in 1952 with the release of *Son of Paleface.* By late 1957 Roy had left the first-run battlefields of radio and television and was content to spend more time with his family, which now included an ever-increasing brood of grandchildren. Briefly in 1959 Roy, along with such other television and movie cowboys as Gene Autry, James Arness, Ward Bond, and James Garner, made a cameo guest appearance in the comic finale of Bob Hope's *Alias Jesse James* feature.

Roy and Dale still made many personal appearances at rodeos and fairs across the country and were always box-office favorites. Each television season they would make occasional guest appearances on popular television variety programs, singing a few songs, participating in comedy skits with the host, and often working in an "inspirational" moment or two. A few of their television and personal appearances were in connection with revivals and television crusades headed by such evangelists as Oral Roberts and Billy Graham.

In 1964 Roy, Dale, and the family moved to Apple Valley, California, where eventually they opened the Roy Rogers Museum—a fortlike structure with a larger-than-life-sized statue of the rearing Trigger on the overhanging marquee entrance. (In 1976 the construction on a new museum site was completed in Victorville, a few miles away, and a move was made.)

In addition to the museum and other business interests, a Roy Rogers Family Restaurant Franchise began in the late 1960s, and by the mid 1970s there were over two hundred Family Restaurants in the United States, with over a dozen in Canada.

In May of 1973 an Associated Press story datelined Apple Valley, California, appeared in newspapers across the country. The story caught Roy in a reflective mood. When asked about his health (Roy had developed angina pectoris in the late fifties), Roy said, "I get around OK—I just can't go killing snakes. But I expect to keep right on doing what I'm doing until I'm called." Strumming a guitar as he talked, Roy commented that some actors aren't what they seem. "Gabby Hayes, my sidekick in a lot of movies, was in reality a man of culture who had a lot of years experience on the stage before he ever got into Western movies. But as soon as the camera got on him, there was that old slouch and toothless grin again."

Rogers, though, is one actor who has always been what he seemed. A man known for his loyalty

Roy, Dale, and the children (circa 1950s). Front row, left to right: Dusty (Roy Rogers, Jr.), Sandy (died while in the service), Debbie (killed in a bus accident), and Dodie. Back row, left to right: Roy, Linda, Marion (their Scottish ward), Cheryl, and Dale. Robin (not pictured), born in 1950, suffered from birth defects and died in 1952. *Photo courtesy of Roy Rogers.*

and long lasting personal and business relations, Roy commented that he and his agent, Art Rush, had never had a contract in their thirty-three years together. "Never needed one. Our word is our bond."

In early 1974 Roy hosted a syndicated television series entitled "Roy Rogers Great Cowboy Movies." In each of twenty-six one-hour programs Roy presented a brief nostalgic introduction to an edited version of an old Western film. The films starred many of the B Western greats including: John Wayne, Bob Steele, Wild Bill Elliott, Allan "Rocky" Lane, Sunset Carson, Monte Hale, Eddie Dean, Lash LaRue, Rex Allen, and Tex Ritter.

In late summer of 1974 Snuff Garrett, a fantastically successful young record producer (a multimillionaire five years before at age thirty when he sold his record and publishing company

Roy is seen here in a more recent photograph. *Photo courtesy of Roy Rogers.*

for six million dollars), was asked by a friend what goals or ambitions he still had in life after slaying the dragons of the record business at such a tender age. Snuff Garrett's response was, "I want to meet Roy Rogers."

Shortly thereafter Snuff and Roy were introduced, and a friendship bloomed. To Snuff, whose father had died when he was still a child, Rogers became like a second father for the second time in his life—the first time having been when Snuff was only a youngster and idolized Roy on the movie and television screens.

The story is told that one day while they were out shooting skeet, Snuff asked Roy if he'd like to make a record with him. Rogers's response was, "Sure, what's it called?" To which Snuff replied almost instantly, "Hoppy, Gene, and Me." "How's it go?" Roy asked. Laughing, Snuff Garrett responded, "I don't know; I haven't written it yet."

But write it he did; and a short time later Roy recorded it. The result was, of course, the first hit record for Roy Rogers in around twenty-five years.

Suddenly Roy Rogers was a "hot" commodity in show business again. His hit recording of "Hoppy, Gene, and Me" was packaged with eleven other newly recorded country-Western songs in an album entitled *Happy Trails To You.* The album was also produced by Roy's new-found friend, Snuff Garrett, on the 20th Century Records label in the spring of 1975.

About this same time wire service stories datelined Dickens, Texas, were announcing, "Roy Rogers Is Back in the Saddle Again" (with apologies to Gene Autry) and "Roy Rogers To Make New Western Feature." In mid-July in a story designed to coincide with the start of production on the movie entitled *Mackintosh and T.J.,* the UPI reporter commented:

Roy Rogers, who at 63 still looks young

enough to be King of the Cowboys on the Saturday matinee circuit, returns to movie making Tuesday after 21 [sic] years.

Instead of Trigger, Roy will ride a pickup truck. Gone will be the twin silver six-shooters. Gone will be Dale Evans, his wife and heyday co-star. Gone will be strains of "Happy Trails to You," Rogers' old theme song.

Roy started location filming of the contemporary Western on July 22nd at two large ranches in the Texas Cap Rock high plains country, seventy-five miles east of Lubbock—the 6666 (Four-Sixes Ranch) and the Pitchfork Ranch. Associate producer Dave Garland commented to reporters at the start of production, "It'll be a new character for Roy. He will spend more time in a pickup than on horseback. He's a loner who picks up a stray thirteen-year-old boy, and they have only each other as they return to the old ranch." Roy told a *Time* reporter, "There's no leading lady, no shooting, some fights, but no blood spurting, and that's the way I wanted it."

On February 5, 1976, the premiere of *Mackintosh and T.J.* was held in Lubbock, Texas, not far from the two ranches where it was filmed. The premiere was a benefit for the Ranching Heritage Center at the Museum of Texas Tech University. Roy and Dale were both scheduled to be in attendance, but at the last minute Roy was

Roy signs an autograph for a modern-day cowboy buckaroo at Houstoncon '77.

felled with a respiratory infection and confined to bed. Dale Evans carried on alone at the press conferences prior to the premiere. Against his doctor's orders, Roy flew to Lubbock the day of the premiere. As usual, he and Dale were a huge success with the audiences.

*   *   *

The drive from Los Angeles to San Bernardino to Victorville should have taken me a couple of hours at most. But in the wintry nighttime blackness I was ambushed by heavy rains and a wind that bucked my car from side to side. Then, clouds of fog cut me off at the passes. It took four hours to get to Victorville and the weather forecast was for more of the same—not a very auspicious start for my next-day visit with Roy Rogers.

But what do meteorologists know? The next morning the sky was clear as the sun sprayed over the distant mountains into the little Western community out in the desert. It was just the kind of landscape you'd expect for the Roy Rogers and Dale Evans Museum where Roy had said he'd meet me around 9:00 A.M.

Roy's secretary escorted me into the small, unpretentious office where sat the King of the Cowboys himself looking fit enough at sixty-five to still take on Roy Barcroft and Grant Withers in their prime. He was clad in a checked cowboy shirt, blue jeans, and a working cowboy's "rough-out" boots. The hair was gun metal; the famous squinty eyes showed nary a sign of age around them as he smiled and welcomed me. His hand, when we shook, was that of an outdoorsman, and gripped strongly.

The ten-week-old German short-haired pointer

Roy greets his many friends at Houstoncon '77, "Southwest Fandom's Largest Convention." That's Roy's friend Snuff Garrett in the background.

The Roy Rogers and Dale Evans Museum in Victorville, California.

A larger-than-life statue of Trigger greets visitors at the front entrance of the museum.

Roy had told me about the week before on the telephone was amusing itself chewing up scraps of paper on the floor next to Roy's desk. Roy told me that lately the pup had been keeping Dale and him awake at night so they'd temporarily banished it to a make-shift kennel at the museum.

Roy suggested we tour the museum before a lot of people arrived. As we started down the corridors lined with glass-encased photo displays and room exhibits, Roy commented that the museum, now located just off Interstate 15, had only been open a short time and that he still had a few exhibit areas to complete. A huge storage room was filled with memorabilia waiting to be displayed—each item a memento from some occurrence in his and/or Dale's show business or personal lives. And this cowboy and his lady had saved it all!

But the museum is not an ego trip for Roy and Dale. It's just a practical way of sorting and organizing their past lives—the happy and sad

times, the personal and professional moments that went into forging two lifetimes. We all like to keep souvenirs, remembrances of other times in our lives. Roy and Dale have just done it better and grander than the rest of us. And now their fans all over the world can visit the museum and share the experiences and physical remembrances from the lives of the Rogerses.

So we toured the museum together, Roy commenting on each exhibit as we came to it. Hundreds of photos lead us through his life: the early days in southern rural Ohio and the journey to California; singing and playing with Western· musical groups; the first marriage and children; stardom at Republic Pictures; Dale's entrance into his life and their combined careers in pictures, radio, television, and personal appearances. Along the way their many children were pictured from birth, through the stages of childhood, to tragic deaths in several cases, or to adulthood and, eventually, their own families.

Then, too, there were the personal sides of each displayed—Roy's passion for hunting, fishing, and other sports was well documented with photos, trophies, and weapons of all kinds; Dale's religious work and many writings were prominently displayed. There were examples of the many Roy Rogers commercial tie-ups throughout the museum—comic books, lunch pails, cowboy boots, and six-shooters, to name only a few. The famous Rose Parade saddle and bridle and other saddles and accessories, inlaid with jewels and precious metals, were there to be seen.

And, finally, most popular of all with visitors was the real Trigger, mounted in the famous rearing position, fully saddled and bridled, while beside him Bullet, "The Wonder Dog," looked up in quizzical rapture.

(ROY ROGERS: When Trigger died I had mixed thoughts about what to do. I'd seen what a beautiful job they do mounting animals. If I put him in the ground, I knew what would happen to him. If I put him here in the museum, people could see him from now on. So I had him mounted. He's been here nine years and looks beautiful. I'm so happy I did it. He appeared in all my pictures and TV programs over all those years, plus those countless personal appearances. It would have been a crime to bury him.) Standing next to Bullet and Trigger was Dale's television series horse, Buttermilk. A little further on Trigger, Jr. was poised in one of his famous dance steps.

By the time we finished the tour, a posse of museum visitors had gathered around us listening to Roy reflect upon the events and objects of his life. Prior to heading back to his office, autographs were signed, pictures snapped, and hands shaken.

Roy's secretary went for sandwiches as we started going through the draft pages of the profile I had sent in advance. Whenever the office door was opened, Roy's pointer pup, exiled in the outer office while we talked, scampered without success to get to Roy before the door was quickly shut. A frustrated whimper slid under the door after each frantic scramble.

As late afternoon rolled around, Roy narrowed in on some of the good-old bad-old days at Republic Pictures—the less glittery side of the business the fans rarely heard about.

ROY ROGERS: The old man (Herbert Yates) wouldn't pay a nickel to see an ant eat a bail of hay. I began starring in pictures at Republic at seventy-five dollars a week, doing six to eight pictures a year. When they decided they were going to star me in pictures, Mr. Yates took all of my contract options and cut them down by anywhere from twenty-five to fifty dollars a week. I worked there for six months for seventy-five dollars a week. Then I was supposed to go to one hundred and twenty-five dollars, but he had that cut to a hundred. The next jump was to be to one hundred and fifty dollars, which he cut to one hundred and twenty-five. It went on that way for the whole seven years of the contract.

By the time I had been there five years, I was still only making about three or four hundred dollars a week [though Roy was the second highest cowboy box-office star]. It was especially rough my first two or three years. My first picture had been voted the best picture of the series Westerns for the year. I had gone to third place in the box-office listings after the first picture, but I couldn't afford to pay to answer my fan mail on the seventy-five dollars a week I was making. One time I had four girls doing nothing but answering fan mail. I felt it was important that it be answered. If a kid thought enough of me to write a letter, it should be answered. I went to the old man several times and tried to get him to pay for answering the fan mail, but he wouldn't. A lot of the other studios answered their stars' fan mail, but he wouldn't touch it.

One time I loaded a five-ton dump truck full of fan letters I'd already answered and took them over to Republic. I backed the truck onto the lawn of the studio and dumped the whole thing. Mr. Yates came out waving his arms and yelling, "What do you think you're doing?" I said, "Here's some of those letters the people you called morons wrote to me. They've already been answered, but I

thought maybe you'd like to read some of them." And I just drove off.

So I had to go out and do one-night stands to supplement my film salary. I carried three musicians with me. I mean we really worked! We'd play those little theaters where if you got one hundred and fifty bucks for eight shows in one day you were doing well. Then we'd drive all night to the next town. One time we made appearances at one hundred and thirty-eight different places in twenty days.

By 1943 I was starting to get pretty good money for the personal appearances. I played Madison Square Garden in 1943. While I was in New York, I got acquainted with some people who were interested in some commercial tie-ups such as cap guns, T shirts, sweatshirts, and stuff like that. I told them I couldn't do it unless I got an okay from Mr. Yates. So I went to him and said, "Mr. Yates, I just can't make it on the amount of money I'm getting from you, and I'm killing myself doing one-night stands. I've got a chance to do some commercial tie-ups, but I have to have a release from you to do it." He said, "I'll be glad to give it to you because you're not going to get a raise." That's the way he talked.

So my lawyer drew up a contract specifying that I had the commercial rights to my name, voice, and likeness. And the old man signed it. I'm the only one that had those rights in my contract. He gave me that instead of giving me a raise. At one time we had around four hundred articles with my name on them and we were doing terrifically with them. We were second only to Walt Disney in commercial tie-ups.

DAVID ROTHEL: Did you ever want to do any other type of pictures?

ROY ROGERS: No, I didn't, because I had established myself as a cowboy and I wanted to keep my pictures clean for the kids. We were playing to the youth of America. One time, though, Mr. Yates came to me with a script he wanted me to do. I read it and found that I was to play the part of a smart-alecky Pulitzer Prize writer who drank and smoked—everything the opposite of what I stood for as a cowboy. I took it back and said, "Mr. Yates, I can't do this." "You have to," he said. "You're under contract." I said, "I'm sorry, but I just won't do it." So I went home and I was off the lot for about two weeks. Finally, I got a call from him, and he said he had gotten somebody else to play the part.

Another time we had a similar run-in. He wanted me to do something that I didn't feel I could do. So he said, "Okay, we'll just take you off Trigger

Roy Rogers and Dale Evans as they appear today. *Photos courtesy of Roy Rogers.*

and put somebody else on him. We'll get another cowboy." I said, "I'm sorry, Mr. Yates, but Trigger belongs to me." I'd bought him from Hudkins and Mr. Yates didn't know it.

It isn't that I don't appreciate what the studio did for me. But these are some of the things I struggled through that never got into print. The publicity was paid by the studio, of course, and they wouldn't put in any of these heartache things—the other side of the fence, you know.

DAVID ROTHEL: You made the most lavishly produced musical Westerns of all the singing cowboys during the mid to late forties. They were unique to you since Gene Autry, who came closest to your type of picture, never really featured production numbers such as you had. How did this type of musical Western happen to come about?

ROY ROGERS: I think the reason Mr. Yates went all out on the musical Westerns was the success of *Oklahoma* on Broadway. It impressed him very much. For the next several years I remade *Oklahoma* as a movie—only generally in different states. There was *Idaho, Song of Texas, Song of Nevada, Rainbow Over Texas,* and *Song of Arizona,* to name just a few. We did a picture about almost every Western state. And we always tried to get a Spanish line or two in the songs because our

pictures were big in Mexico. Duncan Renaldo would always help me with my Spanish lyrics or any Spanish words I had to say in the script.

DAVID ROTHEL: One of the main criticisms of musical Westerns over the years has been the sometimes awkward integration of the music into the pictures. Were you ever concerned about this?

ROY ROGERS: I used to argue to change a script to have a reason for a song—some kind of celebration or something—not to just pull a guitar off a cactus bush and start singing. We'd always try to figure out a situation where there was going to be a party or barbecue or something like that, and that's when the singing would take place. It didn't stop the action that way. If you just put a song right in the middle of the action, the audience would laugh at you. So I always watched that.

I also watched my shooting scenes to try to get a place where I was reloading the gun once in a while. The old saying is that the reason they called the gun a .45 was that it would shoot forty-five times without reloading. Actually, the kids would count the shots. You don't have a more critical audience than children.

DAVID ROTHEL: Which are your favorite pictures from your Republic series?

ROY ROGERS: I liked to keep as many animals

in my pictures as I could because I always felt that children liked the animals—especially dogs and horses. Therefore, I especially liked *The Golden Stallion, My Pal Trigger,* and *Trigger, Jr.* Of course, I think I got a bigger thrill out of making my first picture, *Under Western Stars,* because it *was* my first one and everything was new. I was scared to death, but I still enjoyed making it.

DAVID ROTHEL: Have you seen any of your Republic pictures in recent years?

ROY ROGERS: It's funny you should ask that. With our big family it's hard to get them all together for the holidays—they're scattered all over. So about a week before Christmas we generally have the kids come to our place for a day or so and bring their children to celebrate the holiday with us. Then they can go back and have regular Christmas at their own homes. This last Christmas I ran one of my old pictures, *Under Nevada Skies,* for everybody, and they just loved it. And, you know, it's a good picture. I'm not saying that because it was mine, but it had action—good fights and chases, a slight hint of romance with Dale, good songs—The Sons of the Pioneers were in it, and Trigger. I really got a kick out of it.

DAVID ROTHEL: Could you lose yourself in the picture as you watched it, or were you constantly remembering the things that were going on at the time you shot the picture?

ROY ROGERS: It was almost like reading a new book. It had been so long since I had seen it that I'd forgotten scenes I did, forgotten what Dale and I looked like thirty-five years ago. In fact, I'm going to run it again some night for just Dale and me to see if it's really as good as I thought it was.

We wrapped it up suddenly a little after five o'clock when Roy remembered, "I'm bowling tonight. I've got to get home and get a bite to eat." He invited me to join him at the Victorbowl later, which I did. Between his bowling turns we continued our conversation—only this time I did more of the talking, answering his questions about my home and family. During the evening Roy wasn't bothered by talkative fans (except me) or autograph seekers—the folks of Victorville treat him more like a friendly neighbor than a show business personality.

The next morning Roy scrounged through file cabinets packed with photos of him, Dale, the kids, Trigger, and Bullet—looking for pictures I could use in this chapter. Then, after autographs for myself, my daughter, and a couple of friends, I was ready to head back to Los Angeles and eventually my plane home. We said our goodbyes.

There was still a morning nip in the air as I put my briefcase and camera into the rental car, got in, and started to leave the museum grounds. As the car rounded the building, I saw Roy walking where the paved parking lot met the desert, the German shorthair romping by his side. Roy's white cowboy hat was in place, a bright plaid shirt-jacket kept out the chilly desert breeze. I got a big wave as I passed, which I returned. Then Roy picked up a stick and gave it a throw. The pup, all feet and energy, took off in joyous pursuit, eager to play the game with the King of the Cowboys.

I watched them in my rear-view mirror until I turned onto the highway and they were out of sight.

ROY ROGERS ANNOTATED FILMOGRAPHY

The filmography only includes information on the films in which Roy Rogers starred or guest starred. The films preceding his first starring feature, *Under Western Stars,* in which he appeared as a member of The Sons of the Pioneers are simply listed for the record.

*   *   *

The Old Homestead (Liberty, 1935)
Slightly Static (MGM, Short Subject, 1935)
Tumbling Tumbleweeds (Republic, 1935)
Way Up Thar (Educational, Short Subject, 1935)
Gallant Defender (Columbia, 1935)
The Mysterious Avenger (Columbia, 1936)
Rhythm On the Range (Paramount, 1936)
The Big Show (Republic, 1936)
The Old Corral (Republic, 1936)
The Old Wyoming Trail (Columbia, 1937)
Wild Horse Rodeo (Republic, 1937)
The Old Barn Dance (Republic, 1938)

*   *   *

Under Western Stars (Republic, 1938) 65 M.

Producer, Sol C. Siegel; director, Joseph Kane; screenplay, Dorrell and Stuart McGowan and Betty Burbridge; camera, Jack Marta; songs, Jack Lawrence, Johnny Marvin, Eddie Cherkose, Peter Tinturin, Charles Rosoff.

CAST: Roy Rogers, Smiley Burnette, Carol Hughes, Maple City Four, Guy Usher, Tom Chatterton, Kenneth Harian, Alden Chase, Brandon Beach, Earle Dwire, Jean Fowler, Dora Clemant, Dick Elliott, Burr Caruth, Charles Whitaker, Jack Rockwell, Frankie Marvin, Trigger.

Coming out of the Republic star stable and into the center ring for the first time, Roy Rogers makes a good showing for himself.

The contemporary (1930s) Western story deals with Rogers getting elected to Congress by ranchers on a free-water platform. In Washington he shows a film displaying the dust bowl conditions in which his constituants find themselves and puts over his plan for public ownership of utilities.

As is noted elsewhere, the critics were extremely complimentary to the cowboy newcomer, and prophesied accurately a bright future in films.

*   *   *

Billy the Kid Returns (Republic, 1938) 53 M.

Producer, Charles E. Ford; director, Joseph Kane; screenplay, Jack Natteford; camera, Ernest Miller; songs, Eddie Cherkose, Smiley Burnette, Alberto Colombo, Vern (Tim) Miller.

CAST: Roy Rogers, Smiley Burnette, Lynne Roberts, Morgan Wallace, Fred Kohler, Sr., Wade Boteler, Edwin Stanley, Horace Murphy, Joseph Crehan, Robert Emmett Keane, Trigger.

Discounting entirely the crazy-little-killer image of history, Roy Rogers's Billy the Kid is a likable, crooning cowboy who finds himself on the badge-side of the law, at least long enough to ride through this Western feature.

Seven songs are integrated nicely into the scant fifty-three minutes of the feature. "Born to the Saddle," "Trail Blazin'," "When Sun Is Setting on the Prairie," "When I Camped Under the Stars," and "Dixie Instrument Song" are among the songs sung by Rogers and his sidekick Burnette, who accounts for the novelty numbers in his role of a musical instrument drummer—the salesman type.

*   *   *

Come On, Rangers (Republic, 1938) 57 M.

Producer, Charles E. Ford; director, Joseph Kane; screenplay, Gerald Geraghty and Jack Natteford; camera, Al Wilson; musical director, Cy Feuer; editor, Edward Mann.

CAST: Roy Rogers, Mary Hart (Lynne Roberts), Raymond Hatton, J. Farrell MacDonald, Purnell Pratt, Harry Woods, Bruce MacFarlane, Lane Chandler, Chester Gunnels, Lee Powell, Trigger.

In this fairly ambitious feature the script calls for former Texas Ranger Roy Rogers to gather together members of the now disbanded Rangers to assist the U. S. Cavalry, which has been encountering rampaging outlaws in the unfamiliar expanses of the new state of Texas. Action rather than cactus crooning is stressed in this lively Western.

*   *   *

Shine On, Harvest Moon (Republic, 1938) 55M.

Director, Joseph Kane; screenplay, Jack Natteford; camera, William Nobles; editor, Lester Orlebeck.

CAST: Roy Rogers, Mary Hart, Lulubelle and Scotty, Stanley Andrews, William Farnum, Frank Jacquet, Chester Gunnels, Matty Roubert, Pat Henning, Jack Rockwell, Joe Whitehead, Trigger.

The weakest of the Roy Rogers starrers to this time, *Shine On, Harvest Moon* never seems to get off the ground. The title has nothing to do with the story and only serves to inform ticket buyers of the featured song in the proceedings.

The plot concerns a former range partnership between William Farnum and Stanley Andrews that turns into a range war when Andrews takes up cattle rustling. Rogers plays the son of good rancher Andrews; femme lead, Mary Hart, is cast as Farnum's daughter. National Barn Dance performers, Lulubelle and Scotty, of radio station

Photo courtesy of NTA.

WLS in Chicago are brought in to supply comic relief.

*   *   *

Rough Riders' Roundup (Republic, 1939) 55 M.

Director, Joseph Kane; screenplay, Jack Natteford; camera, Jack Marta; editor, Lester Orlebeck; musical director, Cy Feuer.

CAST: Roy Rogers, Mary Hart, Raymond Hatton, Eddie Acuff, William Pawley, Dorothy Sebastian, George Meeker, Jack Rockwell, Guy Usher, George Chesebro, Glenn Strange, Duncan Renaldo, Trigger.

This action-packed episode takes place immediately after the Spanish-American War. Rogers and other former Rough Riders join up with the border patrol to round up outlaw George Meeker and his gang, who are robbing gold from stages and express offices.

*   *   *

Frontier Pony Express (Republic, 1939) 58 M.

Producer and director, Joseph Kane; screenplay, Norman Hall; camera, William Nobles; editor, Gene Milford; musical director, Cy Feuer.

CAST: Roy Rogers, Mary Hart, Raymond Hatton, Edward Keane, Noble Johnson, Monte Blue, Donald Dillaway, William Royals, Ethel Wales, Bud Osborne, Trigger.

Western-with-songs is a more accurate designation than musical Western for this feature. Only Civil War standards are utilized and they are worked into the plot as naturally as is possible under the circumstances.

Rogers plays a California-to-the-frontier pony express rider who becomes embroiled with Miss Hart's confederate spy brother, Donald Dillaway, and Edward Keane, a Southern politician. The plot thickens as Yankee and Rebel forces vie for the

ROY ROGERS CARRIES THE MAIL

Danger lurks at every crossroad as the heroes of the old west ride to new rangeland adventures with the U. S. Mail.

ROY ROGERS
KING OF THE COWBOYS

Frontier Pony Express

A RE-UELEASE

RAYMOND HATTON

Republic

Photo courtesy of NTA.

allegiance of California. Keane, as it turns out, is actually a traitor who is after the new territory for his own profit.

* * *

Southward Ho (Republic, 1939) 58 M.

Producer and director, Joseph Kane; screenplay, Gerald Geraghty; original story, John Rathmell and Jack Natteford; camera, Jack Marta; editor, Lester Orlebeck; musical director, Cy Feuer.

CAST: Roy Rogers, Mary Hart, George Hayes,

Wade Boteler, Arthur Loft, Lane Chandler, Tom London, Charles Moore, Edwin Brady, Trigger.

Again Roy finds himself in a feature episode set in the Civil War period. His new sidekick is George "Gabby" Hayes, rustled by Republic from William Boyd's Hopalong Cassidy series.

Roy and Gabby, fresh out of the Confederate Army, travel to Texas to assume half-ownership of a large ranch that has been willed to Gabby. They are dismayed to discover that the other half of the ranch belongs to an ex-Union officer with whom they had a run-in during the war. Soon the federal government places the area under martial law and names the former Union officer colonel of the cavalry troop assigned to enforce the law and to collect back taxes. It is soon discovered that the cavalry troop captain and his men are the outlaws who have been pillaging and terrorizing the area. Rogers, the colonel, and the local ranchers join forces to rout the evildoers.

Throughout the story a few cactus carols are sung, but they never get in the way of the fisticuffs and shoot-outs.

* * *

In Old Caliente (Republic, 1939) 55 M.

Director, Joseph Kane; screenplay, Norman Houston and Gerald Geraghty; camera, William Nobles; editor, Edward Mann.

CAST: Roy Rogers, Mary Hart, George Hayes, Jack LaRue, Katherine DeMille, Frank Puglia, Harry Woods, Paul Marian, Ethel Wales, Merrill McCormick, Trigger.

The coming of the Americans to California in hopes of peaceful settlement in the land of the Dons serves as the plot line to carry Roy Rogers through this adventure.

Half-breed Jack LaRue tries to pin a robbery on the newcomers, but Rogers, in the employ of the Don but sympathetic to the plight of the wrongly accused pioneers, suspects foul play. After the appropriate mixture of hard riding, smashing fists, and smoking guns, the immigrating gringos are cleared of blame.

* * *

Wall Street Cowboy (Republic, 1939) 66 M.

Producer and director, Joseph Kane; screenplay, Gerald Geraghty and Norman Hall; original story, Doris Schroeder; camera, Jack Marta; editor, Lester Orlebeck; musical director, Cy Feuer.

CAST: Roy Rogers, George Hayes, Raymond Hatton, Ann Baldwin, Pierre Watkin, Louisiana Lou, Craig Reynolds, Ivan Miller, Reginald Barlow, Adrian Morris, Jack Roper, Jack Ingram, Trigger.

Thanks to the singing of Roy Rogers and the combined comic support of Gabby Hayes and Raymond Hatton, this sagebrush-on-Wall Street episode is passable but not up to the Rogers standards.

It seems that a Wall Street syndicate learns that Rogers's ranch is rich in molybdenum, a metallic element used in the mining of steel, and attempts to bring about a foreclosure on the ranch when Rogers has problems meeting the mortgage payment.

Again the writers have attempted a variation on the stereotype program Western situation. Unfortunately, this time they have come up with a losing hand. Lacking in rootin'-tootin' action, the result is largely ho-hum.

* * *

The Arizona Kid (Republic, 1939) 61 M.

Producer and director, Joseph Kane; screenplay, Luci Ward and Gerald Geraghty; original story, Luci Ward; camera, William Nobles; editor, Lester Orlebeck; musical director, Cy Feuer.

CAST: Roy Rogers, George Hayes, Sally March, Stuart Hamblen, Dorothy Sebastian, Earl Dwire, David Kerwin, Peter Fargo, Fred Burns, Trigger.

The Civil War again serves as the focus for this Rogers adventure. Roy finds himself a Confederate captain in this story built around Missouri's pledge of allegiance to the North and the resultant defection of certain factions that formed outlaw gangs in the pretense of supporting the Confederacy. At one point Captain Rogers is forced to order his friend David Kerwin shot for his involvement in the marauding led by Stuart Hamblen.

Traditional songs of the plains are worked as logically as possible into the tight script.

(Stuart Hamblen, the villain, was to later make his mark in the country music field. Briefly in

Photo courtesy of NTA.

1952, he threw his Stetson into the political ring when he ran for president on the Prohibition ticket.)

*　　*　　*

Jeepers Creepers (Republic, 1939) 69 M.

Producer, Armand Schaefer; director, Frank McDonald; screenplay, Dorrell and Stuart Mc-Gowan; camera, Ernest Miller; editor, Ernest Nims; musical director, Cy Feuer.

CAST: Leon Weaver, Frank Weaver, Elviry, Roy Rogers, Maris Wrixon, Billy Lee, Lucien Littlefield, Thurston Hall, Loretta Weaver, John Arthur.

This little epic is just one big cornfield into which Roy Rogers was contractually led by Republic. It's a Weaver Brothers starrer all the way. Roy's involvement is definitely secondary. He plays the town sheriff and leather lothario (*Variety's* words) of Maris Wrixon (whose name sounds and looks like an anagram). Roy's best scene in the picture is the one in which he sings the title tune, a popular song of a year or so earlier, to Miss Wrixon.

Typical of the Weaver Brothers series turned out by Republic during the thirties and forties, the story concerns the discovery of coal on the Weaver family land by unscrupulous capitalist Thurston Hall. The discovery occurs when Hall is sentenced by justice of the peace Leon Weaver to use a pick for a day because he has been careless with matches out in the parched landscape. Hall acquires the ore-loaded land by paying the back taxes and then moves in a crew to get the coal. Their carelessness results in a forest fire in which villain Hall almost dies but instead has a spark of human kindness kindled.

*　　*　　*

Saga of Death Valley (Republic, 1939) 55 M.

Producer and director, Joseph Kane; screenplay, Karen DeWolf; camera, Jack Marta; editor, Lester Orlebeck.

CAST: Roy Rogers, George Hayes, Donald Barry, Doris Day, Frank M. Thomas, Hal Taliaferro, Jack Ingram, Tommy Baker, Buz Buckley, Trigger.

This Rogers feature is only average for the series. The plot concerns the cutting off of a water supply to area ranchers by an unscrupulous gang that seeks to extort the ranchers.

Donald Barry (who was just starting a film

career that continues even today) plays Rogers's long-lost, kidnapped brother whose identity is revealed just prior to his being done in by the villains.

Roy's leading lady in the film is (according to one critic) a "pop-eyed ingenue who shows nothing special." Her name is Doris Day. (No, it isn't *the* Doris Day!)

*　　*　　*

Days of Jesse James (Republic, 1939) 63 M.

Producer and director, Joseph Kane; screenplay, Earle Snell; original story, Jack Natteford; camera, Reggie Lanning; musical director, Cy Feuer.

CAST: Roy Rogers, George Hayes, Donald Barry, Pauline Moore, Harry Woods, Arthur Loft, Wade Boteler, Ethel Wales, Scotty Beckett, Michael Worth, Glenn Strange, Olin Howland, Monte Blue, Jack Rockwell, Fred Burns, Trigger.

In this sagebrush sizzler the James Boys, for once, don't do it—rob the bank, that is. The deed is done by the bank officials, and guess who figures it out? You got it, Roy Rogers. In just over an hour of gun-slinging, robber-wrangling, and tune-crooning, Rogers triumphs in this pleasing series entry.

*　　*　　*

Young Buffalo Bill (Republic, 1940) 59 M.

Producer and director, Joseph Kane; screenplay, Harrison Jacobs, Robert Yost, Gerald Geraghty; original story, Norman Houston; camera, William Nobles; editor, Tony Martinelli; musical director, Cy Feuer.

CAST: Roy Rogers, George Hayes, Pauline Moore, Hugh Sothern, Chief Thundercloud, Julian Rivero, Trevor Bardette, Gaylord Pendleton, Wade Boteler, Anna Demetria, Estelita Zarco, Trigger.

In this, as in so many other early films in the Rogers career, the emphasis is on fast action with a slighting of the music. Only one cowboy ballad, "Blow, Breeze, Blow," is provided for the diversion of those who expect to hear Buffalo Bill (Roy) sing.

The yarn is fairly typical of the genre, but neatly done. Events include a fight over mining lands in New Mexico, Indians besieging a Spanish ranch, and a U. S. Cavalry detachment riding to the rescue.

*　　*　　*

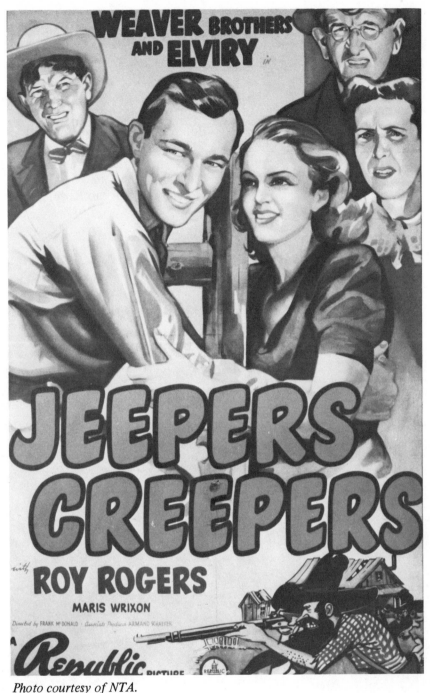

Photo courtesy of NTA.

The Dark Command (Republic, 1940) 91 M.

Producer, Sol C. Seigel; director, Raoul Walsh; screenplay, Grover Jones, Lionel Houser and F. Hugh Herbert based on novel by W. R. Burnett; camera, Jack Marta; editor, William Morgan; assistant director, Kenneth Holmes.

CAST: Claire Trevor, John Wayne, Walter Pidgeon, Roy Rogers, George Hayes, Porter Hall, Marjorie Main, Raymond Walburn, Joseph Sawyer, Helen MacKellar, J. Farrell MacDonald, Trevor Bardette.

In 1939 John Wayne, who had been performing in Republic B Westerns for years, surprised Hollywood veterans by turning in a first-rate acting performance in John Ford's memorable *Stagecoach.* In the heady excitement of this unexpected glory for contractee Wayne, Republic decided to invest heavily ($700,000) in its own super-Western. The result was *The Dark Command,* and the investment proved both financially and artistically rewarding for the studio. The film was not a Roy Rogers starrer. His role was that of the impressionable, impulsive brother of Claire Trevor, the daughter of town banker Porter Hall.

The story takes place in Lawrence, Kansas, during the Civil War and recounts the efforts of the townspeople, already torn by the North-South conflict, to forget their differences and to join with the new town marshal in fighting the common enemy—a guerrilla band led by William Contrell (Walter Pidgeon in a change-of-pace role).

* * *

The Carson City Kid (Republic, 1940) 66 M.

Director, Joseph Kane; screenplay, Robert Yost and Gerald Geraghty; original story, Joseph Kane; camera, William Nobles; editor, Helen Turner; songs, Peter Tinturin.

CAST: Roy Rogers, George Hayes, Bob Steele, Noah Beery, Jr., Pauline Moore, Francis MacDonald, Hal Taliaferro, Arthur Loft, George Rosener, Chester Gan, Trigger.

The Carson City Kid presents Roy Rogers with an opportunity to play a vengeance-seeking gunslinger out to get the man who killed his brother. Bob Steele, who until a short time before this was firmly mounted as a star of similar saddle sagas, plays the owner of a gambling hall and no-good who has killed Rogers's brother. This is just an average entry in the Rogers series.

* * *

The Ranger and the Lady (Republic, 1940) 59 M.

Producer and director, Joseph Kane; screenplay, Stuart Anthony and Gerald Geraghty; original story, Bernard McConville; camera, Reggie Lan-

Roy Rogers, Claire Trevor, Walter Pidgeon, and John Wayne in a scene from *The Dark Command. Photo courtesy of NTA.*

Marjorie Main (right) created a moving character study as the mother of Walter Pidgeon, the guerrilla leader in *The Dark Command*. *Photo courtesy of NTA.*

ning; editor, Lester Orlebeck; songs, Peter Tinturin; musical director, Cy Feuer.

CAST: Roy Rogers, George Hayes, Jacqueline Wells, Harry Wends, Henry Brandon, Noble Johnson, Si Jenks, Ted Mapes, Yakima Canutt, Trigger.

Rogers is the Texas Ranger and Jacqueline Wells is the lady owner of a wagon train of trading goods traveling the old Santa Fe Trail. While Sam Houston is off in Washington trying to get the Texas territory admitted to the United States, his assistant is back home trying to acquire power and impose new taxes—namely a passage tax on anyone using the Sante Fe Trail. This tide of events brings the Ranger and the lady together in an attempt to see that justice and fair play prevail—and they eventually do.

During all the action Rogers is hard pressed to get even two songs sung, with "As Long as We Are Dancing" the favored.

*   *   *

Colorado (Republic, 1940) 57 M.

Producer and director, Joseph Kane; screenplay, Louis Stevens and Harrison Jacobs; camera, Jack Marta; editor, Edward Mann; songs, Peter Tinturin; musical director, Cy Feuer.

CAST: Roy Rogers, George Hayes, Pauline Moore, Milburn Stone, Maude Eburne, Arthur Loft, Hal Taliaferro, Vester Pegg, Fred Burns, Lloyd Ingraham, Trigger.

The much-repeated plot line of brothers on opposing sides in a conflict is offered again in *Colorado*. Rogers has the task of bringing in his treasonous brother who forsook the Unionist cause during the Civil War.

Again, the emphasis is on action with the saddle songs serving only as an infrequent interlude to the other goings on.

*   *   *

Young Bill Hickok (Republic, 1940) 59 M.

Producer and director, Joseph Kane; screenplay, Norton S. Parker and Olive Cooper; camera, William Nobles; editor, Lester Orlebeck; musical director, Cy Feuer.

CAST: Roy Rogers, George Hayes, Jacqueline Wells, John Miljan, Sally Payne, Archie Twitchell, Monte Blue, Hal Taliaferro, Ethel Wales, Jack Ingram, Monte Montague, Trigger.

This yarn is fiction all the way with Rogers as the youthful Hickok during and just after the Civil War. The fanciful plot involves a foreign agent who is attempting to gain control of Western territory with the assistance of his guerrilla band. Even Calamity Jane (Sally Payne) gets involved in the fracas before it's all over.

Roy Rogers in *The Ranger and the Lady*. *Photo courtesy of NTA.*

151

Photo courtesy of NTA.

Gabby, Pauline Moore, Roy, and Fred Burns in *Colorado*.
Photo courtesy of NTA.

Roy, Joseph Sawyer (holding cards up). and Jay Novello
(with guitar). *Photo courtesy of NTA.*

The real Hickok just might look askance at the cowboy ballads he's represented as having rendered.

* * *

The Border Legion (Republic, 1940) 58 M.

Producer and director, Joseph Kane; screenplay, Olive Cooper and Louis Stevens based on a novel by Zane Grey; camera, Jack Marta; editor, Edward Mann; musical director, Cy Feuer.

CAST: Roy Rogers, George Hayes, Carol Hughes, Joseph Sawyer, Maude Eburne, Jay Novello, Hal Taliaferro, Dick Wessel, Paul Porcasi, Robert Emmett Keane, Trigger.

Unfortunately, this Rogers Western unreels at a gait considerably slower than Trigger's gallop. Roy plays an Eastern doctor on the run from the law because of a mix-up back in his home state of New York. He quickly learns his way around in the wide open spaces (including how to handle a gun, his fists, and an occasional Western ballad) and helps his new-found friends rout the Idaho territory of some pillaging outlaws who have been making a nuisance of themselves.

* * *

Robin Hood of the Pecos (Republic, 1941) 59 M.

Producer and director, Joseph Kane; screenplay,

A wounded but ever-alert Roy Rogers in this scene from
***Robin Hood of the Pecos.** Photo courtesy of NTA.*

Olive Cooper; original story, Hal Long; camera, Jack Marta; editor, Charles Craft; songs, Peter Tinturin, Eddie Cherkose; musical director, Cy Feuer.

CAST: Roy Rogers, George Hayes, Marjorie Reynolds, Cy Kendall, Leigh Whipper, Sally Payne, Eddie Acuff, Robert Strange, William Haade, Jay Novello, Roscoe Ates, Trigger.

In this one we're back in the post-Civil War days again, fighting unscrupulous Northerners who have come down to Texas to plunder the localites. Gabby Hayes (in a change-of-pace role) becomes a "night rider" who organizes the citizenry to fight the interlopers. Rogers is Gabby's aide (rather than the reverse, as is usually the case) and together with the other good folks they bring justice to the Pecos.

Between shoot-outs Rogers gets a few chances to do some strummin' and croonin' to Marjorie Reynolds (Peg Riley years later on television's "Life of Riley" series).

*   *   *

Arkansas Judge (Republic, 1941) 71 M.

Producer, Armand Schaefer; director, Frank McDonald; screenplay, Dorrell and Stuart McGowan; adapted by Ian Hunter, Ring Lardner, Jr., Gertrude Purcell from Irving Stone's novel; camera, Ernest Miller; editor, Ernest Nims; musical director, Cy Feuer.

CAST: Leon Weaver, Frank Weaver, June Weaver, Roy Rogers, Spring Byington, Pauline Moore, Frank M. Thomas, Veda Ann Borg, Eily Malyon, Loretta Weaver, Minerva Urecal, Beatrice Maude, Harrison Greene, Barry Macollum, George Rosener, Monte Blue, Frank Danien, Russell Hicks, Edwin Stanley.

This is another in the Weaver family cornball series that Republic popped regularly for appreciating rustics during the late 1930s and early 1940s. In one sense the Weavers might be considered Republic's down home answer to the Hardy family adventures over at MGM.

This time around the Weavers have a script based on an Irving Stone novel and an excellent supporting cast to work with, so the results are somewhat better than usual. The script takes us to Peaceful Valley where (up to now) the locale has lived up to its tranquil billing. Suddenly life in this hillbilly haven is disrupted when fifty dollars is stolen from the Widow Smithers's cracker-barrel. Well, as you might guess, everyone in Peaceful Valley is soon in

a snit, with accusations flying hither and thither.

Soon the long finger of the law is pointing to scrubwoman Spring Byington as the guilty party. Fortunately, kindly old Judge Abner presides in Peaceful Valley and sees to it that mob rule is squelched and that justice prevails.

Roy Rogers has little to do as the young lawyer who is befriended by the judge and does it well.

*   *   *

In Old Cheyenne (Republic, 1941) 58 M.

Producer and director, Joseph Kane; screenplay, Olive Cooper; original story, John Krafft; camera, William Nobles; editor, Charles Craft; musical director, Cy Feuer.

CAST: Roy Rogers, George Hayes, Joan Woodbury, J. Ferrell MacDonald, Sally Payne, George Rosener, William Haade, Hal Taliaferro, Jack Kirk, Trigger.

As with so many of the musical Westerns of this era, the songs in this Roy Rogers celluloid rodeo could be eliminated with no erosion of the plot. So the Western music lover's loss is the action fan's gain, for there is action aplenty.

Cowboy newspaper reporter Roy Rogers goes to Cheyenne to cover the supposedly nefarious goings on of Arapahoe Brown (Gabby Hayes). The local constabulary is after the wrong man, of course, so Rogers, with the help of Cheyenne's crusading newspaper editor, J. Farrell MacDonald, rounds up the bad guy (George Rosener) and gets his story— all in less than an hour of fast drawing, riding, crooning, and fisticuffing.

*   *   *

Sheriff of Tombstone (Republic, 1941) 54 M.

Producer and director, Joseph Kane; screenplay, Olive Cooper; original story by James Webb; camera, William Nobles; editor, Tony Martinelli; songs, Jules Styne, Sol Meyer, Peter Tinturin, Bob Nolan.

CAST: Roy Rogers, George Hayes, Elyse Knox, Addison Richards, Sally Payne, Harry Woods, Zeffie Tilbury, Hal Taliaferro, Jay Novello, Jack Ingram, Trigger.

Much of the playing time of this musical Western is taken up utilizing the old mistaken identity device. It seems that when Roy and Gabby arrive in Tombstone, Roy is mistaken for Shotgun Cassidy (no relation to Hoppy), a gunslinger that the double-dealing mayor has sent for to supposed-

Photo courtesy of NTA.

ly clean up the town, but who is in reality in the mayor's hire to further his plan for town domination.

Roy becomes sheriff and begins to gather evidence against the mayor when—you guessed it—who should ride into town but the real Shotgun Cassidy. But never fear, Roy manages to straighten out the complicated plot details, put the owlhoots behind bars, and sing two of the four songs allotted to the film.

Rogers sings "Ridin' On a Rocky Road" (Styne and Meyer) and "Sky Bald Paint" (Nolan). Elyse Knox, who plays a saloon singer, trills "You Should Have Seen Pete" (Styne and Meyer) and "Don't Gamble with Romance" (Tinturin).

*   *   *

Nevada City (Republic, 1941) 56 M.

Director, Joseph Kane; screenplay, James Webb; camera, William Nobles; editor, Lester Orlebeck; musical director, Cy Feuer.

CAST: Roy Rogers, George Hayes, Sally Payne, George Cleveland, Billy Lee, Joseph Crehan, Fred Kohler, Jr., Jack Ingram, Pierre Watkin, Trigger.

In this one Roy and Gabby attempt to mediate a battle between stage line owner Joseph Crehan and railroader George Cleveland, and at the same time capture the real villains who are encouraging the conflict by means of sabotage. Ultimately Roy and Gabby are successful at both tasks, but not before a slew of gun battles and a climatic ride on a dynamite-loaded train. Not much stress is placed on the music-making in this outing.

*   *   *

Bad Man of Deadwood (Republic, 1941) 61 M.

Producer and director, Joseph Kane; screenplay, James R. Webb; camera, William Nobles; editor, Charles Craft; musical director, Cy Feuer.

CAST: Roy Rogers, George Hayes, Carol Adams, Henry Brandon, Herbert Rawlinson, Sally Payne,

156

Hal Taliaferro, Jay Novello, Horace Murphy, Monte Blue, Raif Harolde, Jack Kirk, Trigger.

In this entry in the Rogers series a group of unscrupulous businessmen in Deadwood attempt to stifle competition by running out all newcomers before they can successfully establish their businesses. Rogers, playing a good badman unjustly forced to go on the lam from the law, takes up with medicine show operator Gabby Hayes and together they help the good men reestablish free enterprise in Deadwood.

Something less than the most impressive tumbleweed saga, it nevertheless has a pleasing cast of mostly familiar faces and some pleasant tenoring of country standards by our cowboy hero.

*   *   *

Jesse James at Bay (Republic, 1941) 56 M.

Producer and director, Joseph Kane; screenplay, James R. Webb; original story, Harrison Jacobs; camera, William Nobles; editor, Tony Martinelli.

CAST: Roy Rogers, George Hayes, Sally Payne, Pierre Watkin, Ivan Miller, Hal Taliaferro, Gale Storm, Roy Barcroft, Jack Kirk, Trigger.

Jesse James (Roy) shows his Robin Hood side in this film as he joins with Missouri settlers in their battle with a land-grabbing railroad outfit. He commits a series of train holdups and gives the loot to the oppressed so that they can better fight the rich railway magnates.

*   *   *

Red River Valley (Republic, 1941) 62 M.

Director, Joseph Kane; screenplay, Malcolm Stuart Boylan; camera, Jack Martin; editor, William Thompson; musical director, Cy Feuer.

CAST: Roy Rogers, George Hayes, Sally Payne, Trevor Bardette, Gale Storm, Robert Homans, Hal Taliaferro, Lynton Brent, The Sons of the Pioneers, Trigger.

The title *Red River Valley* caused some concern and confusion (mostly from movie exhibitors) because back in 1936 Republic had released a Gene Autry film with the same title. Fans were not confused, though, and were inclined to go see any film that promised to feature the popular Western song of the title.

The plot of this sagebrusher gets Rogers involved with water problems way out West. He helps the ranchers raise one hundred and eighty-two thousand dollars toward the construction of a government-subsidized reservoir only to have it snatched up by a gambler and his cohorts as they rig a stock deal while pretending to be assisting the cattlemen. After the regulation number of pistol and fist hassles, Rogers saves the leading lady, the reservoir, and the day.

The main distinction of this release is that it once more unites Roy Rogers with the singing group he helped to organize back in the years prior to his film career—The Sons of the Pioneers.

*   *   *

Man from Cheyenne (Republic, 1942) 60 M.

Producer and director, Joseph Kane; screenplay, Winston Miller; camera, Reggie Lanning; editor, William Thompson.

CAST: Roy Rogers, George Hayes, Sally Payne, Lynn Carver, William Haade, James Seay, Gale Storm, Jack Ingram, The Sons of the Pioneers, Trigger.

Man from Cheyenne is a slam-bang musical Western with some fairly novel twists. For example, Rogers kisses not one, but two girls in the film and the heavy is a female. The subject for the film is modern-style cattle rustling in Wyoming by undercover gal Lynn Carver, who wants to get enough loot to go back East and live in style with her rich society friends. By batting her beautiful eyes at the unsuspecting ranchers, she is able to gain information and plan rustling strategy for her

Gabby, Gale Storm, and Roy in a scene from *Red River Valley*. *Photo courtesy of NTA.*

gang. Rogers, a government agent, is sent in to help the ranchers. The roundup finds the other film femmes taking charge of the capture of the villainess in a hair-pulling tug of war that is straight out of *Destry Rides Again*.

* * *

South of Santa Fe (Republic, 1942) 60 M.

Director, Joseph Kane; screenplay, James E. Webb; camera, Harry Newman; editor, William Thompson.

CAST: Roy Rogers, George Hayes, Linda Hayes, Paul Fix, Judy Clark, Bobby Beers, Arthur Loft, Charles Miller, Sam Flint, Jack Kirk, The Sons of the Pioneers, Trigger.

Quite a departure from Rogers's historical Westerns of the late 1930s, *South of Santa Fe* contains Tommy guns, an airplane, high-powered cars, two-way radios, and big-city mobsters in a tale of kidnapping and undeveloped gold mines in modern New Mexico.

Considerable emphasis is placed on the musical content of this opus, with Rogers and The Sons of the Pioneers vocalizing such country ballads as "We're Headin' for the Home Corral," "Down the Trail," and "Open Range Ahead."

* * *

Sunset on the Desert (Republic, 1942) 63 M.

Producer and director, Joseph Kane; screenplay, Gerald Geraghty; camera, Reggie Lanning; editor, Lester Orlebeck; musical director, Cy Feuer.

CAST: Roy Rogers, George Hayes, Lynne Carver, Frank M. Thomas, Beryl Wallace, Glenn Strange, Douglas Fowley, Fred Burns, Roy Barcroft, Henry Wills, Forrest Taylor, The Sons of the Pioneers, Trigger.

Photo courtesy of NTA.

Roy takes dead aim in this scene from *Sunset on the Desert. Photo courtesy of NTA.*

The mistaken identity ruse is given another go-around in this just average entry in the Rogers series. Rogers is his usual good-guy self, but bears a striking resemblance to an owlhoot that is expected to arrive in town any minute to heighten the nefarious activities of an outlaw gang.

When Rogers arrives, he is mistaken for the bad guy and joins the gang undercover to get the goods on them. Just as he is about to spring the trap on the gang, the real bad guy shows up to complicate the resolution for our look-alike hero.

The few songs are pleasantly done but are unmemorable. The film title, as usual, bears only minimal relationship to the goings-on.

*   *   *

Romance on the Range (Republic, 1942) 63 M.

Producer and director, Joseph Kane; screenplay, J. Benton Cheney; camera, William Nobles; editor, Lester Orlebeck; songs, Tim Spencer, Glen Spencer, Sam Allen, Bob Nolan.

CAST: Roy Rogers, George Hayes, Sally Payne, Linda Hayes, Edward Pawley, Harry L. Woods, Hal Taliaferro, Glenn Strange, Roy Barcroft, The Sons of the Pioneers, Trigger.

Trappers, trading posts, and fur thieving provide a change of atmosphere for this entry in the series. Five songs are performed by Rogers and The Sons of the Pioneers without allowing the action to fall into a slumber. The songs are: "Coyote Serenade," "When Romance Rides the Range," "Sing as You Work," "O, Wonderful World," and "Rocky Mountain Lullaby."

*   *   *

Sons of the Pioneers (Republic, 1942) 55 M.

Producer and director, Joseph Kane; screenplay, M. Coates Webster, Mauri Grashin, Robert T. Shannon; original story, Mauri Grashin and Robert T. Shannon; camera, Bud Thackery; editor, Edward

From left to right: Bob Nolan, Gabby Hayes, Roy, Lynne
Carver, Frank M. Thomas, Fred Burns. *Photo courtesy of
NTA.*

The Sons of the Pioneers. From left to right: Bob Nolan,
Lloyd Perryman, Tim Spencer, Carl Farr, Pat Brady, Hugh
Farr.

Roy stalks the villains in this scene from *Sons of the Pioneers. Photo courtesy of NTA.*

Entomologist Rogers prefers studying bugs to fighting night raiders in this scene from *Sons of the Pioneers*. *Photo courtesy of NTA.*

Schroeder; songs, Bob Nolan, Tim Spencer; musical director, Cy Feuer.

CAST: Roy Rogers, George Hayes, Bob Nolan and The Sons of the Pioneers, Maris Wrixon, Forrest Taylor, Minerva Urecal, Bradley Page, Hal Taliaferro, Chester Conklin, Fred Burns, Trigger.

Well, you see, there are these night raiders who just get the biggest kick out of burning barns and poisoning cattle, and doing other dastardly deeds. The townspeople tell Sheriff Gabby that he's got to do something about it or they're going to get themselves a new lawman.

In desperation Gabby goes back East to get help from Roy Rogers, the descendent of two famous wild West sheriffs—his father and grandfather. Roy, an entomologist, would rather study bugs than chase night raiders but finally agrees to help Gabby. Using the old Zorro bit of pretending to be a simp, Roy throws the villains off guard long enough to get the evidence he needs to put them behind bars.

*   *   *

Sunset Serenade (Republic, 1942) 58 M.

Director, Joseph Kane; screenplay, Earl Felton; original story, Robert Yost; camera, Bud Thackery; editor, Arthur Roberts; songs, Tim Spencer and Bob Nolan.

CAST: Roy Rogers, George Hayes, Bob Nolan and The Sons of the Pioneers, Helen Parrish, Onslow Stevens, Joan Woodbury, Frank M. Thomas, Roy Barcroft, Jack Kirk, Trigger.

A top-flight action entry in the series, *Sunset Serenade* has a script that utilizes most of the cactus clichés available to Western scenarists, but never offensively so.

The plot concerns the attempts of bad guy Onslow Stevens to bilk the newly arrived Eastern girl (Helen Parrish) out of her ranch. Roy intercedes for the sweet young thing, scraps with the villain and his gang, sings a few tunes with The Sons of the Pioneers, and eventually saves the ranch.

The best of the songs are "Song of the San Joaquin," "I'm a Cowboy Rockefeller," and "I'm Headin' for the Home Corral," which was also sung in *South of Santa Fe* earlier in 1942.

*   *   *

Heart of the Golden West (Republic, 1942) 65 M.

Producer and director, Joseph Kane; screenplay, Earl Felton; camera, Jack Marta; editor, Richard Van Enger.

CAST: Roy Rogers, Smiley Burnette, George Hayes, Bob Nolan and The Sons of the Pioneers, Ruth Terry, Walter Catlett, Paul Harvey, Edmund MacDonald, Leigh Whipper, William Haade, The Hall Johnson Choir, Trigger.

The upped budget is very evident in this Rogers episode as Smiley Burnette (available now that Gene Autry was in the service) joins Gabby Hayes to give Roy two sidekicks. In addition, The Hall Johnson Choir is around to perform "Carry Me Back to Old Virginny" when Roy and The Sons of the Pioneers are not crooning their tunes.

The plot revolves around the competition between a trucking company and a steamboat company for the job of hauling the ranchers' cattle to market. The truckers are the bad guys this time and lose no underhanded opportunity to ensure their success in getting the lucrative contract. Roy and his pals thwart the truckers and give the cattle, themselves, and us a ride on an old-time steamboat.

*   *   *

Ridin' Down the Canyon (Republic, 1942) 55 M.

ROY ROGERS and GEORGE "Gabby" HAYES in "SUNSET SERENADE"

A REPUBLIC PICTURE

with
BOB NOLAN and
THE SONS OF THE PIONEERS
HELEN PARRISH
ONSLOW STEVENS
JOAN WOODBURY
FRANK M. THOMAS

JOSEPH KANE *Director*
Screen play by Earl Felton

Photo courtesy of NTA.

Producer, Harry Grey; director, Joseph Kane; screenplay, Albert DeMond; original story, Robert Williams and Norman Houston; camera, Jack Marta; editor, Edward Mann; songs, Tim Spencer, Bob Nolan.

CAST: Roy Rogers, George Hayes, Bob Nolan and The Sons of the Pioneers, Dee (Buzzy) Henry, Linda Hayes, Addison Richards, Lorna Gray, Olin Howlin, James Seay, Hal Taliaferro, Forest Taylor, Roy Barcroft, Trigger.

In this one the ranchers are having a wild horse roundup because the government is in need of horses for wartime uses. Villain Addison Richards and his gang of ne'er-do-wells try to rustle the horses from the ranchers so that they can get all that money from the government for themselves. Roy stops them and still has time to join The Sons of the Pioneers for a number of songs. They include: "Sagebrush Symphony," "Who Am I?" "Blue Prairie," and "Curley Joe."

*   *   *

Idaho (Republic, 1943) 70 M.

Director, Joseph Kane; screenplay, Roy Chanslor and Olive Cooper; camera, Reggie Lanning; editor, Arthur Roberts; musical director, Morton Scott.

CAST: Roy Rogers, Smiley Burnette, Bob Nolan and The Sons of the Pioneers, Virginia Grey, Harry L. Shannon, Ona Munson, Dick Purcell, Onslow Stevens, Arthur Hohl, Hal Taliaferro, Robert Mitchell Boy Choir, Trigger.

Republic was now on the move to promote Roy Rogers into the same class of cowboy star as Gene Autry, and *Idaho* was a great stride in the right direction with its fast action, pleasant songs, appropriate comedy, and heartwarming story.

The plot concerns Judge Harry Shannon's attempt to rid the county of the gambling and drinking emporium run by villainess Ona Munson.

The judge wants the community to be a fit place for the young people in his "Boys' Town" to grow up. Rogers, a state ranger, comes to the aid of the judge, his lovely daughter, and the boys. He gets the goods on Miss Munson and her roughnecks and clears the judge.

The judge's boys are played by the Robert Mitchell Boy Choir who also take part in the music portions of the feature. Of the seven songs in the score, "Lone Buckaroo," "Holy, Holy, Holy," and the title tune are most impressive.

*   *   *

King of the Cowboys (Republic, 1943) 67 M.

Director, Joseph Kane; screenplay, Olive Cooper and J. Benton Cheney; original story by Hal Long; camera, Reggie Lanning; editor, Harry Keller.

CAST: Roy Rogers, Smiley Burnette, Bob Nolan and The Sons of the Pioneers, Peggy Moran, Gerald

Mohr, Dorothea Kent, Lloyd Corrigan, James Bush, Russell Hicks, Irving Bacon, Norman Willis, Trigger.

The title "King of the Cowboys" became official with this feature and would, of course, cling to Roy throughout his career.

Rogers is an undercover investigator/rodeo star attempting to track down and capture a band of saboteurs who go around blowing up government warehouses. Roy's investigation leads him to a mysterious traveling tent show, code words uttered during a spiritualist's performance, and a rip-snorting climax as he and his pals break up the ring.

A vastly increased budget is indicated by the classy supporting cast and production values.

*   *   *

Song of Texas (Republic, 1943) 69 M.

Producer, Harry Grey; director, Joseph Kane;

The Sons of the Pioneers, Roy, and Virginia Grey. *Photo courtesy of NTA.*

163

Smiley Burnette, Roy Rogers, and The Sons of the Pioneers. *Photo courtesy of NTA.*

screenplay, Winston Miller; camera, Reggie Lanning; editor, Tony Martinelli.

CAST: Roy Rogers, Shelia Ryan, Barton MacLane, Harry Shannon, Arline Judge, William Haade, Eve March, Hal Taliaferro, Alex Nahera Dancers, Bob Nolan and The Sons of the Pioneers, Trigger.

Another top-notch, high-budget entry for Rogers, *Song of Texas* places a heavy emphasis on the music with the only major action, a thrilling chuck wagon race, coming during the final few minutes.

The story is nothing new, but is told in an engaging manner. Sheila Ryan comes from the East to visit her father, Harry Shannon, whom she believes owns the ranch on which he is really only a hired hand. In an attempt to allow Shannon to save face, Roy and his friends at the ranch pretend Shannon is indeed the owner. The girl's involvement, however, finally results in the sale of half the ranch to villain Barton MacLane, and the next thing you know Roy has to win a chuck wagon race to keep from losing the entire ranch.

Ten songs are squeezed into the running time with "Mexicali Rose" and "Moonlight and Roses" being the most familiar. During a fiesta production sequence, the Alex Nahera Dancers strut their stuff to nice results.

* * *

Silver Spurs (Republic, 1943) 68 M.

Producer, Harry Grey; director, Joseph Kane; screenplay, John K. Butler and J. Benton Cheney; camera, Reggie Lanning; editor, Tony Martinelli; musical director, Morton Scott.

CAST: Roy Rogers, Smiley Burnette, John Carradine, Phyllis Brooks, Jerome Cowan, Joyce Compton, Dick Wessel, Hal Taliaferro, Forrest Taylor, Charles Wilson, Byron Foulger, Bob Nolan and The Sons of the Pioneers, Trigger.

Silver Spurs is another big-budget Rogers feature with an excellent supporting cast that helps make this opus one of the best in the series.

Carradine is the heavy who tries to dupe Cowan out of his ranch and the oil well on it. Ranch foreman Rogers saves his boss from making a fool of himself with drink and a mail order bride (both supplied by Carradine), and saves the ranch, oil well, and railroad right-of-way from the evil machinations of Carradine.

* * *

Man from Music Mountain (Republic, 1943) 71 M.

Producer, Harry Grey; director, Joseph Kane; screenplay, Bradford Ropes and J. Benton Chaney; camera, William Bradford; editor, Russell Kimball; musical director, Morton Scott.

CAST: Roy Rogers, Ruth Terry, Paul Kelly, Ann Gillis, George Cleveland, Pat Brady, Renie Riano, Paul Harvey, Hank Bell, Jay Novello, Hal Taliaferro, Bob Nolan and The Sons of the Pioneers, Trigger.

This is another winner in the series. Rogers maintains the high quality that he established earlier in the year when the promotional spotlight was first placed on him by Republic.

In this one Rogers plays a famous, cowboy radio singer who returns to his hometown for a radio appearance. While there he gets involved with the local cattlemen-sheepmen feud and agrees to become deputy sheriff long enough to resolve the fracas. Needless to say, bad guy Paul Kelly and his gang are soon locked up in the hoosegow, and Roy is singing yet another ballad to Ruth Terry, his leading lady.

* * *

Hands Across the Border (Republic, 1943) 72 M.

Producer, Harry Grey; director, Joseph Kane; screenplay, Bradford Ropes and J. Benton Cheney; camera, Reggie Lanning; editor, Tony Martinelli; musical director, Morton Scott; dance director, Dave Gould.

CAST: Roy Rogers, Ruth Terry, Guinn "Big Boy" Williams, Onslow Stevens, Mary Treen, Joseph Crehan, Duncan Renaldo, Frederick Burton, LeRoy Mason, Larry Steers, Julian Rivero, Janet Martin, The Wiere Brothers, Bob Nolan and The Sons of the Pioneers, Trigger.

This excellent Rogers effort has the star displaying all the attributes that make him "King" of the movie cowboys. Again there is an emphasis upon music (two production numbers are included) and plot angles that make the feature appealing to adult as well as juvenile audiences.

The plot revolves around Ruth Terry, the daughter of a murdered rancher, who takes over the job of raising a special breed of horses for the Army. Roy helps her find her father's killer (a rival horse breeder) and also is around to sing a few songs—some of them with the charming Miss Terry.

A lot of the music has a "south of the border" quality befitting the picture's title.

* * *

The Cowboy and the Senorita (Republic, 1944) 77 M.

Producer, Harry Grey; director, Joseph Kane; screenplay, Gordon Kahn; original story, Bradford Ropes; camera, Reggie Lanning; editor, Tony Martinelli; musical director, Walter Scharf; dance director, Larry Ceballos; songs, Ned Washington and Phil Ohman.

CAST: Roy Rogers, Mary Lee, Dale Evans, John Hubbard, Guinn "Big Boy" Williams, Fuzzy Knight, Dorothy Christy, Lucien Littlefield, Hal Taliaferro, Jack Kirk, Specialty Dancers: Cappella and Patricia, Jane Beebe and Ben Rochelle, Tito and Corinne Valdez; Bob Nolan and The Sons of the Pioneers, Trigger.

This is another lavish Rogers musical Western—the first with Dale Evans.

The story concerns the efforts of villain John Hubbard, gambler-overlord of the town, to seize a gold mine that is to be bequeathed to Mary Lee on her sixteenth birthday according to the instructions left in her father's will. Rogers and Williams, prospectors who are searching for ore, come to the aid of the young girl and Dale Evans, her cousin.

Songs in the score include "The Cowboy and the Senorita," "What'll I Use for Money," "The Enchilada Man," "Round Her Neck She Wore a Yellow Ribbon," and "Bunk House Bugle Boy."

* * *

The Yellow Rose of Texas (Republic, 1944) 69 M.

Director, Joseph Kane; screenplay, Jack Townley; camera, Jack Marta; editor, Tony Martinelli; musical director, Morton Scott; dance director, Larry Ceballos.

CAST: Roy Rogers, Dale Evans, Grant Withers, Harry Shannon, George Cleveland, William Haade, Weldon Heyburn, Hal Taliaferro, Tom London, Dick Botiller, Janet Martin, Brown Jug Reynolds, Bob Nolan and The Sons of the Pioneers, Trigger.

The Yellow Rose of Texas (the name of a showboat in the film) has a strong story and some lavish production numbers.

The plot has Roy an undercover insurance investigator working as a singer on the showboat owned by Dale Evans. Roy has gotten the job in

hopes of locating the unrecovered loot from a robbery committed some five years before, for which Dale's father was convicted. When the father (who was framed) breaks jail to clear his name, Roy sides with him and pretty soon they have the whole affair wrapped up in time for a couple more songs.

*   *   *

Song of Nevada (Republic, 1944) 75 M.

Director, Joseph Kane; screenplay, Gordon Kahn and Olive Cooper; camera, Jack Marta; editor, Tony Martinelli; musical director, Morton Scott; dance director, Larry Ceballos.

CAST: Roy Rogers, Dale Evans, Mary Lee, Lloyd Corrigan, Thurston Hall, John Eldredge, Forrest Taylor, George Meeker, Emmett Vogan, LeRoy Mason, William Davidson, Bob Nolan and The Sons of the Pioneers, Trigger.

Called "well-knit, fast-paced and lavishly pro-

Mary Lee and Roy Rogers in a scene from *The Cowboy and the Senorita. Photo courtesy of NTA.*

From left to right: Fuzzy Knight, Hugh Farr, Roy, Guinn "Big Boy" Williams, and Ken Carson. *Photo courtesy of NTA.*

duced" by a trade critic, *Song of Nevada* (the last Rogers film directed by Joseph Kane) contains all the expected ingredients of a Rogers musical Western.

The yarn this time has Dale playing a high-hat Eastern girl who gets her comeuppance from cowboy Rogers when she travels out West to sell her dead father's ranch. (Only he's not really dead; he's only hiding while Roy straightens out Dale, but it's far too complicated to get into.)

The eight songs in the score include "It's Love, Love, Love," "New Moon Over Nevada," "Hi Ho Little Dogies," "The Harum Scarum Baron of the Harmonium," "What Are We Going To Do?" and "A Cowboy Has To Yodel in the Morning."

* * *

San Fernando Valley (Republic, 1944) 74 M.

Producer, Edward J. White; director, John English; screenplay, Dorrell and Stuart McGowan; camera, William Bradford; editor, Ralph Dixon; songs, Gordon Jenkins, Ken Carson, Tim Spencer, Charles Henderson, William Lava, Alyce Walker.

CAST: Roy Rogers, Dale Evans, Jean Porter, Andrew Tombes, Charles Smith, Edward Gargan, Dot Farley, LeRoy Mason, Vernon and Draper, Morell Trio, Bob Nolan and The Sons of the Pioneers, Trigger.

Strong on music and lavish production values, the Rogers-Evans effort has a saddlesore plot that keeps the feature from being one of their best. Again Roy is called upon to tame the "quick-tempered but charming mistress of the ranch."

Among the musical contributions, Roy and Dale duet the title song, juvenile Jean Porter sings a double-talk novelty entitled "I Drotled a Drit Drit," and Edward Gargan (brother of William) joins Roy in the novelty "They Went That A-way."

* * *

167

Roy and director Frank McDonald. *Photo courtesy of Frank McDonald.*

Lights of Old Santa Fe (Republic, 1944) 78 M.

Producer, Harry Grey; director, Frank McDonald; screenplay, Gordon Kahn, Bob Williams; camera, Reggie Lanning; editor, Ralph Dixon; musical director, Morton Scott; dance director, Larry Ceballos.

CAST: Roy Rogers, George Hayes, Dale Evans, Lloyd Corrigan, Richard Powers, Claire DuBrey, Arthur Loft, Roy Barcroft, Lucien Littlefield, Sam Flint, Bob Nolan and The Sons of the Pioneers, Trigger.

A good oatuner in the series, *Lights of Old Santa Fe* reunites Roy and Gabby Hayes (his best sidekick) and features Dale Evans in the strong cast.

The plot has to do with rival rodeos run by villain Richard Powers and good guy Gabby Hayes. Dale Evans, as usual, has trouble early in the story telling the good guy from the bad guy, but soon after Rogers, a radio star, gets embroiled in the hassle, she begins to see the light, sings a few songs with the cowboy and his pals, and ends up "smitten" with the singing troubadour.

Frank McDonald makes his debut as a Rogers series director with this feature, although he earlier directed Roy in two Weaver family films, *Jeepers Creepers* (1939) and *Arkansas Judge* (1941).

* * *

Brazil (Republic, 1944) 91 M.

Roy makes a brief guest star appearance in the final festival sequence of *Brazil* to sing the Hoagy Carmichael, Ned Washington song, "Hands Across the Border."

* * *

Lake Placid Serenade (Republic, 1944) 85 M.

Roy makes a guest star appearance in this "A" budget Republic feature starring the boss's (Herbert J. Yates) wife (Vera Ralston). The distainful *New York Times* reviewer panned the film and had this to say about the cowboy crooner's appearance:

Roy Rogers, Republic's "King of the Cowboys," is virtually hauled in by the heels (minus his horse, Trigger, however), to sing a number ["Winter Wonderland"] and be crowned King of the Lake Placid New Year Carnival.

* * *

Hollywood Canteen (Warner Brothers, 1944) 123 M.

Roy, joined by Trigger and The Sons of the Pioneers in a guest appearance, sings "Don't Fence Me In," the popular Cole Porter song.

* * *

Utah (Republic, 1945) 78 M.

Producer, Donald H. Brown; director, John English; screenplay, Jack Townley and John K. Butler; original story, Gilbert Wright and Betty Burbridge; camera, William Bradford; musical director, Morton Scott; dance director, Larry Ceballos; songs, Charles Henderson, Dave Franklin, Bob Palmer, Glen Spencer, Tim Spencer, Bob Nolan, Ken Carson.

CAST: Roy Rogers, George Hayes, Dale Evans, Peggy Stewart, Beverly Loyd, Grant Withers, Jill Browning, Vivien Oakland, Hal Taliaferro, Jack Rutherford, Emmett Vogan, Bob Nolan and The Sons of the Pioneers, Trigger.

Featuring more singing than shooting, this Rogers epic is nonetheless a good addition to the series.

The story has Dale as an Eastern musical comedy star who needs additional loot to keep her show open in Chicago. To raise the money she heads out to Utah to sell the ranch she owns but has never seen. Rogers plays the foreman, who for practical and sentimental reasons doesn't want to see the ranch sold. Gabby is a neighbor rancher who joins with Roy to bring some sense to Dale. As you might guess, they eventually (with the help of a few cowpoke ballads) succeed in winning her over.

* * *

Bells of Rosarita (Republic, 1945) 68 M.

Producer, Edward J. White; director, Frank McDonald; screenplay, Jack Townley; camera, Ernest Miller; musical director, Morton Scott.

CAST: Roy Rogers, George Hayes, Dale Evans, Adele Mara, Grant Withers, Janet Martin, Addison Richards, Roy Barcroft, Robert Mitchell Boy Choir, Bob Nolan and The Sons of the Pioneers, Trigger. Guest Stars: Wild Bill Elliott, Allan Lane, Donald Barry, Robert Livingston, Sunset Carson.

This feature is enjoyable to a great extent *because* of the rather absurd plot situation. The story finds Roy and Bob Nolan playing themselves, Republic Western movie stars. They are filming a movie on location at a circus recently inherited by Dale after the death of her father. Evil Grant Withers, her father's former partner, is attempting to cheat her out of the inheritance. When Rogers gets wind of all this intrigue, he calls his cowboy star friends at Republic (see guest stars in cast listing above) and asks them to help him round up Withers and his thugs. The first thing you know the movie cowboys are proving that they can cut the villains off at the pass in real life as well as in "reel" life.

The songs, action, and comedy are plentiful in this "fun," if illogical, Western.

* * *

The Man from Oklahoma (Republic, 1945) 68 M.

Producer, Louis Gray; director, Frank McDonald; screenplay, John K. Butler; camera, William Bradford; musical director, Morton Scott.

CAST: Roy Rogers, George Hayes, Dale Evans, Roger Pryor, Arthur Loft, Maude Eburne, Sam Flint, Si Jenks, June Bryde, Charles Soldani, Elaine Lange, Edmund Cobb, George Sherwood, Eddie Kane, Bob Nolan and The Sons of the Pioneers, Trigger.

Rex Rogers (as one clever critic was wont to call him), as usual, spends the better part of the running time of this feature saving Dale from danger and heavies. For action fans there's a wagon chase reenacting the early rush for land in the Oklahoma territory. The music is typical for this genre with "I'm Beginning To See the Light" as the

Roy, cameraman William Bradford, Dale, and director Frank McDonald at a postproduction barbecue. *Photo courtesy of Frank McDonald.*

standout. "The Martins and the Coys" is good for a few hillbilly chuckles.

Some reviewers of this film felt that Republic might be trying to get some marquee strength from the Rogers and Hammerstein musical *Oklahoma,* which was currently the biggest hit on Broadway.

* * *

Sunset in El Dorado (Republic, 1945) 66 M.

Producer, Louis Gray; director, Frank McDonald; screenplay, John K. Butler; original story, Leon Abrams; camera, William Bradford; editor, Tony Martinelli.

CAST: Roy Rogers, George Hayes, Dale Evans, Hardie Albright, Margaret Dumont, Roy Barcroft, Tom London, Stanley Price, Bob Wilke, Ed Cassidy, Dorothy Granger, Bob Nolan and The Sons of the Pioneers, Trigger.

A weaker than usual script dry-gulches this Rogers feature and keeps it from coming up to the usual series standards.

Dale, bored with her job working for a bus company, quits and journeys to El Dorado where her late grandmother was the notorious Kansas Kate in years past. Through a dream sequence we learn first-hand about grandmother's adventures—amorous and otherwise—in old El Dorado. It seems that granny fell in love with a cowpoke very much like Roy, and the present reincarnation displays a similar yearning.

Roy, Trigger, and the musical cast in the finale production number from *Don't Fence Me In. Photo courtesy of NTA.*

* * *

Don't Fence Me In (Republic, 1945) 71 M.

Director, John English; screenplay, Dorrell Mc-Gowan, Stuart McGowan; camera, William Bradford; editor, Charles Craft; musical directors, Morton Scott and Dale Butts; dance director, Larry Ceballos; songs, Cole Porter, Morton Shore, Zeke Manners, Jack Scholl and M. K. Kerome, Billy Hill, Larry Marks, Dick Charles, Eddie DeLange, Freddie Slack, F. Victor, R. Herman, Bob Nolan.

CAST: Roy Rogers, George Hayes, Dale Evans, Robert Livingston, Moroni Olsen, Marc Lawrence, Lucille Gleason, Andrew Tombes, Paul Harvey, Tom London, Douglas Fowley, Stephen Barclay, Edgar Dearing, Bob Nolan and The Sons of the Pioneers, Trigger.

Don't Fence Me In is the epitome of the type of musical Western movie that Western purists deride as plastic, banal, and degrading to the Western genre; and that fans flocked to see in record numbers in the war-torn days of the mid-forties. The film is just good fun and pleasant diversion, and never tries to be anything else.

The plot concerns femme Eastern magazine photographer Dale Evans going West to seek the true story about a long-dead Western character known as Wildcat Kelly. During her story-seeking and shutter-bugging, she meets Roy, Gabby, and some bad guys that Roy eventually cleans up on.

When there's a lull, Roy, Dale, or the Pioneers step in to sing a song, and there are some good ones including "The Last Roundup," "Tumbling Tumbleweeds," and the title song.

* * *

Along the Navajo Trail (Republic, 1945) 66 M.

Producer, Edward J. White; director, Frank McDonald; screenplay, Gerald Geraghty, based on a novel by William C. MacDonald; camera, William Bradford; editor, Tony Martinelli; musical director, Morton Scott; dance director, Larry Cabellos; songs, Larry Markes, Dick Charter, Eddie DeLange, Charles Newman, Arthur Altman, Bob Nolan, Gordon Forster, Jack Elliott.

CAST: Roy Rogers, George Hayes, Dale Evans, Estelita Rodriguez, Douglas Fowley, Nester Paiva, Sam Flint, Emmett Vogan, Roy Barcroft, David Cota, Edward Cassidy, Bob Nolan and The Sons of the Pioneers, Trigger.

The comment can be made about this and so many other Rogers films that the players are so appealing, attractive, and apparently enjoying themselves so much that the audience can only exit after the roundup feeling well entertained. In recently re-viewing this film, I was struck by the happy effortlessness of the relaxed performers—a relaxed exuberance, really.

Roy, director Frank McDonald, Dale, and Nat Burns on the set for *Along the Navajo Trail. Photo courtesy of Frank McDonald.*

The plot has Rogers, a U. S. deputy marshal, investigating the disappearance of another government agent who was sent out to the Ladder A Ranch (owned by Dale's father). As it turns out, a syndicate is trying to purchase the ranch because an oil pipeline is coming through, but Dale and her father have no desire to sell. Douglas Fowley and his cohorts pressure them with "accidents," sabotage, and even murder. Rogers clears up the whole mess and joins the others to sing some crowd-pleasing songs including "How Are You Doing in the Heart Department," the title tune, and The Sons of the Pioneers specialty, "Cool Water." Some traveling gypsies get involved in the action and also stage a festival, which serves as the background for a couple of production numbers.

* * *

Song of Arizona (Republic, 1946) 68 M.

Producer, Edward J. White; director, Frank McDonald; screenplay, M. Coates Webster; original story, Bradford Ropes; camera, Reggie Lanning; editor, Arthur Roberts; songs, Jack Elliott, Ira Schuster, Larry Stock, J. Cavanaugh, Mary Ann Owens, Bob Nolan, Gordon Forster.

CAST: Roy Rogers, George Hayes, Dale Evans, Lyle Talbot, Tommy Cook, Johnny Calkins, Sarah Edwards, Tommy Ivo, Michael Chapin, Dick Curtis, Edmund Cobb, Tom Quinn, Kid Chissell, Robert Mitchell Boy Choir, Bob Nolan and The Sons of the Pioneers, Trigger.

The movie, make-believe, "modern" West with its old West traditions (six-guns, buckboards, and saddle horses) is again successfully juxtaposed with modern conveniences (airplanes, cars, and radio) without the anachronism of it all boggling the mind.

Gabby is running a ranch for homeless boys in this episode. One of the youngsters has an outlaw father who is killed just after he leaves some stolen bank money with the boy. When the killers learn the boy has the loot, they go after it. Gabby calls upon Roy and The Sons of the Pioneers to help the boy. With the cowboy crusader and his pals riding the outlaw trail, the gang is soon captured and on its way to jail.

Whenever there is a free moment, Roy, Dale, and The Sons of the Pioneers break into song with such numbers as "Round and Round—The Lariat Song," "Did You Ever Get the Feeling in the Moonlight?," "Will Ya Be My Darling," "Michael O'Leary, O'Bryan, O'Toole," "Half-A-Chance Ranch," "Way Out There," "Mr. Spook Steps Out," and the title tune. With all the harmonizing, it's a wonder there is any story at all.

* * *

Rainbow Over Texas (Republic, 1946) 65 M.

Producer, Edward J. White; director, Frank McDonald; screenplay, Gerald Geraghty; original story, Max Brand; camera, Reggie Lanning; editor, Charles Craft; songs, Jack Elliott, Glen Spencer, Gordon Forster.

CAST: Roy Rogers, George Hayes, Dale Evans, Sheldon Leonard, Robert Emmett Keane, Gerald Oliver Smith, Minerva Urecal, George J. Lewis, Kenne Duncan, Pierce Lyden, Dick Elliott, Bob Nolan and The Sons of the Pioneers, Trigger.

This is a typical Rogers musical Western of the period with the star playing himself on a personal appearance tour that takes him to his Texas home town. The action is pegged to a pony express race the town is sponsoring and in which Rogers plans to participate. This riles some local hoods, who conspire against him and help to raise the action quota for the film. It's all good fun, if not the best in the series.

The music content is rather light with the standout number being "Little Senorita."

* * *

My Pal Trigger (Republic, 1946) 79 M.

Producer, Armand Schaefer; director, Frank McDonald; screenplay, Jack Townley and John K.

171

Butler; camera, William Bradford; editor, Harry Keller; special effects, Howard and Theodore Lydecker; musical director, Morton Scott.

CAST: Roy Rogers, George Hayes, Dale Evans, Jack Holt, LeRoy Mason, Roy Barcroft, Sam Flint, Kenne Duncan, Ralph Sanford, Francis McDonald, Harlan Briggs, William Haade, Alan Bridge, Paul E. Burns, Frank Reicher, Bob Nolan and The Sons of the Pioneers, Trigger.

Jack Holt, the father of Western performers Tim and Jennifer Holt, plays the villain in this production, which director Frank McDonald and star Rogers have called one of their favorite films in the series.

Roy is a horse trader who wants to wed his mare to the prize palomino stud on Gabby's horse ranch. Gambling house operator Holt has similar plans for his mare. Holt tries to steal Gabby's horse and in the process lets it escape long enough to mate with Roy's mare. During the ensuing events Holt accidentally shoots the stud, but Roy gets blamed and sent to jail. In time Roy is released, and the mare's colt is born, grows to maturity, and wins the wrap-up race on which Gabby has recklessly bet his ranch against old gambling debts. Through a slip of the tongue Holt reveals himself as the horse killer and is taken away by the sheriff.

Strong story values and moving performances take the lead in this entry with music very much in a runner-up position.

* * *

Under Nevada Skies (Republic, 1946) 69 M.

Producer, Edward J. White; director, Frank McDonald; screenplay, Paul Gangelin, J. Benton Cheney; original story, M. Coates Webster; camera, William Bradford; editor, Edward Mann; musical director, Dale Butts; assistant director, Yakima Canutt.

CAST: Roy Rogers, George Hayes, Dale Evans, Douglas Dumbrille, Leyland Hodgson, Tristram Coffin, Rudolph Anders, LeRoy Mason, George Lynn, George J. Lewis, Tom Quinn, Bob Nolan and The Sons of the Pioneers, Trigger.

Six sagebrush songs, a solid story, and plenty of shoot-'em-up action make this Rogers adventure a pleaser. In this one Roy, with the help of Gabby and Dale, gets lassoed into locating a missing jewelled crest that contains a map indicating the location of a pitchblende deposit. The whirlwind windup finds Roy leading a posse of Indians in a raid on the villains who have the missing crest.

Songs include "I Want To Go West," "Anytime That I'm With You," "Sea Goin' Cowboy," and "Ne-hah-nee."

With this film Frank McDonald dismounts and hangs up his guns as a Rogers film director. (Look out, here comes "Wild Bill" Witney!)

* * *

Roll On Texas Moon (Republic, 1946) 67 M.

Producer, Edward J. White; director, William Witney; screenplay, Paul Gangelin, Mauri Grashin; original story, Jean Murray; camera, William Bradford; editor, Lester Orlebeck; musical director, Dale Butts; songs, Jack Elliott, Tim Spencer.

CAST: Roy Rogers, George Hayes, Dale Evans, Dennis Hoey, Elizabeth Risdon, Francis McDonald, Edward Keane, Kenne Duncan, Tom London, Harry Strang, Edward Cassidy, Lee Shumway, Steve Darrell, Pierce Lyden, Bob Nolan and The Sons of the Pioneers, Trigger.

William Witney's first directing effort for the Roy Rogers series is very much on the plus side. The fast action that Witney was noted for in his many serials is evident in this feature.

The *Roll On Texas Moon* plot is another version of the cattlemen-sheepmen conflict with Dale the owner of a sheep ranch and Gabby a cantankerous cattleman. Rogers is a troubleshooter for the cattle combine but really just wants to bring peace between the factions by capturing the villains who are causing the turmoil.

A number of pleasant Western songs are sprinkled throughout the plot with no flooding of the action fare. Songs include the popular title tune (a hit Rogers recording), "Wontcha' Be a Friend of Mine?" and "The Jumpin' Bean," a novelty song performed by The Sons of the Pioneers and written by Pioneer Tim Spencer.

* * *

Home in Oklahoma (Republic, 1946) 72 M.

Producer, Edward J. White; director, William Witney; screenplay, Gerald Geraghty; camera, William Bradford; editor, Lester Orlebeck; songs, Jack Elliott, Tim Spencer.

CAST: Roy Rogers, George Hayes, Dale Evans, Carol Hughes, George Meeker, Lanny Rees, Ruby Dandridge, George Lloyd, Arthur Space, Frank Reicher, Bob Nolan and The Sons of the Pioneers, Trigger.

Photo courtesy of NTA.

Again the Rogers-Evans-Hayes combination works to excellent results in this change-of-pace Western mystery with music.

Roy, a crusading, small-town newspaper editor, is on the trail of the killers of a prosperous rancher. Big-city newshen Dale Evans joins Rogers in his search for evidence and the killer. The appropriate mix of hard riding, fisticuffs, and mesquite music (the best song being the Rogers-Evans duet of "Miguelito") makes this film another winner.

*   *   *

Out California Way (Republic, 1946) 67 M.

Roy and Dale (and other Republic Western stars) make a walk-on guest star appearance in this early Monte Hale musical Western. (See the Monte Hale filmography for complete credit listings.)

*   *   *

With Hoover Dam as a location background, director Frank McDonald talks to LeRoy Mason, Dale, and Roy before shooting a scene for *Heldorado*. Although Frank McDonald started as director of *Heldorado*, he had to leave the production prior to its completion. William Witney went on to complete the picture. *Photo courtesy of Frank McDonald.*

Roy and Gabby on location for *Heldorado*. Director Frank McDonald is at right with the megaphone. *Photo courtesy of Frank McDonald.*

Dale, Gabby, Frank McDonald, and Roy between scenes for *Heldorado*. *Photo courtesy of Frank McDonald.*

Heldorado (Republic, 1946) 70 M.

Producer, Edward J. White; director, William Witney; screenplay, Gerald Geraghty and Julian Zimet; camera, William Bradford; editor, Lester Orlebeck; songs, Jack Elliott, Denver Darling, Roy Rogers, Bob Nolan.

CAST: Roy Rogers, George Hayes, Dale Evans, Paul Harvey, Barry Mitchell, John Bagni, John Phillips, James Taggart, Rex Lease, Steve Darrell, Doye O'Dell, LeRoy Mason, Charlie Williams, Eddie Acuff, Bob Nolan and The Sons of the Pioneers, Trigger.

The annual Heldorado parade and rodeo in Las Vegas serve as the background for another Rogers bullseye in Western film marksmanship.

This high-budget gitty-up adventure concerns Rogers's efforts to round up a syndicate of black market racketeers who are involved in some money hanky-panky at the local gambling dens. The film has both an action-filled plot and plenty of music.

"Good Neighbor" is an okay duet number for Roy and Dale; Roy and The Sons of the Pioneers join for "My Saddle Pals and I," written by Rogers; and the star nicely solos "Silver Stars, Purple Sage, Eyes of Blue."

* * *

Apache Rose (Republic, 1947) 75 M. Trucolor

Producer, Edward J. White; director, William Witney; screenplay, Gerald Geraghty; camera, Jack Marta; editor, Lester Orlebeck; songs, Jack Elliott, Tim Spencer, Glen Spencer.

CAST: Roy Rogers, Dale Evans, Olin Howlin, George Meeker, John Laurenz, Russ Vincent, Minerva Urecal, LeRoy Mason, Donna DeMario, Terry Frost, Conchita Lemus, Tex Terry, Bob Nolan and The Sons of the Pioneers, Trigger.

Roy Rogers's first Trucolor feature is only an average entry in the long-running series. A mite more action and an upped pace would have moved the feature into the front ranks of Rogers Western fare.

The plot concerns Rogers, an oil prospector, attempting to get drilling rights to an old Spanish landgrant. He's thwarted at every turn by gamblers from an off-shore gambling boat who know there's oil on the land and are attempting to get the land through a collection of unpaid gambling debts from the owner.

A less impressive roster of tunes is also to be found in *Apache Rose,* with probably the best being Rogers's rendition of "Wishing Well." Also in the score are "There's Nothing Like Coffee in the Morning," "José," "Ride Vaquero," and the title tune.

* * *

Hit Parade of 1947 (Republic, 1947) 90 M.

Roy, Trigger, and Bob Nolan and The Sons of the Pioneers make a brief guest appearance in this "A-" musical that starred Eddie Albert, Constance Moore, and Woody Herman and his orchestra.

* * *

Bells of San Angelo (Republic, 1947) 78 M. Trucolor

Producer, Edward J. White; director, William Witney; screenplay, Sloan Nibley; original story, Paul Gangelin; camera, Jack Marta; editor, Lester Orlebeck; songs, Jack Elliott, Tim Spencer.

CAST: Roy Rogers, Dale Evans, Andy Devine, John McGuire, Olaf Hytten, David Sharpe, Fritz Leiber, Hank Patterson, Fred S. Toones, Eddie Acuff, Bob Nolan and The Sons of the Pioneers, Trigger.

This is the first of the "violent" Rogers films that caused some critics' and parents' brows to furrow. It is nonetheless relatively mild by today's violence standards.

Rogers, a Mexican border investigator, is joined by Dale, a Western novelist, in a search for smugglers that eventually leads to a border silver mine where Roy gets royally clobbered by the bad guys before the appropriate climactic roundup.

Andy Devine joins the cast as the comic character Cookie Bullfincher (a role he continued for a couple of years in the series).

Musical moments include "A Cowboy's Dream of Heaven," sung by Roy, while Dale provides "I Love the West" as her main solo.

* * *

Springtime in the Sierras (Republic, 1947) 75 M. Trucolor

Producer, Edward J. White; director, William Witney; screenplay, Sloan Nibley; camera, Jack Marta; editor, Tony Martinelli; musical director, Morton Scott; songs, Jack Elliott, Bob Nolan, Tim Spencer.

CAST: Roy Rogers, Jane Frazee, Andy Devine, Stephanie Bachelor, Hal Landon, Harry V.

Photo courtesy of NTA.

Cheshire, Roy Barcroft, Chester Conklin, Hank Patterson, Whitey Christy, Pascale Perry, Bob Nolan and The Sons of the Pioneers, Trigger.

This is one of my favorite Rogers films. The William Witney direction is at its best and offers an action fan all the vicarious adventure he could wish for in seventy-five thrill-packed minutes.

Rogers is attempting to break up a gang dealing in the indiscriminate out-of-season killing of game for profit. Stephanie Bachelor is the villainess in the operation. Her top thug is Roy Barcroft (Republic's "best" villain), who just about outdoes himself in the blackguard business when he tries to quick-freeze Roy by throwing him into a meat locker.

The six songs in the score are shared by the musical stars. "Oh, What a Picture" is a novelty number rendered by Roy and comic photographer Devine. The Sons of the Pioneers and Roy perform the title tune, "The Quilting Party," and "A Cowboy Has To Sing." "Pedro from Acapulco" is dueted by feminine lead Jane Frazee and Rogers, and the Pioneers provide "What Are We Gonna' Do Then?"

*   *   *

On the Old Spanish Trail (Republic, 1947) 75 M. Trucolor

Producer, Edward J. White; director, William Witney; screenplay, Sloan Nibley; original story, Gerald Geraghty; camera, Jack Marta; editor, Tony Martinelli; musical director, Morton Scott.

CAST: Roy Rogers, Tito Guizar, Jane Frazee, Andy Devine, Estelita Rodriguez, Charles McGraw, Fred Graham, Steve Darrell, Marshall Reed, Wheaton Chambers, Bob Nolan and The Sons of the Pioneers, Trigger.

This tune-filled horse opera boasts a beautiful title song and the usual Witney style of breakneck action. It rates satisfactory even if (as one critic cited) the logic and credulity of the script are as leaky as a bullet-riddled watering trough—for example, slugfests from which the principals emerge unmarked.

Estelita Rodriguez and Tito Guizar are on board to help lend additional south-of-the-border atmosphere to the proceedings and to add to the musical content.

*   *   *

The Gay Ranchero (Republic, 1948) 72 M. Trucolor

Producer, Edward J. White; director, William Witney; screenplay, Sloan Nibley; camera, Jack Marta; editor, Tony Martinelli; songs, Abe Tuvim, Francia

Roy and Jane Frazee are pictured singing a duet from *The Gay Ranchero*. Miss Frazee bears a striking resemblance to singer Patti Page, who was just beginning her show business career about this same time. *Photo courtesy of NTA.*

Roy is embroiled here in a typical William Witney knock-down-drag-out fight from *The Gay Ranchero*. *Photo courtesy of NTA.*

This is another Rogers epic with the south-of-the-border sombrero motif that seemed to be popular in the postwar years. The old West and the new West are again shown in vivid contrast as Rogers plays a horseback-riding, six-gun-toting sheriff trying to capture a gang of hoodlums who are attempting to gain control of an airport by sabotaging the planes.

The musical slots are filled by a multitude of performers in the film with The Sons of the Pioneers offering a couple of numbers; Tito Guizar tenoring "Granada," and "You Belong to My Heart"; Jane Frazee and Roy Rogers dueting "Wait'll I Get My Sunshine in the Moonlight"; and Estelita singing and dancing the title tune.

*   *   *

Luban, J. J. Espinosa, Harry Glick, Jimmy Lambert, Dave Olsen, Augustin Lara, and Ray Gilbert.

CAST: Roy Rogers, Tito Guizar, Jane Frazee, Andy Devine, Estelita Rodriguez, George Meeker, LeRoy Mason, Dennis Moore, Keith Richards, Betty Gagnon, Robert Rose, Ken Terrell, Bob Nolan and The Sons of the Pioneers, Trigger.

Under California Skies (Republic, 1948) 70 M. Trucolor

Producer, Edward J. White; director, William Witney; screenplay, Sloan Nibley and Paul Gangelin; original story, Paul Gangelin; camera, Jack Marta; editor, Tony Martinelli.

CAST: Roy Rogers, Jane Frazee, Andy Devine, George H. Lloyd, Wade Crosby, Michael Chapin,

ROY ROGERS
KING OF THE COWBOYS
TRIGGER
SMARTEST HORSE IN THE MOVIES
EYES OF TEXAS
in TRUCOLOR   A *Republic* PRODUCTION

Photo courtesy of NTA.

House Peters, Jr., Steve Clark, Joseph Garro, Paul Power, John Wald, Bob Nolan and The Sons of the Pioneers, Trigger.

This average Rogers Western received trade criticism for the sloppy use of a double for Roy (particularly on a trick mounting of Trigger) and the obvious use of a stuffed dummy to double an actor who was supposedly kicked in the face by Trigger. (Yes, Wild Bill Witney was at it again!)

The plot has Trigger kidnapped and held for ransom by a gang of toughs. Rancher Rogers and his range hands take out after them and eventually retrieve Rogers's palomino pal.

*　　*　,　*

Eyes of Texas (Republic, 1948) 70 M. Trucolor

Producer, Edward J. White; director, William Witney; screenplay, Sloan Nibley; camera, Jack Marta; editor, Tony Martinelli.

CAST: Roy Rogers, Lynne Roberts, Andy Devine, Nana Bryant, Roy Barcroft, Danny Morton, Francis Ford, Pascale Perry, Stanley Blystone, Bob Nolan and The Sons of the Pioneers, Trigger.

This excellent Rogers film—filled with typical Witney action and suspense, frescoed with Trucolor, and "festuned" with songs—nevertheless was disturbing to some parents because of the use of a pack of highly frightening killer dogs to murder the villainess's unsuspecting victims.

Nana Bryant (the villainess), out to acquire by whatever means necessary some valuable ranch land in the area, has trained dogs (both animal and human) at her command and doesn't hesitate to use them in discouraging landowners from sticking around. U. S. Marshal Rogers eventually sniffs out the evildoers and sends them on their way to the pen.

*　　*　　*

179

Melody Time (RKO Radio Pictures, 1948) 75 M. Technicolor

Roy Rogers and Bob Nolan and The Sons of the Pioneers make a standout guest appearance in this Walt Disney movie pastiche. After first singing "Blue Shadows on the Trail" (one of their biggest hit recordings), Roy and the Pioneers spin the delightful tale of "Pecos Bill" with words and music while Disney's staff provide their cartoon magic.

*   *   *

Night Time in Nevada (Republic, 1948) 67 M. Trucolor

Producer, Edward J. White; director, William Witney; screenplay, Sloan Nibley; camera, Jack Marta; editor, Tony Martinelli; musical director, Dale Butts; songs, Richard W. Pascoe, Will E. Dulmage, H. O'Reilly Clint, Tim Spencer, Edward Morrissey, Bob Nolan.

CAST: Roy Rogers, Adele Mara, Andy Devine, Grant Withers, Marie Harmon, Joseph Crehan, George Carleton, Holly Bane, Steve Darrell, Jim Nolan, Hank Patterson, Bob Nolan and The Sons of the Pioneers, Trigger.

From the opening cattle train holdup to the climactic fistic duel in a speeding, out-of-control truck, this Rogers Trucolor feature is an adventure-filled showcase for the directorial deftness of William Witney.

When Roy's hands are not filled with fists or guns, they're strumming a guitar while he sings such hitching-post traditionals as "Big Rock Candy Mountain" or the title song. The Sons of the Pioneers, making their final movie appearance with Roy, blend nicely for "Sweet Laredo Lou" and "Over Nevada."

*   *   *

Grand Canyon Trail (Republic, 1948) 67 M. Trucolor

Producer, Edward J. White; director, William Witney; screenplay, Gerald Geraghty; camera, Reggie Lanning; editor, Tony Martinelli; musical director, Nathan Scott; songs, Jack Elliott, Foy Willing.

CAST: Roy Rogers, Jane Frazee, Andy Devine, Robert Livingston, Roy Barcroft, Charles Coleman, Emmett Lynn, Ken Terrell, James Finlayson, Tommy Coats, Foy Willing and The Riders of the Purple Sage, Trigger.

Roy steps in to break up an altercation between Roy Barcroft (right) and Francis Ford (center) in this scene from *The Far Frontier. Photo courtesy of NTA.*

Clayton Moore (who was to become the Lone Ranger on television in 1949) played villains in many Republic features during the 1940s. He seems to have lost this fight with Roy in *The Far Frontier. Photo courtesy of NTA.*

Cooking up the usual chuck wagon recipe of Western action, music, and story spinning, this Rogers sagebrush saga is a tasty offering.

The plot has Roy heavily in debt as the owner of a less than promising silver mine. The mining engineer-villain, Robert Livingston (a Republic cowboy star just a few short years before—how fleeting is fame!), is attempting to swindle Roy out of the mine because he knows there's silver "down thar."

Foy Willing and The Riders of the Purple Sage join Roy for the first time in this film. The singing group is a carbon of The Sons of the Pioneers, and that can be translated as topnotch.

* * *

The Far Frontier (Republic, 1948) 67 M. Trucolor

Producer, Edward J. White; director, William Witney; screenplay, Sloan Nibley; camera, Jack Marta; editor, Tony Martinelli; musical director, Dale Butts.

CAST: Roy Rogers, Gail Davis, Andy Devine, Francis Ford, Roy Barcroft, Clayton Moore, Robert Strange, Holly Bane, Lane Bradford, John Bagni, Clarence Straight, Edmund Cobb, Foy Willing and The Riders of the Purple Sage, Trigger.

The Far Frontier is a lively cowboy caper that contains the stuff and such that popcorn munchers have always expected from Roy and his cohorts.

The story concerns the smuggling of American outlaws back into the United States from Mexico when the heat is off and the coast appears to be clear. Roy and Trigger (who out performs just about everyone with his tricks) come to the assistance of the border patrol and eventually bring the dastardly doings to a proper denouement.

* * *

Susanna Pass (Republic, 1949) 67 M. Trucolor

Producer, Edward J. White; director, William Witney; screenplay, Sloan Nibley and John K. Butler; camera, Reggie Lanning; editor, Tony Martinelli; songs, Jack Elliott, Sid Robin, Foy Willing, Oakley Haldeman, Clem White, Jimmy Lee.

CAST: Roy Rogers, Dale Evans, Estelita Rodriguez, Martin Garralaga, Robert Emmett Keane, Lucien Littlefield, Douglas Fowley, David Sharpe, Robert Bice, Foy Willing and The Riders of the Purple Sage, Trigger.

The one distinguishing feature of this episode is the reuniting of Roy with his real life wife, Dale Evans, as the leading lady; otherwise, the film is somewhat of a letdown with criticism leveled primarily at the predictableness and (at times) improbableness of the goings on.

Roy plays a game warden investigating the dynamiting of a local fish hatchery. The crooks, it soon becomes clear, are not interested in fish or hatcheries but want the oil that's under the lake. Roy, with the help of Trigger, Dale, and a few other friends, soon has the bad guys captured and spending a term up the river.

The big number in the score is "Brush Those Tears from Your Eyes," performed by Roy, Dale, and Foy Willing and The Riders of the Purple Sage. The same performers also get together on "A

Good, Good Mornin' " and the title tune. "Two-Gun Rita" is a novelty number performed by Mexican chili pepper Estelita Rodriguez.

* * *

Down Dakota Way (Republic, 1949) 67 M. Trucolor

Producer, Edward J. White; director, William Witney; screenplay, John K. Butler and Sloan Nibley; camera, Reggie Lanning; editor, Tony Martinelli; musical director, Dale Butts; songs, Sloan Nibley, Dale Butts, Sid Robin, Foy Willing, George Morgan.

CAST: Roy Rogers, Dale Evans, Pat Brady, Monte Montana, Elizabeth Risdon, Byron Barr, James Cardwell, Roy Barcroft, Emmett Vogan, Foy Willing and The Riders of the Purple Sage, Trigger.

This fast-paced oater has villain Roy Barcroft attempting to market his hoof-and-mouth disease-infested herd before their discovery by government officials. To buy some time, he has a henchman murder the local vet, who is wise to the diseased cattle. Roy, a stranger who stumbles into the situation, straps on his shootin' irons and in a little over an hour has the whole situation in hand.

The country hit song of the era, "Candy Kisses," is the featured number in the musical score. Pat Brady gets in some comedy licks as a character called Sparrow Biffle.

* * *

The Golden Stallion (Republic, 1949) 67 M. Trucolor

Foy Willing (left of Roy) and The Riders of the Purple Sage, Roy, Pat Brady, and Dale in this church scene from *Down Dakota Way. Photo courtesy of NTA.*

Photo courtesy of NTA.

Producer, Edward J. White; director, William Witney; screenplay, Sloan Nibley; camera, Jack Marta; editor, Tony Martinelli; musical director, Nathan Scott; songs, Sid Robin, Foy Willing, Nathan Gluck, Anne Parentean, Eddie Cherkose, Sol Meyer, Jule Styne.

CAST: Roy Rogers, Dale Evans, Estelita Rodriguez, Pat Brady, Douglas Evans, Frank Fenton, Greg McClure, Dale Van Sickel, Clarence Straight, Jack Sparks, Chester Conklin, Foy Willing and The Riders of the Purple Sage, Trigger.

The horses steal the spotlight in this excellent entry in the series. As the *Variety* critic commented, *"Golden Stallion* should kick up plenty of gold dust in the action situations."

The clever, if improbable, plot has a ring of smugglers sneaking diamonds across the Mexican border into the United States by using a pack of wild horses led by a palomino mare as the carriers. When Roy captures the herd, the mare and Trigger have a romance. Presently, one of the smugglers arrives to collect the hidden diamonds from the mare. She bolts, killing the crook in the process, and escapes. Thinking that Trigger is responsible for the death, the sheriff demands that he be destroyed. Roy "confesses" that he did the killing, thus saving Trigger, but causing his own jailing for manslaughter.

While Roy is in jail, the outlaws acquire Trigger and train him to smuggle the diamonds just as the mare had earlier. Time passes; Trigger, Jr. is born

of the wild mare and raised by Roy's friends. Finally released, Roy uses the young offspring to assist him in trapping the smugglers.

Four melodies are scattered throughout the story for added adult appeal, but ultimately it's the equine stars who gallop off with most of the glory.

* * *

Bells of Coronado (Republic, 1950) 67 M. Trucolor

Producer, Edward J. White; director, William Witney; screenplay, Sloan Nibley; camera, John MacBurnie; editor, Tony Martinelli; songs, Sid Robin, Foy Willing, Aaron Gonzales.

CAST: Roy Rogers, Dale Evans, Pat Brady, Grant Withers, Leo Cleary, Clifton Young, Robert Bice, Stuart Randall, John Hamilton, Edmund Cobb, Eddie Lee, Rex Lease, Lane Bradford, Foy Willing and The Riders of the Purple Sage, Trigger.

The theft of uranium ore doesn't sound like the makings of a saddle saga, but in the "modern" Westerns turned out by Roy Rogers it's oats for the gristmill.

Rogers is an undercover insurance investigator looking into the missing ore. By the time his Sherlocking has unraveled the mystery, he has participated in the requisite quota of six-gun duels

Photo courtesy of NTA.

Photo courtesy of NTA.

From left to right: Estelita, Dale, Roy, Foy Willing, and
The Riders of the Purple Sage. *Photo courtesy of NTA.*

From left to right: Grant Withers, Leo Cleary, Dale, Roy,
and Stuart Randall. The hapless patient is Pat Brady. *Photo
courtesy of NTA.*

Photo courtesy of NTA.

Pat Brady doesn't seem too pleased that Estelita has taken a liking to him. *Photo courtesy of NTA.*

Roy is seen here on the hunt for a mountain lion. *Photo courtesy of NTA.*

and fisticuffs. The climax is a brutal brawl between Roy and the thugs who are attempting to load the ore on a plane for takeoff and escape to a foreign country.

Even with all this action, Roy still finds time to sing the title song as well as join Dale and The Riders for "Save a Smile for a Rainy Day." "Got No Time for the Blues" is performed by Dale, Foy, and The Riders of the Purple Sage.

*   *   *

Twilight in the Sierras (Republic, 1950) 67 M. Trucolor

Producer, Edward J. White; director, William Witney; screenplay, Sloan Nibley; camera, John MacBurnie; editor, Tony Martinelli; musical director, Stanley Wilson; songs, Sid Robin, Foy Willing.

CAST: Roy Rogers, Dale Evans, Estelita Rodriguez, Pat Brady, Russ Vincent, George Meeker, Fred Kohler, Jr., Edward Keane, House Peters, Jr., Pierce Lyden, Joseph A. Garro, William Lester, Foy Willing and The Riders of the Purple Sage, Trigger.

A regulation amount of rough-and-tumble rowdiness is presented in this outdoor opus to satisfy Roy Rogers fans. In addition, the score complements the proceedings with (among others) "It's One

Wonderful Day" and "Rootin', Tootin' Cowboy." Estelita, playing a Cuban visitor to the United States, warbles "Pancho's Rancho" for nice novelty effect.

Counterfeiting is the name of the game this time, and United States Marshal Rogers is there to see that the varmints don't succeed. Some good suspense is developed in a subplot concerning a mountain lion hunt.

*   *   *

Trigger, Jr. (Republic, 1950) 68 M. Trucolor

Producer, Edward J. White; director, William Witney; screenplay, Gerald Geraghty; camera, Jack Marta; editor, Tony Martinelli; musical director, Dale Butts; songs, Peter Tinturin, Foy Willing, Carol Rice.

CAST: Roy Rogers, Dale Evans, Pat Brady, Gordon Jones, Grant Withers, Peter Miles, George Cleveland, Frank Fenton, I. Stanford Jolley, Stanley Andrews, Raynor Lehr Circus, Foy Willing and The Riders of the Purple Sage, Trigger, Trigger, Jr.

After the success of 1949's *The Golden Stallion*, it was only natural that Republic should whip up another horse story for Roy and Trigger. Though somewhat less successful in execution than its predecessor, *Trigger, Jr.* is nonetheless a film with much appeal for kids and adults.

In order to make his range patrol service of more pressing need to ranchers, villain Grant Withers acquires a killer horse he lets loose to destroy valuable horses on ranches in the area. After the usual plot frustrations, Rogers and his pal Splinters (Gordon Jones) track down Withers and his henchmen only to suddenly find themselves trapped by the crooks. Peter Miles, portraying a youngster deathly afraid of horses, gives a moving performance as he surmounts his fear to ride for help in order to save Roy and his pal.

* * *

Sunset in the West (Republic, 1950) 67 M. Trucolor

Director, William Witney; screenplay, Gerald Geraghty; camera, Jack Marta; editor, Tony Martinelli; special effects, Howard and Theodore Lydecker; songs, Jack Elliott, Foy Willing, Aaron Gonzales.

CAST: Roy Rogers, Estelita Rodriguez, Penny Edwards, Gordon Jones, Will Wright, Pierre Watkin, Charles LaTorre, William J. Tannen, Gaylord Pendleton, Paul E. Burns, Dorothy Ann White, Foy Willing and The Riders of the Purple Sage, Trigger.

Gunrunning is the villainy Roy must stamp out in this above-average Republic Western, and that he does in his usual heroic manner. Roy has a new leading lady, Penny Edwards. (While she doesn't have a great deal to do in this film, succeeding appearances will reveal her to be a pleasant film personality, if not an Academy Award challenger.)

The title song by Foy Willing is given heightened appeal at one point with a set of Spanish lyrics tacked on for variation. Roy does nicely by the title song as well as "Rollin' Wheels." Estelita, playing her now familiar south-of-the-border senorita, has fun with "When a Pretty Girl Passes By."

* * *

North of the Great Divide (Republic, 1950) 67 M. Trucolor

Producer, Edward J. White; director, William Witney; screenplay, Eric Taylor; camera, Jack Marta; editor, Tony Martinelli; songs, Jack Elliott.

CAST: Roy Rogers, Penny Edwards, Gordon Jones, Roy Barcroft, Jack Lambert, Douglas Evans, Keith Richards, Noble Johnson, Foy Willing and The Riders of the Purple Sage, Trigger.

Roy plays an Indian agent in this average entry in the series. Sent into the north country to check out trouble between an Indian tribe and a new salmon cannery run by villain Roy Barcroft,

Roy, Foy Willing (right) and The Riders of the Purple Sage.
Photo courtesy of NTA.

Rogers discovers that the cannery is blocking the salmon from traveling upstream to where the Indians are camped, thus causing a food shortage. Roy has his hands full trying to get the goods on Barcroft and his henchmen before the Indians hit the war path.

Only three songs complement the action this time: "By the Laughing Spring," done by Roy and his leading lady, Penny Edwards, "Just Keep a' Movin'," and the title song, performed by Roy and Foy Willing and The Riders of the Purple Sage.

*　　*　　*

Trail of Robin Hood (Republic, 1950) 67 M. Trucolor

Producer, Edward J. White; director, William Witney; screenplay, Gerald Geraghty; camera, John MacBurnie; editor, Tony Martinelli; songs, Jack Elliott, Foy Willing.

CAST: Roy Rogers, Penny Edwards, Gordon Jones, Jack Holt, Emory Parnell, Clifton Young, James Magill, Carol Nugent, George Chesebro, Edward Cassidy, Foy Willing and The Riders of the Purple Sage, Trigger. Guest stars: Rex Allen, Allan "Rocky" Lane, Monte Hale, William Farnum, Tom Tyler, Ray Corrigan, Kermit Maynard, Tom Keene.

Roy has one of his best screen adventures in this last color feature in the series. Guest appearances by several past and (then) present cowboy film stars add to the enjoyment of the sixty-seven-minute ride and help to keep it moving at a suitable gait.

The plot has retired movie actor Jack Holt raising and selling Christmas trees at cost to poor people. Who should appear on the scene but a Grinch-like fiend running a commercial tree outfit that gets the woodsmen (for a percentage) to cause Holt trouble getting the trees harvested and to their destination. When Roy hears about this, he calls his cowboy friends for assistance, and soon a merry Christmas is being had by all except the villains.

Rogers and The Riders sing "Ev'ry Day Is Christmas in the West" and "Get a Christmas Tree For Johnny," while Foy and the group do "Home Town Jubilee" in their usual pleasant manner.

*　　*　　*

Spoilers of the Plains (Republic, 1951) 68 M.

Producer, Edward J. White; director, William Witney; screenplay, Sloan Nibley; camera, Jack

Marta; editor, Tony Martinelli; songs, Jack Elliott, Aaron Gonzales, Foy Willing.

CAST: Roy Rogers, Penny Edwards, Gordon Jones, Grant Withers, William Forrest, Don Haggerty, Fred Kohler, Jr., House Peters, Jr., George Meeker, Keith Richards, Foy Willing and The Riders of the Purple Sage, Trigger, Bullet.

The title of this episode undoubtedly has special meaning to Western purists who have little respect for singing cowboys and bizarre Western scripts. This feature has both. Regardless, Rogers fans have a treat in store as they watch this feature unwind with its story of foreign spies, desert rocket-launching sites, and weather forecasting satellites (remember, this film was released back in 1951!).

After the usual ration of chases, fights, and shoot-outs, Roy wraps up the adventure with a knuckle-buster atop an oil derrick with heavy Grant Withers. Roy is joined by Trigger and a new partner, a dog named Bullet (who would continue with Roy in the remaining features and then go into the television series).

*　　*　　*

Heart of the Rockies (Republic, 1951) 67 M.

Producer, Edward J. White; director, William Witney; screenplay, Eric Taylor; camera, Reggie Lanning; editor, Tony Martinelli; musical director, Dale Butts; songs, Jack Elliott, Foy Willing, Geri Gallian.

CAST: Roy Rogers, Penny Edwards, Gordon Jones, Ralph Morgan, Fred Graham, Mira McKinney, Robert "Buzz" Henry, William Gould, Pepe Hern, Rand Brooks, Foy Willing and The Riders of the Purple Sage, Trigger, Bullet.

A high-riding entry in the Rogers series, *Heart of the Rockies* offers the usual blend of music, action, and comedy.

The plot has Roy in charge of the construction of a highway going through a portion of rancher Ralph Morgan's land. Morgan fears that the influx of people across his property might cause authorities to discover that years before he acquired the land illegally through dirty doings. To discourage the road builders Morgan sends his henchmen out to sabotage the project. Roy, displaying his usual grit, triumphs in the end.

*　　*　　*

In Old Amarillo (Republic, 1951) 67 M.

Producer, Edward J. White; director, William

Roy and Estelita are accompanied by The Roy Rogers
Riders as they sing a duet. *Photo courtesy of NTA.*

Witney; screenplay, Sloan Nibley; camera, Jack
Marta; editor, Tony Martinelli; songs, Jack Elliott,
Foy Willing.

CAST: Roy Rogers, Estelita Rodriguez, Penny
Edwards, Pinky Lee, Roy Barcroft, Pierre Watkin,
Ken Howell, Elizabeth Risdon, William Holmes,
The Roy Rogers Riders, Trigger, Bullet.

In Old Amarillo Is not one of the better Roy
Rogers features, lacking the usual sustained interest
and excitement. (Perhaps it was because the series
was nearing its end and there was less effort
expended on the part of all concerned, or maybe
budget cuts were taking their toll—whatever, the
series had lost its momentum, and it showed.)

The story deals with a drought in Texas that is
about to drive the cattle ranchers to bankruptcy
since there is no water to keep the cattle alive for
market. Roy Barcroft, hoping to buy the dying
cattle at a fraction of their true price for the
canning factory he is establishing, sends out his
henchmen to foil efforts to bring water to the area
by train or to seed clouds by plane so that it might
rain. Roy is sent by a packing house firm to see
what can be done about the problem. Eventually he
brings justice and (with some help) rain to Texas.

Pinky Lee (fresh from a television series that was
popular with the kiddies) is in the last three Rogers

pictures to provide comic relief and, for the most
part, fails. Foy Willing and The Riders of the
Purple Sage are gone from the series, being
replaced by a group called The Roy Rogers Riders,
apparently a cheaper Republic in-house group.

Roy and Estelita sing the title tune; Roy and
Penny Edwards duet "Under the Lone Star Moon";
"Wasteland" is done by Roy and his Riders; and
Estelita sings "If I Ever Fall in Love" to her
boyfriend Pinky Lee.

*   *   *

South of Caliente (Republic, 1951) 67 M.

Producer, Edward J. White; director, William
Witney; screenplay, Eric Taylor; camera, Jack
Marta; editor, Harold Minter; musical director,
Dale Butts; songs, Jack Elliott, Lee Wainer.

CAST: Roy Rogers, Dale Evans, Pinky Lee, Doug-
las Fowley, Rick Roman, Leonard Penn, Willie
Best, Lillian Molieri, Charlita, Pat Brady, Frank
Richards, The Roy Rogers Riders, Trigger, Bullet.

Another below-average entry, *South of Caliente*
suffers from some apparent dollar saving on the
production budget and an anemic script almost
devoid of the usual Witney action. The one bright

spot is the return of Dale Evans to the Rogers films—although the script offers her little opportunity to display her thespic ability.

The story deals with the horsenapping of Dale's prize racehorse by Douglas Fowley, its trainer. After the usual fistics, chases, shoot-outs, and wrong trails followed, Roy hogties the villains and carts them off to the clink.

During the many action pauses, Roy, Dale, and Pinky Lee sing four songs: "My Home Is Over Yonder," "Gypsy Trail," "Won'tcha Be a Friend of Mine," and "Yascha the Gypsy."

*   *   *

Pals of the Golden West (Republic, 1951) 68 M.

Producer, Edward J. White; director, William Witney; screenplay, Albert DeMond, Eric Taylor; story, Sloan Nibley; camera, Jack Marta; editor, Harold Minter; songs, Jack Elliott, Aaron Gonzales, Jordan Smith.

CAST: Roy Rogers, Dale Evans, Estelita Rodriguez, Pinky Lee, Anthony Caruso, Roy Barcroft, Eduardo Jiminez, Ken Terrell, Emmett Vogan, Maurice Jara, The Roy Rogers Riders, Trigger, Bullet.

Bearing a fitting title for the final series film, *Pals of the Golden West* is, unfortunately, only an average celluloid ride into the sunset.

The script is another hoof-and-mouth disease opus with Rogers, an officer of the U. S. Border Patrol, responsible for keeping the disease from coming into the United States from Mexico. Roy faces and eventually overcomes opposition from nature (a sand storm) and man (villains Anthony Caruso and Roy Barcroft) in his efforts to contain the disease.

Roy and his Riders sing "Beyond the Great Divide" and the title number, and are joined by Dale for "Slumber Trail." "You Never Know When Love May Come Along" provides Estelita with her usual solo number.

*   *   *

Son of Paleface (Paramount, 1952) 104 M. Technicolor

Producer, Robert L. Welch; director, Frank Tashlin; screenplay, Frank Tashlin, Robert L. Welch, and Joseph Quillan.

CAST: Bob Hope, Jane Russell, Roy Rogers, Bill Williams, Lloyd Corrigan, Paul E. Burns, Douglas Dumbrille, Harry Von Zell, Iron Eyes Cody, Wee Willie Davis, Charley Cooley, Hank Mann, Chester

Conklin, Johnathan Hale, Oliver Blake, Cecil B. DeMille, Bing Crosby.

As Roy's Republic contract was running out, he signed for this top-budget musical-comedy Western that was destined to be very popular with fans. Trigger, too, was along for the belly laugh ride that reminded many critics and fans of the Hope-Crosby road pictures of previous years.

Roy sings "There's a Cloud in My Valley of Sunshine" and joins the other two stars, Hope and Russell, for a reprise of "Buttons and Bows," the big hit from the original *Paleface* film.

*   *   *

Alias Jesse James (United Artists, 1959) 92 M. Deluxe Color

Along with many other movie and television cowboy stars, Roy makes a very brief guest appearance in the finale of this Bob Hope Western comedy.

*   *   *

MacKintosh and T. J. (Penland Productions, 1975) 96 M. Technicolor

Producer, Tim Penland; director, Marvin J. Chomsky; screenplay, Paul Savage; camera, Terry Mead; editor, Howard Smith; art director, Alan Smith; assistant director, Claude Binyon, Jr.; music composed and performed by Waylon Jennings.

CAST: Roy Rogers, Clay O'Brien, Billy Green Bush, Andrew Robinson, Joan Hackett, James Hampton, Dennis Fimple, Luke Askew, Larry Mahan, Walter Barnes, Edith Atwater, Ted Gehring, Jim Harrell, Dean Smith, Ron Hay, Guich Kooch, Autry Ward, Steve Ward, Troy Ward.

Twenty-three years after *Son of Paleface*, his last starring movie role, Roy Rogers was again being seen on theater screens in a new Western; indeed, new in many ways: gone were Trigger and Bullet, Dale Evans, the fancy regalia, and the songs. The only link between the old Republic series and the present film was the surprisingly fit cowboy star himself.

Variety described the new film as ". . . an amiable family market film, slick and pleasantly corny, which has no particular distinction except that it marks the first screen appearance of Roy Rogers since *Son of Paleface* in 1952." (*Variety*, like so many others, overlooked or didn't count the very brief guest shot in *Alias Jesse James.*)

The plot deals with Rogers, a ranch hand-drifter,

Photo courtesy of Roy Rogers.

taking young Clay O'Brien under his wing and helping him get through some troublesome times as a teenager. The *Variety* critic commented that basically it is a recycled *Captains Courageous* set in the modern West. While certainly not in the superstar class as far as acting goes, Roy brings a feeling of warmth and sincerity to the character that is at times very moving.

*   *   *

ROY ROGERS DISCOGRAPHY

Although a fairly popular recording artist, Roy Rogers never came close to attaining the stature of fellow movie singing cowboys Gene Autry and Tex Ritter in the recording field. During the height of his film career Roy recorded for RCA Victor. Many of his more successful recordings for Victor are included in the Camden reissue *The Best of Roy Rogers.* Most of Roy's recordings during the fifties and sixties were of a religious nature and featured duets with his wife, Dale Evans. *Happy Trails to You* was recorded in the 1970s and featured his hit single of "Hoppy, Gene and Me."

Currently available recordings by Roy Rogers include the following:

The Best of Roy Rogers Camden (RCA) Records
Selections:

> My Chickashay Gal
> Don't Fence Me In
> I Wish I Had Never Met Sunshine
> Blue Shadows on the Trail
> My Heart Went That-A-Way
> A Gay Ranchero
> The Yellow Rose of Texas
> That Palomino Pal O'Mine
> Along the Navajo Trail
> On the Old Spanish Trail
> Roll On Texas Moon
> Rock Me to Sleep in My Saddle

*   *   *

The Bible Tells Me So Capital Records
    With Dale Evans
Selections:

> The Bible Tells Me So
> Whispering Hope
> Just a Closer Walk with Thee
> In the Sweet By and By
> Peace in the Valley
> Pass Me Not
> It Is No Secret
> Amazing Grace
> Take My Hand
> Precious Lord
> Love of God
> I'd Rather Have Jesus
> How Great Thou Art

*   *   *

Happy Trails To You 20th Century Records
Selections:

> Cowboy Heaven
> A Very Fine Lady
> Hoppy, Gene and Me
> Tennessee Stud
> Happy Trails to You
> Don't Cry, Baby
> Movie Trail Medley:
>   On the Old Spanish Trail
>   Along the Navajo Trail

Blue Shadows on the Trail
Cold, Cold Heart
Good News, Bad News
Don't Ever Wear It for Him

*   *   *

In the Sweet By and By Word Records
    With Dale Evans
Selections:

    Jesus in the Morning
    If I Can Help Somebody
    In the Sweet By and By
    I'll Fly Away
    On the Wings of a Snow White Dove
    Peace in the Valley
    Cowboy's Prayer
    Softly and Tenderly
    This Little Light of Mine
    Stars of Hope
    Whispering Hope

*   *   *

Jesus Loves Me Camden Records (re-released by Pickwick)
    With Dale Evans
Selections:

    Read the Bible and Pray
    I'll Be a Sunbeam
    The Bible Tells Me So
    Watch What You Do
    Did You Stop To Pray This Morning?
    Jesus Loves Me
    The Lord Is Counting on You
    A Cowboy Sunday
    (I'll Pray for You) Until We Meet Again

*   *   *

All-Star Country Christmas Capital Records
    With Dale Evans

Selections:

    I'll Be Home for Christmas
    It's the Most Wonderful Time of the Year
        and additional selections by other Capital artists.

*   *   *

The Great American Singing Cowboys Republic Records
Selections:

    Blue Shadows on the Trail
    Yellow Rose of Texas
        and ten additional selections by other singing
        cowboys.

*   *   *

Great Gospel Songs Word Records
Selections:

    On the Wings of a Snow White Dove (with Dale Evans)
    Cowboy's Prayer
        and additional selections by other artists.

*   *   *

Great Gospel Songs Encore Word Records
Selections:

    Softly and Tenderly (with Dale Evans)
        and additional selections by other artists.

*   *   *

Single recordings available:

    Cowboy Heaven, 20th Century Records
    Don't Ever Wear It for Him, 20th Century Records
    Good News, Bad News, 20th Century Records
    Hoppy, Gene and Me, 20th Century Records
    Happy Anniversary, Capital Records
    Lovenworth, Capital Records

*   *   *

6 Eddie Dean

"You see, our business is usually, to a great extent, feast or famine. Now I'm one of the fortunate few. I've never had the great, tremendous feast of being the super-star, and yet I've never been to the point where I had nothing to eat. I've been lucky."

I have never forgotten my childhood fascination with the fan-magazine-acquired knowledge that Eddie Dean was the seventh son of a seventh son of a seventh son. Someone once told me that meant that he was supposed to be a lucky person. I know as a youngster I marveled at how the chancy dominoes of life would have to fall with inexplicable precision to bring about such a phenomenon as being the seventh son of a seventh son of a seventh son. In my childhood innocence of the 1940s it all seemed rather amazing and not a little mystical. But now, in the second half of the 1970s, with that piece of fan magazine puffery only a dim memory (but still usable for trivia quizzes: What singing cowboy was the seventh son of a seventh son of a seventh son?) and with Eddie Dean and his charming wife, Dearest, sitting across from me at the hotel coffee shop, I was more interested in putting together the pieces of an interesting and varied show business career.

*   *   *

I had done my homework in preparation for this interview with Eddie. I had traced his career from an initial tour through the Midwest singing with a quartet in the late twenties to singing with his brother, Jimmie (not the "Big John" sausage king, Jimmy Dean), on WIBW radio in Topeka for two years starting in 1930. Acting in radio serials in Chicago during the early 1930s led to performing

Eddie Dean.

in radio's "National Barn Dance" program; then it was off to Hollywood and scrounging for roles in cowboy pictures during the late thirties and early forties while serving as vocalist on Judy Canova's radio show. A recording contract and some popular country-Western recordings followed during the 1940s, and finally there was the series of PRC

594-1A

Eddie Dean in a publicity still taken during the time he was
starring in a musical Western series for PRC Pictures.

(Producer's Releasing Corporation) motion pictures between 1945 and 1948. During these years he was also building a reputation as a composer of some note.

A review of his film career indicated that he certainly had not been the darling of the critics. Eddie's film performances were generally described as "so-so," "self-conscious," or "indifferent." Occasionally a critic would describe his performance as "relatively good," "okay," "credible," or "pleasing." The following comment by a *Variety* critic reviewing Eddie Dean's performance in his first starring feature (*Song of Old Wyoming,* 1945) could almost be counted as a rave notice:

> . . .pleasantest aspect of the picture is Eddie Dean's performance as a casual, peace-loving cowhand who, in a pinch, knows how to use his dukes.

The best comments about Dean's performance were reserved for his singing talent: "voice is excellent," "one of the better sets of pipes among cowboy Carusos."

But newspaper and trade critics generally missed the point or else could not appreciate the point of the B Westerns—that they were made primarily for youngsters and dyed-in-the-wool Western fans. The audiences flocked to the theaters to see a particular cowboy personality or to spend an hour vicariously living the adventures of a semifictional time in our past—the early West as depicted on the movie screens of the nation. Most of the singing cowboys of the movie screens were pleasant, appealing country-Western singers who happened to stumble into a profitable side-endeavor—motion-picture-making. Their previous acting training was generally limited, if it existed at all. Such was the case of Eddie Dean, who was in my opinion without peer among Western singers, and who—though lacking formal acting training—acquitted himself very adequately in the thesping and fisti-cuffing departments in the eyes of his fans despite the carping of some critics.

Eddie Dean's Cinecolor series for PRC Pictures was definitely a couple of cuts above the usual screen fare produced by this very small, independent company. PRC's pictures generally failed to camouflage the haste and limited resources that had gone into their production. Often, however, there was an appeal generated by the breezy characterizations of the leading men that seemed to result from the unstudied, frantic pace of production. The Buster Crabbe Billy the Kid series and the Texas Rangers series (with Dave O'Brien,

James Newill, and Guy Wilkerson) produced by PRC had appeal that certainly transcended their limited production values. The early Eddie Dean films, particularly those which co-starred Al "Lash" LaRue or Dave Sharpe, such as *Song of Old Wyoming, The Caravan Trail, Colorado Serenade,* and *Wild West,* exuded much of this same "breezy" quality and surely represent some of the finest product turned out by PRC and Eddie Dean.

The Dean films, unlike so many of the Gene Autry and Roy Rogers "modern" Westerns, all took place in the early West of the late 1800s. There were no lavish production numbers in his films—the saddle serenades were worked into the plots as logically as possible given the peculiarities of the musical Western genre.

Eddie Dean was fortunate in having two appealing comic sidekicks during his film career—Emmett Lynn and Roscoe Ates. Although Emmett Lynn appeared in the first three Eddie Dean films (as Ezra or Uncle Ezra) and was very popular in his familiar role of the crotchety, but still lovable, old codger, he was to gain his greatest recognition in the Red Ryder series produced by Republic and Eagle-Lion during the 1940s. Roscoe Ates put in longer service with Eddie Dean (fifteen films) playing the comic character called Soapy in his standard bumbling, popeyed, stuttering manner that he had utilized repeatedly in films since 1930—mostly to the delight of his many fans.

* * *

With breakfast now over and a second cup of coffee poured by the waitress, Eddie Dean was ready to reflect on his long career—eager almost, it appeared. Dearest, his wife for over forty years, sat quietly at his side obviously proud of his accomplishments having lived with him through the good years and the not-so-good years of his multifaceted career.

DAVID ROTHEL: I know that you were in a lot of pictures in small roles before you starred in the series for PRC. How did you happen to get into pictures?

EDDIE DEAN: Well, actually I went from Chicago to Hollywood on the flip of a coin. I was on CBS radio coast to coast from the Wrigley Building in Chicago with a show for General Mills—what they call a soap opera. When the show left the air, I had to go somewhere, so I flipped a coin to see whether it would be New York or Hollywood. The man who wrote the radio show wanted me to go to New York and go into musical

Dearest Dean and Eddie Dean at the time of the interview with David Rothel.

comedy. Well, I couldn't see myself doing that, but anyway, I flipped a coin and it came up heads and so I went to Hollywood. Mainly, I wanted to get into radio as a singer. Some of the biggest shows were coming out of there [Hollywood] and I thought if I could hit one of those I'd have it made. I almost got on the Jack Benny show. I was up for it when Kenny Baker left, but they wanted another tenor and Dennis Day took over. They said they wanted a tenor that could play a sort of dumb role, which this Irish boy did so beautifully. I'm glad he got it; it worked out fine.

As I said, basically, I went out to Hollywood for radio, but finally it got to the point where I couldn't get a job anywhere except working in a few little nightclubs. I ran into a friend who said, "Why don't you go out and do some Western pictures? You can ride a horse, can't you?" I said, "Sure." He said, "Well, why don't you go out to Republic and see the casting director. But when you go, if he asks you if you can ride a horse, tell him you can ride anything." So I went out and I got an appointment with the casting director. One of the first things he said was, "Can you ride a

horse?" I said, "Sure." That was all I said. "Well, we'll see," he said. So about three days later I ran into my friend again and he said, "What did you tell him?" I said that I told him I could ride a horse. He said, "I told you to tell him you could ride *anything*. They won't hire you unless you tell them that. You got to brag on yourself."

So I went back to Republic and the casting director didn't even remember my being there before. So again he asked me if I could ride a horse. I said, "I can ride anything you've got." He said, "Well, that's good. Can you read a script?" I said, "Sure." "Well, take this outside and in about five or ten minutes come back and read for me." So I went out and read two parts and memorized them right quick—two or three pages—and went back in. He said, "Which part do you want to do?" I said, "It doesn't matter." He said, "Well, I'll read one. Don't you want the script?" I said, "No." So he read for me and I spoke the lines to him and he said, "Fine." So he got me into the Guild. You see, at that time it was a closed shop, the Screen Actor's Guild. And that's how I got into pictures.

DAVID ROTHEL: What year was that?

EDDIE DEAN: That was in 1938. I went out in the fall of '37. It was around early fall or late summer of '38. It was almost a year before I got any break at all. The morning I was supposed to go to work on my first picture I couldn't get to the studio because of a tremendous rain and flooding that occurred. The river had washed out all the bridges; we saw houses going down the river. I had to go from Burbank way around through Glendale and back through Hollywood and over to North Hollywood to get to Republic studios across the river. When I got there, they were waiting on me. I was so upset because it was my first day to do a picture and here I was late. The production manager laughed and said, "Well, none of us could get to work on time this morning." So we went out on location and did a couple of scenes. That was all I did in the picture, but that started me, and from then on I guess I worked in over a hundred pictures for Republic. I worked in the Lone Ranger serial with Bob Livingstone [*The Lone Ranger Rides Again* (1939)] just doing a little ole part, you know, that ran for thirteen weeks for me. It fed my family, which was great.

DAVID ROTHEL: You did a few Gene Autrys, too, I believe.

EDDIE DEAN: I did a couple, yes, and I did one little bit part in a Roy Rogers, and I did a lot of Bob Steeles and Red Barrys and Powells and . . . .

DAVID ROTHEL: Lee Powell who was one of the Lone Rangers in the first Lone Ranger serial?

[*The Lone Ranger* (1938). There were five actors who played the Lone Ranger in the serial, but that's another book.]

EDDIE DEAN: That's right. I did a picture with Lee Powell in which I had a fight with him. He was awful rough to fight with because he didn't know how to pull a punch. He'd hit you! The other actors tipped me off. They said, "Don't let him hit you; he's big! Don't let him hit you because he doesn't know how to do a fight without hitting somebody. He doesn't know how to angle it." There was quite an art to doing picture fights without getting hurt. I studied the technique so I wouldn't get hurt.

I think I worked on the last picture Lee Powell made—at least one of the very last before he went into the service and was killed. I did nine Hopalong Cassidy pictures. I sang in some of them, which Hoppy didn't like. I didn't blame him.

DAVID ROTHEL: He came out against singing cowboys, didn't he?

EDDIE DEAN: Yes, he didn't want songs in his pictures, but he was nice to me. There wasn't really any call for somebody to sing in his pictures, but "Pop" Sherman [the producer] put me in them in an attempt to get me a series with Paramount—a musical series which never materialized. That's why I was in the Cassidy pictures. I told Hoppy one day that I knew how he felt about singing in his pictures and that I didn't want to sing in them any more.

DAVID ROTHEL: How did you happen to get the series with PRC?

EDDIE DEAN: Bill Crespinel, who had developed Cinecolor, had up to that time only done commercials and little shorts with the color process. He'd been trying and trying to get the big studios interested in using it for color features. Of course Technicolor more or less had everything sewed up. Bill just couldn't get started. So he came to me and told me he would give me an exclusive on Cinecolor for one year if I would sell a series in his color. That is really what sold my pictures—the color—because they had singing cowboys out there like crazy. You could go around every corner and run into a singing cowboy.

DAVID ROTHEL: There weren't many good ones, though.

EDDIE DEAN: No, there weren't many good ones, that's true. The first series picture I had the lead in was called *Song of Old Wyoming* [PRC, 1945]. However, I had been featured in a picture with Ken Maynard, Max Terhune, and Ruth Roman a couple of years before called *The White Stallion* [Astor Pictures, 1944]. After I starred in my first couple of pictures they changed the billing on *The White Stallion,* giving me the lead billing, and re-released it. I guess they thought Ken was through; that was Ken Maynard's last picture. It was a sad day for me, but it was also a break for me when they gave me that top billing on *The White Stallion.*

DAVID ROTHEL: You were the first singing cowboy to do movies in color, weren't you?

EDDIE DEAN: I was, yes. That's right.

DAVID ROTHEL: I think the film that really turned me on to your work was *Caravan Trail,* in which you sang "Wagon Wheels." I haven't seen the movie since I was a kid, but I've always remembered that song and the way you sang it.

EDDIE DEAN: I'm glad you were impressed by it, because I've been identified with that song almost as if I had written it. I wish I had written it. I guess I'm the one who popularized it as much as anybody by singing it in that film.

DAVID ROTHEL: I remember seeing the previews to the movie and for some reason being turned on by that one song and the fact that the film was going to be in color. They had a John Wayne re-release called *Rainbow Valley* coming up that same week at the theater. Somehow I got the two films confused—perhaps because the word "rainbow" in the title of the Wayne film reminded me of the color in your film—and a few days later I saw *Rainbow Valley* by mistake. I discovered, of course, that the song wasn't there and you weren't there. So I had to go back a few days after that to see you and hear you sing the song. Emmett Lynn was your sidekick in *Caravan Trail,* wasn't he?

EDDIE DEAN: Yes. I had first worked with Emmett Lynn when I had the CBS radio show out of Chicago. He was my comedian on the program. Emmett was the type of guy that, if he didn't like you, would chew up the scenery around you and not give you a break. If he liked you, he'd be nice to you. Well, he liked me, and he was nice to me; he was a great guy to work with. One of the greatest comedians and actors that ever lived was Emmett Lynn.

DAVID ROTHEL: How long did it take to shoot one of your Westerns?

EDDIE DEAN: About ten days. The average Western in black and white went five to six days.

DAVID ROTHEL: Budgets were around fifty thousand dollars, weren't they?

EDDIE DEAN: I think my first picture cost thirty-six thousand dollars. Before it was in release three weeks, it made over a million. That's why they signed me up right quick—took up my option.

DAVID ROTHEL: In the years you worked at

PRC was there one particular director that you enjoyed working with?

EDDIE DEAN: I think Ray Taylor was my favorite. Ernie Miller was my favorite cameraman. He was such a fine cameraman; he wouldn't let anything happen to make me look bad. The lighting and makeup had to be right. He'd always check to see if there was perspiration on my face; he wanted me to look good, you know. Ray Taylor thought I had a certain resemblance to the great William S. Hart.

DAVID ROTHEL: You certainly do.

EDDIE DEAN: Ray had directed William S. Hart and Ernie Miller had photographed him in years past. They thought my eyes were like his; that I had the same steely eyes and expression. Of course, I thought it was a great compliment because Bill Hart had a certain charisma about him that was good. We saw one of my films recently, and I could see the Bill Hart resemblance.

DAVID ROTHEL: What's your reaction to seeing one of your films—one that you haven't seen for many years?

EDDIE DEAN: It's as if it's not me. It's somebody else. A lot of the scenes I don't remember, because I was working so hard at the time.

DAVID ROTHEL: Which is the favorite of your films, or do you have a favorite?

EDDIE DEAN: No, I don't think so. There are some song sequences that I especially like. I like the "On the Banks of The Sunny San Juan" sequence.

DAVID ROTHEL: That's one you wrote, isn't it?

EDDIE DEAN: Yes, along with Glenn Strange. It had a mood . . . .

DAVID ROTHEL: You wrote that with Glenn Strange? The actor, Glenn Strange?

EDDIE DEAN: Yes.

DAVID ROTHEL: I never realized he did any song writing.

EDDIE DEAN: Glenn Strange was one of the top men of the original Arizona Wranglers years ago. He played fiddle and sang. He was also a protégé of Jack Dempsey until he busted his hands up. He was a fighter and a real, true cowboy; he was raised on a ranch out in New Mexico.

DAVID ROTHEL: You wrote many of the songs for your films, didn't you?

EDDIE DEAN: Most of the title songs except for "Wagon Wheels" and "Hills of Old Wyoming" were written by Hal Blair and myself. We wrote "Stars Over Texas," "West to Glory," all of those big-sounding songs that make good title songs.

DAVID ROTHEL: Do you have any idea how many songs you have written?

EDDIE DEAN: It would be difficult to sing all of them or remember all of them. When I joined BMI as a writer some years ago, I had to go through and give them a list of songs that I'd written and recorded. I found out that there were about forty songs of mine that had been recorded that I'd forgotten about in the past. I would say that I've written close to a hundred songs all together. I've had a few pretty good hits. The biggest, of course, are "One Has My Name, The Other Has My Heart" and "I Dreamed of a Hillbilly Heaven."

DAVID ROTHEL: What inspired you to write "Hillbilly Heaven?"

EDDIE DEAN: "Hillbilly Heaven" was written because Hal Southern had a dream something like the story the song tells. We then got together and wrote the song and I recorded it on a small label called Sage and Sand. When I saw that the song wouldn't have the distribution on a small label that it should have, I went to Capital Records in hopes that they would let Tex Ritter do the song. I got the message that they didn't believe in commercializing on the deceased. Well, that floored me a little bit, because I felt that "Hillbilly Heaven" was paying tribute to many of the friends I'd known in the business for many years. About five years later I finally called Tex and said, "You've got to do 'Hillbilly Heaven' on Capital." He said he'd go to work on it. Then one day I went over to Capital to see Lee Gillette who was head A and R man. I had my record of "Hillbilly Heaven" with me. When I started to leave, he said, "What's this?" I said, "You don't want to hear this. It's just a song of mine." "Well, I'd like to hear it," he said. He played it and said, "That's a great song, Eddie." I said, "Why don't you let someone on Capital do it?" He said, "I don't have an artist on Capital that could do it." I said, "You have one of the greatest, Tex Ritter." He swiveled in his chair and in a moment said, "We've got an album coming up with Tex next week. We'll throw it into the session." And that's the way Tex Ritter got to do "Hillbilly Heaven."

Now "One Has My Name" came about in an entirely different way. My wife Dearest and I had been discussing the idea for a song for about six years, but couldn't come up with the right title. One day Hal Blair and I were out writing a song—actually a rewrite—entitled "Wake Me in the Morning by the Swanee River." I was going to record it. Dearest came out to our little studio and said, "I have the title for the song we've been trying to write." I said, "Honey, we're busy; wait just a minute. We're just finishing this song." She said, "But I have the title; forget everything else. I've got the title." I said, "What title?" She said, "One Has My Name, The Other Has My Heart." Well, we put "Swanee River" aside. Each one of us wrote lyrics and I started singing it. I did the music and within fifteen minutes I had it on the tape. That's the way that song came about.

DAVID ROTHEL: Recently I have had the opportunity to see a good sampling of the films made by the singing cowboys. I've seen films starring Monte Hale, Jimmy Wakely, Rex Allen, Tex Ritter, Gene Autry, Roy Rogers, and you. Seeing the singing cowboys in their films during such a short period of time has given me a chance to evaluate them as singers. You know, you are really a much better singer than the others, and, of course, they are pretty darned good singers. You really are the best in my opinion.

EDDIE DEAN: Well, that's a nice compliment. I think I've probably been a better singer than actor. I think I could have been a good actor if I had had the opportunity to really get in and study acting. I did a lot of radio acting. I must say I did well on radio as an actor. I did a lot of different character parts as well as playing myself. But when it came to pictures, that was a different phase of the business. I was thrown into it without any experience, any *real* experience. I had done little bit parts where you throw an occasional line here and there, but the rest of the time you stood with egg on your face. You never really got into a part. When I went into my own picture series, I thought, well, the only thing I can do is just be myself as much as I can and hope that I'm not too hammy—let it come out as best as it will and depend on the singing, which is my forte anyway, to put me over. The way it worked out, I think it did. Don't misunderstand, I'm not putting myself down as an actor. I think I could have been—without bragging—a super actor if I'd had the experience some had, really.

DAVID ROTHEL: Do you still live in California today?

EDDIE DEAN: Yes. Dearest and I live in a place called West Lake Village about forty miles out of Los Angeles, northwest out of the smog. We live on a lake. We've traveled all over, but we think it's the most beautiful place in the world.

DEAREST DEAN: I always say it's like living in a beautiful resort without having to check out in the morning. (laugh)

DAVID ROTHEL: Mrs. Dean, your first name is very unusual. Is it your real given name?

DEAREST DEAN: My name is really Lorene, but everybody calls me Dearest.

EDDIE DEAN: She writes under that name, too. She's helped write a lot of songs. When we first went out to California, she had an opportunity to go into pictures. They came to her and said, "Listen, we'd like to get you a screen test." She said, "One in the family is enough. If he does his work, that'll be enough." She's a beautiful, intelligent girl, but she cares nothing about that end of it. Incidentally, we've been married forty-three years, and she's been as much a part of my life as any other thing in existence. She's helped me and stuck by me. Dearest happens to be a Libra and I'm a Cancer, so I go in all directions, you know. (laugh) She's my balance wheel. She's been very good for me; I love her and she loves me, and that's unusual today. When some of the young folks talk to me about their problems of getting along with each other, I tell them I'm listening, but I don't understand because that's something that never happened to us.

DEAREST DEAN: I know one little tidbit of information that Eddie won't tell you that I'm real proud of. Eddie's listed in *Who's Who in the West*.

DAVID ROTHEL: I didn't know that. I do know that you were listed among the top box-office cowboys for a period of time in the late forties.

EDDIE DEAN: Yes. *Fame Magazine* did a survey of exhibitors. The first year that I did a series of pictures [1946] I hit the top ten. There were a lot of big cowboy stars then, you know.

DAVID ROTHEL: There sure were.

EDDIE DEAN: And the competition wasn't just the leading men; it was also against the comics like Smiley Burnette and Gabby Hayes. So to me that was just fabulous for the first year, unbelievable. I was very proud of that.

DAVID ROTHEL: What have you been doing in recent years? You're still singing, aren't you?

EDDIE DEAN: Oh, yes. Lately mostly in nightclubs, because there's not much else to do. I wouldn't have left the pictures if it hadn't been for television coming in and closing all the theaters at that time. Then I worked rodeos and fairs, but now mostly it's nightclubs. But if you get a hot recording or get a little break in a picture, then everything starts to turn again.

DAVID ROTHEL: Roy Rogers got back into films a while ago.

EDDIE DEAN: Yes. I saw Roy not too long ago. He's a nice man; he is a good man. You see, if you get a few good shots as he did not so long ago, then everything turns around. Roy made a record

["Hoppy, Gene, and Me"] and that got him started again. Well, I need a good record. If I get a record album that comes out with a good single, makes an impression with the distributors, sells a lot of copies, there's no limit to what you can do then. You can work shows til you have to turn them down. Man, it's unbelievable, because if you go and do a good job then everybody starts wanting you. The main thing is to be in a position to get on. You see, our business is usually, to a great extent, feast or famine. Now I'm one of the fortunate few. I've never had the great, tremendous feast of being the super-star, and yet I've never been to the point where I had nothing to eat. I've been lucky; I've been able to work consistently, continually, all the time. A lot of artists—what you call stars—are unable to do that. So I'm very fortunate. I think maybe in my case it's because I'm a singer. I play an instrument so I can go out and do a show by myself, if necessary, or I can work with a big band. I do a variety of material. I do everything from the classics, as you know, down to real country music, and I do a lot of the modern country stuff. Thank God the fans remember me because of the name I've built up on records and in pictures, so I don't have too much trouble getting bookings.

DAVID ROTHEL: In your years of filmmaking you only worked in B Westerns. How do you feel they compare with the big-budget A Westerns?

EDDIE DEAN: I only had the chance to do what we call small, budget Westerns, so when you talk about the big boys, you know, the big Westerns, you're talking about something I know nothing about. On the screen they didn't look much better than what we called the small ones, but maybe they took more time, many more months and much more money, and the big stars got paid more. But it seems to me that small Westerns were the ones that really made the money for the studios, really.

DAVID ROTHEL: Thank you, Eddie Dean and Dearest Dean, for taking time to talk with me.

Eddie Dean and his wife, Dearest, pose for David Rothel's camera.

Harmony Trail (also known as *White Stallion*) (Astor Pictures, 1944) 54 M.

Producer, Walt Mattox; director, Robert Emmett; screenplay, Frank Simpson; camera, Edward Kull; editor, Fred Bain; musical director, Frank Sanucci.

CAST: Ken Maynard, Eddie Dean, Rocky Camron, Max Terhune, Glenn Strange, Ruth Roman, Bob McKenzie, Charles King, Bud Osborne, Al Ferguson, Dan White, Fred Gildart, Jerry Shields, Hal Price, John Bridges.

*   *   *

EDDIE DEAN
SELECTED FILMOGRAPHY

The following filmography only includes the Western films in which Eddie Dean starred.

*   *   *

Song of Old Wyoming (PRC Pictures, 1945) 66 M. Cinecolor

Producer and director, Robert Emmett; screenplay, Frances Kavanaugh; camera, Marcel LePicard; editor, Hugh Winn; musical director, Carl Hoefle; songs, Ralph Rainger, Leo Robin, Eddie Dean, Milt Mabie, Carl Hoefle.

CAST: Eddie Dean, Sarah Padden, Al LaRue, Jennifer Holt, Emmett Lynn, Ray Elder, John Carpenter, Ian Keith, Lee Bennett, Bob Barron, Horace Murphy, Pete Katchenaro, Rocky Camron, Bill Lovett, Richard Cramer, Steve Clark.

* * *

Romance of the West (PRC Pictures, 1946) 58 M. Cinecolor

Producer and director, Robert Emmett; screenplay, Frances Kavanaugh; camera, Marcel LePicard; editor, Hugh Winn; color supervisor, W. T. Crespinel; musical director, Carl Hoefle; songs, Sam Franklin, Bob Nolan, Bernard Barnes, Carl Wiage.

CAST: Eddie Dean, Joan Barton, Emmett Lynn, Forrest Taylor, Robert McKenzie, Jerry Jerome, Stanley Price, Chief Thundercloud, Dan Reynolds, Rocky Camron, Lee Roberts, Leslie Harrison, Don Williams, Jack Richardson, Matty Roubert, Forbes Murray, Jack O'Shea.

* * *

Chief Thundercloud and Eddie Dean in a scene from *Romance of the West.*

Eddie Dean and Emmett Lynn in the "Wagon Wheels" musical sequence from *The Caravan Trail.*

The Caravan Trail (PRC Pictures, 1946) 53 M. Cinecolor

Producer and director, Robert Emmett; screenplay, Frances Kavanaugh; camera, Marcel LePicard; editor, Hugh Winn; musical director, Carl Hoefle; songs, Billy Hill, Peter DeRose, Eddie Dean, Lew Porter, Johnny Bond.

CAST: Eddie Dean, Al LaRue, Emmett Lynn, Jean Carlin, Robert Malcolm, Charles King, Robert Barron, Forrest Taylor, Bob Duncan, Jack O'Shea, Terry Frost.

*   *   *

Colorado Serenade (PRC Pictures, 1946) 68 M. Cinecolor

Producer and director, Robert Emmett Tansey; screenplay, Frances Kavanaugh; camera, Robert

Shackelford; editor, Hugh Winn; songs, Eddie Dean, H. L. Canova, Sam Armstrong, Carl Hoefle.

CAST: Eddie Dean, David Sharpe, Roscoe Ates, Mary Kenyon, Forrest Taylor, Dennis Moore, Abigail Adams, Warner Richmond, Lee Bennett, Robert McKenzie, Bob Duncan.

* * *

Down Missouri Way (PRC Pictures, 1946) 73 M.

Producer and director, Josef Berns; screenplay, Sam Neuman; camera, Vincent J. Farrar; editor, W. Don Hayes; musical director, Karl Hajos; songs, Kim Gannon, Walter Kent.

CAST: Martha O'Driscoll, John Carradine, Eddie Dean, William Wright, Roscoe Ates, Renee Godfrey, Mable Todd, Eddie Craven, Chester Clute, Will Wright, Paul Scardon.

* * *

Driftin' River (PRC Pictures, 1946) 59 M.

Producer and director, Robert Emmett Tansey; screenplay, Frances Kavanaugh; songs, Eddie Dean, Hal Blair.

CAST: Eddie Dean, Shirley Patterson, Roscoe Ates, Lee Bennett, William Fawcett, Dennis Moore, Lottie Harrison, Forrest Taylor, Robert Callahan, Lee Roberts, Don Murphy, The Sunshine Boys.

* * *

Tumbleweed Trail (PRC Pictures, 1946) 58 M.

Producer and director, Robert Emmett Tansey; screenplay, Frances Kavanaugh; camera, Ernest Miller; editor, Hugh Winn; songs, Eddie Dean, Glenn Strange, Johnny Bond, Ernest Bond, Lou Wayne, Bob Shelton.

CAST: Eddie Dean, Roscoe Ates, Shirley Patterson, Johnny McGovern, Bob Duncan, Ted Adams, Jack O'Shea, Kermit Maynard, Bill Fawcett, The Sunshine Boys.

* * *

Stars Over Texas (PRC Pictures, 1946) 57 M.

Producer and director, Robert Emmett Tansey; screenplay, Frances Kavanaugh; camera, Ernest Miller; editor, Hugh Winn; musical director, Karl Hajos; songs, Eddie Dean, Hal Blair, Glenn Strange.

CAST: Eddie Dean, Roscoe Ates, Shirley Patterson, Lee Bennett, Lee Roberts, Kermit Maynard, Jack O'Shea, Hal Smith, Matty Roubert, Carl Mathews, Bill Fawcett, The Sunshine Boys.

* * *

Wild West (PRC Pictures, 1946) 73 M. Cinecolor

Producer and director, Robert Emmett Tansey;

screenplay, Frances Kavanaugh; camera, Fred Jackson, Jr.; editor, Hugh Winn; musical director, Karl Hajos; songs, Dorcas Cochran, Charles Rosoff, Eddie Dean, Ruth and Louis Herscher.

CAST: Eddie Dean, Roscoe Ates, Al LaRue, Robert "Buzzy" Henry, Sarah Padden, Louise Currie, Jean Carlin, Lee Bennett, Terry Frost, Warner Richmond, Lee Roberts, Chief Yowlachie, Bob Duncan, Frank Pharr, Matty Roubert, John Bridges, Al Ferguson, Bud Osborne.

* * *

Wild Country (PRC Pictures, 1947) 60 M.

Producer, Jerry Thomas; director, Ray Taylor; screenplay, Arthur E. Orloff; camera, Robert Cline; editor, Hugh Winn; songs, Eddie Dean, Hal Blair, Pete Gates.

CAST: Eddie Dean, Roscoe Ates, Peggy Wynn, Douglas Fowley, I. Stanford Jolley, Lee Roberts, Forrest Mathews, Bill Fawcett, Henry Hall, Charles Jordan, Richard Cramer, Gus Taute, The Sunshine Boys.

* * *

Range Beyond the Blue (PRC Pictures, 1947) 58 M.

Producer, Jerry Thomas; director, Ray Taylor; camera, Robert Cline; editor, Hugh Winn; musical director, Walter Greene; songs, Eddie Dean, Bob Dean, Pete Gates, Hal Blair.

CAST: Eddie Dean, Roscoe Ates, Helen Mowery, Bob Duncan, Ted Adams, Bill Hammond, George Turner, Ted French, Brad Slavin, Steve Clark, The Sunshine Boys.

* * *

West to Glory (PRC Pictures, 1947) 60 M.

Producer, Jerry Thomas; director, Ray Taylor; screenplay, Elmer Clifton, Robert B. Churchill; camera, Milford Anderson; editor, Hugh Winn; songs, Eddie Dean, Hal Blair, Pete Gates.

CAST: Eddie Dean, Roscoe Ates, Dolores Castle, Gregg Barton, Jimmy Martin, Zon Murray, Alex Montoya, Harry Vejar, Carl Mathews, The Sunshine Boys.

* * *

Black Hills (PRC Pictures/Eagle-Lion Release, 1947) 60 M.

Producer, Jerry Thomas; director, Ray Taylor; screenplay, Joseph Poland; camera, Ernie Miller; editor, Hugh Winn; songs, Eddie Dean, Hal Blair, Pete Gates.

CAST: Eddie Dean, Roscoe Ates, Shirley Patterson, Terry Frost, Steve Drake, Nina Bara, Bill Fawcett, Lane Bradford, Lee Morgan, George Chesebro, The Plainsmen: Andy Parker, Earl Murphy, Paul Smith, George Bamby, Charles Morgan.

* * *

Shadow Valley (PRC Pictures/Eagle-Lion Release, 1947) 61 M.

Producer, Jerry Thomas; director, Ray Taylor; screenplay, Arthur Sherman; camera, Ernest Miller; songs, Pete Gates.

CAST: Eddie Dean, Roscoe Ates, Jennifer Holt, George Chesebro, Eddie Parker, Lee Morgan, Lane Bradford, Carl Mathews, Budd Buster, The Plainsmen: Andy Parker, Earl Murphy, Paul Smith, George Bamby, Charles Morgan.

* * *

Check Your Guns (PRC Pictures/Eagle-Lion Release, 1948) 55 M.

Producer, Jerry Thomas; director, Ray Taylor; screenplay, Joseph O'Donnell; camera, Ernie Miller; editor, Joseph Gluck; songs, Pete Gates, Hal Blair.

CAST: Eddie Dean, Roscoe Ates, Nancy Gates, George Chesebro, Stan Jolley, Mike Conrad, Lane Bradford, Terry Frost, Mason Wynn, Dee Cooper, Bill Fawcett.

* * *

Tornado Range (PRC Pictures/Eagle-Lion Release, 1948) 56 M.

Producer, Jerry Thomas; director, Ray Taylor; screenplay, William Lively; camera, James Brown, Jr.; editor, Joseph Gluck; songs, Eddie Dean, Curt and Alan Massey.

CAST: Eddie Dean, Roscoe Ates, Jennifer Holt, George Chesebro, Brad Slaven, Marshall Reed, Terry Frost, Lane Bradford, Russell Arms, Steve Clark.

* * *

Jennifer Holt, the sister of Tim and the daughter of Jack, was a frequent leading lady in both Eddie Dean and Tex Ritter films.

The Westward Trail (PRC Pictures/Eagle-Lion Release, 1948) 56 M.

Producer, Jerry Thomas; director, Ray Taylor; screenplay, Robert Alan Miller; camera, Ernie Miller; editor, Hugh Winn; songs, Pete Gates, Hal Blair, Eddie Dean.

CAST: Eddie Dean, Roscoe Ates, Phyllis Planchard, Eileene Hardin, Steve Drake, Bob Duncan, Carl Mathews, Lee Morgan, Bob Woodward, Budd Buster, Charles "Slim" Whitaker, Frank Ellis.

* * *

The Hawk of Powder River (PRC Pictures/Eagle-Lion Release, 1948) 54 M.

Producer, Jerry Thomas; director, Ray Taylor; screenplay, George Smith; camera, Ernie Miller; editor, Joe Gluck; songs, Eddie Dean, Hal Blair, Pete Gates.

CAST: Eddie Dean, Roscoe Ates, Jennifer Holt, June Carlson, Andy Parker and The Plainsmen, Terry Frost, Lane Bradford, Eddie Parker, Carl Mathews, Ted French, Steve Clark, Tex Palmer.

* * *

Prairie Outlaws (PRC Pictures/Eagle-Lion Release, 1948) 55 M.

This feature is a re-edited, re-released, black and white version of Eddie Dean's 1946 Cinecolor feature, *Wild West*. As can be seen in the picture's title lobby card, there is no indication of the feature's origin.

* * *

The Tioga Kid (PRC Pictures/Eagle-Lion Release, 1948) 54 M.

Producer, Jerry Thomas; director, Ray Taylor; screenplay, Ed Earl Repp; camera, Ernie Miller; editor, Hugh Winn; songs, Eddie Dean, Johnny Bond, Pete Gates, Lewis Porter, Robert Tansey.

CAST: Eddie Dean, Roscoe Ates, Jennifer Holt, Dennis Moore, Lee Bennett, Bill Fawcett, Eddie Parker, Bob Woodward, Louis J. Corbett, Terry Frost.

* * *

EDDIE DEAN
DISCOGRAPHY

Eddie Dean has been a recording artist since the mid forties when he starred in his musical Western series. The *Sincerely, Eddie Dean* and *Dean of the West* albums were recorded in the 1970s and reveal that Eddie's voice has lost none of its luster with the passing of the years.

Dean of the West WFC (Western Film Collector) Records

Selections:

> Hills of Old Wyoming
> Wagon Wheels
> Courtin' Time
> Tumbleweed Trail
> Black Hills
> Driftin' River
> Ain't No Gal
> Stars Over Texas
> Way Back in Oklahoma
> Banks of the Sunny San Juan

*   *   *

Sincerely, Eddie Dean Shasta Records

Selections:

> One Has My Name
> Release Me
> Tumbling Tumbleweeds
> I Fall to Pieces
> Make the World Go Away
> That Silver-Haired Daddy of Mine
> Green Green Grass of Home
> Born To Lose
> Old Shep
> Just a Closer Walk with Thee
> Hillbilly Heaven

*   *   *

The Great American Singing Cowboys Republic Records

Selections:

> Banks of the Rio Grande
> Hillbilly Heaven
>   and ten additional selections by other singing cowboys.

7   Jimmy Wakely

"Through the grace of God and Gene Autry, I got a career."

Jimmy Wakely answered the phone on the first ring, causing me to be somewhat taken aback at the suddenness of my being thrust into the telephone presence of this singing cowboy. The voice was unmistakable and you knew immediately that he could break into "Slippin' Around" with Margaret Whiting or "One Has My Name, The Other Has My Heart" and that the songs would sound the same as they had in the late forties when he first recorded them and became one of the leading recording artists in the country.

Over the years I had forgotten just how popular Jimmy Wakely had been as a recording artist. In the *Cash Box* poll of "Best Western Recording Artists" Jimmy placed first in both 1949 and 1950. In the *Billboard* poll of "Top Artists on Juke Boxes" in the folk category Jimmy placed third behind Eddy Arnold and Hank Williams. And in the *Billboard* "Top Male Singers on Juke Boxes" poll he placed third behind Perry Como and Frankie Laine. Bing Crosby was fourth!

I quickly explained to Jimmy what I was up to—putting together this book on all the singing cowboys and their films and records. I asked if I might tape an interview with him sometime soon about his career as a singing cowboy for Monogram Pictures in the mid to late forties and other related matters. He coughed, excused himself and commented that he'd just caught a cold while making a singing appearance up in Anchorage.

"I just came home from Alaska," he said. "We flew in here [Los Angeles] last night. I looked out at this beautiful blue sky and at this gorgeous city—it was seventy degrees—and I said to my

Jimmy Wakely. *Photo courtesy of Jimmy Wakely.*

daughter, 'What a beautiful thing it is to come out of a land of darkness into this.' When you called I was just sitting here thinking I'd go out after a bit and get a half-hour's sunlight; it's a gorgeous day. All I've got to do today is get some sun. I was going to play golf and I decided not to. I've just got some loose ends to catch up with. I would be glad to talk with you right now."

I slid my notes and a list of questions over next to the phone (I would never call anyone without being prepared, just in case). In recent days I had been reviewing Wakely's career, which had been long and varied—providing musical support for nonsinging Western stars with his Jimmy Wakely Trio during the late thirties and early forties; being a top recording artist for many years, especially during the late forties and early fifties; starring in his own modestly successful musical Western series for Monogram Pictures during the mid to late forties; headlining his own CBS radio show during the fifties; and throughout his career appearing at fairs, rodeos, clubs, and theaters all over the country, including such prestigious watering holes as the Thunderbird in Las Vegas and Harrah's Club.

I had heard that his main concern now was watching over his Shasta Records Company, one of the more successful mail-order record businesses around according to *Billboard* magazine; and an item in *Variety* indicated that he was now hosting a daily radio program for Radio Iran.

I punched the record button on my telephone cassette recorder. It purred into motion as Jimmy coughed and cleared his throat again—he undoubtedly needed that thirty minutes of sun for his sore throat and cold more than he needed to use his voice talking to me about his career.

We skipped over his earliest years out in

Jimmy Wakely today. *Photo courtesy of Jimmy Wakely.*

Mineola, Arkansas, and various dust-bowl, four-corner towns in Oklahoma because he promised to send me some material he had prepared on those gritty childhood days marked by frequent family poverty. He was as good as his word and in a few days I was reading over the packet of information he had prepared. Excerpts follow:

"I was born in a ghetto, a hundred miles from town/ Where copperheads and rattle-snakes crawl on the worthless ground/ Where fugitives from justice would hide out from the law/ In those Oklahoma hills just west of Arkansas."

The above words from a song I wrote tell a true story except for the fact that I was born on the Arkansas side of the line near a little town called Mineola, Arkansas. My dad decided to move to Octavia, Oklahoma, when I was three and then to Ida—later named Battiest, Oklahoma—when I was four. It was then that my mind started to record memories of day to day events.

Our locality was inhabited by seed ticks, snakes, chiggers, log cutters, bootleggers, outlaws on the run, and just plain folks. The strength of a man was measured by how much he could lift or who he could whip in a fist fight. If a young boy went to church with his parents, he was called a sissy by some. In all my years I have never witnessed as much ignorance per square acre. In October, 1927, the Wakely family moved to western Oklahoma to pick cotton. We stayed and farmed near Cowden.

1931-1932 were terrible years. Those black clouds of dust would form and people would drive with headlights on in the daytime. You might go to bed at night knowing you had a green wheat field and tomorrow it was gone—blown out of the ground.

Thousands of dust bowl victims migrated to California while others headed for the hills. Papa said, "We will have water, wood to cook with, and I can always shoot a deer if we get hungry." We loaded up the old model T truck with two pigs, a cage of chickens, our personal things, and Papa, Mama and I moved back to Battiest.

"My daddy was a workin' man, part time at the mill/ My uncle had a better job, he ran a whiskey still/ The whistle of that lonesome train made chills run up my spine/ But how can a young man get away, when he hasn't got a dime."

We left western Oklahoma with a total of $28.00, and arrived in Battiest with only five bucks. Come spring of 1933 the hogs died with cholera and the hens stopped laying eggs.

Wood and water were not enough, and cooked fresh peaches from the tree without sugar or cream were not very tasty. Papa would often go up to old man Evans' saw mill hoping for a day's work. Sometimes he worked a day or two.

I remember well the day I heard Franklin Roosevelt say, "All we have to fear is fear itself." His words came to life in a real way. I worked on the road three days per month for $5.00, which went a long way at the local store. I wanted to get out of there—go anywhere. I would hear the whistle of a distant log train, see the black smoke from its stack, and wish I were on it. Ol' Jimmie Rodgers' hobo songs started to pull at my imagination. I knew that somewhere people had electric lights, indoor plumbing, rugs on the floor, and food that was tasty. I also knew that it would take time to make that dream come true.

Then came the long hot summer. Our well went dry and we carried water from a spring a quarter of a mile away. Mosquitoes were all over the place and I came down with malaria. My mother would put wet sheets across my body to try to cool my fever while I would look up at the rafters in my room and watch them change places as if in a kaleidoscope. When I got well I weighed 125 pounds. It was then that I resolved to escape from that ghetto. . . .

My dad was a hard working man, and mama worked in the field along side of the rest of us—my brothers John and Fletch, and my sister, Effie. We never had a generation gap at our house as my parents understood and supported our wishes as well as they could. My family would go to bed on a summer night and I would often sit out on the front porch and sing Jimmie Rodgers' songs and play an old guitar, or play the piano and sing the current popular songs. The family never put me down for this although none of them were musically inclined. Looking back, I must have seemed a little weird because of my attitude that prompted me to depart from the accepted practices of our surroundings. . . .

When we moved to Rosedale I met several very nice people, and I especially liked the George Miser family. The boys, Grady and Harvey, and I used to sit around playing guitars. We were all fans of Milton Brown and His Musical Brownies who were heard each morning on radio on a Ft. Worth, Texas, station. I remember when their sister, Inez, cooked a box of candy and sent it to Milton who acknowledged it on the air and sent her an 8 x 10 autographed picture of him and his band.

Inez was like that, always doing something for somebody. I paid little attention to her even though we used to double date—she with my friend and I with her girl friend. Then Inez broke up with her boy friend and I broke up with my girl friend. Inez went to Oklahoma City to go to college. It was then that I realized that she had already become a part of my life. I went to the City and brought her back. We were married on Friday, December 13, 1935, when I was operating a filling station in Rosedale. She has been with me all the way. . . .

Times were hard in 1937, but we didn't know it. We were unaccustomed to the frills of life and anything we did was an improvement on our life style.

My wife Inez and our first born, Deanna, and I moved into an apartment in Oklahoma City. The rent was $3.25 per week. It was so small you could sit on the bed and take the biscuits out of the oven. Inez taught me love, faith and patience. We worked together and dreamed of a future, maybe even Hollywood some day.

I got a job playing piano with Merle Salathiel and his Barnyard Boys on Friday nights for $2.00 and on Saturday nights from 9:00 P.M. to 4:00 A.M. for $4.00. There were no intermissions on Fridays and only one, at midnight, on Saturdays. I also got a job singing on KTOK for fifteen minutes each morning for $2.50 per week. I would sing popular songs and play piano, and sing a cowboy song or two and play my guitar. As you can see, I was making $8.50 per week.

In the summer of 1937 I got a job with Little Doc Roberts' Medicine Show at $14.00 per week. It was showing near the stockyard in Oklahoma City. The medicine show then located at Chickasha for three weeks in September and closed for the season. In Chickasha I was paid $17.00 per week. My wife was paid $5.00 per week for handing out Little Doc's Tonic to the folks. She also sang on the stage with me. . . .

Allen Clark, program director of radio station WKY, called me and offered me a job singing in a trio to be known as The Bell Boys. It was for three mornings a week, fifteen minutes, five dollars—unheard of money! WOW! Things were getting better. The trio was composed of Scotty Harrel, Jack Cheney and me. Staff guitar man, Mel Osborne, played for us. I soon concluded that this was a dull act. It had no fire, just stale arrangements. It had to fail and I didn't want a failure because WKY was a big station and this was a real opportunity.

Then I met a man who was destined to be my biggest boost along the way, Phil Esterline, the owner of the Bell Clothing Stores in Oklahoma City and Tulsa that were our sponsors. Phil had an open mind and believed in me. I suggested several changes to him. I wanted to do concerts in high schools and theaters; he agreed. I wanted to get some Western clothing and sing cowboy songs; he agreed. I wanted to drop Jack Cheney and Mel Osborne and bring in my pal, Johnny Bond, who could take both their places as he not only sang but played a fine guitar; Phil agreed. . . .

When Phil put us on the air five days per week, The Bell Boys started to take hold in that part of the country. Phil loaned me enough money for a down payment on a car. Then we bought one of those solid spare tire covers and painted a big red bell on it and words advertising our sponsor, station, and broadcast time. . . .We were a struggling trio of singers—Johnny Bond, Scotty Harrel and me—appearing in concert in local high schools around the state.

One night after such an engagement for which we earned about fifteen dollars, we started home. As we approached the main highway to Oklahoma City, a sudden flash of lightning lit up the sky and I caught a glimpse of a face that caused me to stop. I backed the car to where I could turn it so that the car lights would let me see it clearly. It was a placard photo of my favorite star, Gene Autry, tacked to a tree and anouncing that he would appear at Okemah for the annual celebration.

Instead of turning towards home, I turned right to Okemah to see Bill Slepka, the manager of the local theater. Bond and Harrel must have thought I was nuts. It *was* a long shot.

I offered Mr. Slepka our trio and radio broadcast from his theater stage the day of the parade for thirty dollars. He accepted. I arranged for the sponsor to pay for the line charges provided Gene would appear on my broadcast. The price of a Gene Autry guest appearance was about five thousand dollars. I hoped he would appear for my price—nothing.

When the parade started, we climbed to the top of an old store building and waited, hoping Gene would recognize us—we had met a few times previously. As he approached on his horse, we waved our cowboy hats. He spotted us and waved his white stetson and with that famous grin yelled out, "Come on over to my hotel."

When he arrived there, we were waiting. That is one time old Champ lost a race. I told Gene of my promise to my sponsor. He

walked to the theater with us as hundreds followed, packing the theater and making Bill Slepka happy. Gene sang "South of the Border," making my sponsor happy. He then hired our trio to come to Hollywood and join him on his CBS radio show, "Melody Ranch," making us happy.

I will always be grateful for that flash of lightning and for the kindness of Gene Autry.

*   *   *

Our telephone interview continued. . .

DAVID ROTHEL: After a number of years supporting other cowboy stars with your Jimmy Wakely Trio, you acquired your own film series at Monogram. How did that happen to come about?

JIMMY WAKELY: I got lucky. I guess I am the only person who became a star in the forties type shoot-em-up Westerns who supported almost every other star prior to my own stardom. I worked with Roy Rogers in one picture [*Saga of Death Valley* (1939), Jimmy's first], Autry with one picture [*Heart of the Rio Grande* (1942)], two Hopalong Cassidy pictures, two Johnny Mack Brown pictures, and seven Johnny Mack Brown and Tex Ritter pictures when they were starring together. And then I worked with Charlie Starrett at Columbia in eight pictures. I worked with the Range Busters in their very first movie together at Monogram. The three Range Busters were Ray Corrigan, Max Terhune and, I think, John "Dusty" King. I did all of these pictures before I got my own movies. In the Universal pictures with Johnny Mack Brown and Tex Ritter my parts started getting bigger. By the time I did eight pictures with Charlie Starrett at Columbia, my parts were getting to be important and Columbia kept pushing me up. Then I signed with PRC and did one movie called *I'm from Arkansas*. It was a variety show. Even though my billing was number three, when the picture hit the theaters many of them put my name on top of the title because I had started to draw at the theaters. That helped me get my starring contract with Monogram.

DAVID ROTHEL: Was there any one particular person who was responsible for your getting the contract with Monogram?

JIMMY WAKELY: Well, I had some help from Phil Isley, Jennifer Jones's father, from Dallas, Texas.

DAVID ROTHEL: Monte Hale also got some help from him.

JIMMY WAKELY: Yes, in the same way. We were on the same tour together—a savings bond trip. Well, Phil Isley got Monte in at Republic and got me in at Monogram. Monogram had asked Phil to find them a cowboy star for four movies only. Monogram had proposed to shoot eight pictures a year with the Cisco Kid. The first one they made ran way over the budget and they decided to cut back and shoot four Ciscos and four of just anything else to fill out the program. My pictures were to be their "anything else" releases. My first picture, *Song of the Range* [1944], came out, and within sixty days it was in the black. So they decided to drop Cisco after a year and keep my pictures. I was there for five years and a total of twenty-eight movies.

DAVID ROTHEL: You've said that *Song of the Sierras* [1946] was your favorite film from your series.

JIMMY WAKELY: Yes, and it was the biggest grossing picture we made. But Monogram wouldn't spend any money on my pictures. They were trying to hold them down to thirty thousand. Then they went up to thirty-six, and then to forty-two thousand. To make the pictures today it would cost about 250-300 thousand dollars. Finally I talked them into letting me go up to the high Sierras to shoot two movies back to back. They raised the budget and I went up there. *Song of the Sierras* was the first of the two. When it was released, it immediately became the biggest grosser we ever had. But I couldn't get Monogram to follow through. They just wanted to keep me down. The person responsible for this was Scotty Dunlap, the man who had charge of the Johnny Mack Brown features. Scotty had a private production release deal with Monogram for the Johnny Mack Brown pictures. He owned the Mack Browns. Unfortunately for me Scotty Dunlap became studio production manager. He called me in one day and said, "Wakely, I'm going to take you out of those fancy clothes and make an actor out of you." I said, "Scotty, I'm not an actor. You'll destroy my picture career."

I figured Scotty had only one thing in mind: to kill me off so that his Johnny Mack Brown pictures would look better in the stockholder reports. There was a fellow in Memphis, Tennessee, who was the chief stockholder of Monogram. He was a Wakely fan, and he used to send me photo copies of the stockholder reports. They would include—I haven't told this to any publication in the world, ever—but he would send me the reports which would include the cost of each picture, the gross, and how many theaters it played. Well, my pictures were ahead of Mack Brown's about ten to fifteen percent in about a year. Scotty panicked and made it pretty rough on me. In the last few pictures I had to wear Levis, you know, much more rugged-looking clothing. In those days it was the fancy dressed, glamorous cowboys who made the money, as witnessed by Rogers and Autry, all the way back to Tom Mix.

DAVID ROTHEL: He had you cut back on the musical content of the pictures, too, didn't he?

JIMMY WAKELY: Yes, he cut my songs down, cut out the fancy wardrobe, and didn't want me to use my silver saddle.

DAVID ROTHEL: I saw a couple of your later films a few months ago and noticed that there didn't seem to be as many songs as I remembered from some of the earlier ones.

JIMMY WAKELY: Yes, and in '48 I was the number four cowboy star in America. I've got the reprints from *Motion Picture Trade Review,* the magazine that gave the ratings every year. Rogers, Autry, and Starrett were one, two, three. I was four; Mack Brown was five.

DAVID ROTHEL: And then the pressure was put on.

JIMMY WAKELY: The pressure was *on;* it was *really* on.

DAVID ROTHEL: You had quite a few leading ladies over the years. You've probably been asked a million times, but was there any one particular leading lady you especially enjoyed working with?

JIMMY WAKELY: The one that I thought had the most promise was Gail Davis. She did her first picture with me, and I recommended her to Gene Autry for one of his pictures at Columbia. He used her and then signed her up and made her Annie Oakley [in the television series]. In my picture *Across the Rio Grande* [1949] you'll find Polly Bergen singing a song. That was her first movie. She sang a song in it by Ray Whitley originally called "West of the Alamo," but I think she sang it as "West of the Rio Grande."

I also started Whip Wilson. He did one with me called *Silver Trails* [1948]. Scotty Dunlap was trying to make another Buck Jones out of him. Scotty was a close friend of Buck's and was with Buck the night he got killed in the Coconut Grove fire in Boston. Scotty always wanted another Buck Jones type of actor for Monogram. So he brought in this man with the whip and dressed him in a Buck Jones hat, shirt, and pants to try to make him look like Buck Jones. He did the whip act in my picture, *Silver Trails,* and he looked good, so they decided to star him in several pictures.

DAVID ROTHEL: Unfortunately, Whip Wilson wasn't the actor that Buck Jones was.

JIMMY WAKELY: That's right. But I always enjoyed watching young guys come along in pictures. When I was at Universal I used to sit with the director in an extra chair and watch what was happening. I remember one day I was sitting back behind the scene where I couldn't see who came in, but I heard this booming voice. Oliver Drake was doing the picture and he had brought in this actor who was working at Lockheed all night. It was Bob Mitchum. I always said that's where Mitch got those sleepy eyes, working swing shift over at Lockheed and making Westerns during the day. He was playing heavies then—third heavies; he was not even number one heavy. So when I went over to Columbia later, I talked with Jack Fier who was my boss there. I said, "You've got to sign up Bob Mitchum. He's going to be a big star." He said, "Ah, hell, he'll never amount to anything. He's just a 'henchie.'" A henchie was an also-ran heavy.

Then Mitch did a picture with Hoppy that I saw at the Hitching Post Theatre in Hollywood. In about five minutes Mitch got killed and the picture might as well have ended right there.

The next morning I was in to see Fier. I told him I had seen Mitch and said some good things about his performance. Now Mitch and I weren't close friends; I just got inspired when I saw somebody do a good job. Well, Mr. Fier opened *Variety* and saw a review of the film, which said, "Mitchum outdistances Hoppy in five minutes." Fier called his secretary and said, "Get Mitchum's agent." Well, they offered him three hundred a week for a forty-week contract, but the agent said, "RKO just called and we're going with them." And then Mitch did *G. I. Joe* and the lid blew off. This is the kind of thing I like to remember—people who came along and you knew you were looking at a future star.

DAVID ROTHEL: Have you seen any of your films in recent years?

JIMMY WAKELY: No, I haven't seen any of my pictures in many, many years. I had a chance to down at the film festival, but I didn't go. It's not that I'm against it, I just didn't go. I wish I'd gotten copies of my films, but I didn't.

DAVID ROTHEL: Is the Western series you made in the forties a happy memory for you?

JIMMY WAKELY: Oh yes, it had a purpose in my life, very much so. I had wanted to be a cowboy star when I came here, but about halfway through the series I decided it really wasn't what I wanted. When you're working for a studio like Monogram Pictures, you are not going to get any place, not really. Republic Pictures specialized in making Westerns; Monogram was just going to take the leavings. I don't care how good you were, you were not going to get anywhere at Monogram. So I

started looking for a way to bypass all of this. Finally I recorded "Slippin' Around" with Margaret Whiting. It came out in August of 1949. When my contract with Monogram came to an end in September, "Slippin' Around" was number one on all the trade charts. I just sneaked out of one career into another.

DAVID ROTHEL: That was a nice way to leave films.

JIMMY WAKELY: It sure was.

DAVID ROTHEL: Have you seen Margaret Whiting in recent years?

JIMMY WAKELY: I saw her a year or so ago. She played the Playboy Club in Century City out here. A bunch of old-timers went out there, twenty-eight of us, to her opening: Freddie Martin, the bandleader; Jane Withers; the late Johnny Mercer; and myself were the entertainers in the group to wish Margaret well. She did a good job. You know Margaret and I also had the first record of "Silver Bells" in 1950. Bing Crosby had it recorded when we recorded it, but we beat him out with it.

DAVID ROTHEL: Was "Slippin' Around" your biggest seller?

A profile shot of Jimmy Wakely taken near the beginning of his career as a Western star. *Photo courtesy of Don Martin.*

JIMMY WAKLEY: Yes, by far. The second biggest was my single of "One Has My Name, The Other Has My Heart."

DAVID ROTHEL: Eddie Dean's song.

JIMMY WAKELY: Yes, he wrote it. You know Eddie got a tough break on that. He made it on a very small label, Sage and Sand. It started like crazy in Los Angeles but nobody ever heard of it anywhere else. I put it out on Capitol and it was number one in six weeks. Eddie did the same act exactly with "Hillbilly Heaven." He put it out on a little ole label. Tex Ritter got on it, and it was a smash. And everybody forgot Eddie did it.

DAVID ROTHEL: He told me about going to Capitol and getting Tex Ritter to put "Hillbilly Heaven" in one of his recording dates.

JIMMY WAKELY: Eddie had those two bad breaks as an artist. He deserved better, but it just worked out that way. I didn't record "One Has My Name" to hurt Eddie; I just did it to sell records. I knew somebody was going to cover it. Eddie's quite a gentleman. I see him quite often. We released one of his albums, *Sincerely, Eddie Dean,* on Shasta Records. He sells them on tours, you know. He's made a lot of money on that album. Let me tell you what happened, David, when he made that album. Everybody has always tried to make a hillbilly out of Eddie. They've always said, "Eddie Dean sings too good." Well, that's nonsense; nobody's too good. Eddie came over here and made some of the tracks—all we needed was the voice. I said, "Now, Eddie, you go into that booth, put on the headset, and I want the best Eddie Dean there is. You know, the one that causes people to give standing ovations at the Palomino [nightclub]. That's the singer I want; the best there is. I don't want you to try to sound like a Hank Williams or anybody else." Well, he went in there and wasn't inhibited like he'd been many times before. We'd given him the best selections we could find: "Tumbling Tumbleweeds," "Just a Closer Walk with Thee," "Green Grass of Home," "Hillbilly Heaven"—it's pretty hard to beat those kinds of tunes.

Later I got a beautiful letter from his daughter. She wrote to my wife and me and said, "Thank you for believing in my daddy. He never sang as well on a record in his life." Well, we had turned him loose and let him be the Eddie Dean that he is. He's not lost a thing; he sings as well today as he ever did.

You know, David, the Shasta Records mail order business has been one of the most enlightening things that's ever happened to me. Did you see the story *Billboard* did on it? They gave us half a page one week and a column another week on the success of Shasta. We ship records all over the world.

DAVID ROTHEL: Is Gene Autry a partner or associated with you in Shasta Records?

JIMMY WAKELY: No. And many people think I'm part of Gene Autry's Republic Records. Republic and Shasta have a two-way contract. They can deliver our records and we can deliver theirs on a predetermined basis so that each one of us, as a result, has a larger catalog.

DAVID ROTHEL: I recently purchased a couple of Gene's Republic records. Aren't many of his Republic records taken from the old "Melody Ranch" radio programs?

JIMMY WAKELY: Yes. And many of my records on Shasta are taken from my CBS radio show of the fifties. The difference between Gene's records from "Melody Ranch" and my albums is that mine were recorded from tape; his "Melody Ranch" programs were originally recorded on disc. Because of the erosion of the discs through the years, you get scratches, little noises here and there. The technicians have trouble filtering them out. I stored the tapes from my radio shows in a constant seventy degrees for twenty-odd years. When we started dubbing them off for records, they sounded like they were made the day before yesterday. I've got one album called *The Way They Were Back When,* which features Tex Ritter, Merle Travis, and myself. It sounds like it was recorded last week and it was done in 1956. I'm sorry that Gene Autry's are not on tape. If they had been, he'd have an endless supply of material.

DAVID ROTHEL: Some of Gene's Republic recordings sound as if they may have been "sweetened." I mean by adding newly recorded bass, guitar, or other rhythm instruments.

JIMMY WAKELY: Some of Gene's have been sweetened. His musical director, Carl Cotner, added some voices and in some cases a bass fiddle and other instruments. In "Blues Stay Away from Me," for instance, they put almost a rock bass in there—that old 1950s sound. I don't think the rock bass back of Gene fits very well.

DAVID ROTHEL: You mentioned your CBS radio show. I believe that started about 1952. Did that show just evolve out of your recording success?

JIMMY WAKELY: Well, no. CBS had a possible sponsor for a country show on the network that they decided to call the "Hollywood Barn Dance." They needed a star and I was with MCA, which was an agency then. MCA set me on the show. After, I think, the first season, I was in New York doing

Photo courtesy of Jimmy Wakely.

the show one night from the factory of Bristol-Myers, the sponsor. I had invited Mr. Bristol to come over and visit the show. I'd never met him before, but I soon discovered he was a hammy old gentleman and a real sweet guy. He walked in and looked at the script that had been written in Hollywood and sent air mail to us. The script read, "We wish to welcome the 'Hollywood Barn Dance' to Hillside, New Jersey." He read it and said, "Wait a minute. What's your name, young man?"—to me, the star of the show. I said, "Jimmy Wakely." He took a pencil and marked out what was there and said, "We wish to welcome Jimmy Wakely and his show to Hillside, New Jersey." Well, the CBS bosses were there and CBS owned the title "Hollywood Barn Dance." Mr. Bristol's doing this caused them no end of grief. But the boss, the sponsor, had written my name in so there was nothing they could do. I'd never seen him before; I'd never asked for·it. He just gave it to me, gave me "The Jimmy Wakely Show." Bristol-Myers sponsored me all the way through until 1958 when network radio was through. I was one of the last to leave CBS. I lasted two years longer than Gene. I think he finished in 1956 and mine lasted through '58, which left me in company with "Gunsmoke," Jack Benny, and Arthur Godfrey. There were very few network radio shows left.

DAVID ROTHEL: I read in *Variety* that you're doing a radio program for Radio Iran.

JIMMY WAKELY: Yes, I am. I'm doing an hour program a day. I record the five shows on one day each week. It's called "Jimmy Wakely and Friends." I play records and do guest interviews on the program, and I also draw upon a library of interviews with famous people that I have done for my armed forces show. I'm now in my tenth year with American Forces Radio. That's how Iran happened to sign me—because they heard my armed forces shows and their Washington bureau chief called the colonel in charge. He called me from Washington and we made the deal over the telephone.

DAVID ROTHEL: And the program is only running in Iran.

JIMMY WAKELY: That's it! Five days a week for the Americans there.

DAVID ROTHEL: I heard that Bob Hope was on your first show.

JIMMY WAKELY: I went over to Bob's house—he lives three blocks from me—and got his interview. You don't by any chance have a book by Bob Hope called *The Last Christmas Show*? I'm in five pages of the book. When I interviewed Bob the other day, he told my director, "This man did the first Christmas show with me in 1949 in Anchorage, Alaska." It was just Bob and his wife and me. From then on he did twenty-four more.

I'm going to run my television show in Iran, too. I'm producing a series of specials, half-hour taped television shows. One of them has already run here in Hollywood. It has also run in some other West Coast cities and in Phoenix and Alaska.

DAVID ROTHEL: Is it being syndicated?

JIMMY WAKELY: We haven't syndicated it yet. The stations we've presented it to so far bought it just through my office. Gene Autry is my partner. As you know, he owns Golden West Broadcasting, which owns a half interest in the television series. We jointly finance the series.

DAVID ROTHEL: You used to perform quite often in nightclubs. Do you still do any of that?

JIMMY WAKELY: Yes. You see, I didn't want to retire, and I didn't want to beat my brains out on one-night stands like some of the "Grand Ole Opry" people do. I'm not that greedy for money, and I'm fortunate that I don't need it that much. So what I do is play clubs about fourteen or fifteen weeks a year here on the West Coast. In the sixties I played Harrah's 120 weeks in seven years, but that was too tough and I got sick of it. Because of the resurrection of my records through the mail orders, I'm going to start playing again a little bit on a national basis, but not a great deal. It's not that I'm that tired, but I like to play as long as I'm fresh and then come back to the house. I wouldn't pack and run every day for anybody—you know, like so many of these kids. They pack up and drive all night and all that stuff. This I won't do. I don't need that.

DAVID ROTHEL: I read an interview you gave where you said that a career should work for you, should fit into your life in a natural way.

JIMMY WAKELY: You shouldn't serve your career; you should let it serve you. So many people become slaves to their careers. They will go all the way to give everything to it. I've been married forty years; I'm sixty-two years old and I'm blessed with good health. I figure I'm ahead of the game, and there's no point in pushing myself.

DAVID ROTHEL: Coming back to the Western films, I know you wrote many of the songs that were included in your films. Did you record many of your own songs?

JIMMY WAKELY: Very few. I recorded other people's songs. I could pick them better that way. I've written a few songs for movie themes over the years. In 1954 I appeared with Sterling Hayden in a picture called *Arrow in the Dust* in which I sang a song I wrote called "The Weary Stranger." In 1955

I wrote another song called "Silver Star" for a picture of the same title. I sang it off camera during the picture like Tex Ritter did in *High Noon*. Jock Mahoney starred in a thing called *Slim Carter* [1957] for which I wrote a theme called "Cowboy." It did quite well.

DAVID ROTHEL: Did you sing it off camera?

JIMMY WAKELY: No. A later song I did for Jock Mahoney called "Lonely Is the Hunter" I sang in the background. The picture was called *Money, Women and Guns* [1959].

DAVID ROTHEL: Do you have any feeling as to why there is this continuing interest after so many years in B Western films and the musical Westerns with the singing cowboys?

JIMMY WAKELY: I think these people are just terribly sentimental and they want to see once again that guy they used to see on the screen. Let me give you an example. We were playing a show over at Phoenix at the state fair recently. My car was parked on the fairgrounds by the stage. A man about forty, forty-five years old walked over to my wife, who was sitting in the car, and handed her an envelope. She thought it was a song or something and brought it home. It turned out to be one of the most beautiful poems that I have ever read in my life. The writer started by saying that when he was in Amarillo recently he heard that Jimmy Wakely had passed away. When he walked into the fairgrounds and saw my advertisement, he realized I wasn't dead. He wrote that poem dedicated to the way he felt when he thought his hero had gone away. He put no name on it, no address. I haven't the slightest idea who he is or even where he lives. He didn't even say hello to me—that I know of, that is.

DAVID ROTHEL: Doing research for this book I've been constantly, pleasantly surprised at the enthusiasm of people for the performers that were in these films. The people are still interested; they still remember, have fond memories of these films from the past and the stars of the films. Can you see the possibility of the singing cowboy type of films of the past ever coming back?

JIMMY WAKELY: Yes, I can. It's not wishful thinking either, because I obviously wouldn't be doing it myself. But if some young guy comes along willing to cut his hair, look nice, and wear good clothes, he can make it today because there's not enough good music being sung or played, and the people are looking for it as evidenced by what's happening on these mail-order things. I think it will happen. The singing cowboy movies were escapism; that's all they were, adventure and escapism. ABC television has made suckers out of NBC and CBS in the ratings race lately. Know how they're doing it? With the escapist fare, all of these things that present an escape from reality. People are looking for escape pictures.

DAVID ROTHEL: When you look upon your career in show business, what do you look upon as the high point for you personally?

JIMMY WAKELY: You mean in pleasure?

DAVID ROTHEL: Yes, not necessarily in financial reward.

JIMMY WAKELY: Playing guitar for Gene Autry. You see, Gene was my favorite singer and he was my best friend. I played guitar, led the band for Gene, and set up his music for him. He was a great boss and a great guy, still is. When I was with Gene on the "Melody Ranch" radio program, we [The Jimmy Wakely Trio] were under contract with Hoppy at Paramount for pictures and so we couldn't do Autry's pictures. After we left Paramount we did one Autry picture then went to Universal under contract. The "Melody Ranch" program, though, was the first good job I'd ever had in my life. I had a boss that never got mean, paid well, and treated all of us kindly. He was a very popular star in those days. We'd play a rodeo tour with Gene and I'd be billed as Jimmy Wakely and the Melody Ranch Boys. In Madison Square

Jimmy Wakely is seen here in a recent portrait photograph. *Photo courtesy of Jimmy Wakely.*

Garden in New York and the other places, we'd open the show and then Gene would come out with his horse, Champion, and do all the tricks. Then later in the show he'd come out and sing his songs. That's when I would perform with him with the band. I guess that was the height of my pleasure in show business. By the time I got to be a star, I was rather blasé. There'd been so much happening to me that it wasn't anything new, you know. I had come straight from Oklahoma onto the CBS network with Gene Autry. I had gotten a picture contract and a record contract almost immediately and four hits on the first recording session. Everything just went Bingo! I had the records, the Autry radio show, and I was working in the Hoppy pictures. That was a happy position to be in. As I've told Gene so many times since, "Through the grace of God and Gene Autry, I got a career." And I've never forgotten him for it. He is a great man.

The interview drew to a close. I thanked Jimmy and we said our goodbyes. I punched the stop button on the recorder. There was still plenty of time for him to get those thirty minutes of California sunshine.

JIMMY WAKELY SELECTED FILMOGRAPHY

The following filmography only includes the Western films in which Jimmy Wakely starred.

Song of the Range (Monogram, 1944) 55 M.

Producer, Phil Krasne; director, Wallace Fox; screenplay, Betty Burbridge.

CAST: Jimmy Wakely, Lee "Lasses" White, Dennis Moore, Cay Forrester, Bud Osborne, George Eldredge, Carl Mathews, Pierre Watkin, Steve Clark, Edmund Cobb, Ken Terrell, Carl Sepulveda,

Dennis Moore and Jimmy Wakely stop the press of Horace Murphy in this scene from *Springtime in Texas.*

Johnny Bond and His Red River Boys, The Sunshine Girls, Jimmie Dean, Wesley Tuttle.

* * *

Springtime in Texas (Monogram, 1945) 57 M.

Producer, Lindsley Parsons; director, Oliver Drake; screenplay, Frances Kavanaugh.

CAST: Jimmy Wakely, Lee "Lasses" White, Dennis Moore, Marie Harmon, Rex Lease, Horace Murphy, I. Stanford Jolley, Hal Taliaferro, Budd Buster, Ted French, Pat Patterson, Rusty McDonald, Spud Goodale, Frankie Marvin, Terry Frost, Roy Butler, Lloyd Ingraham, Pearl Early, Johnny Bond, The Callahan Brothers and Their Blue Ridge Mountain Boys.

* * *

Lonesome Trail (Monogram, 1945) 57 M.

Producer, Lindsley Parsons; director, Oliver Drake; screenplay, Louise Rousseau from an original story by Oliver Drake.

CAST: Jimmy Wakely, Lee "Lasses" White, Lorraine Miller, Iris Clive, John James, Horace Murphy, Eddie Majors, Zon Murray, Roy Butler, Jasper Palmer, Frank MacCarroll, Jack Rivers, Tom Smith, The Sunshine Girls, Arthur (Fiddlin') Smith, The Saddle Pals.

* * *

Saddle Serenade (Monogram, 1945) 56 M.

Producer and director, Oliver Drake; screenplay, Frances Kavanaugh.

CAST: Jimmy Wakely, Lee "Lasses" White, John James, Kay Deslys, Jack Ingram, Jack Spears, Carl Mathews, Jack Henricks, Frank MacCarroll, Al Sloey, Jimmie Dean, Nancy Brinckman, Pat Gleason, Roy Butler, Alan Foster, Elmer Napier, Johnny Paul, Clarie James, Bob Duncan, Dee Cooper, Foy Willing and The Riders of the Purple Sage.

* * *

Riders of the Dawn (Mongram, 1945) 57 M.

Producer and director, Oliver Drake; screenplay, Louise Rousseau; camera, William Sickner; editor, William Austin.

CAST: Jimmy Wakely, Lee "Lasses" White, John James, Sarah Padden, Horace Murphy, Phyllis Adair, Jack Baxley, Bob Shelton, Dad Picard,

Arthur (Fiddlin') Smith, Eddie Taylor, Brooks Temple, Bill Hammond, Michael Joseph Ward, Wesley Tuttle and His Texas Stars.

* * *

Moon Over Montana (Monogram, 1946) 56 M.

Producer and director, Oliver Drake; screenplay, Louise Rousseau from an original story by Oliver Drake.

CAST: Jimmy Wakely, Lee "Lasses" White, Jennifer Holt, Terry Frost, Jack Ingram, Jesse Ashlock, Jack Rivers, Woody Woodel and His Riding Rangers, Kenne Duncan, Arthur (Fiddlin') Smith, Art Mix, Ray Jones, Eddie Majors, Brad Slavin, Stanley Blystone, Louise Arthur, John Elliott, Bob Duncan.

* * *

West of the Alamo (Monogram, 1946) 57 M.

Producer and director, Oliver Drake; screenplay, Louise Rousseau; camera, Harry Neumann; editor, William Austin; musical director, Frank Sanucci.

CAST: Jimmy Wakely, Lee "Lasses" White, Iris Clive, Jack Ingram, Red Holton, Budd Buster, Eddie Majors, Ray Whitley, Billy Dix, Betty Majors, Jack Rivers, Ted French, Steven Keys, Ray Jones, Rudy Bowman, Arthur (Fiddlin') Smith Trio, The Saddle Pals.

* * *

Trail to Mexico (Monogram, 1946) 58 M.

Producer and director, Oliver Drake; screenplay, Oliver Drake.

CAST: Jimmy Wakely, Lee "Lasses" White, Dolores Castelli, Julian Rivero, Terry Frost, Horace Mathews, Jonathan McCall, Alex Montoya, Dora Del Rio, Juan Duval, Jack Rivers, Don Weston, Arthur (Fiddlin') Smith, Brad Slavin, Cactus Mack, Wheaton Chambers, Dee Cooper, Billy Dix.

* * *

Song of the Sierras (Monogram, 1946) 58 M.

Producer and director, Oliver Drake; screenplay, Oliver Drake; camera, Marcel LePicard; editor, Ralph Dixon; musical director, Frank Sanucci.

CAST: Jimmy Wakley, Lee "Lasses" White, Jean Carlin, Jack Baxley, Iris Clive, Jonathan Black, Bob Docking, Jasper Palmer, Zon Murray, Ray Jones, Budd Buster, Billy Dix, Robert Gilbert, Horace

Mathews, Brad Slavin, Jack Rivers, Wesley Tuttle and His Texas Stars, Carl Sepulveda, Jesse Ashlock, Artie Ortego.

*   *   *

Rainbow Over the Rockies (Monogram, 1947) 54 M.

Producer and director, Oliver Drake; screenplay, Elmer Clifton from an original story by Oliver Drake; camera, Marcel LePicard; editor, Ralph Dixon; musical director, Frank Sanucci.

CAST: Jimmy Wakely, Lee "Lasses" White, Dennis Moore, Pat Starling, Carl Sepulveda, Budd Buster, Jack Baxley, Zon Murray, Billy Dix, Jasper Palmer, Robert L. Gilbert, Wesley Tuttle and His Texas Stars.

*   *   *

Six Gun Serenade (Mongram, 1947) 54 M.

Producer, Barney Sarecky; director, Ford Beebe; screenplay, Ben Cohen.

CAST: Jimmy Wakely, Kay Morley, Lee "Lasses" White, Cactus Mack, Chick Hannon, Jimmie Martin, Bud Osborne, Steve Clark, Pierce Lyden, Jack Rivers, Jack Hendricks, Stanley Ellison, Arthur (Fiddlin') Smith, Rivers Lewis.

*   *   *

Song of the Wasteland (Monogram, 1947) 56 M.

Producer, Barney Sarecky; director, Thomas Carr; screenplay, J. Benton Cheney.

CAST: Jimmy Wakely, Lee "Lasses" White, Dottye Brown, John James, Henry Hall, Marshall Reed, Holly Bane, Pierce Lyden, Chester Conklin, Ted Adams, John Carpenter, George Chesebro, Richard Reinhart, Jack Rivers, Milburn Morante, Johnny Bond, The Saddle Pals, Gary Garrett.

*   *   *

Ridin' Down the Trail (Monogram, 1947) 53 M.

Producer, Bennett Cohen; director, Howard Bretherton; screenplay, Bennett Cohen.

CAST: Jimmy Wakely, Dub "Cannonball" Taylor, Beverly Jons, Charles King, Milburn Morante, Douglas Fowley, John James, Kermit Maynard, Don Weston, Stanley Ellison, Doug Farnsworth, Brad Slavin, Henry Carr, Ted French, Post Park, Dick Reinhart, Jesse Ashlock, Wayne Burson.

The thugs have the drop on Jimmy and "Lasses" White in this scene from *Trail to Mexico*. The villain in the black hat and suit is popular character actor Terry Frost.

Lee "Lasses" White and Jimmy Wakely in a scene from *Six Gun Serenade*.

*   *   *

Song of the Drifter (Monogram, 1948) 53 M.

Producer, Louis Gray; director, Lambert Hillyer; screenplay, Frank H. Young.

CAST: Jimmy Wakely, Dub "Cannonball" Taylor, Mildred Coles, Patsy Moran, Bud Osborne, William Ruhl, Marshall Reed, Frank LaRue, Carl Mathews, Steve Clark, Wheaton Chambers, Bob Woodward, Dick Reinhart, Cliffie Stone, Arthur (Fiddlin') Smith, Wayne Burson, Bill Callahan.

*   *   *

Oklahoma Blues (Monogram, 1948) 56 M.

Virginia Belmont looks as if she just might go after the thousand-dollar reward for Jimmy in this scene from *Oklahoma Blues*. *Photo courtesy of Don Martin.*

Jimmy Wakely is involved in a little "sparkin'" with Mildred Coles in this scene from *Song of the Drifter*.

Jimmy is serenading Virginia Belmont in the moonlight in this scene from *Oklahoma Blues*.

From left to right: George J. Lewis, I. Stanford Jolley, Zon Murray, Dub Taylor, Jimmy, and Steve Clark in a scene from *Oklahoma Blues*. *Photo courtesy of Don Martin.*

Producer, Louis Gray; director, Lambert Hillyer; screenplay, Bennett Cohen.

CAST: Jimmy Wakely, Dub "Cannonball" Taylor, Charles King, Virginia Belmont, George J. Lewis, Zon Murray, I. Stanford Jolley, Steve Clark, Frank LaRue, Milburn Morante, Don Weston, Arthur (Fiddlin') Smith, Bob Woodward, J. C. Lytton.

*　　　*　　　*

Partners of the Sunset (Monogram, 1948) 56 M.

Producer, Louis Gray; director, Lambert Hillyer; screenplay, J. Benton Cheney.

CAST: Jimmy Wakely, Dub "Cannonball" Taylor, Christine Larson, Ray Whitley, Leonard Penn,

Steve Darrell, Marshall Reed, Bob Woodward, Boyd Stockman, John Weston, Jack Rivers, Jay Kirby, Arthur (Fiddlin') Smith, J. C. Lytton, Carl Mathews, Carl Sepulveda, Agapito Martinez.

* * *

Range Renegades (Monogram, 1948) 54 M.

Producer, Louis Gray; director, Lambert Hillyer; screenplay, Ronald Davidson and William Lively.

CAST: Jimmy Wakely, Dub "Cannonball" Taylor, Dennis Moore, Jennifer Holt, John James, Riley Hill, Steve Clark, Frank LaRue, Cactus Mack, Milburn Morante, Don Weston, Arthur (Fiddlin') Smith, Bob Woodward, Roy Garrett, Agapito Martinez.

* * *

Silver Trails (Monogram, 1948) 53 M.

Producer, Louis Gray; director, Christy Cabanne; screenplay, J. Benton Cheney; camera, Harry Neumann; editor, John C. Fuller; musical director, Edward Kay; songs, Jimmy Wakely, Don Weston, Jimmy Rogers.

CAST: Jimmy Wakely, Dub "Cannonball" Taylor, Christine Larson, George J. Lewis, Whip Wilson, George Meeker, Pierce Lyden, William Norton Bailey, Connie Asins, Fred L. Edwards, Glenn Strange, Bob Woodward, Bud Osborne.

* * *

The Rangers Ride (Monogram, 1948) 56 M.

Producer, Louis Gray; director, Derwin Abrahams; screenplay, Basil Dickey.

CAST: Jimmy Wakely, Dub "Cannonball" Taylor, Virginia Belmont, Cactus Mack, Bud Taylor, Bud Osborne, Riley Hill, Marshall Reed, Steve Clark, Pierce Lyden, Boyd Stockman, Bob Woodward, Milburn Morante, Carol Henry, Don Weston, Arthur (Fiddlin') Smith, James Diehl, Jack Sparks, Louis Armstrong.

* * *

Outlaw Brand (Monogram, 1948) 57 M.

Producer, Louis Gray; director, Lambert Hillyer; screenplay, J. Benton Cheney.

CAST: Jimmy Wakely, Dub "Cannonball" Taylor, Kay Morley, Bud Osborne, Leonard Penn, Nolan Leary, Christine Larson, Tom Chatterton, John

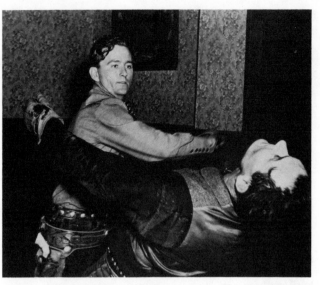

Jimmy Wakely seems to have matters well in hand in this scene from *Courtin' Trouble*.

James, Boyd Stockman, Frank MacCarroll, Jack Rivers, Dick Reinhart, Ray Whitley, Louis Armstrong, Jay Kirby.

* * *

Courtin' Trouble (Monogram, 1948) 56 M.

Producer, Louis Gray; director, Ford Beebe; screenplay, Ronald Davidson; camera, Harry Neumann; editor, Carl Pierson; musical director, Edward Kay; songs, Jimmy Wakely, Oliver Drake, Tommy Dilbeck.

CAST: Jimmy Wakely, Dub "Cannonball" Taylor, Virginia Belmont, Leonard Penn, Marshall Reed, Steve Clark, House Peters, Jr., Frank LaRue, William N. Bailey, Bud Osborne, Bill Hale, Bob Woodward, Carol Henry, Bill Potter, Don Weston, Louis Armstrong, Arthur (Fiddlin') Smith.

* * *

Cowboy Cavalier (Monogram, 1948) 56 M.

Producer, Louis Gray; director, Derwin Abrahams; screenplay, J. Benton Cheney and Ronald Davidson.

CAST: Jimmy Wakely, Dub "Cannonball" Taylor, Jan Bryant, Bud Osborne, Douglas Evans, Steve Darrell, Carol Henry, Steve Clark, Bob Woodward, William Ruhl, Milburn Morante, Claire Whitney, Louis Armstrong, Don Weston.

* * *

Jimmy, Noel Neill, and Dub Taylor are out for a ride and a song in this scene from *Gun Runner*. *Photo courtesy of Don Martin.*

Sheriff Bud Osborne and Jimmy look on as Cannonball tries the old milk-in-the-paper trick in this scene from *Gun Runner.*

Gun Runner (Monogram, 1949) 59 M.

Producer, Louis Gray; director, Lambert Hillyer; screenplay, J. Benton Cheney; camera, Harry Neumann; editor, John Fuller; musical director, Edward Kay.

CAST: Jimmy Wakely, Dub "Cannonball" Taylor, Noel Neill, Mae Clarke, Kenne Duncan, Marshall Reed, Carol Henry, Bud Osborne, Steve Clark, Ted Adams, Pascale Perry, Eddie Majors, Clem Fuller, Bob Woodward, Tex Atchinson, Ray Jones.

* * *

Gun Law Justice (Monogram, 1949) 54 M.

Producer, Louis Gray; director, Lambert Hillyer; screenplay, Basil Dickey.

CAST: Jimmy Wakely, Dub "Cannonball" Taylor, Ray Whitley, Jane Adams, Lee Phelps, Bud Osborne, John James, Edmund Cobb, Myron Healey, Ray Jones, Zon Murray, Tom Chatterton, I. Stanford Jolley, Carol Henry, Bob Curtis, Eddie Majors, Tex Atchinson, George Morrell.

* * *

Across the Rio Grande (Monogram, 1949) 56 M.

Producer, Louis Gray; director, Oliver Drake; screenplay, Ronald Davidson; camera, Henry Neumann; editor, John C. Fuller; musical director, Edward Kay; songs, Jimmy Wakely.

CAST: Jimmy Wakely, Dub "Cannonball" Taylor, Reno Browne, Riley Hill, Terry Frost, Dennis Moore, Kenne Duncan, Ted Adams, Myron Healey, Bud Osborne, John James, Bob Curtis, Carol Henry, Boyd Stockman, William Bailey, Polly Burgin (Bergen), Bob Woodward, Bill Potter.

* * *

Brand of Fear (Monogram, 1949) 56 M.

Producer, Louis Gray; director, Oliver Drake; screenplay, Basil Dickey.

CAST: Jimmy Wakely, Dub "Cannonball" Taylor, Gail Davis, Ray Whitley, Myron Healey, Marshall Reed, Frank MacCarroll, Holly Bane, Tom London, William Norton Bailey, William H. Ruhl, Boyd Stockman, Bill Cooper, Bob Woodward, Bob Curtis, Bill Potter, Don Weston, Joe Galbreath.

* * *

Roaring Westward (Monogram, 1949) 55 M.

Producer, Louis Gray; director, Oliver Drake; screenplay, Ronald Davidson; camera, Marcel LePicard; editor, Carl Pierson; musical director, Edward Kay.

CAST: Jimmy Wakely, Dub "Cannonball" Taylor, Dennis Moore, Lois Hall, Jack Ingram, Claire Whitney, Marshall Reed, Kenne Duncan, Holly Bane, Buddy Swan, Nolan Leary, Bud Osborne, Ted French, Bob Woodward, Al Haskell, Art Mix, Rudy Bowman.

* * *

Lawless Code (Monogram, 1949) 58 M.

Jimmy, Edmund Cobb (in vest), and an unidentified gun-slinger prepare for action in this scene from *Gun Law Justice.*

Dub "Cannonball" Taylor and Jimmy Wakely in a scene from *Gun Law Justice. Photo courtesy of Don Martin.*

Producer, Louis Gray; director, Oliver Drake; screenplay, Basil Dickey.

CAST: Jimmy Wakely, Dub "Cannonball" Taylor, Bud Osborne, Riley Hill, Tristram Coffin, Terry Frost, Myron Healey, Kenne Duncan, Ellen Hall, Bob Curtis, Steve Clark, Frank MacCarroll, Beatrice Maude, Carl Deacon Moore, Michael Royal.

* * *

JIMMY WAKELY DISCOGRAPHY

In the late forties and early fifties Jimmy Wakely recordings were among the most popular in the country. Singles on such songs as "I Love You So Much It Hurts Me," "My Heart Cries for You," "Signed, Sealed and Delivered," and "Beautiful

Photo courtesy of Don Martin.

Brown Eyes" were big sellers throughout the United States.

In 1949 Jimmy and Margaret Whiting teamed up for a series of duets that had phenomenal success with record buyers. In addition to their runaway hit recording of "Slippin' Around," Jimmy and Margaret also had success with such recordings as "I'll Never Slip Around Again," "Till the End of the World," "Let's Go to Church Next Sunday Morning," and "Broken Down Merry-Go-Round."

The following are currently available Jimmy Wakely recordings:

Country Million Sellers Shasta Records

Selections:

Slippin' Around
I'll Never Let You Go
Anytime
San Antonio Rose
I Love You So Much It Hurts Me
Tennessee Waltz
Your Cheating Heart
Beautiful Brown Eyes
Oklahoma Hills
One Has My Name
You Are My Sunshine
Too Late

*   *   *

The Gentle Touch Shasta Records

Selections:

Slippin' Around (with Lindalee Wakely, Jimmy's
   daughter)
You'll Never Walk Alone (with Lindalee)
This Night I'll Remember (Lindalee solo)
To Each His Own
I Don't Want To Be Free Anymore (with Lindalee)
Sunshine on My Shoulders (with Lindalee)
The Sun Is Shining (with Lindalee)
Dear Mama and Daddy (Lindalee solo)
Hey Good Lookin' (with Lindalee)
Have You Ever Seen a Big Man Cry?
Mood Indigo (with Lindalee)

*   *   *

Jimmy Wakely Country Shasta Records

Selections: (Recorded live from the Wakely CBS
   radio shows of the fifties.)

Ridin' Hidin' Teardrops
Twilight on the Trail
The One Rose
Mother
I Cried for You
Let the Rest of the World Go By
When the Moon Comes Over the Mountain
Where the Blue of the Night Meets the Gold
   of the Day
A Melody from the Sky
Carry Me Back to the Lone Prairie
When Your Hair Has Turned to Silver
Where the Mountains Meet the Sky
That Silver-Haired Daddy of Mine

*   *   *

Jimmy Wakely On Stage Shasta Records

Selections: (Recorded live from the Wakely CBS
   radio shows of the fifties.)

Smiles
Someday
Around the World
Swinging Sweethearts
Song of the Sierras
Gonna Find Me a Blue Bird
Singin' the Blues
All the Way
It's Not for Me To Say
Fascination
September Song

*   *   *

Jimmy Wakely Sings Shasta Records

Selections:

My Heart Cries for You
I Know How It Feels
My Mother's Eyes
Tomorrow
Me and My Shadow
This Night I'll Remember
When I Lost You
The Keeper of the Key
Sleep Kentucky Babe
Out in the Cold Again
I Heard an Angel Cry
As Time Goes By

*   *   *

Jimmy Wakely with Russ Morgan Shasta Records

Selections: (Recorded live from the Wakely CBS
   radio shows of the fifties.)

Marie
Molly Darling
Pagan Love Song (Russ Morgan)
Object of My Affections (Russ Morgan)
Wabash Blues (Russ Morgan)
I'm Movin' On (The Three Rays)
The Moon of Manakoora
Ridin' 'Round in the Rain
Undecided (Russ Morgan)
The One Rose
Does Your Heart Beat for Me? (The Three Rays)

The Doll Dance (Russ Morgan)
It Is No Secret (Russ Morgan and Choir)

*   *   *

Merry Christmas from Jimmy Wakely Shasta Records

Selections:

    Swingin' Jingle Bells
    Winter Wonderland
    Silver Bells
    It's Christmas
    It Came Upon a Midnight Clear
    Joy to the World
    White Christmas
    Rudolph the Red-Nosed Reindeer
    Away in a Manger
    That's Santa Claus
    O Come All Ye Faithful
    Frosty the Snowman
    Silent Night

*   *   *

Reflections By Jimmy Wakely Shasta Records

Selections:

    Cimarron
    Happy Rovin' Cowboy
    Tenting Tonight on the Old Camp Ground
    Silver Trails
    Try To Understand
    I Wish I Had a Nickel
    Let's Go to Church
    Freight Train Blues
    If I Had My Way—Lovesong of the Waterfall
    Softly and Tenderly
    Star of Hope
    Too Bad Little Girl

*   *   *

Singing Cowboy Shasta Records

Selections:

    I'm an Old Cowhand
    Tumbling Tumbleweeds
    Song of the Sierras

Empty Saddles
Blue Shadows on the Trail
When the Bloom Is on the Sage
Lonely Is the Hunter
The Yellow Rose of Texas
It's a Lonely Trail
There's a Goldmine in the Sky
The Last Roundup
Call of the Canyon
Saddle Pals
Cowboy's Prayer

*   *   *

A Tribute to Bob Wills Shasta Records

Selections:

    A Tribute to Bob Wills
    Take Me Back to Tulsa
    Time Changes Everything
    Steel Guitar Rag
    I Knew the Moment I Lost You
    Faded Love
    Stay a Little Longer
    San Antonio Rose
    Corrine, Corrina
    Dusty Skies
    I Wonder If You Feel the Way I Do
    Maiden's Prayer

*   *   *

The Wakely Family Show Shasta Records

Selections: (with son Johnny and daughter Lindalee)

    Cimarron
    Your Cheatin' Heart
    Release Me
    Snowbird
    Cool Water
    Green, Green Grass of Home
    Crazy Arms
    Rocky Top
    How Can You Mend a Broken Heart?
    Welcome to My World
    I'm a Fool To Care
    Blue Moon of Kentucky
    Peace in the Valley

*   *   *

The Wakely Way with Country Hits Shasta Records

Selections: (with son Johnny and daughter Lindalee)

Easy Lovin'
Delta Dawn
Top of the World
Tweedle O' Twill
Tears on My Pillow
The Wayward Wind
Take Me Home Country Roads
For the Good Times
Behind Closed Doors
Daddy Don't You Walk So Fast
Let Me Be There
You Are My Sunshine

*   *   *

The Way They Were—Back When Shasta Records

Selections: (Transcribed from the Wakely CBS radio shows, 1953 through 1958)

The following artists discuss and perform the songs that made them famous: Jimmy Wakely, Tex Ritter, Hank Penny, Johnny Bond, Wesley Tuttle, Tommy Duncan, Merle Travis, Tex Williams.

*   *   *

Country and Western Spectacular Shasta Records

Selections:

Love Me Tender
Please Don't Hurt Me Anymore
Dreams That Won't Come True
and additional selections by other artists.

*   *   *

Country Hits of the '40s Capitol Records

Selections:

Slippin' Around (with Margaret Whiting)
One Has My Name, The Other Has My Heart
and additional selections by other Capitol artists.

*   *   *

The Great American Singing Cowboys Republic Records

Selections:

Tumbling Tumbleweeds
Ghost Riders in the Sky
and additional selections by other singing cowboys.

8   Monte Hale

"I just never could get used to the idea that I was in show business."

He was sitting, talking with Ben Johnson in the lobby of the Hyatt House in Orlando when I arrived in the early evening. I was surprised at the in-person size of the man—six-two at least, and bulky, but in good shape. The hair was silvery white; the clothes—sport coat and slacks, buttoned sport shirt—were casually elegant with only a suggestion of Western showing in the jewelry, a rather large ring and a chain pendant. I noticed his hands as we shook—big-boned and possessing a hint that at one time they had done manual labor. Monte Hale had changed considerably since I had last seen him on the screen perhaps twenty-eight years ago, but then we all had. And now he and Ben Johnson and some other stars were in Orlando for the Florida Mid-Winter Western Film Round-up—a three-day festival for B Western film buffs.

Monte asked me if I had met his old friend Ben. I said that I hadn't, but before the introduction could occur, a youngster came up to Ben Johnson and asked for an autograph and then there were others who crowded around him. Everyone recognized Ben from all his movies or they remembered him from when he won the Oscar for *The Last Picture Show*.

I asked Monte if he and I could meet after breakfast the next morning to talk about his singing cowboy Westerns. "Sure, Pal, we'll get together; I'll tell you everything you want to know," he said in a Texas drawl that was thick enough to cut with a Bowie knife—a pleasant, rolling, low-pitched drawl that lopped off "ing's" as he spoke.

Later that evening Monte joined about forty of us in a viewing room to see one of his early films, *Along the Oregon Trail*. When it was over, he thanked everyone for "sittin' through this turkey." It wasn't one of his better films, and he knew it.

*   *   *

I had found it enjoyable, though, watching Monte Hale on the screen again after so many years. Although he did not have an extremely forceful screen personality, there was a pleasant warmth that he exuded in his films. His singing voice possessed the familiar "down-home" quality of most cowboy singers and was very appealing. For some reason his Texas drawl was not as apparent in his films as one might expect from talking with him. The drawl that did come through on the sound track only added to the folksy quality that was always a plus in his film appearances. He handled the fisticuffs and riding well, but sometimes seemed a bit ill at ease in straight dramatic scenes that relied upon only dialogue rather than physical action. This appeared to be especially true in the earliest films he made when he had little acting experience to fall back on.

I was reminded as I viewed the film that I had had the general feeling that his films during the forties did not have as much action in them as, say, the Roy Rogers or Gene Autry films, but that they had more "romance." (I was unable to verify this remembrance based upon the Monte Hale films I viewed for this chapter.)

For the first three years (starting in 1946) the Monte Hale films were in Trucolor—the first B Westerns to be filmed by Republic in color. Trucolor, to those of us who had seen mostly black-and-white B Westerns up to that time, was a

Monte Hale.

big boost and increased our want-to-see interest. The addition of color perhaps gave the impression to us (in our tender years) that Monte's films were special or maybe better than the black-and-white Westerns we had been seeing.

While the Monte Hale Westerns stressed the musical aspects for the first few years, the series finally settled into more of a Western-with-music series with Monte only singing a song or two in an entire film. In some of the later films (the "six-day wonders" as he referred to them) the singing was cut entirely. In fact, Monte does not perceive of himself as having been a singing cowboy. When I mentioned my wish to interview him for a book on the singing cowboys, he said he probably didn't qualify since he had only sung a few songs now and then in his films.

Monte was not a singing cowboy in the Gene Autry or Roy Rogers sense. There were no lavish production numbers in his films, and there was not the great quantity of buckskin ballads that could

Monte signs his autograph for a newly acquired fan at the film festival.

be found in the Autry and Rogers pictures. But from 1946 through 1948—until the budgets were cut and the Trucolor lensing forsaken—Western music and singing were an integral part of the Monte Hale films with Foy Willing and The Riders of the Purple Sage usually around to assist the star.

*   *   *

When I arrived at the coffee shop the next morning, Monte was finishing his breakfast with Chill Wills, another Western star who was a guest at the film festival. I caught Monte's eye and indicated I would wait for him in a booth across from where they were sitting.

Chill was his usual boisterous self and from all appearances was still recovering from the night before. Presently Chill (and someone else who had joined them) got up and left the table to view a film that Chill seemed eager to see.

A few moments later Monte moved over to my booth and slid in across from me. After exchanging a few pleasantries, we got to the business of his singing cowboy days in motion pictures.

DAVID ROTHEL: Can you give me a little background on how you happened to get into motion pictures in the mid forties?

MONTE HALE: You bet! I'm originally from San Angelo, Texas, Tom Green County [born June 8, 1921]. I went to school in San Angelo and Sterling City, Texas, where Fess Parker and Ernest Tubbs were from. We're all very good friends; over the years we've crossed trails and shook hands with each other many times.

When I was a youngster, I picked up a little bit on the guitar, just enough to get by. At one point during the war I was workin' at a theater in Galveston, Texas, the Jean Lafitte Hotel. I had heard that a bunch of movie stars had come out from Hollywood to sell war bonds. I was walking over from the theater one afternoon after the first show to restring my guitar when I looked up and saw Chill Wills walkin' through the lobby, only I didn't know it was him. I walked up to him and said, "Excuse me, I hear there's a bunch of movie stars including Chill Wills that just got into town. I'm lookin' for them." He said, "Well, you can stop right here. I'm Chill." So I got his autograph and later found out that Huntz Hall of the Dead End Kids was there with them, Lasses White, who did comedy with Jimmy Wakely in all those Monogram movies, Gale Storm, Big Boy Williams—so many I can't think of them all now, but there were about twenty-eight that came out to sell war bonds.

It happened that they needed a guitar accompanist for Lasses White. Phil Isley, who was the president of the Stars Over Texas War Bond Drive Committee, asked me if I would play guitar for Lasses for two weeks on that bond drive. I said, "Yes, Sir, but how am I goin' to eat and get along? I'm just down here makin' a livin'." I said, "What I'm makin' at this theater today, Mr. Isley, is just enough to pay for the hotel room. I'll probably have to wind up hitchhiking back to Houston." He kind of laughed. Phil Isley, as you probably know, is Jennifer Jones's father. But, anyhow, to make a long story short, I went with them on the bond drive. Mr. Isley paid me a nominal little fee to take care of my expenses and everything. It was a beautiful experience for me and I got a chance to play and sing a little, too. I was with them for about two, two and a half weeks, and they sold over sixty million dollars worth of bonds.

They liked me, I guess, enough to write a letter to Mr. Herbert Yates [the president] of Republic Studios. Then somebody called Mr. Yates and told him what I'd done on that war bond drive, singin' and everything. He said, "Well, I can't promise you that we'll give Hale a job, but if he wants to come out to Republic Studios, we'll have him meet with the producers and directors. If he lives up to expectations and qualifications, there might be a good chance he'll be employed."

So I took the gamble. I went to a friend of mine—I didn't have any money to get out there—I went to Bill Williams in Houston. They call him the Chicken King down there. He came to Houston with a dollar and eighty cents in his pocket many years ago and wound up a multimillionaire. Not just sellin' fried chicken, but in the oil business also. So I told Bill, I said, "Bill, I got this telegram here to come to Hollywood and I don't know how I'm goin' to get out there. It's a helluva walk." He read the telegram and said, "Here, take this and go." He handed me five one hundred dollar bills. I never saw so much money in my life; I couldn't believe what I was lookin' at.

So I went to California. I stayed at a place called the Biltmore Hotel. It was the only hotel I ever saw pictures of in a magazine, you know, in those tourist pages. That was the only place I knew to stay, so I stopped there.

The next morning I went out to Republic Studios in a cab. I saw Victor McLaglen walkin' along the studio walk there; I asked him where the office was. He pointed it out to me, and I got his autograph. I had a ball! But I don't want to bore you with all this. This is about how I got started. I signed a seven-year contract the followin' day after I met Mr. Yates.

DAVID ROTHEL: I know you were in a few bit roles and then all of a sudden you were starring in a musical Western series. How did it suddenly happen that you were made a star?

MONTE HALE: Well, they put me under contract. Naturally, when you're under contract, you're their property so they can do what they want to with you. And I was glad, because I'd never had any experience acting. At first they just put me in the background in films with Alan "Rocky" Lane and. . . .

DAVID ROTHEL: Bill Elliott in one of the Red Ryder series. You appeared long enough to get one line spoken before you disappeared from the film.

MONTE HALE: *California Gold Rush* [1946], I think, was the name of it. Earlier they had put me in one with—oh, who was it?—Richard Arlen called *The Big Bonanza* [1944].

DAVID ROTHEL: Yes. In doing some research on your career I discovered that you were listed at the bottom of the credits of *The Big Bonanza* as "a singer."

MONTE HALE: Oh, man, how they lied! Actually, they took a screen test of me in that movie. They liked it, I guess, left it in there, and

Monte, astride his horse named Partner, is seen here galloping into action.

gave me bottom billing on the film. I was happy about it.

DAVID ROTHEL: After a few bit parts you suddenly starred in *Home On the Range* [1946]. That was quite a jump from bottom billing to starring position.

MONTE HALE: Let me tell you how I got into *Home On the Range,* my first starring picture. They wrote a picture for me called *Don't Fence Me In.* It was to have all of Roy's [Rogers] cast in it: Gabby Hayes, Dale Evans, The Sons of the Pioneers—the whole bunch. This was when they thought Roy was going into the Army. They wrote it for me and gave me the script. I learned every part in it. I studied that script day and night. Then one day they called me up to the office and told me Roy was not goin' into the service and that I wasn't goin' to make the movie, that Roy wanted to make it.

It broke my heart a little bit. They knew that, I guess, because it wasn't long after that that Lou Gray, the producer, started dreamin' up a little script about animals that he called *Home On the Range.* It was to be Republic's first color film, and they put me in it. Robert Blake was in it, too. He was a little boy about, oh, ten or eleven years old—a great little kid. I remember Robert Blake from the last movie he and I were in together, *Out California Way* [1946]. That's the last time I saw him. I've talked to him on the phone a few times, but we've never gotten together. But he's really been a great success, that kid.

DAVID ROTHEL: Yes, he sure has. Did you have any acting experience before you went into films?

MONTE HALE: Nothing!

DAVID ROTHEL: I heard you say last night in the viewing room that you had no business ever getting into show business.

MONTE HALE: That's the truth. I should have stayed right down on the farm or on a ranch in Texas.

DAVID ROTHEL: (laugh) I can't agree with that.

MONTE HALE: But that's the truth! That's how I really have felt about it all my life.

DAVID ROTHEL: Did you have any riding experience before going into Western films?

MONTE HALE: I never had ridden many horses. I'd been bucked off a bunch of them, but not because I was a rodeo performer; I'd just fall off because I was so damned clumsy. (laugh)

DAVID ROTHEL: How long did it generally take to shoot one of your Republic pictures?

MONTE HALE: Well, when they were in color they took a little more time with makeup and lighting. It took a little longer than the six-day wonders, the black-and-white ones. We averaged around thirty to thirty-five days on each color picture.

DAVID ROTHEL: That long!

MONTE HALE: Yes.

DAVID ROTHEL: I know the fact that they were using color would alter the budgets quite a bit.

MONTE HALE: Yeah, they had budget hassles, I know, over it. But it wasn't anyone's fault; it was just that they were tryin' to perfect this new color process called Magnacolor [later called Trucolor], and it took a little more time.

DAVID ROTHEL: Can you tell me what the budgets were on those first color films?

MONTE HALE: Not the first one, but I understand that *Out California Way* cost over a million dollars. Now, I don't know this for sure. I know they didn't spend too much money on the cast. It was just the technical part of it that cost so much—what they were doing to perfect the color. I know there was a cameraman—Jack Marta—who was fired from the picture because he took so long to film it. He wanted to do as good a job as he knew how, with correct lighting and everything, so they let the man go. He was a wonderful cameraman.

DAVID ROTHEL: Yes, he shot a lot of Republic films. Over the years, who was your favorite director?

MONTE HALE: Well, I think Buddy Springsteen was my favorite director, but I liked Lesley Selander very much, too. He directed Randolph Scott and Hoppy in a lot of movies. And I liked Philip Ford; he's John Ford's nephew. He's a nice little guy.

DAVID ROTHEL: I didn't realize he was related to John Ford.

MONTE HALE: A nephew. Phil Ford, a good little director. He's been doin' a lot of TV directin' in the past few years.

DAVID ROTHEL: Lesley Selander has, too, of course.

MONTE HALE: Oh, yes.

DAVID ROTHEL: Of all your films, is there one that's a particular favorite?

MONTE HALE: (laugh) I don't know. I don't really even like to look at them because I was so green when I started. I didn't know what to do with my thumbs. (laugh) I'd just stand around lookin' silly, you know. The first four or five pictures I was just anxious to read the lines, not even knowin' when the answers were comin' to me. I wouldn't even listen after I gave someone a line. I wasn't even payin' attention to their answers. I just memorized my lines and wanted to get them out of the way. Finally, about the sixth or seventh one, I got to payin' attention to what I was sayin'. But I really wasn't interested in it [making motion pictures]. I didn't take interest in it as a craft.

DAVID ROTHEL: Did you look upon it as something you were going to do for a year or so. . . .

MONTE HALE: Or twenty minutes. (laugh) That sounds stupid and silly to say, but that's the way I felt. Show business wasn't for me.

DAVID ROTHEL: What have you been doing in the years since then?

MONTE HALE: Pretty good, and you?

DAVID ROTHEL: (laugh) Well, I . . . .

MONTE HALE: I'm just kidding. Not a heck of a lot. I did a few "Gunsmokes." About 1955 I was on *Giant* for six months with all that bunch. We lost a good boy, too. Killed in a wreck—James Dean.

DAVID ROTHEL: Did you know him well?

MONTE HALE: Very well. I taught him the rope trick he did in *Giant* in that scene where we were trying to buy the land back from him. One day he saw me spinnin' a rope out and tying trick knots with it. He said, "I sure wish I could do something like that." I said, "Well, how about me teachin' you a little deal right here?" He said, "I sure would appreciate it." So I taught him how to tie a knot with a rope by just throwin' a loop down it. I said, "Now use it somewhere in this picture." And he used it in the scene where we were tryin' to buy the land back. It was a good scene. People who have seen *Giant* will know what I'm talkin' about.

DAVID ROTHEL: What have you been doing in recent years outside of show business?

MONTE HALE: Well, I'm like most kids who go to Disneyland. I like to go bye-bye once in a while. I like to get in the car and just drive all over the country, or get on an airplane and go somewhere for a few days and just see the people and shake hands with them.

DAVID ROTHEL: I was referring to work over the years to keep yourself. . . .

MONTE HALE: I haven't done any work; I haven't wanted to. Believe me, I'm not a wealthy man; I'm just here by being careful.

DAVID ROTHEL: Tell me about some of the people you worked with over the years. How about Roy Barcroft, the king of the Republic villains? Was he as great a guy as just about everybody says?

MONTE HALE: Oh, was he ever!

DAVID ROTHEL: And he was such a horrendous villain; just the most despicable character on the screen.

MONTE HALE: He was a great musician, too. He played the saxophone and clarinet just beautifully.

DAVID ROTHEL: I didn't realize that.

MONTE HALE: I'll never forget one time Roy Barcroft and I were having lunch out at Iverson's Ranch where we were doing some location shooting. Roy and I went over to the catering truck to get a little beef and peas and mashed potatoes, and then sat down near a big boulder. He was sitting on the ground, leaning up against the rock; I was sitting on a limb that was torn out of a tree. As we were eating, I looked down under Roy by the rock and saw a little gopher snake crawlin' right beside him around the rock. Roy hadn't seen it. I said, "Roy, sit real still." I reached back and picked up a rock in my hand. He said, "What's the matter?" I said, "There's a snake crawlin' there, hold it." He yelled, "No, wait a minute! Don't kill it. It may be someone from the front office." (laugh) That actually happened. It sounds like a joke, but it really, really happened, and I laugh about it to this day.

DAVID ROTHEL: Do you know Rex Allen?

MONTE HALE: Oh, sure. I met him the day he walked on the lot. I hugged his neck and wished him the best of luck, and he did pretty good. He's a wonderful personality. You can't help but like him, and he can sing his heart out. He and Eddie Dean are the two greatest singers I've ever heard in this field; they are fantastic. I could never hold them a light. I admire those boys. They are entertainers. But I will say this, when I was singin' and workin' theaters, rodeos, and fairs, I loved to do that work. My shows sometimes would run an hour and forty-five minutes with me alone on the stage. And I loved the work; I really did. I felt always that I could entertain people, especially children. I used to go to the hospitals, all the crippled children's hospitals, and meet all those kids. I imagine I've played every Shrine Hospital in the United States. It was just a wonderful feeling to know you could go in and maybe get a smile out of some kid that probably would never walk. I had photographs made at darned near every one of the hospitals I worked. I look at them sometimes and just can't help but well-up in the eyes a little bit. But we were talkin' about Eddie Dean and Rex Allen; they're good friends, as are Sunset Carson, Bob Nolan and The Sons of the Pioneers, Don "Red" Barry; all of them were very close friends.

DAVID ROTHEL: Is Bob Nolan still working?

MONTE HALE: Yes. I took Marty Robbins to his home a few weeks ago. I hadn't seen Bob in—well, twenty years or more. He and Marty Robbins kept passing the guitar back and forth to each other, singing. I just sat there and relished it all because they are two greats.

DAVID ROTHEL: They sure are. Did you ever know Tex Ritter?

MONTE HALE: Knew him well. I was with him the week before he passed away. He drove me all over Nashville. I'd never seen Nashville before, and he drove me all over there with his wife's car; showed me everything. A week later he was gone.

DAVID ROTHEL: Roy Rogers and Gene Autry?

MONTE HALE: We weren't clubby at all, but I knew them. We nodded, shook hands, visited with each other.

DAVID ROTHEL: Is there any truth to the story that you were brought in to Republic as singing cowboy competition to keep Roy Rogers in line at contract time?

MONTE HALE: I know what people say about that, but I don't believe that was the case. Roy was the king and, by gosh, he's goin' to remain that as far as I'm concerned. I love him. You never knew what a front office was liable to hold over a star's head, but I will never believe that they brought me in there to hang over him.

DAVID ROTHEL: What was your reaction to Herbert Yates, the president of Republic Pictures? What kind of a person was he?

Monte Hale as he appeared at the peak of his singing cowboy career in the late 1940s. *Photo courtesy of Monte Hale.*

MONTE HALE: He could spit tobacco juice as far as anybody. I mean he was pretty cold.

DAVID ROTHEL: Pretty cold?

MONTE HALE: Pretty cold, but you had to like him. He was a cold person, but I think down deep he had a lot of soul. I really believe that. Although he was a businessman, I can buy that.

DAVID ROTHEL: From everything I've heard, he was a really tough fellow.

MONTE HALE: He was rough, but he was business, and I think he had a big heart in him—somewhere.

DAVID ROTHEL: Monte, as you well know, B Western film festivals have been sprouting all over the United States during the last few years. What do you think accounts for the continuing popularity of these Western films? Is there any particular thing that you see—a sort of enduring quality—that causes so many people after all these years to still want to see them?

MONTE HALE: You know, I'm glad you brought this up. I can't understand what they really mean, these film festivals. I don't know if it's a commercial thing or. . . .

DAVID ROTHEL: I don't think they could be making much money on them; the promoters aren't charging enough for that.

MONTE HALE: I think it's just the love of it.

It's the love of the restoration of the past through the B Westerns. I think the people, the fans, really love these men, the people who were in the films. I really believe that.

DAVID ROTHEL: I think you're right. It's great enjoyment after all these years to come and look at the films again. I am astounded by how well they hold up. So many times when you go back and look at something you saw years before—especially something you saw during your youth—you find it's a disappointment now. But these B Western films hold up surprisingly well.

MONTE HALE: As far as Westerns ever coming back like in the old days, that'll never happen. Not like it was. Nothing like that can ever happen again because they're gone, all those people are gone who made them, and there are no youngsters coming up to take their places.

DAVID ROTHEL: But it sure is enjoyable to look back on them.

MONTE HALE: Yes, it is. It's a good feeling, but when I look at them—look at something old like that—it doesn't give me reason to want to be back in the business. I just come down to meet the people, and wipe it out of my mind when I leave on the airplane.

DAVID ROTHEL: When you sit in the viewing

Monte Hale smiles for the author's camera at a recent Western film festival.

room watching your films as you have during the last couple of evenings, do you ever have the feeling that it's somebody else you are seeing up there on the screen?

MONTE HALE: No, I know it's me.

DAVID ROTHEL: Does it seem like another world to you?

MONTE HALE: I know what you're talkin' about. When I first started making these things and goin' to the rushes, I couldn't wait for the editor to get a film all together—to piece it together—just so I could look at it to see what it really was. Boy, I found out what it was; it was a bunch of nothin'. But it was a job, and I met lots of nice people in the business. I just never could get used to the idea that I was in show business. It just wasn't my cup of tea. It just wasn't it!

DAVID ROTHEL: Where are you living now?

MONTE HALE: I live in Burbank. Redd Foxx lives about two doors from me. We have a lot of laughs.

DAVID ROTHEL: Thank you, Monte, for this opportunity to talk with you.

MONTE HALE: I'd like to say this, a little thing I threw together a few years ago. I'd just like to close out with this:

Life is like a journey taken on a train,
With a pair of travelers at each windowpane.
I may sit beside all you folks
    the whole journey through,
or I may sit elsewhere never knowing you.
But if fate should mark us all to
    sit there side by side,
Let's be pleasant travelers because it's such
    a short old ride.

MONTE HALE
SELECTED FILMOGRAPHY

The following filmography only includes the Republic Western series in which Monte Hale starred.

* * *

Home On the Range (Republic, 1946) 55 .M. Magnacolor

Producer, Louis Gray; director, Robert Springsteen; screenplay, Betty Burbridge; original story by Betty Burbridge and Bernard McConville; camera, Marcel LePicard; editor, Charles Craft; musical director, Morton Scott; songs, Gordon Forster, Ken Carson, Glen Spencer.

CAST: Monte Hale, Adrian Booth, Tom Chatterton, Bobby Blake, LeRoy Mason, Roy Barcroft, Kenne Duncan, Budd Buster, Jack Kirk, John Hamilton, Bob Nolan and The Sons of the Pioneers.

* * *

Man from Rainbow Valley (Republic, 1946) 56 M. Trucolor

Producer, Louis Gray; director, Robert Springsteen; screenplay, Betty Burbridge; camera, Bud Thackery; editor, Edward Mann; songs, Eddie Cherkose, Cy Feuer, Roy Rogers, Glen Spencer.

CAST: Monte Hale, Adrian Booth, Jo Ann Marlowe, Ferris Taylor, Emmett Lynn, Tom London, Bud Geary, Kenne Duncan, Doyle O'Dell, Bert Roach, The Sagebrush Seranaders: Enright Busse, John Scott, Frank Wilder.

* * *

Out California Way (Republic, 1946) 67 M. Trucolor

Producer, Louis Gray; director, Lesley Selander; screenplay, Betty Burbridge; original story, Harry Shipman; camera, Bud Thackery; editor, Charles Craft; songs, Paul Westmoreland, Foy Willing, Jack Meakin, Foster Carling, Tex Carlson, Jack Statham, Gus Snow, Eddie Dean, Hal Blair.

CAST: Monte Hale, Adrian Booth, Bobby Blake, John Dehner, Nolan Leary, Fred Graham, Tom London, Jimmy Starr, Edward Keane, Bob Wilke, Brooks Benedict, St. Luke's Choristers, Foy Willing and The Riders of the Purple Sage.

* * *

Last Frontier Uprising (Republic, 1947) 67 M. Trucolor

Producer, Louis Gray; director, Lesley Selander; screenplay, Harvey Gates; original story, Jerome Odium; camera, Bud Thackery; editor, Charles Craft; musical score, Mort Glickman.

CAST: Monte Hale, Adrian Booth, James Taggart, Roy Barcroft, Tom London, Philip Van Zandt, Edmund Cobb, John Ince, Frank O'Connor, Bob Blair, Doyle O'Dell, Foy Willing and The Riders of the Purple Sage.

* * *

Monte seems to have the situation well in hand in this scene from *Out California Way*. *Photo courtesy of NTA.*

It is a tense moment for old Tom London, the pooch, and Monte Hale in this scene from *Last Frontier Uprising*. *Photo courtesy of Monte Hale and NTA.*

238

Photo courtesy of NTA.

Along the Oregon Trail (Republic, 1947) 64 M. Trucolor

Producer, Melville Tucker; director, R. G. Springsteen; screenplay, Earle Snell; camera, Alfred S. Keller; editor, Arthur Roberts; musical director, Mort Glickman; songs, Foy Willing.

CAST: Monte Hale, Adrian Booth, Clayton Moore, Roy Barcroft, Max Terhune, Will Wright, Wade Crosby, LeRoy Mason, Tom London, Forrest Taylor, Foy Willing and The Riders of the Purple Sage.

*   *   *

Under Colorado Skies (Republic, 1947) 65 M. Trucolor

Producer, Melville Tucker; director, R. G. Springsteen; screenplay, Louise Rousseau; camera, Alfred S. Keller; editor, Arthur Roberts; musical director, Mort Glickman; songs, Bob Wills, Foy Willing, Sid Robin.

CAST: Monte Hale, Adrian Booth, Paul Hurst, William Haade, John Alvin, LeRoy Mason, Tom

Clayton Moore (television's Lone Ranger) is on the wrong side of the law in this scene from *Along the Oregon Trail*. *Photo courtesy of NTA.*

London, Steve Darrell, Gene Evans, Ted Adams, Steve Raines, Hank Patterson, Foy Willing and The Riders of the Purple Sage.

* * *

California Firebrand (Republic, 1948) 63 M. Trucolor

Producer, Melville Tucker; director, Philip Ford; screenplay, J. Benton Cheney and John K. Butler; adapted by Royal K. Cole; camera, Reggie Lanning; editor, Tony Martinelli; songs, Foy Willing, Sid Robin.

CAST: Monte Hale, Adrian Booth, Paul Hurst, Alice Tyrrell, Tristram Coffin, LeRoy Mason, Douglas Evans, Sarah Edwards, Daniel M. Sheridan, Duke York, Lanny Rees, Foy Willing and The Riders of the Purple Sage.

* * *

The Timber Trail (Republic, 1948) 67 M. Trucolor

Producer, Melville Tucker; director, Philip Ford; screenplay, Bob Williams; camera, Reggie Lanning; editor, Tony Martinelli; musical director, Mort Glickman; songs, Tim Spencer, Ned Washington, Phil Ohman.

CAST: Monte Hale, Lynne Roberts, James Burke, Roy Barcroft, Francis Ford, Robert Emmett

Monte and James Burke are about to ambush the outlaws in this scene from *The Timber Trail*. This stock set was used in many Republic features and serials. *Photo courtesy of NTA.*

Keane, Steve Darrell, Fred Graham, Wade Crosby, Eddie Acuff, Foy Willing and The Riders of the Purple Sage.

* * *

Son of God's Country (Republic, 1948) 60 M.

Producer, Melville Tucker; director, R. G. Springsteen; screenplay, Paul Gangelin; camera, John MacBurnie; editor, Harry Keller.

240

CAST: Monte Hale, Pamela Blake, Paul Hurst, Jim Nolan, Jay Kirby, Steve Darrell, Francis McDonald, Jason Robards, Fred Graham.

*   *   *

Prince of the Plains (Republic, 1949) 60 M.

Producer, Melville Tucker; director, Philip Ford; screenplay, Louise Rousseau, Albert DeMond; camera, Bud Thackery; editor, Richard L. Van Enger.

CAST: Monte Hale, Paul Hurst, Shirley Davis, Roy Barcroft, Rory Mallinson, Harry Lauter, Lane Bradford, George Carleton.

*   *   *

Law of the Golden West (Republic, 1949) 59 M.

Producer, Melville Tucker; director, Philip Ford; screenplay, Norman S. Hall; camera, Ernest Miller; editor, Richard L. Van Enger.

Photo courtesy of NTA.

CAST: Monte Hale, Paul Hurst, Gail Davis, Roy Barcroft, John Holland, Scott Elliott, Lane Bradford, Harold Goodwin, John Hamilton.

*   *   *

South of Rio (Republic, 1949) 60 M.

Producer, Melville Tucker; director, Philip Ford; screenplay, Norman S. Hall; camera, John MacBurnie; editor, Harold Minter.

CAST: Monte Hale, Kay Christopher, Paul Hurst, Roy Barcroft, Douglas Kennedy, Don Haggerty, Rory Mallinson, Lane Bradford, Emmett Vogan, Myron Healey, Tom London.

*   *   *

Outcasts of the Trail (Republic, 1949) 59 M.

Producer, Melville Tucker; director, Philip Ford; screenplay, Olive Cooper; camera, Bud Thackery; musical director, Stanley Wilson.

CAST: Monte Hale, Paul Hurst, Jeff Donnell, Roy Barcroft, John Gallaudet, Milton Parsons, Tommy Ivo, Minerva Urecal, Ted Mapes, George W. Lloyd, Steve Darrell.

*   *   *

San Antone Ambush (Republic, 1949) 60 M.

Producer, Melville Tucker; director, Philip Ford; screenplay, Norman S. Hall; camera, John MacBurnie; editor, Tony Martinelli.

CAST: Monte Hale, Bette Daniels, Paul Hurst, Roy Barcroft, James Cardwell, Trevor Bardette, Lane Bradford, Francis Ford, Tommy Coats, Tom London, Edmund Cobb.

*   *   *

Ranger of Cherokee Strip (Republic, 1949) 60 M.

Producer, Melville Tucker; director, Philip Ford; screenplay, Bob Williams; original story, Earl Snell; camera, Ellis W. Carter; editor, Irving M. Schoenberg; musical director, Stanley Wilson.

CAST: Monte Hale, Paul Hurst, Alice Talton, Roy Barcroft, Douglas Kennedy, George Meeker, Frank Fenton, Monte Blue, Neyle Morrow.

*   *   *

Pioneer Marshal (Republic, 1950) 60 M.

Producer, Melville Tucker; director, Philip Ford;

Jeff Donnell, Sheriff Monte Hale, and John Gallaudet seem apprehensive as they await the arrival of one of the *Outcasts of the Trail. Photo courtesy of NTA.*

screenplay, Bob Williams; camera, John MacBurnie; editor, Robert M. Leeds; musical director, Stanley Wilson.

CAST: Monte Hale, Paul Hurst, Nan Leslie, Roy Barcroft, Damian O'Flynn, Myron Healey, Ray Walker, John Hamilton, Clarence Straight, Robert Williams.

* * *

The Vanishing Westerner (Republic, 1950) 60 M.

Producer, Melville Tucker; director, Philip Ford; screenplay, Bob Williams; camera, Ellis W. Carter; editor, Richard L. Van Enger; musical director, Stanley Wilson.

CAST: Monte Hale, Paul Hurst, Aline Towne, Roy Barcroft, Arthur Space, Richard Anderson, William Phipps, Don Haggerty, Dick Curtis, Rand Brooks, Edmund Cobb, Harold Goodwin.

* * *

The Old Frontier (Republic, 1950) 60 M.

242

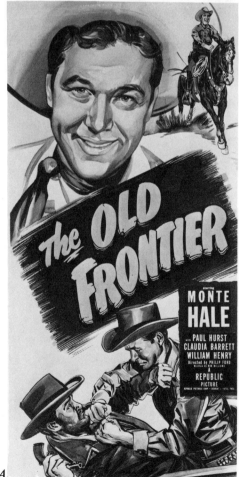

Photo courtesy of NTA.

Photo courtesy of NTA.

Monte struggles with Lane Bradford for the gun in this scene from *The Old Frontier. Photo courtesy of NTA.*

Producer, Melville Tucker; director, Philip Ford; screenplay, Bob Williams; camera, Ellis W. Carter; editor, Harold Minter.

CAST: Monte Hale, Paul Hurst, Claudia Barrett, William Henry, Tristram Coffin, William Haade, Victor Kilian, Lane Bradford, Denver Pyle, Almira Sessions, Tom London.

*   *   *

The Missourians (Republic, 1950) 60 M.

Producer, Melville Tucker; director, George Blair; screenplay, Arthur E. Orloff; camera, John Mac-Burnie; editor, Robert M. Leeds.

CAST: Monte Hale, Paul Hurst, Roy Barcroft, Lyn Thomas, Howard J. Negley, Robert Neil, Lane Bradford, John Hamilton, Sarah Padden, Charles Williams, Perry Ivins.

MONTE HALE DISCOGRAPHY

Monte Hale would be the first to acknowledge that he didn't make too much headway as a recording artist. He made only a few recordings in the late forties, none of which is available today.

Among Monte Hale's single recordings were the following:

Is It Wrong? Beltone Records
In My Stable Beltone Records
I'm Roundin' Up My Love for You
    Beltone Records
I'm Ridin' the Rails MGM Records
Statue in the Bay MGM Records

9 Rex Allen

THE LAST OF THE SINGING COWBOYS

"Sure, gimme a call in our room. We're going to be here for the next three days, so I don't know why we can't get together for a little whittlin' and gigglin'." Great! That was the main reason I had come to Nashville in the barefoot-blistering, egg-frying heat of late July—to whittle and giggle with the last of the singing cowboys, Rex Allen.

It was just after lunch and we were in the lobby of the Sheraton. Rex was dressed in a tan-colored business suit that had an indiscernible something about it that bespoke Western. The conventional white shirt and tie fit the quiet tone of the suit. It was only when my eyes reached the boots that the hint of cowboy in the conservative duds was confirmed, but tastefully.

The voice, clothes, and husky, masculine good looks gave the impression of an Oklahoma businessman—confident, comfortable in the brief give-and-take of words with a total stranger. Like some other Southerners and Westerners I had encountered over the years, Rex enjoyed employing the old shibboleth of feigning to be just a plain ole country boy with the "whittlin' and gigglin' " routine. But he wasn't fooling anybody. It was obvious that he had been around the barn a couple of times, knew the price of wheat, and how to skin a cat—a fat cat in a business deal. And this ole country boy reeked of class and the type of easy, quiet sophistication that comes with success in your chosen field rather than necessarily from a formal education. This was the type of man who could be as comfortable at a White House dinner as he would be "jawin' " with a hand on his ranch. It seemed to me that you would really have to

Rex Allen. *Photo courtesy of Rex Allen.*

"The Arizona Cowboy," Rex Allen, today.

riding the Disney range as narrator for many of the nature features and shorts. Rex's slow, Oklahoma, bass-baritone drawl exuded by the bucketful a quality that was to most people's ears what the cowboy, the true Westerner, should sound like when he opened his mouth. It was a warm, down-home, country voice, intelligent and masculine. Therefore, when Walt Disney was looking for such a voice to tell us about *The Hound That Thought He Was a Racoon* (1960), *The Legend of Lobo* (1962), *The Incredible Journey* (1963) of two dogs and a cat, or the furlong-eating horse in *Run, Appaloosa, Run!* (1966), he called on Rex Allen—"The Voice of the West."

Rex's wonderful world of Disney was not confined to just theatrical features and shorts. Pretty soon he was narrating episodes on Disney's television series such as "Sancho the Homing Steer" (1961), "An Otter in the Family" (1964), "Nosey, the Sweetest Skunk in the West" (1972), and "The Secret of Old Glory Mine" (1976).

When he wasn't voice-overing for Disney, Rex was pushing Dog Chow and other animal dinners on television for the Purina people. Often he could also be seen touting brakes, shock absorbers, batteries, and other wares for numerous commercial companies—but meanwhile, back at the musical Westerns . . . .

The blue shadows had grown long on the musical Western trail by the time Rex Allen hit the singing cowboy saddle in 1950. At Monogram and PRC Tex Ritter, Eddie Dean, and Jimmy Wakely had already bitten the dust. Monte Hale had long since stopped singing in his Republic features and was in production on his last nonmusical series for the company. Roy Rogers, still the king of the Republic lot with his Trucolor musical Westerns, would only last another year, and during that year (1951) his features would revert to black and white and lower budgets. Only Gene Autry over at Columbia was still finding plenty of outlaws to capture and songs to warble.

The whole motion picture industry was in a state of crisis by the early fifties as revenues were dropping (primarily because of the invasion of television) and costs were soaring. The low budget genre films were suffering more than most other types of motion pictures, because television was their nearest direct competition. Many picture companies were contemplating the shutdown of B picture units so that energies and resources could be concentrated on the big-budget, big-screen blockbusters—television being unable to compete with film epics like *Quo Vadis* (1951) and *The Robe* (1953) or such lavish color musicals as *An*

work hard at not liking Rex Allen. I wasn't even going to try. I just liked him immediately.

* * *

I had never really thought about it until I started research on the singing cowboys, but the truth was that I had somehow never seen a Rex Allen musical Western (a deficiency I soon remedied). He had first come down the B Western trail about mid 1950 with a feature appropriately called *The Arizona Cowboy*. I knew about it at the time and that he was the new singing cowboy at Republic, but because I was moseying on into high school and temporarily beyond such things as singing cowboys, ole Rex had to make it without me. My fascination with *Variety*, though, allowed me to keep a watchful eye on his career through reviews and announcements of personal appearances. I knew he was around but never really checked him out.

A few years later in the sixties, Rex showed up

Rex Allen, businessman and television pitchman (circa 1960s). *Photo courtesy of Rex Allen.*

American in Paris (1951). Despite the PR boys' hype that "Movies Are Better Than Ever," many of the fans were staying home to watch Uncle Miltie, Lucy, and the old Hopalong Cassidy films free of charge on the mini screen. Considering the state of the film industry at the time, many people felt that Rex Allen was just riding down the celluloid canyon to watch the sun go down on his kind of pictures—the B musical Westerns.

It was extremely unfortunate that Rex Allen (named after former cowboy star Rex Bell) came along so late in the life of the singing cowboy films. He had it all going for him—looks, voice, riding ability, and a natural, unaffected acting style that made him very appealing on the screen. A cynical critic once commented that Rex Allen was the result of a recipe containing the ingredients of "a pinch of Gene Autry, two tablespoons of Roy Rogers, a half-cup of Jimmy Wakely, and two

shakes of Tex Ritter." Actually, the recipe is not really an unkind appraisal. When Herbert Yates hired Rex Allen, he wasn't looking to break new ground in the musical Western field; he wanted to perpetuate the box-office success of the singing cowboys in yet another incarnation. Therefore Yates *was* looking for someone who possessed a mixture of the ingredients listed above in hopes that they would result in a singing cowboy as successful as the others had been.

What Yates got for his money was the best traits of the other singing cowboys plus a quality that was all Rex Allen's. He looked the part of the singing cowboy probably more than most of his competitors. He was tall and ruggedly handsome with a trim physique. His manner suggested a warmth, grace, and integrity that was appealing to both males and females. Rex was more relaxed and natural in the acting department than most of his predecessors. While some might accuse him of a tendency toward blandness in his performances, he certainly was not as guilty of this as Monte Hale, Jimmy Wakely, or even Gene Autry, for that matter. Concerning Rex's ability to handle his dukes in a screen fight or stay on a horse during a chase, few, if any other singing cowboys could give him competition. He was what he was, an appealing singing cowpoke who was very likable handling the acting and action demands of his type of film.

While Rex's singing voice never had as great an appeal to the hillbilly-Western trade as, say, Gene Autry's or Tex Ritter's, he nevertheless had a fuller, richer voice that had the potential for appealing to a wider, more diverse audience than most of the other singing cowboys. During the fifties when he had his own radio show on the CBS radio network, it ranked as high as seventh in the ratings, attesting to his broad appeal to audiences.

I find it interesting to contemplate the results of a head-on Gene Autry, Roy Rogers, and Rex Allen singing cowboy competition during the years when the musical Westerns were at their peak of popularity. It is the guess of this armchair critic that the name Rex might have taken on its Latin meaning of king, as in King of the Singing Cowboys.

Rex Allen starred in only nineteen Republic Western features, starting in 1950 with *The Arizona Cowboy* and concluding in early 1954 with *The Phantom Stallion.* They were all in black and white, low budget, and generally undistinguished in plot and originality. But the films did have a few things going for them in addition to their star: the excellent technical crew and Western production facilities of Republic Pictures, unusually competent comic sidekicks (Buddy Ebsen and Slim

Rex Allen, his wife, Bonnie, and Monte Hale at a social gathering. Rex is not as heavy now as he appears in this photo. *Photo courtesy of Monte Hale.*

Pickens), generally strong supporting players, and, for many of the pictures, the best B Western action director in the business—William Witney. But the main thing that distinguished the Rex Allen musical Westerns was Rex Allen himself.

*   *

Rex's wife, Bonnie (a former actress), had suggested three o'clock when I called their room to schedule the interview (Rex was taking a nap), so here I was knocking on the door armed with a cassette recorder, notepad, and a sheaf of questions for the last of the line of singing cowboys.

Rex answered the door himself. In the crowded hotel suite there appeared to be a small army of people: Rex, Bonnie, their daughter, Bonita, Rex, Jr. (a budding country-Western singing star in his own right), and an old musician buddy of Rex's, Wade Ray. Pretty soon Rex hustled them all off into the bedroom so that he and I could be by ourselves in the living room area. During our conversation I could hear talking and occasional laughter coming from the next room. Although I figured Rex would rather be whittlin' and gigglin'

with them, he had that intriguing ability to concentrate so completely that you felt you were the most important person in his life for the time you were with him. Doubly amazing was his ability to keep this same concentration while answering de rigueur questions that you knew he must have answered a thousand times before.

He sat relaxed in an easy chair next to the sofa I was on, the recorder between us. He had offered me a drink from the bar set up in the corner. I substituted a Fresca; he had nothing. He smoked two or three cigarettes during the time we talked.

DAVID ROTHEL: You really grew up in cowboy country out in Willcox, Arizona.

REX ALLEN: I was born there in 1921, but I lived the first five years of my life on a homestead about forty miles north of Willcox, back in the mountains. Then after my brother was rattlesnake bit, we moved to town. I was about five at the time. We lived there for about a year and then moved about six miles out of town where I actually grew up. I went to school in Willcox.

DAVID ROTHEL: And you were literally a cowboy, weren't you?

REX ALLEN: I was raised on a ranch and did all the things you're supposed to do, I guess. And I rodeoed for a couple of years before I got involved in the entertainment business.

DAVID ROTHEL: When did you get started singing?

REX ALLEN: Actually when I was just a ten-year-old. My dad was a country fiddle player. He needed somebody to back him on guitar, so he bought me one. I got involved in music that way. Then all through high school I was involved in the glee clubs and church choirs. I used to sing in the Sunday school Baptist choir and then sneak out the back door and go sing in the Methodist choir.

DAVID ROTHEL: You got a job singing on the radio when you were quite young, didn't you?

REX ALLEN: My first radio singing job was at KOY in Phoenix, Arizona, when I first got out of high school. Then I went with the rodeo back East, got banged up and bucked off a bull and ended up in Trenton, New Jersey, about to starve to death. So I had to kind of sing for my supper. That's why I started in radio in Trenton. That was around 1943 during the war.

DAVID ROTHEL: You then went to the "National Barn Dance" radio program out of Chicago.

REX ALLEN: Yes. I'll tell you how that came about. I got a job playing for a group out of Allentown, Pennsylvania, called The Sleepy Hollow Gang. A lot of the "National Barn Dance" acts used to come over there on Sundays and play that big outdoor park. Lulubelle and Scotty were playing there one time and they said, "Hey, you ought to come and take an audition at the 'National Barn Dance.'" I almost beat them back to Chicago. I went to work there in 1945—that's when I started in Chicago.

DAVID ROTHEL: And in about 1949 you were out in Hollywood with a radio program sponsored by Phillips Petroleum called "The Rex Allen Show."

REX ALLEN: Well, yeah. Phillips was one of my sponsors in Chicago. When I left Chicago to go to Republic Pictures, they moved the show out there and we did it from CBS in Hollywood. I didn't take many people with me. I think Wade Ray and Frank Messina [musicians] went with me. The Sons of the Pioneers worked for me on the show.

DAVID ROTHEL: How did you happen to go from the "National Barn Dance" show to your own show?

REX ALLEN: In Chicago the show was originally part of the "National Barn Dance." I was the master of ceremonies and so-called star of that particular section—like Red Foley used to be the star of the "Grand Ole Opry," Prince Albert section. The "National Barn Dance" show was run very similarly to the "Opry." It ran from 7:30 P.M. in the evening until midnight. But certain sections of the show belonged to certain artists as it went along.

DAVID ROTHEL: When you went to Hollywood with your program, was it still affiliated in any way with the "National Barn Dance"?

REX ALLEN: No, it had nothing to do with the "Barn Dance" then. It was all mine.

DAVID ROTHEL: How did the Republic contract come about?

REX ALLEN: The Chicago radio program had been very good for me, and I had several hit records going. Also at that time the Westerns were still very big in Hollywood. I had had a number of movie offers but they had never quite worked out. Paramount was planning to do a new series of Hopalong Cassidys with a younger man and they had been talking to me about doing a Hopalong Cassidy—they owned it still at that time. That never did work out. Then Autry came to me. Autry by that time had gone to Columbia and he was going to do a series of films over there. He had a contract with them to produce another series, too. He was going to do a thing called *The Range Riders*. I talked to Gene for probably three or four months about leaving Chicago and going to do

that. But that didn't quite work out either. Mainly it was because I was doing so well in Chicago with the "Barn Dance" that I couldn't leave there for the kind of money that I could get in Hollywood. So then Roy Rogers came into the picture. Roy was planning on leaving Republic and going to Fox studios. He wanted me to come and do a series with him. We just about had that one put together when I got a call one morning from Mr. Yates of Republic Pictures. He was in Chicago and he said, "I was at the 'Barn Dance' last night and I wonder if you could come down and talk with me this morning?" I didn't know who Mr. Yates was or anything, but I went down and talked with him. The next thing I knew they flew me out for a screen test, and I signed a seven-year deal with them.

DAVID ROTHEL: I understand Herbert Yates could be a cantankerous old cuss when he wanted to be. I've asked this question of other people when Yates's name has come up; how did you get along with him?

REX ALLEN: Mr. Yates was a very strong-willed person. A lot of times you'd think, "Gee, I'm the only guy on the lot." But then the next day you might think, "Well, he couldn't care less whether I'm around here or not." A lot of people had good things, a lot of people had bad things to say about him. But I'll have to say this, he gave me an opportunity that only comes to very few people in this world. The working conditions at Republic were sometimes a little awkward, but I wouldn't take a million dollars for the experience I had. He was good to me; he was a good ole guy to me.

DAVID ROTHEL: Did he keep his finger on the pulse of what was happening at Republic all the time?

REX ALLEN: He was aware of everything that was going on. He actually read all the scripts. If there was something in there he didn't like, he said, "No, let's don't do that." He was not a great motion picture man; he was just a great business-man and a good manipulator. (chuckle)

DAVID ROTHEL: In the Lone Ranger book I had the same sort of character in George W. Trendle who owned "The Lone Ranger" for many, many years. He was the same sort of man—domineering, controversial, tight-fisted in some ways.

REX ALLEN: Well, I think, truthfully, you'll find all of the old studio bosses were like that to their contract players. There are no contract players left in the business anymore, but in those days it was like an athlete today. You signed a seven-year contract and it meant you belonged to him. If he picked up the phone and said, "You get on a plane and meet me tomorrow morning in New York City at the Essex House," you better be there, because it wasn't just making movies, it was the whole spectrum. (chuckle)

DAVID ROTHEL: From what you have said, you apparently weren't brought in to keep Roy Rogers in line at contract time as some people have speculated.

REX ALLEN: Oh, no, Roy wanted to do television and Mr. Yates was just dead against, flat against television. In fact, my contract read that I was not ever allowed to walk in front of a television camera. Never! Not even for publicity purposes or for an interview or anything. When Roy and Gene quit making movies and went into television, the movie exhibitors really felt that this was a kick in the face to them. So one of the selling points that Mr. Yates had with my new series of films was that "You'll never see this guy on that big enemy, television. He belongs to you, the theaters." And I was not allowed to go near it [television].

DAVID ROTHEL: How did you take to being a singing cowboy? Did you feel comfortable accepting everything that went with it? The fancy clothes, the heroics, the super-clean-cut image for the kids?

REX ALLEN: I didn't mind at all.

DAVID ROTHEL: You're smoking a cigarette right now. Obviously you couldn't do it at that time.

REX ALLEN: No, no. You never smoked a cigarette in public or on the screen. It was just a no-no. I don't think that any of us have lived the pious life that we portrayed on the screen—maybe some of us have lived a little closer to it than others—but in those days it was important to keep that image in public, the same as on the screen. It was important to the producer of the motion pictures, and it was important to you—and it's still important to me. I try my best to keep that image. I don't smoke around children and I don't use any foul language. It's been awfully good for me that way, and I think I'll just go on that way.

DAVID ROTHEL: I think the public has a warm feeling for a performer who respects the idea of what the youngsters think of him.

REX ALLEN: I think maybe the youngsters of today should have a little more of that kind of exposure, someone to look up to rather than somebody that's high on narcotics or loaded to the gills, or something of that sort.

DAVID ROTHEL: Who were your favorite cowboy performers?

Rex is seen here in an action scene from one of his early Republic Westerns. *Photo courtesy of NTA.*

REX ALLEN: Whoever was playing at the movie theater when I was a boy was my favorite for that day and I'd go home and try to act like him. Roy hates me for saying this because it makes him sound so old, but the first time I saw Roy Rogers I was about ten years old and I was trying to learn to play the guitar and that kind of stuff, and I thought he was the greatest thing I had ever seen in my life. I think you have to split-up the musical guys and the people who did just straight dramatic Westerns. And in that route I have to go with Duke Wayne.

DAVID ROTHEL: How about the bad guys? Who were your favorite character actors?

REX ALLEN: Most of the guys who played the character roles—the so-called bad guys in the business—were the nicest guys you ever met in your life. One in particular who played heavies in many of my pictures was like an ole teddy bear—Roy Barcroft. One time I went into the front office and asked Mr. Yates if it would be completely out of line to someday cast Roy as my buddy. You know, the minute Roy's face hits the screen everybody in the audience knows that he's the guy that "did it," but it takes a smart cowboy three-fourths of the way through the picture to find out that he's guilty. I said to Mr. Yates, "Why don't we just fool them one time and let Roy turn out to be a good guy?" He said, "No, they'd never buy that." (laugh)

DAVID ROTHEL: You didn't have production numbers in your series the way Roy Rogers and Gene Autry did. Your songs were integrated right into the script.

REX ALLEN: More or less. One of the reasons for that was that they spent a lot less money on my pictures than they did the Roy Rogers and the Autrys. All of mine were done in black and white and a big portion of Roy's were done in color. Where they were spending maybe three-hundred-thousand dollars on Roy Rogers pictures and taking three weeks to shoot them, mine were shot for fifty-thousand dollars in five days. Quite a difference!

DAVID ROTHEL: I have recently seen some of your pictures. They certainly don't look as if they were shot in five days.

REX ALLEN: They were. I have the bruises to prove it. (laugh)

DAVID ROTHEL: Did the budgets of your pictures vary much?

REX ALLEN: Not on mine, no.

DAVID ROTHEL: I know you averaged four or five films a year. I assume that they were sold as a package to exhibitors.

REX ALLEN: Yes. The sales department would just take a bunch of titles that they had dreamed up or maybe the creative department of the studio had given them four or five titles. These titles would be the Rex Allen series for that particular year. If you had a chain of theaters and you wanted that series, you signed a contract to buy those pictures over that period of time. The Rogers, Autrys, and the Rocky Lanes all sold the same way, as a series. People often ask me about titles. I can't remember the titles of half of the pictures I made. In fact, I just saw a picture of mine I'd never seen before in my life. It was the first time, too, that my daughter had ever seen one of my pictures. She's twelve years old. I don't have any prints of them at home, so this was the first time she'd ever seen one.

DAVID ROTHEL: I imagine her reaction to you on the screen from twenty-some years ago must have been interesting.

REX ALLEN: Oh, yes. "Gee, Dad, those were good! You should never be ashamed of them." You know, a twelve-year-old in this day and age—I thought she was going to come up and hold her nose.

DAVID ROTHEL: What's your reaction when you see yourself on the screen?

REX ALLEN: (Chuckle) It's like moving your life back twenty years and watching and trying to remember what went on between the things that you see on the screen. I remember the little funnies. It reminds me of a lot of little things that happened with that particular crew or that particular cast of people.

DAVID ROTHEL: Tell me about your horse, Koko. How did you happen to get him?

REX ALLEN: I didn't have Koko for my first picture. I'd been hunting for a horse, a real different looking animal. I wanted to find one that was different from the horses the other screen cowboys had used before me. I didn't want anybody to ever say that I copied Autry or Rogers or any of the others. Also, I wanted to be as different from the rest as I possibly could from a wardrobe standpoint, from horse gear, hat crease, everything. I wanted to ride a buckskin because it had been a long time since anybody had used as a star horse a good buckskin with a black mane and tail and a black stripe down his back. I'd had a horse like that when I was a kid that I liked very much, but I couldn't find one with a good head and all the conformation I wanted. So I used a sorrel horse in my first picture, one that just belonged to Hudkins Stables. Glen Randall, the horse trainer . . . .

DAVID ROTHEL: He trained Trigger, I believe.

REX ALLEN: Yes, he did. Glen said one day, "I've got a horse on pasture that we bought out in Missouri for Dale [Evans] before she started using Buttermilk. He's a stud and just a little too much horse for Dale. Maybe you ought to go take a look at him." A girl trick rider had owned him for a while. She had done some trick riding on him.

Rex Allen astride "The Miracle Horse of the Movies," Koko.

Rex Allen and Koko on location for a Republic Pictures feature.

Then Glen bought him and brought him out to California. The horse had been running loose for about a year. I drove out and took a look at him. I couldn't get within fifty yards of him, but I thought he was the prettiest thing I'd ever seen in my life. I came back and said, "Glen, that's the horse I want if you'll train him for me." He sold me the horse, brought him back in and went to work on him. When Glen had him trained, he did basically the same tricks as Trigger and all of the other movie horses. I never knew Koko's dame and sire, but most people thought he was probably half Morgan and half Quarter.

DAVID ROTHEL: I've heard that you couldn't find a double for Koko because of his unusual markings.

REX ALLEN: No, no double. The only way we could double him was to take a white horse and mask off the mane and tail and the blaze in the face and the stockings and put vegetable dye on him. We used a chocolate-colored vegetable dye which would last maybe a week. That was long enough to use him for the long shots, like some of the running long shots, but, actually, I just had to run Koko to death on nearly every film because we just couldn't double him that close. For camera

shots within fifty yards we'd have to use Koko. So he earned his oats and hay. Then I traveled him over a half-million miles on the rodeo circuit after that. He earned his keep. He passed away about five years ago and he's buried in the park in my home town. And they've got a hole dug right next to him. I think my head goes . . . . (laugh)

DAVID ROTHEL: Do you have a favorite film from the series you made?

REX ALLEN: Yeah, I think my favorite picture while I was at Republic was a little thing called *Rodeo King and the Senorita*.

DAVID ROTHEL: That was the first one of yours that I saw. And I agree with you, although I haven't seen all of your films. I thought Buddy Ebsen made an excellent sidekick, too.

REX ALLEN: We had some pretty good production in it, and it was a sort of believeable story.

DAVID ROTHEL: I read that the picture was a rewrite of a Rogers film called *My Pal Trigger*.

REX ALLEN: No, it was a rewrite of an old John Wayne film, actually, called *Cowboy and the Lady*. One of the cutest ones I made, I think, was a picture called *Colorado Sundown*. I don't know whether you've seen it. It was the first picture Slim Pickens did with me. That was a good picture.

DAVID ROTHEL: Slim Pickens looks like a kid in those pictures.

REX ALLEN: Yes, he was *slim* then. We *both* were slim. (laugh)

DAVID ROTHEL: Did you have a favorite leading lady in your pictures?

REX ALLEN: Republic, after I went there, decided they did not want to team a cowboy with one leading lady, like they had Roy and Dale for so many years, because then they only had one person to fight instead of two. I wouldn't like to name a favorite, but I was very happy with Penny Edwards, Mary Ellen Kay, and Marjorie Lord, and several other very lovely ladies.

DAVID ROTHEL: Your television series was entitled "Frontier Doctor." It was produced by Republic, wasn't it?

REX ALLEN: Yes, this was after they quit theatrical production—'55 or '56, somewhere in there.

DAVID ROTHEL: Did that series evolve out of your films as they closed down the theatrical operation?

REX ALLEN: No, actually we had decided not to make any more of the B Westerns. What Republic had decided to do then was to gradually get into television and still produce some big features. So what happened was I stayed with Republic in order to do the "Frontier Doctor"

Rex is seen here looking like the rancher he is. *Photo courtesy of Rex Allen.*

series and to do maybe one or two high-budget feature films, maybe not as the star of the things, but possibly with a Duke Wayne or somebody of that stature. "Frontier Doctor" was my own idea. I came up with that and sort of sold the studio on doing it. As it happened, the studio got into a problem with the Screen Actors Guild. Mr. Yates refused to pay residuals. They blacklisted him and he couldn't do any more production at all. So he sold the studio to CBS. (chuckle) He'd made his buck.

DAVID ROTHEL: There again, a tough old guy.

REX ALLEN: You bet!

DAVID ROTHEL: William Witney directed that television series, didn't he?

REX ALLEN: Yes, and quite a few of the features, too. After Roy [Rogers] left, Billy did most of my pictures. I had the same production crew and a lot of the same people who worked on Roy's films.

DAVID ROTHEL: Of the directors you worked with, who was your favorite?

REX ALLEN: By far Billy Witney, by far. He could get more on the screen for a dollar than any director I've ever known. And I've worked with a lot of them since then. Billy is just a superb guy.

DAVID ROTHEL: Does he live down in Mexico now?

REX ALLEN: Well, he travels quite a bit down there, but he lives in Thousand Oaks now and he's still active. He stops by the ranch. My ranch is just between Los Angeles and where Billy lives.

DAVID ROTHEL: Isn't your ranch called the Diamond X?

REX ALLEN: Diamond X Ranch, yeah. Twenty acres. (chuckle) I have a place in Arizona that's considerably bigger. But this is where I live, and it's a beautiful place to live.

DAVID ROTHEL: You have done a lot of work for Walt Disney. How did you get into that?

REX ALLEN: I was sitting at home one night when Walt called me on the phone and asked, "Would you be interested in coming over here and doing some things for us?" I said that I sure would. So I went over. I had no idea what he had in mind. I've been doing [narrating] most of their nature things since then. We counted a while back that I've done about a hundred and fifty of them over the years. And I do a lot of voices for them—cartoon character voices.

DAVID ROTHEL: Are you still doing work for them?

REX ALLEN: Oh yeah. Two weeks ago I finished one that'll be on this fall. Another dog and cat picture. (laugh)

DAVID ROTHEL: Are you doing a lot of personal appearance work?

REX ALLEN: You bet. I still work a lot of rodeos, fairs, auditoriums, but I don't work nightclubs.

DAVID ROTHEL: I read that you have a hotel in Acapulco.

REX ALLEN: John Wayne and I and Johnny Weissmuller and Fred MacMurray owned a hotel there for years. Wayne and I owned a farm in Lancaster, California. I traded Duke my interest in the hotel for his interest in the farm. So I have the farm now and he has the hotel. And I'm happier about it than he is.

DAVID ROTHEL: Do you see much of the other cowboy performers these days?

REX ALLEN: I think I've kept in touch with nearly all the guys in the Western field—Eddie Dean, Ray Whitley, Johnny Bond. I'm happy to say I see Roy and Dale often. Gene Autry and I have lunch together quite often.

DAVID ROTHEL: If you had had to choose music or acting as a career, which would it have been?

REX ALLEN: I would have definitely chosen music because it has been a part of my life all my life, and it really is what got me into the motion picture business. All I ever started out to be was a singer. And I'd rather be remembered for that than anything else.

*　　*　　*

REX ALLEN SELECTED FILMOGRAPHY

The following filmography only includes the Western films in which Rex Allen starred for Republic Pictures.

*　　*　　*

The Arizona Cowboy (Republic, 1950) 67 m.

Producer, Franklin Adreon; director, R. G. Springsteen; screenplay, Bradford Ropes; camera, William Bradford; editor, Harry Keller; musical director, Stanley Wilson; songs, Rex Allen.

CAST: Rex Allen, Teala Loring, Gordon Jones, Minerva Urecal, James Cardwell, Roy Barcroft, Stanley Andrews, Harry V. Cheshire, Edmund Cobb, Joseph Crehan, Steve Darrell, Douglas Evans, John Elliott, Chris-Pin Martin, Frank Reicher, George H. Lloyd, Lane Bradford.

Photo courtesy of NTA.

* * *

Hills of Oklahoma (Republic, 1950) 67 M.

Producer, Franklin Adreon; director, R. G. Springsteen; screenplay, Olive Cooper and Victor Arthur from original story by Olive Cooper; camera, Ellis W. Carter; editor, Arthur Roberts; musical director, Stanley Wilson.

CAST: Rex Allen, Elizabeth Fraser, Elizabeth Risdon, Robert Karnes, Fuzzy Knight, Roscoe Ates, Robert Emmett Keane, Trevor Bardette, Lee Phelps, Edmund Cobb, Rex Lease, Ted Adams, Lane Bradford, Michael Carr, Johnny Downs, Koko.

* * *

Along with his other performing attributes, it would appear that Rex flies, too, in this scene from *Hills of Oklahoma*. *Photo courtesy of NTA.*

Rex is smoking out the villains in this scene from *Redwood Forest Trail*. *Photo courtesy of NTA.*

Jack Larson, Ted Fries, Joseph Granby, Robert E. Burns, Koko.

* * *

Under Mexicali Stars (Republic, 1950) 67 M.

Producer, Melville Tucker; director, George Blair; screenplay, Bob Williams; camera, John MacBurnie; editor, Harold Minter.

CAST: Rex Allen, Dorothy Patrick, Roy Barcroft, Buddy Ebsen, Percy Helton, Walter Coy, Steve Darrell, Alberto Morin, Ray Walker, Frank Ferguson, Stanley Andrews, Robert Bice, Koko.

* * *

Redwood Forest Trail (Republic, 1950) 66 M.

Producer, Franklin Adreon; director, Philip Ford; screenplay, Bradford Ropes; camera, John MacBurnie; editor, Harold Minter.

CAST: Rex Allen, Jeff Donnell, Carl "Alfalfa" Switzer, Jane Darwell, Marten Lamont, Pierre Watkin, Jimmy Ogg, Dick Jones, John Cason, Jimmy Frasher, Bob Larson, Robert W. Wood,

Silver City Bonanza (Republic, 1951) 66 M.

Producer, Melville Tucker; director, George Blair; screenplay, Bob Williams; camera, John MacBurnie; editor, Robert M. Leeds; musical director, Stanley Wilson.

CAST: Rex Allen, Buddy Ebsen, Mary Ellen Kay, Billy Kimbley, Alix Ebsen, Bill Kennedy, Gregg Barton, Clem Bevans, Frank Jenks, Hank Patterson, Harry Lauter, Harry Harvey, Koko.

* * *

Roy Barcroft gets his usual comeuppance from Rex Allen in this scene from *Under Mexicali Stars*. *Photo courtesy of NTA.*

Photo courtesy of NTA.

Rex Allen's rodeo experience came in handy for this scene in *Rodeo King and the Senorita*. Photo courtesy of NTA.

Thunder in God's Country (Republic, 1951) 67 M.

Producer, Melville Tucker; director, George Blair; screenplay, Arthur E. Orloff; camera, John Mac-Burnie; editor, Harold Minter; songs, Irving Beriau, Leonard M. Sive.

CAST: Rex Allen, Mary Ellen Kay, Buddy Ebsen, Ian MacDonald, Paul Harvey, Harry Lauter, John Doucette, Harry Cheshire, John Ridgely, Frank Ferguson, Wilson Wood, Koko.

*   *   *

Rodeo King and the Senorita (Republic, 1951) 70 M.

Director, Philip Ford; screenplay, John K. Butler; camera, Walter Strange; editor, Robert M. Leeds; songs, Fred Howard, Nat Vincent, Curley Fletcher, Caroline Norton.

CAST: Rex Allen, Mary Ellen Kay, Buddy Ebsen, Roy Barcroft, Tristram Coffin, Bonnie De Simone, Don Beddoe, Jonathan Hale, Harry Harvey, Rory Mallinson, Joe Forte, Buff Brady, Koko.

*   *   *

Utah Wagon Train (Republic, 1951) 67 M.

Producer, Melville Tucker; director, Philip Ford; screenplay, John K. Butler; camera, John Mac-Burnie; editor, Edward H. Schroeder; musical director, Stanley Wilson; songs, Rex Allen.

CAST: Rex Allen, Penny Edwards, Buddy Ebsen, Roy Barcroft, Sarah Padden, Grant Withers, Arthur Space, Edwin Rand, Robert Karnes, William Holmes, Stanley Andrews, Frank Jenks, Koko.

*   ,*   *

Colorado Sundown (Republic, 1952) 67 M.

Photo courtesy of NTA.

Producer, Edward J. White; director, William Witney; screenplay, Eric Taylor and William Lively from an original story by Eric Taylor; camera, John MacBurnie; editor, Tony Martinelli.

CAST: Rex Allen, Mary Ellen Kay, Slim Pickens, June Vincent, Fred Graham, John Daheim, Louise Beavers, Chester Clute, Clarence Straight, The Republic Rhythm Riders, Koko.

* * *

The Last Musketeer (Republic, 1952) 67 M.

Producer, Edward J. White; director, William Witney; screenplay, Arthur E. Orloff; camera, John MacBurnie; editor, Harold Minter; new song, Foy Willing.

CAST: Rex Allen, Mary Ellen Kay, Slim Pickens, James Anderson, Boyd "Red" Morgan, Monte Montague, Michael Hall, Alan Bridge, Stan Jones, The Republic Rhythm Riders, Koko.

* * *

Border Saddlemates (Republic, 1952) 67 M.

Producer, Edward J. White; director, William Witney; screenplay, Albert DeMond; camera, John MacBurnie; editor, Harold Minter; new song, Jack Elliott.

CAST: Rex Allen, Mary Ellen Kay, Slim Pickens, Roy Barcroft, Forrest Taylor, Jimmie Moss, Zon

Photo courtesy of NTA.

Estelita, Rex, and The Republic Rhythm Riders serenade Slim Pickens in this scene from *South Pacific Trail*. *Photo courtesy of NTA.*

Murray, Keith McConnell, Mark Hanna, The Republic Rhythm Riders, Koko.

*　　*　　*

Old Oklahoma Plains (Republic, 1952) 59 M.

Producer, Edward J. White; director, William Witney; screenplay, Milton Raison from an original story by Albert DeMond; camera, John MacBurnie; editor, Tony Martinelli.

CAST: Rex Allen, Slim Pickens, Elaine Edwards, Roy Barcroft, John Crawford, Joel Marston, Russell Hicks, Fred Graham, Stephen Chase, The Republic Rhythm Riders, Koko.

*　　*　　*

South Pacific Trail (Republic, 1952) 60 M.

Producer, Edward J. White; director, William Witney; screenplay, Arthur Orloff; camera, John MacBurnie; editor, Harold Minter; songs, Jack Elliott, Aaron Gonzales, Rex Allen.

CAST: Rex Allen, Estelita, Slim Pickens, Nestor Paiva, Roy Barcroft, Douglas Evans, Joe McGuinn, Forrest Taylor, The Republic Rhythm Riders, Koko.

*　　*　　*

Old Overland Trail (Republic, 1953) 60 M.

Producer, Edward J. White; director, William Witney; screenplay, Milton Raison; camera, John MacBurnie; editor, Harold Minter; musical director, R. Dale Butts; song, Jack Elliott.

CAST: Rex Allen, Slim Pickens, Roy Barcroft, Virginia Hall, Gil Herman, Wade Crosby, Leonard Nimoy ("Star Trek's" Mr. Spock), Zon Murray, Harry Harvey, The Republic Rhythm Riders, Koko.

Rex and The Republic Rhythm Riders serenade Virginia Hall around the campfire in this scene from *Old Overland Trail*. Photo courtesy of NTA.

Photo courtesy of NTA.

*   *   *

Iron Mountain Trail (Republic, 1953) 53 M.

Producer, Edward J. White; director, William Witney; screenplay, Gerald Geraghty from a story by William Lively; camera, Bud Thackery; editor, Tony Martinelli.

CAST: Rex Allen, Slim Pickens, Grant Withers, Nan Leslie, Roy Barcroft, Forrest Taylor, Alan Bridge, John Hamilton, George H. Lloyd, Koko.

*   *   *

Down Laredo Way (Republic, 1953) 54 M.

Producer, Rudy Ralston; director, William Witney; screenplay, Gerald Geraghty; camera, John Mac-

Burnie; editor, Harold Minter; musical director, Stanley Wilson.

CAST: Rex Allen, Slim Pickens, Dona Drake, Marjorie Lord, Roy Barcroft, Judy Nugent, Percy Helton, Clayton Moore (television's Lone Ranger), Zon Murray, Koko.

*   *   *

Shadows of Tombstone (Republic, 1953) 53 M.

Producer, Rudy Ralston; director, William Witney; screenplay, Gerald Geraghty; camera, Bud Thackery; editor, Richard L. Ven Enger.

CAST: Rex Allen, Slim Pickens, Jeanne Cooper, Roy Barcroft, Emory Parnell, Ric Roman, Richard Avonde, Julian Rivero, Koko.

*   *   *

Red River Shore (Republic, 1953) 53 M.

Producer, Rudy Ralston; director, Harry Keller; screenplay, Arthur Orloff and Gerald Geraghty; camera, Bud Thackery; editor, Harold Minter.

CAST: Rex Allen, Slim Pickens, Lyn Thomas, Bill Phipps, Douglas Fowley, Trevor Bardette, William Haade, Emmett Vogan, John Cason, Koko.

*   *   *

The Phantom Stallion (Republic, 1954) 54 M.

Producer, Rudy Ralston; director, Harry Keller; screenplay, Gerald Geraghty; camera, Bud Thackery; editor, Harold Minter.

CAST: Rex Allen, Carla Belinda, Slim Pickens, Harry Shannon, Don Haggerty, Peter Price, Rosa Torich, Zon Murray, Koko.

*   *   *

REX ALLEN DISCOGRAPHY

Rex Allen was a popular recording artist from the late 1940s through most of the 1960s. In 1953 he had a hit with "Crying in the Chapel." "Don't Go Near the Indians" was a click single by Rex in the early sixties. LP albums have included *Under Western Skies* and *Mister Cowboy* (Decca), recorded during the late fifties; *Sixteen Favorite Songs,*

Starring **Rex Allen** THE ARIZONA COWBOY with **KOKO** THE MIRACLE HORSE OF THE MOVIES

RED RIVER SHORE

SLIM PICKENS · LYN THOMAS
BILL PHIPPS · DOUGLAS FOWLEY
Written by ARTHUR ORLOFF and GERALD GERAGHTY
Directed by HARRY KELLER
A REPUBLIC PICTURE

Douglas Fowley doesn't look too happy about the fact that
Rex is deputizing Slim Pickens. *Photo courtesy of NTA.*

The Rex Allen star on the Boulevard of the Stars—Hollywood Boulevard in Los Angeles.

Photo courtesy of Rex Allen.

recorded on Disney's Buena Vista label during the early sixties; *Faith of a Man* and *Rex Allen Sings and Tells Tales* (Mercury), released during the 1960s.

Currently available recordings by Rex Allen include the following re-releases:

The Great American Singing Cowboys Republic Records

Selections:

Little Joe the Wrangler
Streets of Laredo
and ten additional selections by other singing cowboys

* * *

The Touch of God's Hand Coral Records

Selections:

Precious Memories
He's Got the Whole World in His Hands
God Walks Those Hills with Me
Daddy Sang Bass

Less of Me
Wasted Years
When God Dips His Love in My Heart
Just a Closer Walk with Thee
Supper Time
The Touch of God's Hand

* * *

Golden Songs of the Golden West Vocalion Records

Selections:

The Trail of the Lonesome Pine
Nothin' To Do
The Last Roundup
The Last Frontier
Ole Faithful
Twilight On the Trail
The Railroad Corral
I'm a Young Cowboy
At the Rainbow's End
Too Lee Roll Um

* * *

Epilogue

SHADOWS ON THE TRAIL

The trail dust kicked up by the singing cowboys in their B musical Westerns has settled. The films are now beyond being an endangered species; they are extinct—none having been produced for over twenty years. Only the shadows remain—flickering from old celluloid at Western film festivals or in the darkened rooms of film collectors or very infrequently on television stations during off hours.

Most of the men who were the singing cowboys of our youth are now shadows of another sort with faces and bodies that reveal only subliminal flashes of the youthful riders of the range who would nonchalantly pick a guitar out of a nearby cactus and yodel us a song of the saddle.

Now the singing cowboys we knew ride a different range. They ride on the shadowy trails of our memories.

Adios.

Selected Bibliography

Aaronson, Charles S. *1963 International Motion Picture Almanac.* New York: Quigley, 1963.

Autry, Gene. "Sour Note." *American Magazine* (April, 1947).

Barbour, Alan G. *A Thousand and One Delights.* New York: Macmillan, 1971.

____.*The Thrill of It All.* New York: Macmillan, 1971.

Becker, Joyce. "Roy Rogers, King of the Cowboys, Is Still Riding Happy Trails." *In the Know* (March, 1976).

Blair, Earl. "FCR Meets Roy Rogers." *Film Collector's Registry* (April, 1976).

Buxton, Frank, and Owen, Bill. *The Big Broadcast.* New York: Viking, 1966.

Cooper, Texas Jim. "The Real Tex Ritter." *Western Film Collector* (November, 1974).

Corneau, Ernest N. "Our Vanished Western Heroes." *Movie Digest* (March, 1972).

"Cowboy in Clover." *Time* (August 18, 1947).

"Cowboy Tycoon." *Newsweek* (January 6, 1964).

Davis, Elise Miller. *The Answer Is God.* New York: Pillar Books, 1975.

"Double Mint Ranch." *Time* (January 15, 1940).

Downey, Linda and Ron, eds. "Under Western Skies: Rex Allen." *The World of Yesterday* (July, 1976).

Dunning, John. *Tune in Yesterday.* New Jersey: Prentice-Hall, 1976.

Everson, William K. *A Pictorial History of the Western Film.* New York: Citadel, 1969.

Fernett, Gene. *Hollywood's Poverty Row.* Satellite Beach, Florida: Coral Reef Publications, 1973.

Glut, Donald F., and Harmon, Jim. *The Great Television Heroes.* New York: Doubleday, 1975.

Goodman, Mark. "The Singing Cowboy." *Esquire* (December, 1975).

Hake, Theodore L., and Cauler, Robert D. *Sixgun Heroes.* Iowa: Wallace-Homestead Book Company, 1976.

Halliwell, Leslie. *The Filmgoer's Companion.* New York: Avon, 1971.

Hanley, Loretta, ed. *Series, Serials and Packages.* New York: Broadcast Information Bureau, Inc., Volume 15: Issue 2D, 1974.

Hemphill, Paul. *The Nashville Sound.* New York: Ballantine Books, 1975.

Horwitz, James. "In Search of the Original Singing Cowboy." *Rolling Stone* (October 25, 1973).

____.*They Went Thataway.* New York: E. P. Dutton and Company, Inc., 1976.

Houston, Mack A. "The Story of a Man Called Tex." *Western Trails Magazine* (July-August, 1975).

Hughes, Carol. "Gene Autry Rides Back to the Top." *Coronet* (June, 1951).

Johnston, Alva. "Tenor on Horseback." *Saturday Evening Post* (September 2, 1939).

Kauffman, Richard M. "Gene Autry Today." *Western Trails Magazine* (March-April, 1975).

"King of the Cowboys." *Newsweek* (March 8, 1943).

Knauth, Percy. "Gene Autry, Inc." *Life* (June 28, 1948).

Lahue, Kalton C. *Riders of the Range.* New York: Castle Books, 1973.

McCarthy, Todd, and Flynn, Charles, Editors. *Kings of the Bs.* New York: E. P. Dutton and Company, Inc., 1975.

McClure, Arthur F., and Jones, Ken D. *Heroes, Heavies and Sagebrush.* South Brunswick and New York: A. S. Barnes and Co., 1972.

Maltin, Leonard, Editor. *The Real Stars No. 2.* New York: Curtis Books, 1973.

"Man and Wife." *Time* (March 7, 1955).

Michael, Paul, ed. *The American Movies Reference Book,*

The Sound Era. New Jersey: Prentice-Hall, Inc., 1970.

Miller, Don. *Hollywood Corral.* New York: Popular Library, 1976.

Mitchell, Curtis. *Cavalcade of Broadcasting.* Chicago: Follett, 1970.

Morgan, James. "Conversations with the Cowboy King." *The Ambassador* (October, 1976).

Nevins, Jr., Francis M. "William Witney." *Films in Review* (November, 1974).

New York Times Film Reviews, 1913-1968, The. New York: The New York Times and Arno Press, 1970.

Ortega, Herbert. "The Many Facets of Eddie Dean." *Western Film Collector* (March-May, 1974).

Osborne, Jerry. *55 Years of Recorded Country/Western Music.* Phoenix, Arizona: O'Sullivan, Woodside and Company, 1976.

Parish, James Robert. *Actor's Television Credits 1950-1972.* New York: Scarecrow Press, 1973.

Parkinson, Michael, and Jeavons, Clyde. *A Pictorial History of Westerns.* London: Hamlyn, 1972.

Parks, Jack. "Hollywood's Singing Cowboys: They Packed Guitars as Well as Six-Shooters." *Country Music* (July, 1973).

Rainey, Buck. "Rex Allen, The Friendly Cowboy." *Film Collector's Registry* (January, 1976).

Reinhart, Ted. "Roy Rogers Today." *Western Trails Magazine* (January-February, 1976).

Rogers, Dale Evans. *Dale.* New Jersey: Fleming H. Revell Company, 1971.

Rogers, Roy. "Don't Shoot, Ma!" *American Magazine* (August, 1949).

Rowlands, Dave. "Riding The Celluloid Range." *Wrangler's Roost* (June, 1976).

Sawyer, Kathy. "An Interview with Tex Ritter, Champion of the West." *Country Music* (July, 1973).

Shelton, Robert, and Goldblatt, Burt. *The Country Music Story.* New Jersey: Castle Books, 1971.

Shestack, Melvin. *Country Music Encyclopedia.* New York: Thomas Y. Crowell Company, 1974.

Smith, H. Allen, "King of the Cowboys." *Life* (July 12, 1943).

Smith, M. P. "The Tex Ritter Family." *Western Film Collector* (March, 1973).

"Spirit." *People* (October 18, 1976).

Stambler, Irwin, and Landon, Grelun. *Encyclopedia of Folk, Country, and Western Music.* New York: St. Martin's Press, 1969.

Tuska, Jon. *The Filming of the West.* New York: Doubleday, 1976.

Twomey, Alfred E., and McClure, Arthur F. *The Versatiles.* New York: Castle, 1969.

Variety (Files from 1934 through 1955).

Vreeland, Frank. *Foremost Films of 1938.* New York: Pitman Publishing Corporation, 1939.

Weaver, John T. *Forty Years of Screen Credits, Volumes 1 and 2.* New York: Scarecrow Press, 1970.

Williams, Nick. "The Film Career of Bob Baker." *Western Film Collector* (July, 1973).

Willis, Lee Roy. "Gene Autry, My Personal View." *Western Trails Magazine* (March-April, 1975).

Young, J. R. "Roy Rogers." *Country Music* (July, 1975).

Zinman, David. *Saturday Afternoon at the Bijou.* New York: Arlington House, 1973.

Index

GENERAL INDEX

(NOTE: Since there are literally thousands of names included in the producer, director, technical crew, and cast listing entries of the filmographies, these have been excluded from the General Index, which includes only names mentioned in the text of the book.)